Modelling World Englishes

Modelling World Englishes
A Joint Approach to Postcolonial and Non-Postcolonial Varieties

Edited by Sarah Buschfeld and Alexander Kautzsch

EDINBURGH
University Press

Edinburgh University Press is one of the leading university presses in the UK. We publish academic books and journals in our selected subject areas across the humanities and social sciences, combining cutting-edge scholarship with high editorial and production values to produce academic works of lasting importance. For more information visit our website: edinburghuniversitypress.com

© editorial matter and organisation Sarah Buschfeld and Alexander Kautzsch, 2020
© the chapters their several authors, 2020

Edinburgh University Press Ltd
The Tun – Holyrood Road, 12(2f) Jackson's Entry, Edinburgh EH8 8PJ

Typeset in 11.5/13 Monotype Ehrhardt by
Servis Filmsetting Ltd, Stockport, Cheshire

A CIP record for this book is available from the British Library

ISBN 978 1 4744 4586 3 (hardback)
ISBN 978 1 4744 4588 7 (webready PDF)
ISBN 978 1 4744 4589 4 (epub)

The right of Sarah Buschfeld and Alexander Kautzsch to be identified as the editors of this work has been asserted in accordance with the Copyright, Designs and Patents Act 1988, and the Copyright and Related Rights Regulations 2003 (SI No. 2498).

Contents

List of Figures and Tables vii
List of Contributors ix
Foreword xi

1 Introduction 1
  Sarah Buschfeld and Alexander Kautzsch

2 English in England: The Parent Perspective 16
  Clive Upton

3 English in Namibia: Multilingualism and Ethnic Variation in
  the Extra- and Intra-territorial Forces Model 38
  Anne Schröder and Frederic Zähres

4 English in the United Arab Emirates: Status and Functions 63
  Saeb Sadek

5 English in India: Global Aspirations, Local Identities at the
  Grassroots 85
  Sachin Labade, Claudia Lange and Sven Leuckert

6 English in Singapore: Two Issues for the EIF Model 112
  Lionel Wee

7 English in the Philippines: A Case of Rootedness and
  Routedness 133
  Bejay Villaflores Bolivar

8 English in South Korea: Applying the EIF Model 154
  Sofia Rüdiger

9 English in Japan: The Applicability of the EIF Model   179
   Saya Ike and James D'Angelo

10 English in Australia – Extra-territorial Influences   202
   Kate Burridge and Pam Peters

11 English in North America: Accounting for its Evolution   228
   Edgar W. Schneider

12 English in The Bahamas and Developmental Models of World
   Englishes: A Critical Analysis   251
   Stephanie Hackert, Alexander Laube and Diana Wengler

13 Standard English in Trinidad: Multinormativity,
   Translocality, and Implications for the Dynamic Model and
   the EIF Model   274
   Philipp Meer and Dagmar Deuber

14 Englishes in Tristan da Cunha, St Helena, Bermuda and the
   Falkland Islands: PCE, non PCE or both? Blurred Boundaries
   in the Atlantic   298
   Daniel Schreier

15 English in Ireland: Intra-territorial Perspectives on Language
   Contact   322
   Patricia Ronan

16 English in Gibraltar: Applying the EIF Model to English in
   Non-Postcolonial Overseas Territories   347
   Cristina Suárez-Gómez

17 English in Ghana: Extra- and Intra-territorial Forces in a
   Developmental Perspective   371
   Thorsten Brato

18 Synopsis: Fine-tuning the EIF Model   397
   Sarah Buschfeld

Index   416

Figures and Tables

FIGURES

1.1	The Extra- and Intra-territorial Forces Model	5
1.2	Depicting internal linguistic variability in the EIF Model	7
5.1	Language of identity indicated in the English and Marathi questionnaires	100
5.2	Educational level of the parents and language of identity	102
5.3	Indicated language of prestige in the English and Marathi questionnaires	102
5.4	Educational level of the parents and most prestigious language	103
8.1	Departures of Koreans from Korea 2003–2017	166
8.2	Visitor Arrivals in Korea 1997–2017	167
13.1	An extended and modified version of the postcolonial component of the EIF Model accounting for multinormative stabilization and translocality	293
16.1	Gibraltar in Europe	349
17.1	Map of Ghana with current regions	373
17.2	Number of pupils attending primary school and secondary school for selected years between 1881 and 1949	383
18.1	The revised Extra- and Intra-territorial Forces Model	411

TABLES

3.1	Namibian households by main language spoken	42
5.1	Schneider's original parameters of the Dynamic Model (2007) and their extension to the Expanding Circle	93
5.2	Languages indicated as mother tongues by Indians living in Maharashtra in descending order of speaker percentage (Census of India 2011) and speaker numbers in the questionnaires	95
5.3	Number of questionnaires according to gender and language of the questionnaire	98
5.4	Knowing ___ is important for people living in Maharashtra	104
5.5	Knowing ___ is an advantage in the job market	105
5.6	Knowing ___ is an advantage at school	106
10.1	Relative frequencies of rubbish, garbage, trash in corpora before and after 2000	215
10.2	Relative frequencies of apartment, flat, condominium, home unit in corpora before and after 2000	217
10.3	Relative frequencies of -ed and -t for past tense/past participle in four GloWbE corpora	219
10.4	Relative frequencies for alternative expressions of dates from four regional corpora	221
16.1	Gibraltar English in the EIF Model	365
17.1	Summary of population figures for the exonormative stabilisation phase	379
17.2	Language policies from the pre-colonial era to today	391

Contributors

Bejay Villaflores Bolivar is a PhD student at the Ateneo de Manila University and a lecturer at the University of San Carlos

Thorsten Brato is an assistant professor at the University of Regensburg

Kate Burridge is a full professor at Monash University

Sarah Buschfeld is a full professor at the TU Dortmund University

James D'Angelo is a full professor at the Chukyo University College of World Englishes

Dagmar Deuber is a full professor at the University of Münster

Stephanie Hackert is a full professor at the Ludwig Maximilian University of Munich

Saya Ike is an associate professor at Meijo University

Alexander Kautzsch was an assistant professor at the University of Regensburg

Sachin Labade is an associate professor at the University of Mumbai

Claudia Lange is a full professor at Technische Universität Dresden

Alexander Laube is a PhD student, lecturer and research assistant at the Ludwig Maximilian University of Munich

Sven Leuckert is an assistant professor at Technische Universität Dresden

Philipp Meer is a PhD student, lecturer and research assistant at the University of Münster and State University of Campinas

Pam Peters is an emeritus professor at Macquarie University

Patricia Ronan is a full professor at the TU Dortmund University

Sofia Rüdiger is an assistant professor at the University of Bayreuth

Saeb Sadek is a PhD student, lecturer and research assistant at Bielefeld University

Edgar W. Schneider is an emeritus professor at the University of Regensburg

Daniel Schreier is a full professor at the University of Zurich

Anne Schröder is a full professor at Bielefeld University

Christina Suárez-Gómez is a full professor at the University of the Balearic Islands

Clive Upton is an emeritus professor at the University of Leeds

Lionel Wee is a full professor at the National University of Singapore

Diana Wengler is a PhD student, lecturer and research assistant at the Ludwig Maximilian University of Munich

Frederic Zähres is a PhD student, lecturer and research assistant at Bielefeld University

Foreword

Sarah Buschfeld

This book is dedicated to our colleague and my late husband Alexander Kautzsch, who died far too young, on March 2, 2018, after a severe heart attack. Back then, the book project was in its initial stages. We received acceptance for publication by Edinburgh University Press on February 23, the very day Alex suffered the heart attack; this is why I am so emotionally attached to the volume. It is based on the Extra- and Intra-territorial Forces (EIF) Model we developed in the summer of 2014. Since the original version of the model was presented in an article in *World Englishes* (John Wiley and Sons Ltd) in 2017, it has undergone further modification in a later article we wrote with Edgar Schneider (Buschfeld et al. 2018). I would therefore like to take the opportunity to thank Edgar for his generosity in helping us to rethink and modify some of the original ideas on his Dynamic Model. The EIF Model was not conceptualized as a counter-model but as a follow-up approach with a broader aim (viz. the integration of non-postcolonial varieties of English, something Edgar never had in mind). It thus has a wider and modified perspective, a reaction in essence to the most recent linguistic changes and scientific trends in the World Englishes paradigm.

The present volume constitutes the deliberate attempt to put the model to the test, a project we started working on in March 2017. The model and also the volume constitute a major achievement in both our academic careers, an achievement Alex will now not reap the fruits of. I have continued and finished this project as best as I could, but I would like to stress that the merit is not only mine. Those who I need to acknowledge and to whom I need to express my gratitude include the following:

First and foremost, of course, Alex needs to be acknowledged. Apart from having been an inspiring colleague, it was in Kautzsch (2014) that he generated the concept of extra- and intra-territorial forces that constitutes the scientific basis of the EIF Model.

My deep gratitude also goes to the authors of the individual chapters for their invaluable contributions, all of which have helped to assess, refine, and further the model in important ways.

I would like to thank Edgar Schneider for providing helpful input and feedback on various chapters from the perspective of his Dynamic Model, and to Patricia Ronan for her fruitful comments and suggestions on the Synopsis and the modified illustration of the EIF Model.

Last but not least, I am indebted to my editorial assistants, Pınar Dağdeviren and Brian Hess, not only for their invaluable support in the final proofreading and formatting process, but also for keeping me in good spirits in the last couple of weeks.

It only remains for me to say thank you to all of you for a fruitful collaboration and for helping me create (in all modesty) a fantastic and valuable new addition to research and theory in the field of World Englishes.

REFERENCES

Buschfeld, Sarah, Alexander Kautzsch and Edgar W. Schneider. 2018. From colonial dynamism to current transnationalism: A unified view on postcolonial and non-postcolonial Englishes. In Sandra C. Deshors, ed. 2018, *Modelling World Englishes in the 21st Century: Assessing the Interplay of Emancipation and Globalization of ESL Varieties*. Amsterdam: John Benjamins, 15–44.

Kautzsch, Alexander. 2014. English in Germany. Spreading bilingualism, retreating exonormative orientation and incipient nativization? In Sarah Buschfeld, Thomas Hoffmann, Magnus Huber and Alexander Kautzsch, eds. 2014, *The Evolution of Englishes: The Dynamic Model and Beyond*. Amsterdam: John Benjamins, 203–227.

CHAPTER 1

Introduction

Sarah Buschfeld and Alexander Kautzsch

1. THE MODEL OF EXTRA- AND INTRA-TERRITORIAL FORCES (EIF)

Powerful and innovative World Englishes theorizing should factor in ongoing developmental processes and aim at explanations for the blurring between major variety types such as ESL (English as a Second Language) and EFL (English as a Foreign Language), or ENL (English as a Native Language) and ESL. To capture current linguistic realities, we believe that it is necessary to jointly approach postcolonial and non-postcolonial settings in which varieties of English have been emerging.

A multitude of forces and factors operating on many varieties, to different extents and maybe also at different times, have been described and addressed for postcolonial Englishes (PCEs): for example, issues such as language policies, language in education, attitudes towards English, English and identity, and language in use, to name but a few. Structural linguistic properties and features of PCEs have been identified and interpreted as results of such forces.

In non-postcolonial territories, the spread and depth of entrenchment of the English language are often determined by the very same factors. Yet, they have traditionally been analyzed and located in a different framework, namely as learner or EFL varieties. Though Kachru's (1985) Three Circles Model is an early acknowledgment of these Englishes, they have been largely neglected by World Englishes theorizing. Despite the fact that Sridhar and Sridhar (1986) issued an early call for an integrated approach to ESL and EFL varieties, it has long gone largely unheard. In recent times, however, this potential interface has experienced renewed research interest, especially by World Englishes researchers (e.g. Buschfeld 2011, 2013; Laporte 2012; Nesselhauf 2009 and the edited volume by Mukherjee and Hundt, eds. 2011) – and with good reason: against the backdrop of recent linguistic realities, such strict separation has turned out to be untimely, if not inadequate. Colonization is, of course, a strong predictor for second-language variety status; however, second-language varieties did not emerge to the same degree of entrenchment and local restructuring in all countries with a colonial past (e.g. Schneider's case study of Tanzania [2007: 197–199] and the cases of Tswana English [Gilquin and Granger 2011] and English in Cyprus [Buschfeld 2013]). On the other hand, recent research has shown that second-language varieties, with a very similar entrenchment and shared sets of linguistic characteristics, have been emerging in countries without a (post)colonial background (e.g. Buschfeld and Kautzsch 2014 on Namibia; Edwards 2016 on the Netherlands; Modiano 2003 on the Swedish context; Rüdiger 2019 on Korea, to mention just a few). Often, these varieties have been described as being of hybrid ESL-EFL status, and to be thus located somewhere in between the Expanding and Outer Circles in Kachru's model. The categories of such earlier models certainly still apply, but they should not be considered as clear-cut entities but rather as points on a continuum (e.g. Biewer 2011; Buschfeld 2013). Most of these Englishes are indeed developing towards second-language variety status (as in the cases mentioned above), but reverse development from ESL to EFL status has also been observed (e.g. for the case of Cyprus; Buschfeld 2013).

Such hybrid statuses, smooth transitions between variety types, and similar linguistic outcomes (i.e. the distinct forms and ways of using English) reported for PCE and non-PCE settings are not surprising.[1] After all, the general mechanisms operating in the early developmental stages of any new type of English are determined by the very same psycholinguistic processes of second-language acquisition (e.g. first-language transfer, simplification, overgeneralization and other universal strategies of language learning, regularization; see also Buschfeld 2013: 63; Davydova 2012: 367–368; Gilquin 2015; Schneider 2007: 88–90; Williams 1987). Additionally, apart from the historical factor of

---

[1] See, for example, Biewer 2011 on the use of modal auxiliaries; Koch et al. 2016 on intrusive *as*; Laporte 2012 on the use of the verb *make*; Nesselhauf 2009 on co-selection phenomena; Rüdiger 2019 on characteristics of English in Korea.

colonization, the sociopolitical forces operating in postcolonial and non-postcolonial territories appear to be very similar in nature (Buschfeld and Kautzsch 2017; Buschfeld et al. 2018; see also Buschfeld and Schneider 2018). If boundaries are becoming more and more blurred and second-language variety status is not linked to postcolonialism in principle but is also strongly guided by general forces of globalization (cf. Blommaert 2010; Coupland, ed. 2010) and other historico-political, demographic, geographic, and social factors (to be elaborated on in the following), this inevitably calls for a joint approach to postcolonial and non-postcolonial varieties of English.

Although Schneider's (2003, 2007) Dynamic Model is explicitly geared towards PCEs, it addresses a number of the forces to be included in a description of PCEs and non-PCEs alike, with the central issue of identity (re)writings as one of its core components. Still, it is explicitly – and deliberately – geared towards postcolonial societies. Because of its scientific appeal, some of the recent approaches trying to integrate PCEs and non-PCEs have nevertheless asked the question whether the Dynamic Model can also account for non-PCEs and attempts have been made to do so. Conclusions have been variably optimistic, though. Schneider himself concludes that "[i]n essence, the Dynamic Model is not really, or only to a rather limited extent, a suitable framework to describe this new kind of dynamism of global Englishes" (2014: 27–28). Instead, he introduces the notion of "Transnational Attraction" (Schneider 2014) to account for the recent developments of global Englishes. It addresses current sociolinguistic realities by viewing English as an "attractor" which exceeds national boundaries in orientation and impact. While not fully worked out, this concept can be viewed as an attempt to cover the infinite diffusion of English today into new contexts and settings. This spread largely takes place beyond national boundaries and is the result of a need felt by many speakers (and also nations) to spend a lot of resources on the acquisition of some proficiency in English; at times, this happens even without norms of correctness in mind ("grassroots" diffusion is a case in point; cf. Schneider 2016). Although "Transnational Attraction" tackles a decisive factor responsible for the constant global spread and local entrenchment, uses, and restructuring of the English language (cf. the notion of "glocalization" frequently employed to depict this twofold development), it merely operates on an abstract level. While it elucidates the more general, global causes for the spread of English and thus has a strong explanatory power, it does not address and describe particular factors and forces operating in specific countries, which would be needed for analyses and comparisons of individual cases.

Indeed, several important factors for integrating non-PCEs are not covered in the Dynamic Model, in particular globalization and its effects (e.g. computer-mediated and other means of transnational communication, language contact via the internet, mass tourism, trade, etc.), but also aspects such as foreign policies and domestic political decisions on trading relationships. What is more, the "colonial trappings of the model" (Edwards 2016: 187) are not easy to surmount. These trappings manifest in three fundamental problems in applying the model: (1) English was taken to non-postcolonial regions in completely different ways than to postcolonial territories (affecting the applicability of phase 1, foundation); (2) in non-postcolonial societies, both a settler strand and an external colonizing power which influences the colony politically, socially, and linguistically from the outside are lacking (mainly affecting the applicability of phase 2, exonormative stabilization); (3) due to the missing settler strand, language contact in non-postcolonial scenarios is of a different nature and the development of identity constructions and consequently linguistic accommodation between the two strands does not take place (relevant for all phases of the model; for further details on these aspects, see Buschfeld and Kautzsch 2017).

In her case study of English in the Netherlands, Edwards shows that "various elements of the Dynamic Model are in evidence in the Netherlands" and concludes that, despite the colonial trappings of the model, "the parallels [between PCEs and non-PCEs] should be salvaged, but placed in a new framework" (Edwards 2016: 190).

In accordance with this suggestion, accepting the notion of "Transnational Attraction" as a precondition for the evolution of further second-language varieties (particularly in non-postcolonial contexts) and building on Schneider's Dynamic Model, the editors of this volume have developed the "Extra- and Intra-territorial Forces Model" (EIF Model; Buschfeld and Kautzsch 2017). The model elaborates on the details of both conceptions and identifies various forces which operate within and beyond national confines and affect and strengthen the role and status of English in a diverse set of environments. These forces, for instance, include language policies and language attitudes, globalization and "acceptance" of globalization, foreign policies, the effects of the sociodemographic background of a country, tourism, and, obviously, colonization and attitudes towards the colonizing power, seen in this context as one out of several forces but not the main or exclusive one.

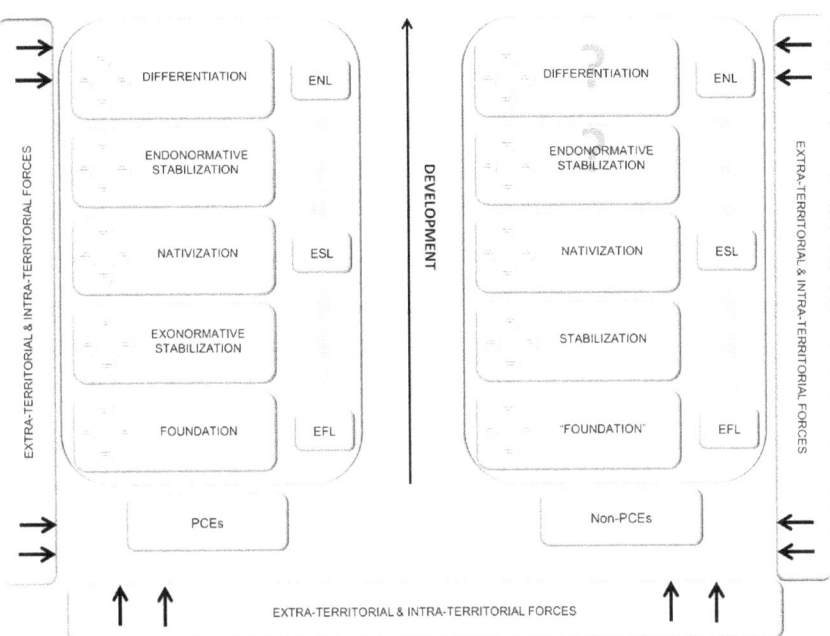

Figure 1.1 The Extra- and Intra-territorial Forces Model
Source: adapted from Buschfeld and Kautzsch 2017: 117;
Buschfeld et al. 2018: 24.

Further forces will be identified and illustrated in the case studies presented in this volume and discussed in the synopsis.

In principle, Buschfeld and Kautzsch (2017) suggest that non-PCEs also emerge and develop following a uniform process, when compared not only to each other but also to PCEs (cf. Schneider's [2007: 21] general assumptions and stages for the development of PCEs). The EIF Model, illustrated in Figures 1.1 and 1.2, postulates that a range of extra- and intra-territorial forces constantly influence the development of all types of English, that is, from their early to their current developmental stages. Although different cases naturally show differences in the manifestations of the individual forces (i.e. in their occurrence, strength, impact, and outcome), our general idea is that a multitude of forces, equally important and worth considering, hold for all settings in which English has experienced entrenchment and use.

Adopting some successful and influential notions already established in categorizing World Englishes and adding some novel conceptions, the model comprises five major components:

1. It integrates the description of both PCEs and non-PCEs and introduces the concept of "extra- and intra-territorial forces" (EIF).
2. Transnational Attraction is seen as the main driving force behind the ongoing entrenchment of English and its diffusion beyond postcolonial contexts and even national borders.
3. The diachronic set-up of the EIF Model is based on Schneider's Dynamic Model and thus assumes that varieties develop along a set of distinct phases (at least the five phases identified by Schneider 2003, 2007 and implemented in the current version of the model; for a discussion of an increased number of phases see Wee's contribution to this volume) and are shaped by the four parameters in Schneider's initial conception.
4. It takes up the traditional categorization of English into EFL/Expanding Circle, ESL/Outer Circle, and ENL/Inner Circle and broadly matches the five developmental phases with these main variety types. It assumes that in the initial foundation phase language acquisition results in EFL status, in the central phases English may acquire increased intra-national functions (typical for ESL varieties) and in the final phase (as, for example, in today's Singapore) the development may eventually give rise to extended intra-national heterogeneity and ultimately even new native speakers and thus ENL varieties. The EIF Model thus follows up on the early influential work of Braj Kachru and others, but does not define the three categories as necessarily clearly distinct from one another. We postulate that (i) transitions from one variety type to another are feasible throughout and that (ii) developments should not be seen as unidirectional only, since reverse development can be witnessed in some cases (e.g. from ESL to EFL for English in Cyprus; Buschfeld 2013).
5. A third dimension (as added to the model in Buschfeld et al. 2018 and illustrated in Figure 1.2) addresses variety-internal heterogeneity, present – to a larger or smaller extent – in nearly all regionally demarcated types of English. This heterogeneity is shaped by situational and sociolinguistic factors such as speakers' proficiency levels, status, identity conceptions, formality of a situation, and so on. This is an important facet of the model, since viewing varieties as a monolithic whole always requires a high degree of abstraction and can merely be a very rough approximation of the status and forms of English in a particular territory. A full grasp of the sociolinguistic realities and of the status, functions, and uses of English entails a higher level

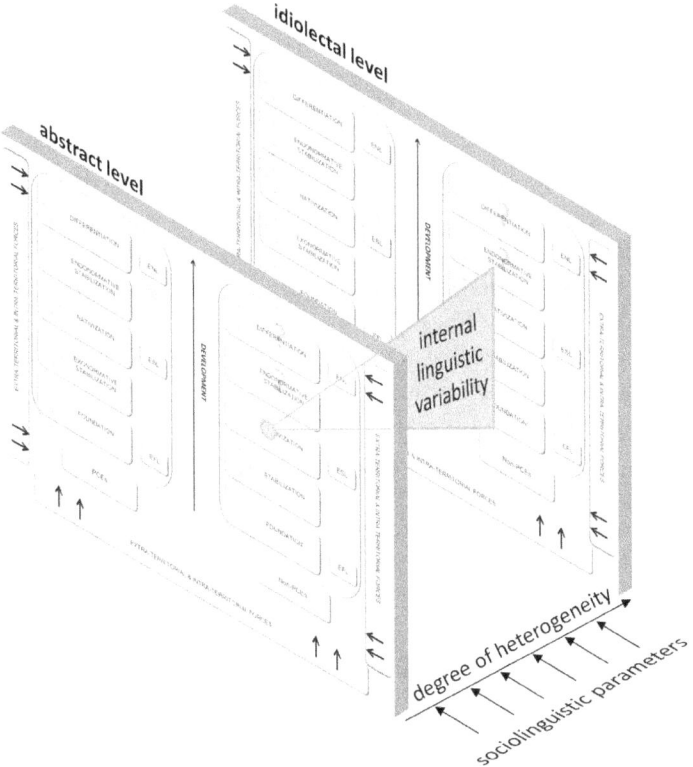

Figure 1.2 Depicting internal linguistic variability in the EIF Model
Source: Buschfeld et al. 2018: 25.

of granularity and can only be obtained by going into the details of potential differences between speaker groups and – on its most fine-grained level – of the idiolects of individual speakers. This heterogeneity can originate in sociolinguistic variables like age (e.g. the case of Cyprus), ethnicity (e.g. the cases of South Africa and Singapore), social status (e.g. the differences between white-collar and blue-collar occupations), gender, and so on.

In Figure 1.2, this heterogeneity is visualized by the branching-off axes. Here, the starting node represents the most abstract level, while language use of the individual is mapped on the vertical plane in the back, thus representing the highest level of detail. Within the triangle, the potential sub-varieties can then be located closer towards the abstract or idiolectal plane, according to the intended level of detail. The more heterogeneous a variety is, the further apart the external points of the fan will be at the level of the individual.

The current volume therefore sets out to contribute to the modelling of World Englishes by proposing a joint approach towards PCEs and non-PCEs as suggested in the EIF Model. In what follows, sixteen case studies on Englishes spoken in a variety of contexts will evaluate the usefulness of the model in comparison to earlier ones. The contributions address individual aspects of the model, with and without reference to the earlier successful models and their legacies (in particular Schneider's 2003, 2007 approach). They point out strengths and weaknesses and potentially make suggestions for improvements or other types of modification. Based on these findings and suggestions, we hope to arrive at a larger set of extra- and intra-territorial forces responsible for shaping the statuses and characteristics of Englishes worldwide. We expect to identify both general forces that operate on a wide range of contexts and specific forces characteristic of individual cases. Ultimately, we hope that this volume will contribute substantially to World Englishes theorizing and that we ultimately arrive at an even more comprehensive understanding of what Mesthrie and Bhatt (2008) aptly call "the English Language Complex" (for an earlier use of the term, see McArthur 2003: 56).

2. CONTRIBUTIONS TO THE VOLUME: CASE STUDIES

Each of the sixteen case studies in the volume investigates the emergence and current characteristics and status of one or more Englishes with respect to the applicability of current models of World Englishes, and in particular the EIF Model, and attempts to identify extra- and intra-territorial forces crucial to the development of individual varieties.

Our goal is to provide a maximally neutral and unbiased approach to the description and assessment of the Englishes covered in this volume. This is why we avoid implications about the statuses of the respective Englishes by grouping them according to given categories such as native or non-native English or foreign-, second-, or first-language variety. Instead, we sort the chapters by geographical longitude of the countries under consideration, moving east from the United Kingdom, that is, from Great Britain, to Namibia, the United Arab Emirates, India, Singapore, the Philippines, South Korea, Japan, Australia, North America, The Bahamas, Trinidad and Tobago, the Atlantic Ocean (more precisely Bermuda, the Falkland Islands, Tristan da Cunha, and St Helena), Ireland, Gibraltar, and Ghana.

We start our journey around the world by looking into the origins of the English language. In the first case study (Chapter 2), "English in England: The Parent Perspective," Clive Upton takes us back to the early days of the English language. He sketches out how "English begins with England" and its sixteen-century-long historical evolution, which has made it grow organically from its beginnings. English in England has put its stamp on the other varieties of English; it is both progenitor and participant in the worldwide spread of English. It is therefore an integral part when accounting for the English Language Complex and yet so different from the other postcolonial and non-postcolonial contexts treated in the present volume. By examining the evolutionary circumstances of (in particular) English English but also broadening the scope to English in Britain beyond England, Clive Upton offers reflections on whether and how the EIF Model can account for the evolution of English English as well as for its special status among the many varieties of English having emerged around the globe.

Chapter 3 takes us to Southern Africa. Anne Schröder and Frederic Zähres give an account of "English in Namibia" and focus on "Multilingualism and Ethnic Variation in the Extra- and Intra-territorial Forces Model." They build on previous research on vowel realizations in English spoken by different ethnic groups to elaborate on implications for the phases of endonormative stabilization and differentiation. They further discuss the influence of South Africa, South African Englishes, and South African (language) policies, in the past and present, and claim that these should be acknowledged as decisive extra-territorial forces when applying the EIF Model to the Namibian case.

Moving on to the Middle East in Chapter 4, Saeb Sadek presents another interesting case, "English in the United Arab Emirates", and investigates its "Status and Functions." Although the United Arab Emirates were a British protectorate until 1971, this did not lead to intensive linguistic contact due to the low numbers of troops and settlers in the country. Rather, the discovery of oil and the ever-increasing influx of a highly diverse workforce led to English becoming an important lingua franca. To describe this unique situation, Sadek resorts to identifying and discussing relevant extra- and intra-territorial forces in the domains of education, media, tourism, and public administration and governance, and discusses the status of English in the UAE as either EFL or ESL.

Next, with Chapter 5, "English in India: Global Aspirations, Local Identities at the Grassroots", we turn to South Asia. Here, Sachin Labade, Claudia Lange, and Sven Leuckert look into the attitudes of users of English in India from two very different strata of society: the young urban middle class and the less affluent rural population. Focusing specifically on Maharashtra, the authors document the use of English in different domains vis-à-vis the local languages as well as Hindi as the other overarching official language of the country and report the speakers' differential attitudes towards English as an identity carrier. Ultimately, they assess the merits of the Dynamic Model and the EIF Model from the perspective of the Indian communicative space.

The next two chapters deal with Englishes in Southeast Asia. In Chapter 6, Lionel Wee uses "English in Singapore" as a case in point to identify "Two Issues for the EIF Model." He argues that, being based on Schneider's Dynamic Model, the EIF Model faces the same problem as the Dynamic Model, namely that a development beyond phase 5 is not addressed and, connected to this, that developments due to globalization, technological innovations, and mobility are not incorporated, yet. Moreover, although the EIF Model proposes an integration of PCEs and non-PCEs in one model, Wee suggests to shun an assumed parallel development of PCEs and non-PCEs and rather go for convergence in the era of late modernity.

In Chapter 7, "English in the Philippines: A Case of Rootedness and Routedness", Bejay Villaflores Bolivar focuses on Bislish, a hybrid form of English and Cebuano-Bisaya, the local language spoken in Cebu. She examines utterances in online interactions as examples of linguistic hybridity involving English and Bisaya and shows how the mixed code emerged and has been propelled through the interplay of various intra- and extra-territorial forces like language policies or the local resistance against the dominance of Tagalog. As suggested in the title of her contribution, she assumes that these forces originate from two general attitudes of Cebuano-Bisaya speakers, a sense of "rootedness" and a sense of "routedness."

Chapters 8 and 9 investigate two non-postcolonial contexts in East Asia. In "English in South Korea: Applying the EIF Model" (Chapter 8), Sofia Rüdiger gives an account of which extra- and intra-territorial forces have contributed to the extraordinary status English has gained in South Korea since the end of World War II. She sheds light on aspects of colonization, language policies and language attitudes, foreign policies, globalization, and sociodemographic background, and ultimately proposes to add "cultural phenomena" and the "presence of English in the linguistic landscape and in the native language (L1)" as additions to the EIF Model as these take center stage in her case study.

Saya Ike and James D'Angelo's chapter (Chapter 9) on "English in Japan: The Applicability of the EIF Model" offers a thorough investigation of English in Japan and the country's historical involvement with the language from the point of earliest contact. The authors present a careful application of the EIF Model and test its utility by means of an in-depth analysis of the forces at work that might place Japan in the second phase of the model. They discuss possible advantages of it as well as some aspects that may need further definition in a refined version of the model.

Chapter 10 takes us down under, where Kate Burridge and Pam Peters investigate "Extra-territorial Influences" on "English in Australia." They focus on the extra-territorial influence of American English on Australian English with comparisons to other World Englishes. Based on several types of data, that is, letters of complaint, online Australian English as represented in GloWbE (Corpus of Global Web-Based English), and attitude surveys on Americanization and American loan words, they find different perspectives on the Americanization of Australian English and shed light on the different attitudes to AmE in Australia.

Continuing with the oldest postcolonial variety in Chapter 11, "English in North America: Accounting for its Evolution," Edgar W. Schneider explicitly addresses the question underlying the present volume, that is whether, or to what extent, the EIF framework is able to account for postcolonial and non-postcolonial contexts on a par. He compares the components of his Dynamic Model (Schneider 2003, 2007) to the mechanisms and factors envisaged as driving forces in the EIF Model. Due to the fact that AmE has gone through all of the evolutionary stages of the Dynamic Model, it provides an excellent case in point for assessing the suitability of both approaches to postcolonial Englishes in general and for identifying and discussing differences between the models.

The following two chapters investigate Englishes in the Caribbean. First, Stephanie Hackert, Alexander Laube, and Diana Wengler's chapter (Chapter 12) on "English in The Bahamas and Developmental Models of World Englishes: A Critical Analysis" aims at assessing if the EIF Model can accommodate the comparatively complex sociolinguistic situation in The Bahamas. They critically discuss the question of whether geography-based models are capable of capturing the intricate linguistic realities of such postcolonial, urbanized and "glocalized" territories at all. In this respect, the authors address a number of ideological complexes revolving around issues of the nature and discreteness of language varieties and their evolution.[2]

In Chapter 13, Philipp Meer and Dagmar Deuber look into "Standard English in Trinidad" and discuss issues of "Multinormativity, Translocality, and Implications for the Dynamic Model and the EIF Model." Based on a large-scale attitude survey in the domain of education, they find that exo- and endonormative orientations coexist. They argue that in contrast to the Dynamic Model, the EIF Model is capable of accommodating such heterogeneity and suggest that postcolonial communities might in fact reach a phase of "multinormative" stabilization. They also introduce "translocality" as an alternative theoretical framework for the conceptualization of forces.

In Chapter 14, "Englishes in Tristan da Cunha, St Helena, Bermuda and the Falkland Islands: PCE, non-PCE or both? Blurred Boundaries in the Atlantic," Daniel Schreier examines the interplay of extra- and intra-territorial forces that have shaped the emergence of these four varieties spoken in the Atlantic Ocean. He describes and evaluates general and locally specific forces that have worked on the formation of these varieties. What all four have in common is the presence of ENL, ESL, and EFL from their evolutionary beginnings, as well as a great deal of population mixing and a high level of mobility, which have led to blurred boundaries between ethnic and social communities. This is then taken as the starting point for a detailed exploration of how such settings can be grasped by models of World Englishes.

Coming back to the British Isles, Patricia Ronan looks into "Intra-territorial Perspectives on Language Contact" in the development of "English in Ireland" (Chapter 15). Drawing on data from historical texts and corpora, she investigates in how far the Dynamic Model and the Extra- and Intra-territorial Forces Model can explain the rise of the English language in Ireland. The chapter shows that the English language, in spite of the strong position of the Anglo-Saxon and Anglo-Norman settlers in Ireland, was a minority language at the beginning of the Early Modern period but developed into the de facto first language in Ireland due to continued extra- and intra-territorial pressure.

Chapter 16 takes us to the southern tip of Western Europe with "English in Gibraltar: Applying the EIF Model to English in Non-

---

[2] Strictly speaking, The Bahamas do not geographically belong to the Caribbean, but politically they do.

Postcolonial Overseas Territories" by Cristina Suárez-Gómez. Since Gibraltar shares similarities with PCEs but continues to be a British Overseas Territory, the English spoken there cannot easily be accounted for by the Dynamic Model. Therefore, the author accounts for the demographic, historical, and sociocultural situation of Gibraltar as well as the status of English spoken in the territory drawing on the EIF Model and tackles the internal heterogeneity of Gibraltar English by identifying several forces that have shaped this variety.

Finally, Chapter 17, the second contribution on English in Africa, is Thorsten Brato's account of "English in Ghana: Extra- and Intra-territorial Forces in a Developmental Perspective." Although Ghanaian English might be placed between the nativization and endonormative stabilization phases of the Dynamic Model (cf. Huber 2014), the absence of a stable settler strand makes this variety a less prototypical PCE, defying a straightforward application of the Dynamic Model. To evaluate if the EIF Model offers a more useful way to describe the development and current linguistic realities of Ghanaian English, Brato sets out to identify relevant intra- and extra-territorial forces. Investigating /t/-affrication, he argues that taking a more fine-grained view at socio-demographic developments helps in identifying possible reasons for the emergence of structured sociolinguistic variation.

In the final chapter, the "Synopsis" (Chapter 18), Sarah Buschfeld aims at "Fine-Tuning the EIF Model" by pulling together the relevant theoretical findings of the preceding chapters. Despite some suggestions for modifications, which Buschfeld bids welcome and incorporates in the overall conception of the model, she concludes that the EIF Model with its integration of PCEs and non-PCEs seems to be a welcome and necessary addition to World Englishes theorizing.

REFERENCES

Biewer, Carolin. 2011. Modal auxiliaries in second language varieties of English: A learner's perspective. In Mukherjee and Hundt, eds. 2011, 7–33.

Blommaert, Jan. 2010. *The Sociolinguistics of Globalization*. Cambridge: Cambridge University Press.

Buschfeld, Sarah. 2011. The English Language in Cyprus: An Empirical Investigation of Variety Status. PhD dissertation, University of Cologne.

Buschfeld, Sarah. 2013. *English in Cyprus or Cyprus English? An Empirical Investigation of Variety Status*. Amsterdam: John Benjamins.

Buschfeld, Sarah and Alexander Kautzsch. 2014. English in Namibia: A first approach. *English World-Wide* 35.2: 121–160.

Buschfeld, Sarah and Alexander Kautzsch. 2017. Towards an integrated approach to postcolonial and non-postcolonial Englishes. *World Englishes* 36.1: 104–126.

Buschfeld, Sarah and Edgar W. Schneider. 2018. World Englishes: Postcolonial Englishes and beyond. In Ee Ling Low and Anne Pakir, eds. 2018, *World Englishes: Re-Thinking Paradigms*. London: Routledge, 29–46.

Buschfeld, Sarah, Alexander Kautzsch and Edgar W. Schneider. 2018. From colonial dynamism to current transnationalism: A unified view on postcolonial and non-postcolonial Englishes. In Sandra C. Deshors, ed. 2018, *Modelling World Englishes in the 21st Century: Assessing the Interplay of Emancipation and Globalization of ESL Varieties*. Amsterdam: John Benjamins, 15–44.

Coupland, Nikolas, ed. 2010. *The Handbook of Language and Globalization*. Malden, MA and Oxford: Wiley-Blackwell.

Davydova, Julia. 2012. English in the Outer and Expanding Circles: A comparative study. *World Englishes* 31.3: 366–385.

Edwards, Alison. 2016. *English in the Netherlands. Functions, Forms and Attitudes*. Amsterdam: John Benjamins.

Gilquin, Gaëtanelle. 2015. At the interface of contact linguistics and second language acquisition research. New Englishes and Learner Englishes compared. *English World-Wide* 36.1: 91–124.

Gilquin, Gaëtanelle and Sylviane Granger. 2011. From EFL to ESL: Evidence from the International Corpus of Learner English. In Mukherjee and Hundt, eds. 2011, 55–78.

Huber, Magnus. 2014. Stylistic and sociolinguistic variation in Schneider's Nativization Phase: The case of Ghanaian English. In Sarah Buschfeld, Magnus Huber, Thomas Hoffmann and Alexander Kautzsch, eds. 2014, *The Evolution of Englishes: The Dynamic Model and Beyond*. Amsterdam: John Benjamins, 86–106.

Kachru, Braj B. 1985. Standards, codification and sociolinguistic realism: The English language in the outer circle. In Randolph Quirk and Henry G. Widdowson, eds. 1985, *English in the World. Teaching and Learning the Language and Literatures*. Cambridge: Cambridge University Press for the British Council, 11–30.

Koch, Christopher, Claudia Lange and Sven Leuckert. 2016. This hair-style called as 'duck tail' – The 'intrusive as'-construction in South Asian varieties of English and Learner Englishes. *Linguistic Innovations: Rethinking Linguistic Creativity in Non-native Englishes.* Special issue of the *International Journal of Learner Corpus Research* 2.2: 151–176.

Laporte, Samantha. 2012. Mind the gap! Bridge between World Englishes and Learner Englishes in the making. *English Text Construction* 5.2: 264–291.

McArthur, Tom. 2003. World English, Euro English, Nordic English? *English Today* 19.1: 54–58.

Mesthrie, Rajend and Rakesh M. Bhatt. 2008. *World Englishes: The Study of New Varieties.* Cambridge: Cambridge University Press.

Modiano, Marko. 2003. Euro-English: A Swedish perspective. *English Today* 19.2: 35–41.

Mukherjee, Joybrato and Marianne Hundt, eds. 2011. *Exploring Second-Language Varieties of English and Learner Englishes. Bridging a Paradigm Gap.* Amsterdam: John Benjamins.

Nesselhauf, Nadja. 2009. Co-selection phenomena across New Englishes. Parallels (and differences) to foreign learner varieties. *English World-Wide* 30.1: 1–26.

Rüdiger, Sofia. 2019. *Morpho-Syntactic Patterns in Spoken Korean English.* Amsterdam: John Benjamins.

Schneider, Edgar W. 2003. The dynamics of New Englishes: From identity construction to dialect birth. *Language* 79.2: 233–281.

Schneider, Edgar W. 2007. *Postcolonial English. Varieties Around the World.* Cambridge: Cambridge University Press.

Schneider, Edgar W. 2014. New reflections on the evolutionary dynamics of world Englishes. *World Englishes* 33.1: 9–32.

Schneider, Edgar W. 2016. Grassroots Englishes in tourism interactions. *English Today* 32.3: 2–10.

Sridhar, Kamal K. and S. N. Sridhar. 1986. Bridging the paradigm gap: Second-language acquisition theory and indigenized varieties of English. *World Englishes* 5.1: 3–14.

Williams, Jessica. 1987. Non-native varieties of English: A special case of language acquisition. *English World-Wide* 8.2: 161–199.

CHAPTER 2

English in England: The Parent Perspective

Clive Upton

1. INTRODUCTION

This chapter focuses specifically on English in England (EE). This territorial concentration deliberately cuts through the complexities of terms relating to the constituent members of 'the United Kingdom' and of 'the British Isles' (which are not the same thing – see section 2 below); in doing so avoiding grouping under one all-embracing and quite misleading name Englishes that are to be found in disparate (if politically conjoined) geopolitical entities. Further, it enables consideration of the relationship which EE has had with those other neighbouring Englishes. The overall intention is to make observations which might be relevant on the wider World Englishes stage. To this end, sections 3 to 10 conclude with 'Reflections' arising from their individual content, the aim of which is to draw conclusions from what has immediately preceded them and to suggest matters which might be addressed by others when postcolonial Englishes (PCEs) and non-postcolonial Englishes (non-PCEs) are being modelled. In no way should the reflections be considered obligatory to the analytic process: to many they will certainly not be a revelation, but some at least might be found helpful in furthering development of a World Englishes model as a whole.

2. ENGLISH AT HOME

The briefest of visits to the distinctions inherent in the political organisation of the British Isles should suffice to establish that English on its native turf is far from uniform at anything other than a quite meaninglessly coarse level of granularity. England, Wales and Scotland together properly constitute 'Great Britain', and together with *Northern* Ireland these constitute 'the United Kingdom of Great Britain and Northern Ireland', simply 'the UK'. These came together politically long after English began its career in England itself. And these alone are not 'the British Isles', the term properly embracing two states, the UK and the *Republic* of Ireland, or Eire. The latter was once part of the UK, but for long now it has been quite separate. Each part of the UK and Eire has its own linguistically expressed identity, with numerous regional and social divisions evident in myriad linguistic permutations. This diversity, born of a long history of conflict and alliance spawning countless (a word carefully chosen) standard and non-standard dialects, cannot be overstated.

As discussed in more detail in section 9 below, the historical relationships of Wales, Scotland and Ireland to EE have not been identical, in consequence of which the resultant Englishes found there are distinctive: see e.g. Hickey (2007) on Ireland; Penhallurick (2008a, 2008b) and Paulasto et al. (forthcoming) on Wales; Corbett et al. (2003) and Corbett and Stuart-Smith (2012) on Scotland. Along with other factors, in all of these Celtic plays a vital role in colouring English phonology, grammar and lexis, properly adding to claims of linguistic distinctiveness. Linguistic forms which can be considered indexical of specific British communities are not confined to specific geographical territories, and it is neither possible nor desirable here totally to ignore the English used beyond the borders of England. Nevertheless, the intention throughout this chapter will be to focus *out* from EE only as required, lest concentration on the essential points of argument prompted by a complicated story of linguistic evolution be diluted to no good purpose.

3. PROBLEMATIC STAGES

Historical complexity in the formation of the 'home' nations of the British Isles, and of their language use, must immediately call into question attempts to apply sequentially modelled 'stages' in an orderly fashion to EE. The Germanic language variety, or more properly varieties, which appeared in what is today England during the European Migration Period did, of course, have a 'foundation' of sorts. But whether or not that foundation was of English as we understand the term today, or whether that was of a precursor to our language, is a moot point to which we shall address ourselves below. Whatever one's view of this particular issue, its introduction was certainly not part of any colonial plan, in the accepted sense of the settling of a people subject to a parent state. Rather, it was an artefact of peoples extending their range in a haphazard fashion into territory adjacent to their ancestral lands. And 'nativisation' was by definition present with the first Anglo-Saxon settlers, as was, and remains, 'differentiation' aplenty between speaker communities and individual speakers. No exonormative stabilisation can be posited, there being no pressure exerted on speakers from a previous homeland. And little endonormative stabilisation can be detected in the foundational Old English (OE) period, this excepting the brief flowering of West Saxon written language prior to the Norman Conquest of the eleventh century.

The unruly sixteen-century history of English has been one of natural evolution driven by the needs of its speakers, piecemeal innovations prompted by contact and use interacting to create the language we now have. Remarking especially English grammar, Smith (1996: 158) puts it well:

> Over time, a major set of changes in the grammatical structure of English has been brought about; but these changes are the result of a series of minor developments which have constantly interacted over a great number of linguistic states. These minor developments are the result of variation, deriving both from within the language and as a result of contact with other languages.

It is not possible neatly to organise these 'minor developments' into any linear sequence. People came, speaking West Germanic dialects, which might or might not have been mutually intelligible one with another. They interacted within and beyond their immediate communities. The communities blended and split, forming and re-forming alliances and associated identities, fashioning their speech and ultimately (after a long gestation) their writings according to need. It is important to recognise the fact that the ancestor of all Englishes is of quite accidental formation, unplanned and, for most of its users always and for all of its users often, for much of its existence quite unregulated.

So the idea of fixed 'stages' of progression for EE must be carefully treated, no attempt being made to squeeze EE into an inappropriate mould. Rather, concentration will be on identifying, and exploring, some of the principal forces which over time have shaped the variety as it is. Some of these are occurrences of large geopolitical moment, some more intimately affecting confined geographical or social groups. But all are chosen with the intention of making some observation which might prove of help in the further contemplation of the EIF Model. As far as is possible, in the interests of creating a coherent narrative an historically linear route is adopted.

3.1 Reflection 3

Here is not even the sketchiest 'potted history' of EE, this being unnecessary for the immediate task in hand. But anyone studying the rise of an English would do well to gain a sound knowledge of the historical course of EE, so as to be able to factor in from this English anything appropriate to the development of their own. The simple variationist principle of the vital importance of an historical focus might profitably be taken as the first implication of this chapter.

4. ANGLO-SAXONS

To establish the place of EE among the pantheon of World Englishes we must immediately emphasise its heterogeneity at 'foundation'. While the date for its arrival in Britain is conventionally given as around 449 CE, versions of the language were in use in the multicultural society that was late-Roman Britannia prior to formal Roman withdrawal in 410 CE, and these versions proliferated as time went on and more and more Germanic settlers arrived in the islands. 'Versions' is the operative word here, differentiation being in-built from the beginning. On 'the origins of Old English', Crystal (2004: 15–28) draws proper attention to synchronic and diachronic dimensions of early English diversity, crucially observing:

> A cross-section of British society in 449 would . . . show people of many different backgrounds – Celts, Romano-Celts, Germanic migrants of various origins, probably some Germano-Celts . . . – living in tiny communities of perhaps just a few hundred people. But this synchronic picture is not the only dimension we have to consider, in understanding the sociolinguistic forces which influenced Old English. The diachronic dimension . . . must also be taken into account. We must not forget that the various waves of

immigration and invasion did not take place all at once. If Germanic people were arriving in, say, 400, their speech would be very different from those who arrived a century later – even if the two groups originated in exactly the same part of the Continent. (Crystal 2004: 22–23)

Here Crystal makes it clear that as English took root in (what was ultimately to become) England, there was no one version of the language. Rather, the different bands – for they can have been no more than that – of West Germanic speakers, participating in a fragmented invasion and settling of the land, had no especial linguistic cohesion. We can legitimately say that linguistic differentiation was the norm at every phase of the early career of the language. Further, the fact of generational change as well as synchronic inter-group and interpersonal differences will have exacerbated varietal distinctions.

4.1 Reflection 4

The salient point here is that, as the EIF Model makes plain, there are forces imposing variation which should be sought at the implanting of any language or language variety. These forces encompass complex considerations of space, time and associated identities. We cannot assume uniformity of language even at the stage of its introduction into a territory, with any time lapse that is part of that introduction likely to add to the distinctions apparent within it.

5. A CELTIC CONTRIBUTION

With no obligations tying them back to past Continental practice other than those of nostalgia and inertia, and no 'mother country as initial power broker' (Buschfeld and Kautzsch 2017: 111), Anglo-Saxon speakers in 'England' were at liberty to express their new-found world in the unfettered way of free settlers everywhere – with one outstanding circumstance, the presence in their new homeland of a pre-existing complex and vibrant indigenous culture, this expressed through the medium of Celtic.

Two distinct views exist regarding the interaction of Celtic and English in the early period of settlement. A 'Germanist' view has long held that Celtic, being the language of a conquered people, exerted little influence on the language of the incomers, what effect there was being largely restricted to lexis and even then not greatly beyond the onomastic. This view continues to be influential in moderated form, a recent iteration of it coming from Crystal (2004: 29–33), who observes the limited extent to which readily verifiable Celtic lexis exists in English. He maintains that comparatively little trace of Celtic survived Germanic settlement in England, the settlers being so dominant as not to 'need' access to more than a limited set of speech forms that were not already their own. Voices dissenting from such reasoning have always been present, however, and a view is today increasingly advanced that some considerable code-mixing must have been a feature from settlement onwards. Wales (2006: 43–45) argues that the settlers' westward progression from their east-coast footholds was not immediate and overpowering of the indigenous Celts. Providing a cogent summary of an extensive literature on both sides of the debate, she rehearses arguments that some significant Celtic influences can be traced especially in former and present-day nonstandard dialects. Such early influences are explored, and beyond that speculated upon, by scholars such as Tristram (2002) and Breeze (2002), and in very considerable depth by Filppula et al. (2008: 24–132), going beyond the usual concentration on lexis into areas of phonology and (especially) grammar.

The opposing views are not wholly irreconcilable, however, and neither should be overstated. At the Germanic invasion there is no evidence of the sweeping away of Celts or their language, and evidence instead of collaboration, intermarriage and the continuing existence of Celtic enclaves in largely Anglo-Saxon territory. Filppula et al. are able to advance a large body of linguistic evidence to suggest Celtic had a part to play in the emergence of OE. The Anglo-Saxons were, however, the dominant force in what ultimately became England, their military, economic, cultural and evolving political structures defining the course of the English future. The Welsh were truly *wealhas*, 'foreigners', on land that had once been theirs. And it must be acknowledged that, in the absence of concrete written evidence that English features thought likely to be of Welsh origin *were* indeed so derived, it is their number, and the erudition with which they are advanced, which lift them beyond the level of informed speculation.

5.1 Reflection 5

At the implanting of a new language in a territory, we can reasonably expect there to be some measure of linguistic accommodation between incomers and the indigenous population (as well as between various groups of the incomers themselves, of course). We cannot too readily predict the extent of that accommodation, however, and must seek definite evidence of its occurrence. When such evidence is not forthcoming, it is possible that the incoming force might largely have blotted out possibilities of interaction. Each case needs to be judged independently in this regard, evidence being sought and rigorously tested before fixed positions are taken.

6. VIKINGS AS EQUAL PARTNERS?

In a thought-provoking paper exploring the effects of linguistic ideology on our conception of the evolution of English, Milroy (1996) persuasively argues against any assertion that the English language has had an uninterrupted progression from that of the first Germanic settlers through to the present day. He sees this unilinear view as reducing to insignificance issues of language contact, specifically between English and Old Norse (ON), and of dialectal variability, issues which the sociolinguist sees as central to an understanding of language in any age. In Milroy's view, concentration on an essentially tidy sequential progression in development focuses attention on the standard dialect at the expense of that variability that should be seen as the mainstream of language through time.

Milroy does not, of course, deny the planting of Germanic speech into England with the first Anglo Saxon settlers. Nor does he discount from his consideration the resulting form of English of the period, which we today term Old English (OE). But, in concentrating his attention on the 'discontinuity' between Old and Middle English which has conventionally been ascribed to the uninformed practices of Anglo-Norman scribes, he asserts:

> It can be argued that Modern English is not the direct lineal descendant of the language known as Old English (or Anglo-Saxon) as represented in documentary sources, but of an Anglo-Norse contact language which developed amongst speakers in the east

midlands and north of England between about 850 and 1050, and which is not attested in writing during that period. (Milroy 1996: 172–173)

It should be readily acknowledged that there was indeed remarkable and quite rapid change from synthetic to analytic grammatical structure between the English that is apparent in the available written records of what we now term 'Old' and 'Middle' English (ME). And, driven by his sociolinguistic stance, Milroy readily moves beyond this evidence in his search for an explanation, finding causation in the same subtle interplay of dialects and languages of an earlier period that is readily observable today.

If one chooses to subscribe to Milroy's view of the foundational nature of what he terms an 'interlanguage' (variously described by some other commentators as a koine or pidgin, with somewhat different implications), we have here a case of endonormative stabilisation writ large as OE and ON merge. The notion is contentious, though demanding of the highest degree of serious consideration, and it is not our purpose here closely to explore the arguments, for and against, that Milroy entertains in his fascinating article. Whatever one's stance on the issue, in the introduction of Norse into the English equation we are presented with a singularly potent instance of extra-territorial force being applied to an existing language, Anglo-Saxon (or Old English if one wishes to impute the longer pedigree).

6.1 Reflection 6

'Interlanguage' aside, two interrelated points emerging from Milroy's thesis warrant consideration. Milroy gives primacy to the spoken over the written word in the search for a true record of what is happening to the language at any point in time – and, we might not unreasonably add, in any place. As our own experience tells us, writing is unquestionably a secondary medium, the written record not closely reflecting what is the current usage of the majority. While contexts vary from one English to another, in each case it is worthwhile to consider the origin of forces operating variously on development of written and spoken language, and the relative prominence of one mode over the other. Further, differentiation is inherent in linguistic production, this most especially being the case when focus is on (primary) speech rather than on (secondary) writing. So some focus must be on variants from the standard dialect, if we are truly to understand what is taking place at any period in the formation and evolution of an English.

7. FRENCH

As both Smith and Milroy assert, 'variation' is the spur for language change, this variation being the result of both intra- and extra-territorial forces. This is no better exemplified for English than in the next phase of its development, which comes with the eleventh-century Norman Conquest and continues throughout the following centuries of the Middle Ages. Although Norman French influence on English did not begin with the invasion of 1066, interaction between the two languages being in evidence much earlier, speakers of English in larger measure had to accommodate to a new linguistic environment only with the coming of French-speaking conquerors in that year. In due course English speakers were provided with further resource for their language as a result. It is a truism, but one that cannot be repeated too frequently, that development of a language is caused by its speakers, and speakers in England experiencing the clash of OE, ON and Norman French were bound to have much to do to fashion their speech to cope with the times in which they lived. Smith (1996: especially 128–140 and 144–150) is instructive in summarising the most telling lexical, morphological and syntactic activity in a period of remarkable linguistic change, as the speakers of three languages interacted.

The result of the coming of French was that EE entered a stage where dialectal variation was the norm. There was now no pre-eminent English variety to which the adjective 'standard' could be applied, since the late West Saxon variety of OE, which was (at least when written) its most influential immediately pre-Conquest form, became increasingly relegated to simple varietal status with the overthrow of the Anglo-Saxon Wessex dynasty. In consequence, English writers of the early Middle English period and up to the late fourteenth century wrote in their own vernaculars: Chaucer in east Midland, Langland in southwest Midland, 'The Gawaine Poet' in northwest Midland and so on. Until the very end of the ME period, at which point a written standard can be seen to be emerging, we are in what Crystal (2004: 194–217) terms 'a dialect age'. Of this he writes exuberantly: 'For a glorious 300 years, people could write as they wanted to, and nobody could say they were wrong' (Crystal 2004: 195). We thus have a fresh external force countering an emerging consensus on a stable language. Into the fourteenth century, however, the linguistic tide was turning somewhat. More than 200 years since the coming to England of Norman French, this to be followed by metropolitan Old French, noble family ties between England and France were weakening. From 1362, government business was conducted in English (Freeborn 1992: 60), this signalling a significant, though not definitive, change of direction. The stage was set for the emergence of an English variety around which official agreement could settle.

7.1 Reflection 7

It must be constantly held in mind that variety is the norm, especially though not exclusively in speech, spoken variation running ahead of changes that eventually become apparent in the written record when that record has a recognised standard dialect available for its transmission. Triggered by the overwhelming forces of external political, social and linguistic upheaval, and sustained by the dynamic force of long-established internal variation, for most of the ME period EE was freed from normative standard-dialectal restraints. It is quite possible for differentiations to prevail unopposed in a thriving linguistic tradition.

8. AN EMERGING STANDARD

In the fifteenth century some agreement begins to be observable on how EE was to be written, the start of the debate about 'right' and 'wrong' in usage which has been evident for English ever since. Crystal (2004: 222–248) succinctly charts the emergence of the standard, identifying psycholinguistic, social and natural evolutionary forces at work to bring this about. He argues that the variation in writing, especially spelling, which had characterised the ME 'dialect age' had become out of control, this being especially problematic for those now aspiring to learn to read and for those seeking to use the language for official administrative purposes: by 1400 many in the population were psychologically ready for some regularity to appear. There was personal need to resolve a socially unsettling and perplexing situation caused by confusion engendered through uncontrolled variation in practice. And, as French increasingly lost its place as a vehicle for administrative documentation, there was practical need for English to achieve some regularity if it was to be used as an official language: it now came to be needed as a tool for expression of all matters of national, not simply local, life. Furthermore, a quite natural tendency is for people linguistically to accommodate one to another and to adopt shared practice in order to communicate efficiently: here, Crystal invokes the sociolinguistic concept of social networks to explain the sharing of forms between speakers and writers possessed of a common purpose. (On networks specifically in a language-historical context, see Milroy 1992.)

At the psychological and social levels, we might also invoke the force of nationalism as a driver towards the upsurge in popularity of English for use in all matters of national life. On this issue, Fasold (1984: 3–4) observes:

> Another role that language plays in nationalism is what Fishman calls 'contrastive self-identification' and Garvin and Mathiot call the 'unifying and separatist functions'. Simply stated, these terms refer to the feeling of the members of a nationality that they are identified with others who speak the same language, and contrast with and are separated from those who do not.

It is significant that French, which had played a large part in administration in England since the Conquest, ultimately never took hold as the national language. Demographics will have played a large part in this, the great majority of the inhabitants of England being of Anglo-Saxon or Norse descent. But the largely French-descended aristocratic class, charged with the country's leadership in peace and war, increasingly veered towards English for pragmatic reasons. There are many arguments to be raised in favour of a language being seen to have both 'unifying' and 'contrastive' functions, but one should suffice here for consideration: England needed to be distinguished from France, the principal enemy of the age. In the constant warfare of the late Middle Ages the language of command will perforce have been English, if for no other reason than that the largely English and Welsh soldiery charged with fighting England's wars would have been less inclined to follow orders couched in French than they would ones in English. And there must have been some meeting of minds on just what the essential forms of that English were.

So, for a complex of reasons there was a movement in late medieval England towards the institution of a standard dialect, this always operating alongside a plethora of other distinct and competing varieties of English. It is important to emphasise the word 'alongside' here: the locally- and socially-located nonstandard dialects of the past were not displaced, but rather they continued to be used and, as living entities, they continued to evolve. However, a new and especially authoritative dialect with a nationwide purpose came to be established. Fasold quotes Fishman (1972) on this subject:

> Nationalisms consciously undertake to produce self-consciously modern, authentic, and unifying standard languages, which are to be consciously employed and conscientiously espoused, where previously there existed only regional and social varieties, unconsciously employed and unemotionally abandoned. (Fasold 1984: 4)

There are problems with this statement. We must question whether the rise of a standard dialect (certainly 'dialect' rather than 'language') was, in the case of Standard English, entirely deliberate. It was certainly not the result of any official dictum, and what consensus there was emerged only slowly over a considerable period. And we can observe that nonstandard dialects were not, and are not, 'unemotionally abandoned' by the many, but rather they persist for reasons of deep-seated regional and social identity. But the essential point is well made, that a standard variety of a language can perform a role in nationhood. English in the emergent medieval state needed to be codified for more than simply administrative reasons.

8.1 Reflection 8

The forces acting in the creation of a standard form of EE should now be clear. Many users of the variety were psychologically ready to see their language at the national level emerge from the anarchy of sole reliance on a multitude of competing varieties of only limited mutual comprehensibility. An agreed linguistic tool was required for the efficient governance of the realm. Especially at the official level, users of EE were subject to the understandable and well-documented tendency linguistically to accommodate one with another. All of these were forces internal to the speaker community. To them may be added one very significant external force, that of the need for language to act as a symbol of unity for an ambitious but frequently embattled nation. In the uncertain and contentious world of medieval Europe, England could close ranks against its Continental rivals by reinforcing its identity with a confident and robust language unique to itself.

9. ENGLISH IN BRITAIN BEYOND ENGLAND

Although concentration so far has been on EE, much of what has been claimed in terms of its evolutionary forces can of course also be claimed for the English varieties to be found in Scotland, Wales and Ireland. Residents in all of these had historically been subject to Anglo-Saxon, Norse, Norman French and later French linguistic influences, these playing their part in shaping emerging and evolving varieties. And all felt the effects of a developing standard dialect serving as a linguistic rallying-point for the wider British Isles. Especially as regards grammar, and to a lesser degree lexis and phonology, the emergence of Standard (English) English and (from the mid-nineteenth century on) Received Pronunciation have had some influence on the cementing together of peoples, especially as they have faced outwards to the world.

Nevertheless, notwithstanding continuing normalising effects from a prestige dialect, reinforced socially and through state education, bureaucracy and mass media, each constituent part of the British Isles has had, from the outset of the planting of English among its speakers, a wide range of dialectal varieties distinctive to itself. And although the minute distinctions that once prevailed have lessened in an age of improved communications and increased geographical and social mobility, robust support for distinctive variation has been maintained: the Irish Republic of course, since its formation in 1922, has had no necessary ties to the UK, and the confidence today engendered by growing political autonomy in Wales, Scotland and Northern Ireland, as separate identifiable nations within the UK, sees added expression in the use of non-EE there.

We recognise varying evolutionary circumstances as speaking to the possibilities of different linguistic forces operating within one overarching polity. Wales is the nation with the longest political attachment to England, and especially in the Marches border area, in the industrial South Wales valleys, and in the extreme southwest, English is long established as the language of the majority of speakers. Indeed, the identification of the southwest as 'Little England Beyond Wales' tells of almost a millennium of entrenched political, cultural and linguistic 'Englishness' there. By contrast, Scotland and Ireland have had only comparatively recent formal ties with England: now, as already mentioned, the larger part of Ireland has again been quite independent of English rule for almost a century; and so entrenched has been the English language in Scotland since Anglo-Saxon times that the versions there, from the most vernacular form to that most closely resembling Standard EE, have status as a language distinct from English, that is 'Scots' (Corbett et al. 2003: 1–4). Internal forces of history, politics and underlying social identity might mean that a language (in this case 'English') that is strongly associated with a territory might nevertheless be subject to diverse pressures and so take different forms, depending on where those pressures have been applied. And the fact that the Englishes of Wales, Scotland and Ireland are in many of their features quite distinct from the EE standard dialect is crucial to an understanding of the English exported to the world, especially given the several diasporas in which the populations of these British nations have been participants over a very long period.

Of course, linguistic variation is not to be tied to national boundaries as they are politically conceived, any more than they can be to regional boundaries as they exist administratively and/or in the minds of local communities and individual speakers. Herein lies a crucial matter of concern for anyone charged with identifying linguistic varieties to which it might be tempting to attach a territorial label. Gaston Paris's dictum of 1888 that 'there really are no dialects' (quoted in Davis et al. 1997: 281) cannot be too often repeated and is rightly to be set in the province of languages as well as dialects. Boundaries imagined or map-drawn between varieties prove illusory in the face of individuals' espousal of linguistic items drawn from a variety of sources, as well as the number of features that are used in any identification process. In his advocating the notion of 'transnational attraction', Schneider (2014: 28) rightly cites Fishkin's remarking the 'arbitrariness of borders'. (For an examination of this as it relates to the issue of non-standard dialects, see Davis et al. 1997; Kretzschmar 2002; Upton 2012, 2013.)

9.1 Reflection 9

Three essential implications emerge here. One is that linguistic features cannot be assigned to territory without there being variability in the stories told for any named region, up to and including national level. The finer the granularity with which the same data are interrogated, the more complexity is seen to exist. If this can be said for English as it is to be found within the confines of the United Kingdom, we can reasonably expect it to exist in World Englishes, so that care must be taken when making observations or claims regarding any one variety. Another message, following from the first, must be that linguistic boundaries are leaky beyond national borders, so that talk of a particular PCE or non-PCE having sway over just one country must be regarded ultimately as a fiction, albeit a useful fiction in certain contexts: this is most properly acknowledged in the unifying titles of chapters in the current book, each concerning 'English in x' rather than 'x English'. And a third point is that the larger territory from which English spread throughout the world, the British Isles, is home to a multiplicity of communities that have always identified themselves by local and regional variants. It is indeed one of the great strengths of the language that its regional forms have remained vibrant and that, while a small if influential elite might deplore the fact, there has been little success in attempts to impose the standard dialect on the majority, among whom variety and change have typically been widely tolerated. Occasional calls for an English equivalent of the Académie Française (a quite recent one by Honey [1997: 164]) have met with singular lack of support. In consequence, the regional and class backgrounds of the colonial settlers and administrators, who will have been linguistically influential in any particular territory overseas, have properly to be taken into account in the deeper analysis of the forms of English in use there.

10. EXPORTING ENGLISH

It is not the intention here to attempt any close analysis of the status of the EIF Model in places beyond the UK to which the language has been passed, others being far better able to undertake such work for their respective varieties. However, some general observations can contribute to the wider debate, these drawing on what has been written above and on personal experience.

We should be cautious about supposing that PCEs have arisen as a result of concerted British policies being implemented consistently in the past. In fact, some large amount of British territorial acquisition historically took place essentially in furtherance of reciprocal trade and the exploitative acquisition of materials to prosper home industry. For this, *any* form of English will have served. Unlike some other European nations, which came late to the colonising project, Britain was active in the expansion of its influence for some centuries before a system of overseas governance was properly formalised. It was not until 1854 that a distinct British Colonial Office came into being with the appointment of a Secretary of State for the Colonies (Kirk-Greene 1999): prior to that date, responsibilities for the colonies were variously, and significantly, linked directly to matters of trade and war. Sometimes, in the early days of Britain's expansiveness, the physical planting of settler communities was even officially frowned upon as taking place quite against the wishes of the home government, as was the initial case for Newfoundland (Government of Canada 1950: 15–41). More usually, when plantation of colonies was encouraged by successive British administrations, there is no great evidence that along with settlement came policy to impose a standard English. Indeed, apart from a short period following World War I, formal control of colonial education was apparently of no great concern to the British government (Whitehead 2005: 443), and what was true of education in the round will surely have applied to the teaching of English. Windel (2009: 16) points to this short period of tighter educational control being essentially inter-war and as ending 'sometime in the late 1950s or early 1960s, when education in Africa stopped being British and stopped being colonial'.

Of course, wherever formal centrally-controlled teaching of the English language was instituted under British rule, as afterwards by independent governments of former British colonies, it is to be expected that textbooks certainly, and teachers to some degree, were and remain oriented towards a standard (usually British) English dialect. My own experience teaching English in universities in Malawi and Papua New Guinea in the immediate postcolonial era was certainly that the baseline for instruction was in and about some standard form of English. But that standard was essentially *international* in form, as I taught with American and Australian as well as British colleagues. And notwithstanding a proper emphasis at political and administrative levels on high standards (see e.g. Kamwendo 2003: 31 on Malawi), a pragmatic grassroots view was typically taken to language acquisition, with emphasis on the ability to communicate effectively rather than on the minutiae of lexical, phonological or even grammatical regularity according to one strict (British) model. Beyond the classroom, variations were to be expected, these born of generations who have inherited and further developed indigenous English variants. In this respect there is no difference between the localised UK dialects and PCEs, all of which have pedigrees deserving of recognition.

Herein might lie a measure of distinction between PCEs and non-PCEs. The former, like EE, draw upon a tradition – sometimes a very long tradition – which might have seen the interaction of English with indigenous languages and between numerous regional and social imported varieties. They will of course have been subject to the same kinds of judgemental pressures to which home-grown British 'nonstandard' dialects have been and continue to be subject, so that the more highly-educated speakers might be conscious of any divergence of their own usage from that formally taught. But even in the case of comparatively newly established PCEs there could exist a marked level of confidence in indigenous forms, confidence in some cases approaching that of the English speakers of the USA and the 'Old Commonwealth'. In contrast to these Englishes, a non-PCE might not (yet, at least) have had time fully to establish its own traditions. Where there has been close contact with surrounding PCEs, we might expect it to have imbibed features from its once-colonial neighbours: this can be expected of non-PCE varieties in southern and south-central Africa, for example, where South African English has its own standard norms and varieties available for transmission. But even in such cases the English of the schoolroom might dominate. Especially in countries with a strict normative education system the rule of long-established teachers and teaching materials might prevail, this at the expense of the realities of recent native-English language developments.

At an academic meeting in Poland some few years ago, I presented a paper on changes to Received Pronunciation transcription that would result in the accent being reproduced accurately by phonetics-literate teachers and learners. Featured transcriptions included those which were then becoming embedded in the Oxford English Dictionaries (Upton et al. 2001) and have now gained the widest acceptance (Cruttenden 2014). While students fully appreciated the desirability of change in theoretical transcription and consequent practical articulation, they were aware of a need to adhere to the prescriptions of their teachers while under instruction. Of course, the brake placed on the development of an indigenous English, be that internally driven or externally influenced, can be expected to be only temporary. But depending on the strength of prescriptive forces at play, the nature of that development might be different in kind from that of an English which has evolved over time in a more relaxed and natural context.

10.1 Reflection 10

English at large in the world has been established in various ways for various reasons, these having less to do with notions of linguistic purity and standard-variety excellence than of control over resources and, more recently in the colonial era, over the territories from which resources were to be obtained. (More recently, of course, increasing communication possibilities have led to the forces of globalisation outstripping all else in this regard.) Traditionally, the varieties of English to which indigenous communities were exposed were many, there being no reason to infer a heavy-handed colonial diktat for transmission of one variety across what (quite belatedly) came to be the British Empire. Broadly, PCEs are in essence unregulated in their evolution. The same might or might not be the case for a non-PCE subject to educational policy imposed in response to the current global influence of English as a resource. Societies differ in their response to the prescriptive, and it is impossible to generalise in this regard. But, when assessing the forms which a World English takes, the psycho-social forces operating within a specific culture might usefully be examined as regards attitudes to deference to authority, formality, correctness and consequent language change.

11. CONCLUSION

Contemplation of aspects of the past career and present position of EE might provide a platform from which to examine development of World Englishes modelling, as it both shares in and differs from the experience of other varieties. The foundation of EE in time did not stem from that 'colonial' state-sponsored imposition implicit in both the foundation and exonormative stabilisation phases of the Dynamic Model, though it did at foundation encounter 'sociolinguistic situations in which different languages and different varieties of English meet', as put forward in the EIF Model (Buschfeld and Kautsch 2017: 115). By definition, its nativisation was present at its foundation, as was (crucially) differentiation of varieties as planted and evolved. An indigenous language was in large measure replaced. It is argued here that for more than a millennium there was little if any endonormative stabilisation and that, furthermore, for the remainder of its career most speakers – and very many writers – have been little troubled by standard-dialect strictures. Of course, access to privileged echelons of British society has long been predicated on an ability to use the standard dialect of the day. But most native users, even many who are masters of the standard dialect, have access to nonstandard dialects, and it is a rich mix of varieties that has spread outwards to the world, communication rather than conventionality being the rule when English has been exported.

Moreover, there is an important sense in which World Englishes are all part of that accepted differentiation which has always characterised English: however independent of EE other Englishes become – and American English has long been a dominant force as the oldest and most influential PCE of all – they are all part of a pantheon of varieties ultimately tied back to their British homeland.

The popular embrace of varietal differences in their language has continued unabated among English people, despite the necessary development of a standard (but constantly evolving) dialect, and it is held that this has done much to foster the worldwide popularity of their language. (Quite properly, Schneider [2003: 235] lists 'the state, business companies, religious communities, missionary and colonization societies, and also simply individuals' as among the agents of colonial expansion: at the linguistic level, 'individuals' can usefully head this list, speakers rather than agencies being the primary agents for the transmission of language in any age or place.) Acceptance and even welcoming of varieties will of course have varied from place to place and time to time, but it is too tempting to see colonisation as involving a controlling linguistic zeal, when in truth communication has mattered much more than, and frequently with total disregard to, conformity. Variation being a norm, the identity of any English implanted elsewhere is not necessarily to be thought of as invested solely in its standard dialect. Extra- and intra-territorial forces of 'Attitude to variation' might be added to the list of forces posited by the EIF Model, a mainly positive interpretation of this being likely to apply to both PCEs and non-PCEs at anything other than the most prescriptive educational and administrative levels. Of course, attitude to variation will be variable in the intra-territorial realm, depending on how prescriptive various regimes have been as regards language policies. It might also as a general rule apply more positively to PCEs than to non-PCEs, the latter being more under the control of prescriptive educationalists than are the former. While it is of course true that 'rules of correctness' 'might come from institutions like the British Council or the implementation of the TOEFL [Test of English as a Foreign Language] or any other factor influencing linguistic choices and norm orientations' (Buschfeld and Kautzsch 2017: 114), as concerns PCEs the embedding of English in pre-colonial and colonial times began long before the rise of agencies of linguistic normalisation, and was largely in the hands of those with primarily utilitarian goals, while even at the educational level British colonial policy was largely laissez-faire. Rather than assuming that British colonialism as an extra-territorial force was concerned with driving home a rigid English-language doctrine in its overseas possessions, it is advisable in each individual case to search the historical record for the facts.

Written significantly into the EIF Model is the importance of foreign policies as a force operating in the development of World Englishes. Touching on this, if somewhat tangentially, is the linguistic stance which a country takes towards others, especially its neighbours. It has been asserted in section 8 above that an important driver in the medieval establishment of EE as the national language, in face (especially) of French, was nationalism. A nation might see its embrace of English solely as a means of it entering a wider regional or global sphere, in which case it will adopt an English as little different as possible from that of others. But to the extent that its inhabitants feel required to assert distinctiveness from others, they might be expected to heighten the uniqueness of the languages available, English included. (Europe at the present time might provide fruitful ground for exploration of this, it being the site of both unifying and separatist imperatives at play in the political arena.) 'Nationalism' might be considered to be both an extra- and an intra-territorial force potentially applying to PCEs and non-PCEs alike.

These final suggestions join the 'reflections' advanced piecemeal in the preceding sections, in the contention that there can be transfer from the realities of the sixteen-century career of EE to the structured codifying of other, newer, Englishes. Whether taken collectively or severally, their consideration should prove instructive as they are applied variously to established and emerging World Englishes.

REFERENCES

Breeze, Andrew. 2002. Seven types of Celtic loanword. In Markku Filppula, Juhani Klemola, and Heli Pitkänen, eds. 2002, *Studies in Languages 37: The Celtic Roots of English*. Joensuu: University of Joensuu, 175–181.

Buschfeld, Sarah and Alexander Kautzsch. 2017. Towards an integrated approach to postcolonial and non-postcolonial Englishes. *World Englishes* 36.1: 104–126.

Corbett, John and Jane Stuart-Smith. 2012. Standard English in Scotland. In Raymond Hickey, ed. 2012, *Standards of English: Codified Varieties Around the World*. Cambridge: Cambridge University Press, 72–95.

Corbett, John, J. Derrick McClure and Jane Stuart-Smith. 2003. A brief history of Scots. In John Corbett, J. Derrick McClure and Jane Stuart-Smith, eds. 2003, *The Edinburgh Companion to Scots*. Edinburgh: Edinburgh University Press, 1–16.
Cruttenden, Alan. 2014. *Gimson's Pronunciation of English*. 8th edn. London: Routledge.
Crystal, David. 2004. *The Stories of English*. London: Allen Lane.
Davis, Lawrence M., Charles L. Houck and Clive Upton. 1997. The question of dialect boundaries: The SED and the American atlases. In Alan R. Thomas, ed. 1997, *Issues and Methods in Dialectology*. Bangor: University of Wales Bangor, 271–283.
Fasold, Ralph. 1984. *The Sociolinguistics of Society*. Oxford: Blackwell.
Filppula, Markku, Juhani Klemola and Heli Paulasto. 2008. *English and Celtic in Contact*. New York and London: Routledge.
Freeborn, Dennis. 1992. *From Old English to Standard English*. Basingstoke and London: Macmillan.
Government of Canada. 1950. Newfoundland history: Early colonization and settlement policy in Newfoundland. In *Newfoundland: An Introduction to Canada's New Province*. Ottawa: Department of External Affairs, 15–41, http://faculty.marianopolis.edu/c.belanger/nfldhistory/NewfoundlandHistory-EarlyColonizationandSettlementofNewfoundland.htm (last accessed September 12 2018).
Hickey, Raymond. 2007. *Irish English*. Cambridge: Cambridge University Press.
Honey, John. 1997. *Language is Power: The Story of Standard English and its Enemies*. London: Faber and Faber.
Kamwendo, Gregory. 2003. Is Malawi guilty of spoiling the Queen's language? *English Today* 19.2: 30–33.
Kirk-Greene, Anthony. 1999. The colonial office: Administering British territories and colonies. *OSPA* 77, https://www.britishempire.co.uk/article/colonialoffice.htm (last accessed September 12 2018).
Kretzschmar, William A. 2002. Dialectology and the history of the English language. In Donka Minkova and Robert Stockwell, eds. 2002, *Studies in the History of the English Language*. Berlin: Mouton de Gruyter, 79–108.
Milroy, James. 1992. *Linguistic Variation and Change: On the Historical Sociolinguistics of English*. Oxford: Basil Blackwell.
Milroy, James. 1996. Linguistic ideology and the Anglo-Saxon lineage of English. In Juhani Klemola, Merja Kytö and Matti Rissanen, eds. 1996, *Speech Past and Present: Studies in English*

Dialectology in Memory of Ossi Ihalainen. Frankfurt am Main: Peter Lang, 169–186.
Paulasto, Heli, Rob Penhallurick and Benjamin Jones. Forthcoming. *Welsh English*. Berlin and Boston: De Gruyter Mouton.
Penhallurick, Rob. 2008a. Welsh English: phonology. In Bernd Kortmann and Clive Upton, eds. 2008, *Varieties of English, 1: The British Isles*. Berlin: Mouton de Gruyter, 105–121.
Penhallurick, Rob. 2008b. Welsh English: Morphology and syntax. In Bernd Kortmann and Clive Upton, eds. 2008, *Varieties of English, 1: The British Isles*. Berlin: Mouton de Gruyter, 360–372.
Schneider, Edgar W. 2003. The dynamics of new Englishes: From identity construction to dialect birth. *Language* 79.2: 233–281.
Schneider, Edgar W. 2014. New reflections on the evolutionary dynamics of world Englishes. *World Englishes* 33.1: 9–32.
Smith, Jeremy. 1996. *A Historical Study of English: Function, Form and Change*. London: Routledge.
Tristram, Hildegard L. C. 2002. Attrition of inflections in English and Welsh. In Markku Filppula, Juhani Klemola and Heli Pitkänen, eds. 2002, *Studies in Languages 37: The Celtic Roots of English*. Joensuu: University of Joensuu, 111–149.
Upton, Clive. 2012. The importance of being Janus: Midland speakers and the 'North-South Divide'. In Manfred Markus, Yoko Inieri, Reinhard Heuberger and Emil Chamson, eds. 2012, *Middle and Modern English Corpus Linguistics: A Multi-dimensional Approach*. Amsterdam and Philadelphia: John Benjamins, 257–268.
Upton, Clive. 2013. Blurred boundaries: The dialect word from the BBC. In Clive Upton and Bethan L. Davies, eds. 2013, *Analysing Twenty-first Century British English: Conceptual and Methodoligical Aspects of the Voices Project*. London: Routledge, 180–197.
Upton, Clive, William A. Jr Kretzschmar and Rafal Konopka. 2001. *The Oxford Dictionary of Pronunciation for Current English*. Oxford: Oxford University Press.
Wales, Katie. 2006. *Northern English: A Cultural and Social History*. Cambridge: Cambridge University Press.
Whitehead, Clive. 2005. The historiography of British Imperial educational policy, part II: Africa and the rest of the colonial empire. *History of Education* 34.4: 441–454.
Windel, Aaron. 2009. British colonial education in Africa: Policy and practice in the era of trusteeship. *History Compass* 7.1: 1–21.

CHAPTER 3

English in Namibia: Multilingualism and Ethnic Variation in the Extra- and Intra-territorial Forces Model

Anne Schröder and Frederic Zähres

1. INTRODUCTION

The English spoken in Namibia is a newcomer to the family of varieties of English around the world. It has been disregarded in most publications on World Englishes (WE) (e.g. Kachru et al. 2009; Kirkpatrick 2010; Kortmann and Schneider 2004; Schneider 2011), although it is sometimes mentioned in passing (e.g. Melchers and Shaw 2011: 159), generally, however, only with reference to (White) South African English (SAfE) (e.g. Trudgill and Hannah 2017: 35). It was not even considered for inclusion in volumes on "lesser-known varieties of English" (Schreier et al. 2010a; Williams et al. 2015), because in Namibia "English has gained a special status only recently" and "fails to meet the criterion of direct transmission" (Schreier at al. 2010b: 10). This fact, however, seems to have attracted the attention of a handful of researchers, who investigate various aspects of English language dynamics in the country (see Schröder forthcoming). Namibia has never been a British colony and the widespread use of English on a nationwide level only started with independence in 1990 and the subsequent introduction of English as the sole official language. This makes this country an interesting case with regard to the purpose of this volume, that is, modeling WE and unifying postcolonial Englishes (PCEs) with non-postcolonial Englishes (non-PCEs).

In their article introducing the Extra- and Intra-territorial Forces Model (EIF), Buschfeld and Kautzsch (2017: 107–111) take the situation in Namibia as a starting point to demonstrate the shortcomings of the Dynamic Model (Schneider 2007), which does not account for the developments of English in non-postcolonial contexts. They reveal that despite the fact that quite obviously "English in Namibia exhibits parallels with postcolonial types of English" (2017: 110), it lacks "important sociopolitical and sociolinguistic factors postulated by the model" (2017: 110), most notably the experience of British colonization. As they elaborate, without British colonists settling the country, the language contact dynamics between the settler strand and the indigenous population are absent. These, however, constitute the central idea of the Dynamic Model, and hence, its applicability to the Namibian case is seriously challenged.

This is why Buschfeld and Kautzsch (2017) propose the EIF Model as "a solution that integrates PCEs and non-PCEs in a unified framework" (2017: 113). They identify a number of forces operating from outside (extra-territorial) and from inside of a country (intra-territorial). These are assumed to exert an influence on the language dynamics "both on the national level but also on the different groups of speakers within and ultimately also across particular countries" (Buschfeld and Kautzsch 2017: 113).

In order to move their theoretical reflections to an application, Buschfeld and Kautzsch (2017: 119–120) use Namibia as a case study. However, for space limitations and their paper having a theoretical focus, they look at the Namibian situation without much detail. We believe that accounts of linguistic features may lead to a deeper understanding of the effects of extra- and intra-territorial forces on the development of English in Namibia.

This is what the present chapter will provide: taking up the discussion from Buschfeld and Kautzsch (2017) and elaborating on observations from Kautzsch and Schröder (2016) as well as Schröder et al. (2020) on Namibian-specific realizations of vowels, we will show that Namibian English (NamE) probably cannot be seen as a monolithic whole. We argue that it should be considered a bundle of local sub-varieties and, hence, we will point to the question marks in the EIF Model (see Buschfeld and Kautzsch 2017: 14, figure 2) concerning the phase of differentiation (and thus possibly also the one on endonormative stabilization). This will necessitate the discussion of the status of (Namibian) English in comparison to Afrikaans, which is still regarded a major lingua franca in parts of the country, and also to minority languages, such as German, as well as majority languages, such as Oshiwambo. We will do so by focusing on identity constructions based on insights gathered from language use and attitude surveys, as well as taking into account the concept of epicenters to investigate the role of South Africa in the Namibian context, both before and after independence.

2. NAMIBIA AND THE EIF MODEL: SOME PRELIMINARY CONSIDERATIONS

Buschfeld and Kautzsch identify a number of extra- and intra-territorial forces which help to systematize the linguistic situation in Namibia vis-à-vis the development of English. Buschfeld (2014) also sketches "possible developmental scenarios" and determines "what role can be attributed to South Africa for the development of [English in Namibia]" (2014: 194). English was very probably first introduced into the territory through the annexation of the seaport of Walvis Bay and its incorporation into the British Cape Colony in 1878/1884 (Dierks 2002: 53, 60; Wallace 2011: 57, 106). This led to this town becoming part of the newly founded Union of Africa in 1910, the predecessor of today's Republic of South Africa. The Union of Africa was also granted the administration of the rest of the territory, that is, the then German colony of South West Africa (SWA), from 1915 onwards. Hence, the first type of English brought into the region "would not have been British English [. . .] but rather an L2 variety, viz. South African English (SAfEng)" (Buschfeld 2014: 195). "The South African takeover conditioned the history of SWA for the rest of the twentieth century" (Wallace 2011: 215).

Referring to Namibia as a non-PCE country implies that the British colonization of Walvis Bay is considered to play a negligible role in the identity constructions and rewritings of the newly formed nation. The same would account for the influence of the South African "colonial style of rule that lasted almost 70 years" (Tonchi et al. 2012: 6), at least with regard to the English language spoken in this country. In fact, according to Buschfeld, English in Namibia is not primarily "the product of early South African influence [. . .] but the result of the 1990 change in language policy" (2014: 195), when English was made the sole official language of the newly independent country. Buschfeld and Kautzsch also point out that the foundation phase probably precedes independence, and that the stabilization phase then sets in with the country's independence; with the subsequent spread of bilingualism and English assuming an important role in present-day Namibia, the country is furthermore described as having entered the nativization phase recently (Buschfeld and Kautzsch 2017: 120).

The attractiveness of Buschfeld and Kautzsch's proposal certainly lies in the fact that they downplay the importance of South Africa, and thus any variety of SAfE in the formation of NamE. Hence, the authors systematically challenge the predominant picture of viewing NamE as an offspring variety of SAfE. Furthermore, possible South African influences are not categorically excluded, but the "many linguistic parallels can just as well be explained by the very similar language contact scenarios, especially with respect to English meeting Afrikaans as *lingua franca* in both countries" (Buschfeld 2014: 296, original italics).

However, any development beyond phase 3 remains speculative in their model (as well as for Namibia) since "Phase 4 status, and thus endonormative stabilization, to our knowledge has never been reported for a non-PCE country" (Buschfeld and Kautzsch 2017: 118). What Mesthrie and Bhatt already suggest for PCEs, namely that "a territory could move from phase 3 to 5, bypassing phase 4" and that "English [becomes] nativized and subsequently differentiated into sub-dialects, without there being a commonly accepted endonormative standard" (Mesthrie and Bhatt 2008: 35), may also be an option for non-PCEs, as the discussion in Edwards (2016: 184) shows. Similarly, Bekker (2009) – with reference to the different varieties of SAfE – "emphasizes the need for sub-varieties to be allowed 'to run their own course'" (as reported in Schneider 2014a: 13). This, however, also runs counter to "the assumption of relative uniformity being characteristic of the endonormativity stage" (Schneider 2014a: 29, endnote 2). We believe that this interplay between stabilization and heterogeneity is of utmost relevance in the Namibian context, and probably for the EIF Model as such.

To overcome these issues, Buschfeld et al. (2018) add a new dimension to the original EIF Model, addressing a number of factors causing heterogeneity. We believe multilingualism and ethnicity to be among the most relevant ones in the Namibian context, but also the purported similarity to and influence of SAfE, which includes the influence of Afrikaans. We will therefore investigate these factors in the Namibian context in more detail in the following sections.

3. ETHNIC DIVERSITY, MULTILINGUALISM AND IDENTITY CONSTRUCTIONS

Namibia is one of the least densely populated countries in the world, but it hosts a variety of ethnic groups, languages and language families.

Table 3.1 Namibian households by main language spoken

Language	Language family	Number of households	Percentages
Oshiwambo	Bantu	227,103	48.9
Nama/Damara	Khoisan	52,450	11.3
Afrikaans	Indo-European	48,238	10.4
Otjiherero	Bantu	40,000	8.6
Kavango	Bantu	39,566	8.5
Caprivi	Bantu	22,484	4.8
English	Indo-European	15,912	3.4
German	Indo-European	4,359	0.9
Other	N/A	14,727	3.2
Total		**464,839**	**100**

Source: cf. Namibia Statistics Agency (2012: 68).

The CIA World Factbook lists the following ethnic groups: the Ovambo (constituting 50 percent of the population), the Kavango (9 percent), the Herero and the Damara (7 percent each), the Nama (5 percent), the Caprivian (4 percent), San (3 percent), Basters (2 percent), and the Tswana (0.5 percent). Only 6 percent of the population are reported to be 'white.' These include Afrikaners, that is, "white South Africans of Dutch descent" (Tonchi et al. 2012: 19), but also German-Namibians. Hence, in the linguistic ecology of the country we find next to English two other languages (Afrikaans and German) from the Indo-European language family, but also approximately sixteen Bantu languages (e.g. Oshiwambo, Otjiherero), and about nine Khoisan languages (e.g. Nama/Damara, San).[1]

The Namibian 2011 Population and Housing Census provides an overview of the distribution of the languages spoken as the main language in households and it roughly reflects the distribution of the ethnic groups within the Namibian population.

The census data seemingly show that comparatively few Namibians

---

[1] As Buschfeld and Kautzsch (2014: 122, footnote 4) point out, the naming conventions of indigenous southern African languages constitute a somewhat challenging and problematic topic. While we are aware of ongoing discussions in this matter, we will refer to the two major African language families as Bantu and Khoisan, respectively. The major Bantu speech communities in Namibia will be referred to as Otjiherero-speaking and Oshiwambo-speaking, respectively. The two major Khoisan languages in Namibia are named San and Nama/Damara in this chapter.

use English as their main language at home as very few Namibians speak English as their L1 (Tonchi et al. 2012: 4). However, the survey did not allow for multiple replies and the numbers thus conceal the fact that "[a]n overwhelming majority of Namibians claim to speak two or more languages with nearly half claiming three or more" and "over 80 percent claim to have a working knowledge of English" (Tonchi et al. 2012: 4).

As Buschfeld and Schröder (2020: 349) show, "English is definitely making inroads even into the homes of non L1-speaking families." In their survey, "one third of the informants [. . .] claimed to speak English often, mostly or always at dinner or when discussing personal matters with family members, and almost half of them to speak English often, mostly or always at home in general" (Buschfeld and Schröder 2020: 349).[2] Furthermore, English has become the primary mode of communication when talking to friends and acquaintances (Buschfeld and Schröder 2020: 350, table 17.8).

Buschfeld and Schröder also corroborate observations by Buschfeld and Kautzsch who describe a "shift from Afrikaans to English outside the family domain for people born 1985 onwards" (2014: 139), since in their survey Afrikaans "seems to have become disfavored and partly been replaced by English as a language in official and administrative contexts and for job interviews" (Buschfeld and Schröder 2020: 350). Moreover, English also seemingly supersedes Afrikaans as the primary medium of inter-ethnic communication (Buschfeld and Kautzsch 2014: 142; Buschfeld and Schröder 2020: 348, table 17.6). However, Buschfeld and Schröder's (2020) results must be taken with a grain of salt. The representativeness of their data cannot be assured and they are also right in pointing out that "Afrikaans is still widely spoken, far from disappearing" with the stigma "left from the Apartheid era [. . .] slowly washing off" (Buschfeld and Schröder 2020: 356–357). When it comes to linguistic and cultural identity constructions, for instance, we can see that for the majority of the Afrikaans L1-speaking Namibians, Afrikaans is also the language they most strongly identify with.

We would like to look at cultural and linguistic identity constructions

---

[2] This survey is based on an expanded version of the questionnaire also applied in Buschfeld and Kautzsch (2014). Two hundred and thirty-seven informants completed the questionnaire; these represent the major ethnic groups, but the majority of the informants are comparatively young and linked to the educational sector as either pupils, university students, teachers or lecturers. See Buschfeld and Schröder (2020: 344–346) for details.

in more detail and complement some observations from Buschfeld and Schröder (2020). Since the focus of their paper lies on English, German, and to some extent Afrikaans in Namibia, Buschfeld and Schröder report on the West Germanic L1-speakers only. In the context of the present discussion, however, we find it necessary to include informants from the Bantu L1-speaking and Khoisan L1-speaking groups. Here, quite obviously, we consider the biggest linguistic group, namely Oshiwambo L1-speakers,[3] but also two other culturally relevant groups, that is, Otjiherero L1-speakers, as well as Nama/Damara L1-speakers.[4] By taking the same survey data as Buschfeld and Schröder (2020), we can see how Namibians from diverse linguistic backgrounds conceive themselves in the multilingual and multicultural ecology of Namibia.[5]

While the Germans were noted "to be the culturally most homogenous" from the Indo-European L1-speaking groups, with "75% (24) of them most strongly identify[ing] with 'German' culture" (Buschfeld and Schröder 2020: 353), we can see that only the Oshiwambo L1-speakers are similarly homogenous; 78.4 percent (58) of them give 'Oshiwambo' as an answer to the question: *With which culture do you most strongly identify?* These figures are decisively higher than for the Otjiherero L1-speaking, of which 52.9 percent (9) identify with the Herero culture most strongly. The same is true for the Nama/Damara-speaking group, with 52.2 percent (12) of them identifying with the Damara culture most strongly, and another 13.04 percent (3) mentioning 'Nama.' However, these results differ markedly from the other two Germanic-speaking groups, for which Buschfeld and Schröder (2020) note that they are culturally rather heterogeneous:

---

[3] Here, the classification 'Oshiwambo' not only includes informants who simply self-identified their L1 as Oshiwambo, but also those listing the two major Oshiwambo dialects Kwanyama and Ndonga as their L1 (cf. Simons and Fennig 2018).

[4] The labels are self-identifications that the informants filling in the questionnaire gave by answering the question: *Which language(s) did you first speak as a child?*

[5] We would like to thank Sarah Buschfeld, Markus Bieswanger and Alexander Kautzsch, who were part of the research team conducting this survey in 2014. We would also like to thank the student assistants at Bielefeld University, most notably Jens Thomas, Daniela Kauschke and Lisa Schumacher, for entering the results into an SPSS grid. Furthermore, we thank the many people who supported the process of data collection, most notably Sarala Krishnamurthy, Ernest Olivier, Ronel Louw, Reiner Stommel, and Gillian Stommel.

> Our Afrikaans L1-speaking informants mainly identify with 'White/Afrikaner' culture, with 'Coloured' culture, or 'Rehoboth Baster' culture. Some even mention an 'Afrikaans' culture, but, possibly more surprising, 'English' and 'German' or 'Damara' and 'Ovambo' are also mentioned among the cultures with which some of these L1-speakers most strongly identify. These are also the cultures with which the English L1-speakers among our informants identify, the only difference being that none of these cultures seems to be dominant in this group. (Buschfeld & Schröder 2020: 353)

When asking the informants with which language they most strongly identify, 71.9 percent (23) of the German L1-speakers give 'German' as their answer. The figures are similarly high for 'Afrikaans' as the language with which 67.9 percent (53) of the Afrikaans L1-speaking informants identify. For 54.1 percent (40) of the Oshiwambo L1-speakers it is 'Oshiwambo,' for 35.3 percent (6) of the Otjiherero L1-speakers it is 'Otjiherero,' and for 26.1 percent (6) of the Nama/Damara L1-speaking informants it is 'Nama/Damara.' As it seems, however, English is also slowly becoming a language of identification for all linguistic groups: almost one third of each of the Afrikaans L1-speakers (25/32.1 percent), the Nama/Damara L1-speakers (7/30.4 percent) and the Oshiwambo L1-speakers (22/29.7 percent) identifies most strongly with the English language. This is also true for 25.0 percent (8) of the German L1-speaking and for 23.5 percent (4) of the Otjiherero L1-speaking respondents.

This observation is further confirmed by looking at the answers given to the question: *Which language do you prefer to use in most situations whenever possible?* This is 'English' for three quarters (55/74.3 percent) of the Oshiwambo L1-speakers, for almost two thirds of the German L1-speaking (20/62.5 percent) and for more than half of the Otjiherero L1-speaking (10/58.8 percent) respondents, as well as for almost half (38/48.7 percent) of the Afrikaans L1-speakers and for 43.5 percent (10) of the Nama/Damara L1-speakers. Their respective L1 is the most preferred language for only 12.2 percent (9) of the Oshiwambo L1-speakers, for one Nama/Damara L1-speaking respondent and for none from the Otjiherero L1-speaking group. 'Afrikaans,' however, is still comparatively firmly rooted within the Afrikaans L1-speaking group, of which 55.1 percent (43) claim it to be the language they prefer to use whenever possible. Afrikaans is also the language that 34.8 percent (8) of the Nama/Damara L1-speakers prefer to use in most situations. For the

German L1-speaking group, 37.5 percent (12) still prefer German over any other language.

Finally, English is the language which the majority of the respondents, irrespective of their L1-background, consider the most prestigious. This is true for 73.1 percent (57) of the Afrikaans L1-speaking, 64.9 percent (48) of the Oshiwambo L1-speaking, 65.2 percent (15) of the Nama/Damara L1-speaking, 58.8 percent (10) of the Otjiherero L1-speaking, and 50.0 percent (16) of the German L1-speaking informants.

What these figures suggest is that many Namibians still identify culturally with one of the ethnic groups, which is largely determined by their respective L1, that is, a German culture for the German L1-speaking respondents or an Ovambo culture for the Oshiwambo L1-speakers. This is seemingly less so for an 'Afrikaans' culture, because the Afrikaans language as an L1 comprises diverse ethnic groups, such as the Rehoboth Basters, Coloureds, and white/Afrikaners. Linguistically, however, a shift of identification from the respective L1 to English appears to be happening at a seemingly more accelerated rate for some groups than for others. All ethnic and linguistic groups do however acknowledge the importance of English in the multilinguistic ecology of the country. As conceptions of cultural identity are still mainly happening along ethnic lines while linguistic identity constructions are slowly shifting towards English, linguistic ethnic differentiation could happen within NamE, which means it could lead to ethnically based varieties of NamE. However, we do acknowledge that the figures of this survey are far from representative. Like the report by Buschfeld and Schröder (2020), the sample in our study is biased towards the younger and more educated stratum of the Namibian society; however, this may possibly point even more accurately towards future developments.

Before we can look at how these identity constructions translate into linguistic practices, which may possibly manifest themselves in the development of Namibian-specific linguistic norms in the English language, we believe that the various links to and ties with South Africa need to be specified in more detail.

4. RELATIONSHIPS TO SOUTH AFRICA

In the past, NamE has been described to "closely resemble [SAfE]" (Trudgill and Hannah 2017: 35) and to orient itself specifically "towards White SAfE, but with features [resembling] those of Black SAfE"

(Gramley 2012: 308). The reasons are, of course, the historical links as well as the influence South Africa still exerts on the country, both linguistically and economically.

Contact between the two territories began early. Dierks (2002: 6–7) reports on a vessel sailing from Cape Town to the mouth of the Kuiseb River and skirmishes between the Dutch and the local Namas at Sandwich Harbour (near Walvis Bay) from as early as 1677. From the eighteenth century onwards, Dutch settlers attempted to explore the territory north of the Orange River and South Africans continuously visited, worked, or even settled permanently in Namibia (Tonchi et al. 2012: 390).[6] At the end of the eighteenth century for example, "the Orlam Afrikaners [left] South Africa permanently and beg[a]n to settle in present-day Namibia" (Dierks 2002: 11). The Oorlams were an ethnically mixed group, "consisting of (Cape) Khoekhoe, descendants of mixed settler-slave/settler-Khoekhoe unions, runaway slaves and Cape outlaws," who "settled primarily in southern and central Namibia, where they intermarried with Khoesan-speaking communities" (Deumert 2009: 355). Some seventy years later, in 1870, they were joined by approximately ninety families from another group of people of mixed origin from the Cape Colony. The offspring of predominantly Dutch settlers and the indigenous Khoikhoi eventually settled in the area of Rehoboth and came to be known as Rehoboth Basters (see Schröder et al. 2020 for details). These two early settler groups from the Cape Colony would have been bilingual, bringing Cape Dutch/Afrikaans as well as Khoisan languages into the territory.[7]

The Cape Colony was also the point of departure for many trading and missionary enterprises towards Namibia (Tonchi et al. 2012: 390). For the first half of the nincteenth century, several missionary activities "cause[d] a cardinal reconstruction of identity and the social space" (Dierks 2002: 23). They interfered massively in local politics, and planned missionary stations and military centers (Dierks 2002: 23). Furthermore, Dierks describes a "destructive trade network with the Cape Colony," which "drain[ed] the country of assets and productive resources and [for which it] receive[d] nothing comparable in exchange" (Dierks 2002:

---

[6] See Dierks (2002: 7–11) for details on explorers coming from the Cape Colony and the South African Dutch East India Company in the eighteenth century.

[7] Deumert uses "the term Cape Dutch/Afrikaans to refer to the continuum of Dutch-based contact varieties that existed in South Africa and Namibia until the early 20th century" (2009: 355, footnote 6).

23). New diseases and alcoholism were by-products brought to the area from the Cape via this route. In 1876, the Cape parliament declared the Hereroland and the Namaland protectorates and appointed William Coates Palgrave as Special Commissioner (later Civil Commissioner), who visited Walvis Bay, Okahandja, Rehoboth, and some other places for negotiations several times in the same year and the years to follow (Dierks 2002: 50–55). On one of his journeys, Palgrave sought to assist a group of trekboers, attempting to settle in Namibia (Dierks 2002: 53), some of whom moved on to Angola (Tonchi et al. 2012: 390). The influence from the Cape Colony probably diminished during German colonial rule in Namibia from 1884 to 1914.

However, "[a] somewhat more direct involvement began in late 1914 when South African soldiers began to invade Namibia in order to defeat Germans there, all part of the European war called World War I" (Tonchi et al. 2012: 390). From 1915 onwards, South African troops occupied the territory, and in 1920 the League of Nations transferred the C-Mandate for Namibia (then South West Africa) to the Union of South Africa (Dierks 2002: 174). Hence started the colonial period under South African rule, which lasted until the country's independence in 1990, as after World War II South Africa "refused to UN requests to place Namibia under a trustee agreement, and instead implemented its own [. . .] legislation in the mandated territory" (Deumert 2009: 356). South Africa's colonization included the "systematic introduction of the apartheid" system (Tonchi et al. 2012: 7) and a "policy in which land was allocated to groups of people based on their race or tribal affiliation [. . .] formally instituted [. . .] in 1964" (Tonchi et al. 2012: 28).

The social and linguistic influences of this policy have been tremendous and long-lasting. Afrikaans, the language of the South Africans of (white) Dutch descent as well as of the Oorlams and the Basters, was firmly established as the language of administration and education under South African colonial rule. Although English and German were both official languages alongside Afrikaans, "the administrators required that Afrikaans be the language for all education from the fifth school year on" (Tonchi et al. 2012: 17). This led to much protest and the image of Afrikaans as "the language of the oppressors" (Frydman 2011: 182), and subsequently, with independence, to English being introduced as the language of liberation to overcome ethnolinguistic fragmentation. However, "many whites and blacks from the central and southern areas still maintain it as a mother tongue" (Tonchi et al. 2012: 17).

Since the end of the Apartheid regime and the attainment of a majority rule in South Africa, the two countries have maintained rather friendly relationships, "although Namibia remains suspicious of South Africa's hegemonic interests in the region" (Tonchi et al. 2012: 391). They are united through several Southern African economic organizations, especially in a monetary union through which South Africa still exerts an influence on monetary policies and foreign exchange regulations.

Namibia depends on South Africa economically due to the fact that 80 percent of its goods are imported from or through the neighboring country, the banking and business services largely operate from South Africa (Tonchi et al. 2012: 391), and South Africa is "the largest source with both drive-in and fly-in traffic that continues from before independence" (Tonchi et al. 2012: 420). Conversely, a number of Namibians, "continue to legally migrate to South Africa temporarily to visit family and friends and [. . .] to pursue tertiary education or better economic opportunities" (CIA The World Factbook 2018). Hence, Tonchi et al. (2012: 9) believe that in Namibia "[t]he structure of the economy continues to reflect the colonial pattern of a resource-exporting economy."

It therefore seems plausible to assume that South Africa still exerts a linguistic influence on Namibia's language ecology. The important role of Afrikaans due to the effects of colonial policy rule has already been mentioned above. With regard to the English language, Schneider (2014b: 208) also attributes "an epicentric status to the country in a southern African perspective," and we may therefore suspect that South African forms of English may have had (and may still have) an influence on the development of English in Namibia. Although we are aware of the fact that the concept of an epicenter "is far from straightforward, both on theoretical and methodological grounds" (Hundt 2013: 182), we may still call upon it in our case. "In many cases of epicentric influence geographical closeness will play an important role," but also "[e]picentric influence is largely a mirror of political and commercial power, and cultural prestige" (Biewer 2015: 71). The effects will be most profound in "smaller neighbouring countries which have formed a close relationship over decades with the mighty neighbour" (Biewer 2015: 71). South African forms of English are very likely to have served as a norm-providing model – probably alongside Standard British English and more recently Standard American English – during the colonial era, but also in the stabilization phase of NamE following independence. We may therefore suspect a process of norm competition (see Biewer 2015: 305) to have taken and possibly to still take place.

This brings us to the study of linguistic features in various forms of NamE. The factors of ethnicity, multilingualism, identity constructions, and South African influence possibly manifest themselves at the structural level of the language.

5. VARIATION AND HETEROGENEITY IN NAMIBIAN ENGLISH

In their first approach to NamE, Buschfeld and Kautzsch suggest that the language exhibits aspects of early nativization and they describe a first set of linguistic features to support their claim (cf. Buschfeld and Kautzsch 2014: 143–147). In their rather "anecdotal and impressionistic" (2014: 146) account, the authors also note some transfer from Afrikaans and Oshiwambo languages in the area of phonology (2014: 146).

5.1 Ethnic Variation in the Phonology of Namibian English

Kautzsch and Schröder (2016) take this up and show that the phonology of NamE seemingly exhibits variation according to ethnicity as well as both parallels and differences to South African varieties of English. Looking at the idiolects of eighteen speakers from different L1 backgrounds, they describe the vowel realizations in the lexical sets TRAP, DRESS, NURSE, and KIT with a focus on the distribution of two mergers and two splits. Their findings suggest that the merging of TRAP and DRESS is a widespread feature, "occurring across all ethnicities" (2016: 282) but being "strongest in the black population with a Bantu and Khoisan L1" (2016: 283). There is a clear distinction between more and less monitored speech for all speaker groups, but it is clearest in the group of German L1-speakers. A TRAP-DRESS-NURSE merger seems to be absent from the speech of German and Afrikaans L1-speakers, whereas it is almost consistently produced by the speakers with a Bantu L1 background (2016: 283). With regard to these two mergers, the variation in NamE seems to parallel some aspects of South African English (SAfE) since the TRAP-DRESS merger has been reported for Broad White SAfE as well as Black SAfE (Bowerman 2008: 170; Van Rooy 2008: 179, 181). The TRAP-DRESS-NURSE merger has only been documented in mesolectal Black SAfE (Van Rooy 2008: 179–180), but not in White SAfE. With regard to the two splits investigated, the results from Kautzsch and Schröder (2016) reveal an entirely different picture when compared to the findings for SAfEs. For one, the KIT split, a well-known feature of White SAfE (Bowerman 2008: 169–170) and possibly emerging in acrolectal Black SAfE (Van Rooy 2008: 182), is found across all ethnic groups although mostly in the less monitored speech style (and hence probably not in acrolectal usage) in the Namibian data. It also seems to follow a somewhat different realization pattern (Kautzsch and Schröder 2016: 286). Second, the NURSE-WORK split described for some Bantu and Khoisan speakers in their sample "has not been reported for any type of English in South Africa" and might therefore be considered "a distinguishing feature for English in Namibia" (2016: 284).

5.2 Splits and Mergers in the Speech of Rehoboth Basters

In their exploratory study of the phonology of one ethnic group, namely the Rehoboth Basters, Schröder et al. (2020) find further evidence for the NURSE-WORK split in NamE. The Basters constitute a particularly interesting group in the country's multi-ethnic make-up because of their unique history and ethnically mixed origin (see section 4). They managed to maintain a high degree of linguistic and political independence throughout Namibia's colonial history. Combining African and European ethnic and linguistic heritage into a strong sense of a separate local and ethnic identity, "the general contradictions and negotiations between the national discourses in Namibia can be illustrated through concrete studies in Rehoboth" (Kjæret and Stokke 2003: 580). Hence, they are a particularly relevant group to investigate in the context of our discussion on stabilization versus heterogeneity.

Concerning the NURSE-WORK split, it seems as if the analysis of the Baster data partly contradicts the results from Kautzsch and Schröder (2016). By finding the split across three registers in the speech of four out of five Basters, who are by definition Afrikaans L1-speakers, the original assumption of this split being exclusively restricted to speakers of the Bantu or Khoisan languages can definitely not be upheld. However, the analysis of the Rehoboth Baster speech nicely supports Kautzsch and Schröder's (2016) hypothesis that the NURSE-WORK split has the potential of becoming a nativized feature of NamE. In fact, we may even speculate that this feature, possibly originally restricted to the Bantu-speaking ethnicities in Namibia, may have been taken over into the speech of the Rehoboth Basters, specifically to signal a pan-Namibian identity. This feature therefore may direct towards nativization, if not endonormative stabilization.

The TRAP-DRESS-NURSE merger, allegedly a feature of Bantu L1-speakers and absent from speakers with Afrikaans as an L1 in Namibia (Kautzsch and Schröder 2016: 282–283), could not be observed in the Baster speakers' sample. Hence, this feature does not easily present itself as a pan-ethnic Namibianism; especially since it is also documented for mesolectal Black SAfE (Van Rooy 2008: 179). The TRAP-DRESS merger and the KIT split have both been observed in the Baster data, albeit with a fair degree of intra-speaker variation across registers. Both phenomena are more consistently realized in the formal, reading style registers, and are somewhat less observable during informal conversation (see Schröder et al. 2020 for details). Their presence in the Basters' speech possibly suggests that both phenomena represent ethnically unconditioned features of NamE. Both phenomena, however, are features also described for South African varieties of Englishes, that is in Broad White SAfE and Cape Flats English (cf. Bekker 2009; Bowerman 2008; Finn 2008). The fact that they are more consistently attested in the rather formal styles in the Rehoboth Baster speech, may hence be interpreted as an instance of exonormative orientation towards some Afrikaans influenced varieties of SAfE. This could also suggest some L1-transfer for the English of the Basters and, perhaps, the upheld, norm-providing function of SAfE for native speakers of Afrikaans.

Similarly, Schröder et al. (2020) describe a phonological phenomenon linked to the KIT vowel: a number of Basters seem to raise their realizations of the vowels in the DRESS set, which subsequently overlap with realizations of the KIT vowel. Since an analogous process of DRESS raising is attested for in SAfEs (cf. Bekker 2009; Bowerman 2008; Watermeyer 1996), the authors conclude

> that parts of the unique Baster identity with its roots between South Africa and Namibia are reflected linguistically. The majority of the phenomena observed concerning the pronunciation of vowels, such as the KIT split, DRESS raising, and the TRAP-DRESS merger, can be found in both NamE and Afrikaans-influenced varieties of South African English. Since Afrikaans is also the native language of all the speakers in the present study, it is not surprising that these features are attested in their speech as well. (Schröder et al. 2020: 213)

Hence, in many ways and not very surprisingly, features of NamE can variously be explained by influences from SAfEs, from Afrikaans, and from local indigenous Namibian languages.

5.3 Stabilization, Differentiation, and Heterogeneity in Namibian English

The preceding sections seem to indicate that NamE oscillates between influences from SAfE, Afrikaans, and the development of local features in different ethnic groups. However, "features described as particular to NamE [...] should not be viewed as interference phenomena, instances of borrowing or substrate/superstrate influences but as independent and local Namibian solutions in the complex linguistic ecology of the speech community" (Schröder and Schneider 2018: 359). The preceding discussion of (phonological) features in NamE and language attitudes therefore rather suggests that forces working towards both (endonormative) stabilization and differentiation are at work in the Namibian context.

The prevailing language attitudes towards English as reported here and in previous publications (Buschfeld and Kautzsch 2014; Buschfeld and Schröder 2020; Kautzsch and Schröder 2016; Pütz 1995) suggest that English is largely welcomed in Namibia and hailed as a language of identification, particularly for the youth, and a connecting factor between different ethnic groups. English helps to overcome ethnolinguistic fragmentation caused by apartheid policy, at least for those who have sufficient access to it. It is the uncontested only official language and a very useful lingua franca in official and, increasingly, private domains. In this, English serves as stabilizing force within the multilingual ecology of the country and presents itself as firmly installed in the territory. This holds especially true for urban contexts as reported by Stell (2016), who identifies either English or a mix of English and Coloured Afrikaans as the predominant language(s) of informal inter-ethnic communication among university students in the country's capital, Windhoek. It has also been shown that English serves as the primary choice for informal digital messaging among young Namibians despite a different shared L1 (Zähres 2016). At the linguistic level, we find phonological features, most notably the NURSE-WORK split, seemingly establishing themselves as a pan-Namibianism, probably spreading from the numerically and politically dominant Bantu/Oshiwambo L1-speaking group to other ethnicities and L1 groups.

In spite of this, we are probably safe to assume that a uniform (phonological) standard for NamE will be very difficult to describe at this stage, given the obvious differences between the various L1 groups reported. These could increase in the future if identity alignments (see Schneider

2017: 47) with one's ethnic group are transferred from the respective ethnic L1 to an ethnic variety of English. Furthermore, we believe a number of different target varieties to operate in the NamE language acquisition process. In the process of norm competition, several varieties of English are involved. These include American English, traditionally still British English, as well as White and, increasingly, Black SAfEs. The attitudes towards these as well as their media presence, however, especially of the last two, need to be investigated in far more detail. From our impressionistic personal observation, the broadcasting of South African comedies, soap operas, and radio shows is rather frequent. The same is true for the overall, strong media representation of American forms of English and other globalization effects reported for other nations (cf. Mair 2013). Furthermore, we have noticed that a number of Namibian teachers have received and still receive their training at South African universities, as do other professionals, who may serve as role models for learners of English in Namibia.

6. NAMIBIA AND THE EIF-MODEL REVISITED

Given the obvious parallels of some phonological developments and, more importantly, the strong historical and economic links between Namibia and South Africa, we would not downplay the influence of South Africa on the development of NamE in the same way as Buschfeld (2014) or Buschfeld and Kautzsch (2017). Nevertheless, we embrace their intention to view NamE as a variety of its own and independent of SAfEs. However, without any claim concerning the theoretical status of the epicenter, we need to investigate synchronically and diachronically in far more detail as to whether a particular emerging feature in NamE can legitimately be seen as an independent development. This will help to rule out that it is triggered "by earlier dialect input into that variety" and also to ascertain whether or not "it is more likely to be due to external influence from another variety that is (currently) acting as a strong role model (either locally or on a global scale)" (Hundt 2013: 198).

Hence, we believe that when applying the EIF Model to the Namibian case, the influence of South Africa, SAfEs, and South African (language) policies, in the past and present, should be acknowledged as decisive extra-territorial forces. This also accounts for attitudes towards South Africa, Afrikaans, SAfEs, and so on as an important intra-territorial force. In addition, the interplay between these forces and the general forces of 'Transnational Attraction' (Schneider 2014a), accounting for the global spread of (American) English and the development of local forms (Buschfeld et al. 2018: 23), need to be investigated in far more detail.

Furthermore, we agree with Buschfeld et al. that the "use of English by Namibians of different ethnicities [...] who mostly also have full command of Afrikaans as a second language, leads to a plethora of contact scenarios, which in turn is likely to give rise to ethnic differences in the use of English" (2018: 27). Some of the observations described in section 5 above certainly corroborate this assumption. We therefore wonder, at a more general level, how this ethnic differentiation can be incorporated more visibly into a model that, as it is graphically presented in Figure 1.1 in the Introduction to this volume, suggests a developmental process with a(n) (endonormative) stabilization phase preceding any kind of differentiation. As Buschfeld and Kautzsch make clear, PCEs and non-PCEs are believed to follow a similar developmental route, "even if the initial forces operating on their development are fundamentally different" (2017: 118) and the "diachronic conception builds on Schneider's Dynamic Model, namely the development of varieties along five phases" (Buschfeld et al. 2018: 23–24). This is strongly underlined by the black arrow for 'development' (Buschfeld et al. 2018: 24; Figure 1.1 in the Introduction to this volume) in the respective graphic representation. In a footnote, Buschfeld et al. (2018: 24, footnote 1) already explicitly state: "the model leave[s] room for reverse developments" and "it also allows for stages to be skipped or to be taken in some other order." But we find this is not yet accurately reflected in its graphic representation. Hence, we believe the model needs to specify in far more detail how the critical comments with respect to the assumption of the consecutiveness of the phases in the Dynamic Model (see section 2 above) can be countered in the EIF Model and how a development past the nativization phase may be described. We suggest that phase 4, 'endonormative stabilization,' and phase 5, 'differentiation,' may actually be conflated into one, or else bi-directional arrows should be used to question the mono-directionality of any such development.

We believe that mistakes made by assuming other so-called 'standard varieties' to be homogenous, and hence to gloss over the dialectal variation that each of these varieties undoubtedly always exhibited diachronically and synchronically (Bruthiaux 2003), should not be repeated when further developing the EIF Model and describing PCEs and non-PCEs. This issue is already addressed in the most recent version of the model in Buschfeld et al., which adequately "accounts for the variety-internal heterogeneity found in almost every regionally defined type of English" (2018: 24–25). However, in the way we interpret the accompanying graphic representation (2018: 25, figure 2), this type of heterogeneity is set apart from the type of differentiation constitutive of the last phase of the model. We are not sure that this does justice to the signs of (ethnic) differentiation we believe to be found in Namibia.

This also accounts for the conflation of 'norms' with 'standards' (see Lange 2012 for an excellent discussion). Does 'endonormative stabilization' require codification and the development of a single, standard variety? After all, "standardization is inseparable from writing" (Lange 2012: 236). Thus, we need to take into consideration "the fundamental difference between spoken norms, spontaneously shared by communities of speakers and hence not easily amenable to deliberate standardization, and written norms" (Bruthiaux 2003: 162), which are more likely to be codified and, in the Namibian case, are very likely to follow British or American English rules for an extended period of time.

Finally, multilingualism as a major intra-territorial force should be given more prominence in the EIF Model, and the model should "discriminate between strongly multiethnic entities [that is, nation-states] and strongly monolingual ones" (Bruthiaux 2003: 164). We believe that differences between non-PCE (as well as PCE) cases in predominantly monolingual countries, such as the Netherlands (Edwards 2016) or Germany (Kautzsch 2014), on the one hand, and multilingual ones, such as Namibia, on the other, should explicitly be paid tribute to.

7. CONCLUSIONS AND OUTLOOK

In this chapter, we have argued that NamE cannot be regarded as a monolithic variety, but rather as consisting of several sub-varieties. Such a view challenges the "linear progression of stages" (Buschfeld et al. 2018: 24) of a non-PCE, and points to the question marks in the EIF Model from stage 3 onwards. While we largely agree with the deliberations on the foundation, stabilization, and nativization stages by Buschfeld and Kautzsch (2017), we feel the need that further, or more detailed, extra- and intra-territorial forces must be taken into account, most prominently represented by the discussed epicenter of South Africa that still has an undeniable impact on Namibia today. Additionally, as of now, there seems to be little evidence suggesting the arrival to the stage of endonormative stabilization. However, the present data rather suggest signs for differentiation during or perhaps following the evident nativization process, as exemplified by the phonological analyses presented in section 5, which also suggest potential candidates for pan-Namibian feature status. Whether this assumption holds true and whether this constitutes a step towards endonormative stabilization after all or whether this reflects only the internal linguistic heterogeneity incorporated in the extended version of the EIF Model, remains to be assessed with further research on the phonology of NamE.

Further research into norms and nativization processes in NamE should definitely also include morpho-syntactic and lexical aspects in addition to phonological research. With the almost total absence of empirical research on these areas of NamE, with Buschfeld and Kautzsch (2014: 144–145) providing only an impressionistic and anecdotal account, and with Buschfeld's (forthcoming) results not being conclusive, any further assessment in the context of the present chapter seemed premature at this research stage. We would suspect, however, that the effects of ethnic variation, identity constructions, South African influence, and further factors might be less clearly visible at the morpho-syntactic or lexical than at the phonological level of language. After all, "when it comes to standardization of [. . .] local norms: these norms have to compete with an already existing international standard of written English" (Lange 2012: 237). We believe that this written exonormative force is less influential at the phonological than at the morpho-syntactic level, with the lexical level possibly lying somewhere in-between. In this context, Lange raises the question "whether endonormative stabilization can be achieved without actual codification, and brings us back to the distinction between norms and standards" (2012: 241). With her, we "would like to argue that many of the most prominent nativized features in [PCEs] are prone to resist standardization and eventual codification" (2012: 241). This issue must be assessed not only with the aforementioned morpho-syntactic and lexical investigation of NamE, but possibly also by taking into account digital forms of communication as these can blur and subvert the traditional distinction between spoken and written.

We do agree with Schneider that "model making [. . .] appears to simplify complex realities and disregard aspects of it" (2017: 26) and that this constitutes "a perfectly reasonable and justified procedure" (2017: 36). However, in our opinion, key aspects of a model need to be spelled out in detail to attain more specificity and less relativization. In the case of the EIF Model, which is characterized by the eponymous extra- and intra-territorial forces influencing PCEs and non-PCEs, the proposed forces (cf. Buschfeld and Kautzsch 2017: 114, table 1) seem very appropriate, but also vague at the same time. In which of the categories or developmental phases do factors such as multilingualism, norm orientation (including epicentric influences), mass media, and tourism play what role? Also, the practicability, discriminatory power, and consecutiveness of the proposed five phases, especially the last two, needs to be assessed for non-PCEs (and possibly for PCEs as well) with further case studies.

Finally, the case of Namibia could raise an additional interesting question: If South African influence is assumed for NamE (as proposed in this chapter), should we still consider NamE to be a non-PCE or rather a PCE? We believe that this should not make much of a difference in a model that tries to treat these Englishes in a joint approach. Therefore, we would argue, Namibia (and NamE for that matter) may not be "a very prototypical case" (Buschfeld and Kautzsch 2017: 119) for a non-PCE, but may be an excellent test case for the EIF Model, which does this country and its socio-historical linguistic situation far more justice than any other model of WE to our knowledge.

REFERENCES

Bekker, Ian. 2009. The Vowels of South African English. PhD dissertation, North-West University, Potchefstroom.

Biewer, Carolin. 2015. *South Pacific Englishes. A Sociolinguistic and Morphosyntactic Profile of Fiji English, Samoan English and Cook Islands English*. Amsterdam and New York: John Benjamins.

Bowerman, Sean. 2008. White South African English: Phonology. In Rajend Mesthrie, ed. 2008, 164–176.

Bruthiaux, Paul. 2003. Squaring the circles: Issues in modelling English worldwide. *International Journal of Applied Linguistics* 13.2: 159–178.

Buschfeld, Sarah. 2014. English in Cyprus and Namibia. A critical approach to taxonomies and models of World Englishes and second language acquisition research. In Sarah Buschfeld, Thomas Hoffmann, Magnus Huber and Alexander Kautzsch, eds. 2014, *The Evolution of Englishes*. Amsterdam: John Benjamins, 181–202.

Buschfeld, Sarah. Forthcoming. The question of structural nativization in Namibian English: Some answers from extended uses of the progressive. In Anne Schröder, ed. forthcoming, *The Dynamics of English in Namibia*. Amsterdam: Benjamins.

Buschfeld, Sarah and Alexander Kautzsch. 2014. English in Namibia: A first approach. *English World-Wide* 35.2: 121–160.

Buschfeld, Sarah and Alexander Kautzsch. 2017. Towards an integrated approach to postcolonial and non-postcolonial Englishes. *World Englishes* 36.1: 104–126.

Buschfeld, Sarah and Anne Schröder. 2020. English and German in Namibia. In Raymond Hickey, ed. 2020, *English in the German-speaking World*. Cambridge: Cambridge University Press, 334–360.

Buschfeld, Sarah, Alexander Kautzsch and Edgar W. Schneider. 2018. From colonial dynamism to current transnationalism: A unified view on postcolonial and non-postcolonial Englishes. In Sandra C. Deshors, ed. 2018, *Modeling World Englishes: Assessing the Interplay of Emancipation and Globalization of ESL Varieties*. Amsterdam: John Benjamins, 15–44.

CIA The World Factbook. Namibia. 2018. https://www.cia.gov/library/publications/resources/the-world-factbook/geos/wa.html (last accessed October 15, 2018).

Deumert, Ana. 2009. "Namibian Kiche Duits": The making (and decline) of a Neo-African language. *Journal of Germanic Linguistics* 21.4: 349–417.

Dierks, Klaus. 2002. *Chronology of Namibian History*. 2nd edn. Windhoek: Namibia Scientific Society.

Edwards, Alison. 2016. *English in the Netherlands: Functions, Forms and Attitudes*. Amsterdam: John Benjamins.

Finn, Peter. 2008. Cape Flats English: Phonology. In Rajend Mesthrie, ed. 2008, 200–222.

Frydman, Jenna. 2011. A critical analysis of Namibia's English-only language policy. In Eyamba G. Bokamba, Ryan K. Shosted and Bezza Tesfaw Ayalew, eds. 2011, *Selected Proceedings of the 40th Annual Conference on African Linguistics: African Languages and Linguistics Today*. Somerville MA: Cascadilla Proceedings Project, 178–189, http://www.lingref.com/cpp/acal/40/paper2574.pdf (last accessed October 15, 2018).

Gramley, Stephan. 2012. *The History of English. An Introduction*. London and New York: Routledge.

Hundt, Marianne. 2013. The diversification of English: Old, new and emerging epicentres. In Daniel Schreier and Marianne Hundt,

eds. 2013, *English as a Contact Language*. Cambridge: Cambridge University Press, 182–203.
Kachru, Braj B., Yamuna Kachru and Cecil L. Nelson, eds. 2009. *The Handbook of World Englishes*. Malden, MA: Wiley-Blackwell.
Kautzsch, Alexander. 2014. English in Germany: Spreading bilingualism, retreating exonormative orientation and incipient nativization? In Sarah Buschfeld, Thomas Hoffmann, Magnus Huber and Alexander Kautzsch, eds. 2014, *The Evolution of Englishes: The Dynamic Model and Beyond*. Amsterdam: John Benjamins, 203–227.
Kautzsch, Alexander and Anne Schröder. 2016. English in multilingual and multiethnic Namibia: Some evidence on language attitudes and the pronunciation of vowels. In Christoph Ehland, Ilka Mindt and Merle Tönnies, eds. 2016, *Anglistentag 2015 Paderborn: Proceedings*. Trier: WVT, 277–288.
Kirkpatrick, Andy, ed. 2010. *The Routledge Handbook of World Englishes*. London: Routledge.
Kjæret, Kristin and Kristian Stokke. 2003. Rehoboth Baster, Namibian or Namibian Baster? An Analysis of national discourses in Rehoboth, Namibia. *Nations and Nationalism* 9.4: 579–600.
Kortmann, Bernd and Edgar Schneider, eds. 2004. *A Handbook of Varieties of English. 2 Volumes*. Berlin: Mouton de Gruyter.
Lange, Claudia. 2012. Postcolonial Englishes: From norms to standards. In Anne Schröder, Ulrich Busse and Ralf Schneider, eds. 2012, *Codification, Canons, and Curricula. Description and Prescription in Language and Literature*. Bielefeld: Aisthesis, 233–246.
Mair, Christian. 2013. The world system of Englishes: Accounting for the transnational importance of mobile and mediated vernaculars. *English World-Wide* 34.3: 253–278.
Melchers, Gunnel and Philip Shaw. 2011. *World Englishes*. 2nd edn. Abingdon: Hodder Education.
Mesthrie, Rajend, ed. 2008. *Varieties of English. Volume 4: Africa, South and Southeast Asia*. Berlin: Mouton de Gruyter.
Mesthrie, Rajend and Rakesh M. Bhatt. 2008. *World Englishes: The Study of New Linguistic Varieties*. Cambridge: Cambridge University Press.
Namibia Statistics Agency. 2012. Namibia 2011 Population and Housing Census Main Report, http://nsa.org.na/page/publications (last accessed October 15, 2018).
Pütz, Martin. 1995. Attitudes and language: An empirical investigation into the status and use of English in Namibia. In Martin Pütz, ed.

1995, *Discrimination Through Language in Africa? Perspectives on the Namibian Experience*. Berlin and New York: Mouton de Gruyter, 245–285.
Schneider, Edgar W. 2007. *Postcolonial English: Varieties Around the World*. Cambridge: Cambridge University Press.
Schneider, Edgar W. 2011. *English Around the World. An Introduction*. Cambridge: Cambridge University Press.
Schneider, Edgar W. 2014a. New reflections on the evolutionary dynamics of world Englishes. *World Englishes* 33.1: 9–32.
Schneider, Edgar W. 2014b. Global diffusion, regional attraction, local roots? Sociocognitive perspectives on the pluricentricity of English. In Augusto Soares da Silva, ed. 2014, *Pluricentricity. Language Variation and Sociocognitive Dimensions*. Berlin: Mouton de Gruyter, 191–226.
Schneider, Edgar W. 2017. Models of English in the world. In Markku Filppula, Juhani Klemola and Devyani Sharma, eds. 2017, *The Oxford Handbook of World Englishes*. Oxford: Oxford University Press, 35–57.
Schreier, Daniel, Peter Trudgill, Edgar W. Schneider and Jeffrey P. Williams, eds. 2010a. *The Lesser-Known Varieties of English. An Introduction*. Cambridge: Cambridge University Press.
Schreier, Daniel, Peter Trudgill, Edgar W. Schneider and Jeffrey P. Williams. 2010b. Introduction. In Daniel Schreier, Peter Trudgill, Edgar W. Schneider and Jeffrey P. Williams, eds. 2010, *The Lesser-Known Varieties of English. An Introduction*. Cambridge: Cambridge University Press, 1–14.
Schröder, Anne, ed. Forthcoming. *The Dynamics of English in Namibia*. Amsterdam: John Benjamins.
Schröder, Anne and Klaus P. Schneider. 2018. Variational pragmatics, responses to thanks and the specificity of Namibian English. *English World-Wide* 39.3: 338–363.
Schröder, Anne, Frederic Zähres and Alexander Kautzsch. 2020. Ethnic variation in the phonology of Namibian English: A first approach to Baster English. *English World-Wide* 41.2: 193–225.
Simons, Gary F. and Charles D. Fennig, eds. 2018. *Ethnologue: Languages of the World*. 21st edn. Dallas, Texas: SIL International. Online version, http://www.ethnologue.com (last accessed October 15, 2018).
Stell, Gerald. 2016. Trends in linguistic diversity in post-independence Windhoek: A qualitative appraisal. *Language Matters* 47.3: 326–348.

Tonchi, Victor L., William A. Lindeke and John J. Grotpeter. 2012. *Historical Dictionary of Namibia*. 2nd edn. Lanham, Toronto, Plymouth: The Scarecrow Press.

Trudgill, Peter and Jean Hannah. 2017. *International English. A Guide to Varieties of English Around the World*. London: Routledge.

Van Rooy, Bertus. 2008. Black South African English: Phonology. In Rajend Mesthrie, ed. 2008, 177–187.

Wallace, Marion. 2011. *A History of Namibia*. London: C. Hurst & Co.

Watermeyer, Susan. 1996. Afrikaans English. In Vivian De Klerk, ed. 1996, *Focus on South Africa*. Amsterdam: John Benjamins, 99–124.

Williams, Jeffrey P., Edgar W. Schneider, Peter Trudgill and Daniel Schreier. 2015. *Further Studies in Lesser-Known Varieties of English*. Cambridge: Cambridge University Press.

Zähres, Frederic. 2016. A case of code-switching in Namibian keyboard-to-screen communication. *10plus1: Living Linguistics* 2: 31–46, 10plus1journal.com (last accessed October 15, 2018).

CHAPTER 4

English in the United Arab Emirates: Status and Functions

Saeb Sadek

1. INTRODUCTION

The United Arab Emirates (UAE) first gained independence in 1971. Prior to that date, the country used to be a British protectorate dating back to 1820. By the time the country gained independence, the oil industry was on the rise, and the investments enabled by the wealth brought in by the oil changed the country on a massive scale. Expatriates originally came to the UAE to work in the oil industry, but after rapid development in all domains, demand on expatriates was no longer exclusive to the oil sector. Today, expatriates constitute up to 90 per cent of the population. The majority of expats come from South Asian countries. Yet, the Emirates is also home to nationalities from all over the world. Mainly due to the population's highly diverse cultural and linguistic backgrounds, the fact that the UAE is a worldwide-famous tourist attraction and the country's role as a regional trade and media centre, English today plays a major role in most domains from tourism to education and the media.

Due to its diverse linguistic and cultural composition, the UAE has attracted a number of studies investigating the linguistic situation and the role of English in the country (cf. Randall and Samimi 2010). More specifically, a study also applied Schneider's Dynamic Model to English in the UAE and concluded that the variety entered phase 3 of the model (Boyle 2012). The aim of this study is threefold. First, it aims at pointing out the complexity of Emirati history and the difficulties it poses to World Englishes categorisations. Second, it aims at discussing some of the main functions of English in the country. Finally, an attempt will be made to apply the Extra- and Intra-territorial Forces Model (EIF) to the variety.

2. THE UNITED ARAB EMIRATES – HISTORICAL BACKGROUND

Located in the southeast corner of the Arabian Peninsula, the United Arab Emirates (UAE) borders Saudi Arabia, Oman, the Gulf of Oman and the Persian Gulf. The UAE is a federation of seven emirates, which are Abu Dhabi (the capital), Ajman, Dubai, Fujairah, Ras al-Khaimah, Sharjah and Umm al-Quwain. While the Emirates poses an interesting case for World Englishes research in general, its history is particularly interesting and challenging for the field. Traditionally, the study of emerging varieties of the English language distinguishes between post-colonial Englishes (PCEs) and non-postcolonial Englishes (non-PCEs). This classification, however, cannot fully represent the Emirati history. This section will present a history of the country and the challenge it poses to the PCEs/non-PCEs distinction.

The Emirati coast has been home to humans for thousands of years. Emirati locals in the twenty-first century could be traced back to waves of migration within the Arabian Peninsula. As early as the sixteenth century, the Bani Yas tribe immigrated from deep within the Peninsula to areas close to today's Abu Dhabi. Both Al Nahyan and the Maktum families (rulers of Abu Dhabi and Dubai, respectively) are traced back to the Bani Yas tribe (Ulrichsen 2017: 20). In the eighteenth century, the Qawasim tribe 'developed into a regional maritime power with control of territory on both the Arabian and Persian coastlines of the Gulf' (Ulrichsen 2017: 19). The ruling families of both Ras al-Khaimah and Sharjah, the Qasimi families, are traced back to the Qawasim tribe. The growing maritime influence of the Qawasim tribe in the Persian Gulf was possibly one of the reasons that attracted the British to the Emirati coastline. Due to their interest in protecting their trade lines with the East India Company, the British saw the Qawasim presence as a threat in the region. Hence, the British-Qawasim tension intensified in the early years of the nineteenth century with direct confrontations between the two parties.

The tension eased by the year 1820 with the signing of the General Treaty between a representative of the East India Company and rulers of the local tribes. Thus, as of 1820 the area (today's UAE) became the

Trucial States. In terms of the General Treaty, 'Article 1 stipulated the "cessation of plunder and piracy by land and sea" while Article[s] 6 and 10 authorised the British to function as a maritime policeman to ensure compliance and settle any disputes arising in Gulf waters' (Ulrichsen 2017: 23). The Trucial Coast's vital and sensitive geographical location made the British seek to strengthen and increase their influence on the Trucial States. The General Treaty was followed by a number of treaties and agreements ending with the Exclusive Agreement signed in 1892, which limited all Trucial foreign affairs to the British (Ulrichsen 2017: 24). The British were not the only player in the region, and thus the Exclusive Agreement protected their footprint in the Trucial States against other colonial or regional powers.

For the British to keep control of Trucial foreign affairs, they needed to keep internal problems at bay. Despite the fact that the British and the Trucial locals never came into direct, full-on armed confrontation, their relationship was never free of tensions. One famous incident, known as the Dubai Incident of 1910, shows how easily British-Trucial tensions could escalate. The affair started after British troops had come on land to inspect a number of houses for smuggled weapons. This escalated into an armed fight with some of the locals, resulting in casualties on both sides. The situation was contained, and a peaceful agreement was reached after the rulers intervened. However, according to Abdullah, '[t]he most important long-term effect of the incident was to provoke hatred among the local people against [. . .] British firms' (1978: 37).

British-Trucial relations, however, improved in the following years. As Peck points out, '[b]y the end of World War I the defeat of the Ottoman Empire and Britain's dominant position in the Arabian Peninsula and the Gulf had made Britain more than ever the arbiter of Trucial States affairs' (1986: 36). The interwar era would reshape British-Trucial relations, especially after oil exploration in the Trucial States began in the 1930s. Both parties signed a number of new agreements which ended with an ultimatum in 1937 that forced all rulers of the Trucial States 'to deal only with Petroleum Concessions Ltd., a wholly owned subsidiary of the London-based Iraq Petroleum Company (IPC)' (Peck 1986: 37).

Oil exploration largely enhanced the country's economy and increased the demand for political and social reform. The British played an important role in shaping these reforms and keeping them within British control. This is best illustrated with the establishment of the British-officered Trucial Oman Levies in 1951, whose 'mission was to keep peace and order throughout the shaikhdoms and serve as an escort for the British representative' (Peck 1986: 44). In the following year, and with British support, the Trucial States Council was founded, which served as a 'mere consultative body' for the Trucial rulers (Khalifa 1979: 26). Despite its limited functions, the council served as a 'forum' for political discussion and provided a ground zero for future similar institutions in the country (Peck 1986: 45).

Due to changes in the political climate both at the local and international levels, in 1968 Britain announced that it was 'terminat[ing] its official treaty obligations with all Trucial States' (Khalifa 1979: 27). In their announcement, the British included their intention to withdraw from the Trucial States by the end of 1971, leaving the country more than three years of political chaos to determine its post-independence fate, something that the Trucial rulers at the time were not necessarily very keen on (Fenelon 1976: 222; Peck 1986: 47). After a period of political confusion and uncertainty in the Trucial States and the Gulf in general, '[t]he UAE was declared a sovereign entity on December 2, 1971, one day after the official British involvement was terminated' (Khalifa 1979: 35).

In the early post-independence years, the UAE made use of the growing oil industry and invested largely in infrastructure. The large-scale infrastructure investments made in the 1970s and 1980s constituted a cornerstone for the development in various sectors. As a result of those investments, the UAE managed gradually to reduce its dependency on oil. Tourism, transportation, media, education and many other sectors became equally important revenues for the federation's economy. By 2013, only 28.2 per cent of the country's GDP was accounted for by oil in comparison to 90 per cent in 1970 (Ulrichsen 2017: 87). Due to its ever-improving economy and its political stability, the UAE became one of the region's most influential players at both the political and economic levels.

In the years between 1820 and 1971, British interests in the then Trucial States were mainly geopolitical and, after the discovery of oil, also economical. Within this period, however, the Trucial States were never colonised by the British. The various agreements signed by both parties during those years granted the British varying degrees of control over the country's internal and foreign affairs. However, the British presence was mainly located at sea, and it only significantly increased on land due to the oil industry and the foreign expertise it required. Thus, it could be argued that the UAE used to be a subjection colony where sparse 'colonial settlements maintained the pre-colonial population in subjection, allowing some of them access to learning English as a second, or additional language' (Leith 2007: 120). Then again, the country's colonial past has very little influence on the UAE's modern image, its demographic, linguistic or cultural repertoires. In comparison, the wealth and infrastructure investments brought in by the discovery of oil had a major effect on the UAE's post-independence trajectory. Hence, the country's history poses a challenge to the PCE/non-PCE categorisation, since the UAE falls somewhere in the middle.

3. SOCIOLINGUISTIC BACKGROUND

As has been pointed out, the Emirati native population extends to tribes from the Arabian Peninsula. Their settlement on the Emirati coast dates back to as early as the sixteenth century. The Arabian Peninsula has been home to the Arabic language with varying degrees of dialectical change (Holes 2004: 2). During the Trucial era (1820–1971), the Arabic-speaking locals came into no significant contact with the British due to the fact that British-Trucial relations mostly took place at the leadership level with agreements and ultimatums. It was only until oil exploration began in the 1930s that the contact increased between some of the locals and the foreign expertise needed for the oil industry. The need for skilled foreign expertise increased after independence as a result of the booming oil industry and the massive investments following that. In 1971, the Emirati population numbered over 278,000; the number today exceeds nine million (Worldometers 2018). Over the years, the demand for a skilled expatriate force in all sectors has increased so much so that expatriates today constitute over 90 per cent of the Emirati population. Most of the population is located in the country's urban centres. Dubai alone hosts over three million people, a third of the country's population (Baldwin 2018).

According to the official portal of the UAE government, the official religion of the country is Islam; Arabic is the official language of the UAE, while '[o]ther widely spoken languages include: Bengali, English, Farsi, Hindi, Malayalam, Mandarin, Nepali, Russian, Sinhalese, Tagalog and Urdu' (About the UAE 2018). While the local population is outnumbered by the expatriate community, 'Indians form the largest foreign community in the UAE, followed by Pakistanis, Bangladeshis, other Asians, Europeans, and Africans' (About the UAE 2018). Clearly, the UAE is home to a colourful mixture of ethnic, cultural and linguistic backgrounds. The Arabic language is still highly used, especially between the locals and other Arabic-speaking expatriates. However, since the majority of the expatriates do not speak Arabic, English is by far the most used lingua franca in the UAE and plays an important role in intra-national communication (cf. Findlow 2006; Randall and Samimi 2010).

3.1 Functions of English in the UAE

Given the mixture of people in the Emirates, English has become a necessity in everyday life. The spread of the English language in the UAE has, in fact, reached every domain and sector in the country. This section sketches some of the main functions of English in the Emirates.

3.1.1 Education

Since independence, and increasingly in the past few decades, education has been a top priority for the Emirati government. According to Höselbarth, '34 percent of the national budget goes into education' (2010: 99). The country has 659 public schools and 567 private schools (United Arab Emirates Ministry of Education 2018). Arabic is the main language of instruction in public schools with the exception of English language classes (Gaad et al. 2006: 293). In comparison, private schools are officially allowed to use English as a language of instruction in all subjects if the Arabic-speaking students in a class total less than 20 per cent (Ibrahim 2011: 333). Private schools are also expected to teach 'Islamic education [and] Arabic language as a basic subject for Arab students and as an additional subject for non-Arab students' (Ibrahim 2011: 333). Private schools, however, are likely to focus less on Islamic education than public schools, and they have mixed gender classes compared to single-gender classes in the public schools. Additionally, only after the school year 2006–2007 were expatriate students admitted into public schools, provided they pay educational fees, whereas Emirati students receive free education (Federal Research Division 2007). The divide between private and public schools is also reflected in the curricula used in both systems. According to Ibrahim, public schools do not address issues 'such as evolution, all topics that relate to sexuality, and topics that question the existence of God' (2011: 332–333). On the other hand, private schools could use their own curricula; however, they need to be approved by the ministry of education (Ibrahim 2011: 332–333).

With regard to public higher education, the UAE has three main public universities. The United Arab Emirates University (UAEU) is the oldest and largest and uses mainly English as a language of instruction. UAEU, established in 1976, provides free education and consists of 90 per cent national students and only 10 per cent non-national students (Ibrahim 2011: 333). The Higher Colleges of Technology (HCT) use English as the language of instruction but admit only national students (Höselbarth 2010: 97; Ibrahim 2011: 334). Zayed University also uses English as its language of instruction; however, the university is exclusive to national female students (Ibrahim 2011: 334). On the other hand, private higher education has been a developing sector in the UAE with '61 internationally accredited universities' (Höselbarth 2010: 101). Most private universities also offer education in English. Emirati private higher education attracts a number of international students. It also is home to most of the expatriate university students since they have certain limitations in access to public universities in the UAE.

3.1.2 Media

The Emirates has 'seven Arabic newspapers, and eight English language newspapers, as well as a Tagalog newspaper' (The Official Portal of the UAE Government 2018). *Al-Etihad* is the country's leading and first Arabic newspaper, established in 1969 (Alittihad.ae 2018). *Khaleej Times* was launched in 1978 to be the first English newspaper in the UAE; the newspaper reaches out to more than 450,000 multinational readerships (*Khaleej Times* 2018). With their online versions, *Gulf News* and *The National* are also very influential English newspapers at the national and regional levels. In 2010, *Gulf News* 'ranked number one among the English-language online newspapers in the Middle East and North Africa' (Badih 2010).

Furthermore, the Emirati government has invested heavily in the media sector. To that end, the country established a number of free zones and media cities or centres. In fact, numerous media agencies and TV broadcasters have their headquarters or regional offices located in the UAE. These TV agencies broadcast 'mainly in Arabic, English, Hindi, Urdu, Malayalam, Tagalog, and Farsi [. . .] with at least 72 free-to-air stations' (The Official Portal of the UAE Government 2018). Additionally, one of the largest and most famous free-to-air broadcasting agencies in the Middle East, MBC Group, is located in Dubai Media City. MBC includes a number of channels that broadcast only in

English; they mainly broadcast Hollywood films, western sitcoms and series, entertainment shows, and also a channel for children's entertainment (MBC Group 2018). Emirati public channels also include the channel Dubai One, which broadcasts content exclusively in English.

3.1.3 Tourism

In 2017, Dubai alone received over 15 million tourists, which makes the city the fourth most visited city in the world (Maceda 2018; Sadaqat 2018). In fact, Dubai and Abu Dhabi, in particular, are now internationally very famous tourist destinations, with their modern yet oriental image. To achieve that, the Emirati government invested largely in the tourism sector. For instance, Abu Dhabi's Department of Culture and Tourism 'regulates, develops and promotes the Emirate of Abu Dhabi as an inspired global destination, rich in cultural authenticity, diverse natural offerings and unparalleled family leisure and entertainment attractions' (Department of Culture and Tourism 2018). As part of its promotional campaign, the department supports the website visitabudhabi.de, which is available in English, Arabic, French, German, Italian, Russian, Portuguese, Dutch and Mandarin. The website even offers an Arabic phrase book which provides tourists with useful phrases for daily activities and socialising. Additionally, the website provides the following information with regard to language use:

> Arabic is the official language, although English is widely spoken and most road and shop signs are in both languages. The further out of town you go, the more Arabic you will find, both written and spoken. Arabic isn't the easiest language to pick up, or to pronounce but if you can throw in a couple of Arabic words here and there they will be warmly received. (Visit Abu Dhabi 2018)

Clearly, English plays a vital role in the tourist sector in the UAE, especially in the country's major centres Dubai and Abu Dhabi.

3.1.4 Public administration and governance

Since the country is home to so many expatriates with varying linguistic and cultural backgrounds, the UAE was bound to accommodate their needs. In fact, the Emirati government does a great job at providing necessary information with regard to visa applications, finding a job, healthcare, education and housing. Such information can be found on the government's website –government.ae – which is available in both Arabic and English. Additionally, the website provides a number of different smartphone applications meant to facilitate public services for residents of the UAE. Many of these applications are also available in English. In order to maintain such services and to run the country's infrastructure, the Emirati public sector has become a fertile job market for expatriates who occupy up to 91 per cent of public positions, whereas they occupy 99 per cent of jobs in the private sector (Ahmed 2008). With such high numbers of expats in the public and private sectors, English is likely to dominate workplace communications. There have been concerns within the Federal National Council's education, media and youth committee as to whether the use of Arabic in government communication is on the decline; the committee recommended taking measures to 'protect the Arabic language' (Salem 2014). A law in Sharjah already 'requires all government offices to use Arabic for their oral and written transactions' (Bassiouney 2009: 255–256).

3.2 English in the UAE – Assessment of the Variety: EFL or ESL?

Having explored the sociolinguistic background of the UAE and various functions of English in the country, there is no doubt that the English language has become a necessity in the Emirates and that its spread and use have reached a variety of important sectors. The question worth asking at this point is whether English in the UAE is merely a learner English or whether it has reached a more complex second-language variety status (ESL).

Traditionally, English counts as a second language in countries where 'only a small proportion of the people have English as their native language' (Quirk et al. 1985: 4). Such countries are often 'former British territories' where English is a 'neutral language that is politically acceptable', and where English serves in many domains as in administration or education (Quirk et al. 1985: 4). On the other hand, English as a Foreign Language is typically 'used by persons for communication across frontiers or with others who are not from their countries: listening to broadcasts, reading books or newspapers, engaging in commerce or travel, for example' (Quirk et al. 1985: 5). More recently, the distinction between English as a Foreign Language (EFL) and English as a Second Language (ESL) has been widely challenged by scholars of

World Englishes, especially on emerging varieties (cf. Buschfeld 2013; Edwards 2016; Mollin 2006). Buschfeld points out that the EFL-ESL divide is rather 'hazy' and that it should be viewed as a continuum (2013: 75). Buschfeld introduced a modification of the EFL-ESL-ENL continuum notion originally suggested by Platt et al. (1984). While in this notion's early form, decrease or increase in functions of a language determined its positon on the continuum, in Buschfeld's modification, decrease or increase of function as a marker of local identity is introduced as another, and equally important, variable for that matter (Buschfeld 2013: 75–76). Additionally, Buschfeld's modification questions the traditional link between aspects of postcolonialism and the emergence of second-language varieties (Buschfeld 2013: 75–76).

In 2006, Mollin observed, and fairly so, that despite the fact that the New Englishes literature was 'replete with criteria of ESL-status', there had been no 'comprehensive catalogue' for that matter (Mollin 2006: 45). Hence, Mollin devised a catalogue of criteria for assessing ESL status focused on function, form and attitude (Mollin 2006: 51–52). Buschfeld offers a comprehensive review of the literature on the EFL-ESL distinction and provides an elaborate checklist for ESL variety status (2013: 56–77). Buschfeld's checklist explores four main aspects: '[e]xpansion in function', '[n]ativisation of linguistic structures', '[i]nstitutionalisation' and '[w]ays of language acquisition' (2013: 68–69).

English in the UAE strongly matches two points from Buschfeld's checklist with regard to its functions and ways of acquisition. As section 3.1 has illustrated, the intra-national use of English in the country is high and has spread to a number of domains. Furthermore, the density and diversity of expatriates in the UAE makes it almost impossible for residents (both locals and expatriates) to maintain their lives without using English to communicate at, for instance, school, university, work, or at the market. Thus, societal bilingualism is very likely to be predominant. Additionally, in such a fast-growing and diverse society as that in the UAE, the language learning process is not restricted to the educational system. It is also worth mentioning that residents of the UAE potentially learn, at varying levels, other languages than just English, influenced by the linguistic communities one would come in contact with through their social circles.

With the exception of few studies, research on the nativisation or institutionalisation of linguistic structures in the UAE lags behind in comparison to other emerging varieties of English. Boyle (2012) observes certain aspects of syntactic restructuring in the variety. In addition to that, a study has investigated the use of English articles in the variety and has detected reoccurring patterns (Sadek 2016). Sadek found out that using *the* instead of *zero article* is the most frequent non-standard use of English articles among Emirati students (2016: 83). Due to a lack of further linguistic evidence, there is no strong argument as to whether there are significant systematic characteristics on all linguistic levels of the variety in question. Thus, points two and three from Buschfeld's checklist remain partly, or largely, vague in this case. Then again, based on the evidence provided thus far, one could argue that 'English in the UAE is closer to an ESL on the ESL-EFL continuum' (Sadek 2018: 23). It is, however, important to point out that this does not necessarily reflect the situation in the UAE as a whole, especially as the country's urban centres (Dubai and Abu Dhabi) contain the majority of expatriates. Thus, the linguistic reality could still differ to a large extent in some parts of the country.

4. MODELLING THE UAE

4.1 A Theoretical Background

The study and investigation of World Englishes came into light particularly in the 1980s with a special focus on postcolonial varieties of English (PCEs). For the study of PCEs, the field generated a number of models and theories that helped researchers understand and map the development of English in postcolonial contexts. However, the spread of English is not exclusive to postcolonial settings. English has also been spreading due to factors such as globalisation, the media, the internet and education. The study of such non-postcolonial Englishes relied on methods and tools originally devised for PCEs and then repurposed them for the investigation of non-PCEs and the comparison between both categories.

World Englishes research could be divided into two waves (cf. Buschfeld 2013: 43–47; Edwards 2016: 2–5). Early models such as the EFL-ESL-ENL distinction or Kachru's Three Circles Model were more synchronic in orientation (Kachru 1992; Quirk et al. 1985). The second wave had a chronological or developmental orientation such as Schneider's Dynamic Model of the Evolution of Postcolonial Englishes (Schneider 2007). The underlying principle of Schneider's Dynamic Model is that postcolonial Englishes evolve through a similar pattern 'which drives their formation, accounts for many similarities between them, and appears to operate whenever a language is transplanted' (Schneider 2007: 29). This process develops through five major phases: (1) foundation, (2) exonormative stabilisation, (3) nativisation, (4) endonormative stabilisation, and (5) differentiation. Along these five phases, contact takes place between two strands. The settler strand (STL) typically brings English to the territory in question, while the indigenous strand (IDG) is the strand that originally inhabited a territory. The Dynamic Model suggests four parameters to observe and account for the contact between both strands in each phase; these parameters are (a) historical and political factors, (b) identity constructions, (c) sociolinguistic factors, and (d) structural effects (Schneider 2007: 30–35).

Since its publication, the Dynamic Model has been applied to numerous postcolonial varieties of English, and it has proven to be a comprehensive tool for that matter. More recently, the Dynamic Model has also been applied to non-PCEs (cf. Edwards 2016; Kautzsch 2014). In his work on English in Germany, Kautzsch concluded that the Dynamic Model is fit for categorising a non-PCE; Kautzsch viewed English teachers in Germany as the 'bodily incarnation of Schneider's STL strand' (2014: 224). By doing that, he offered a solution to the issue of the missing STL strand in non-PCE varieties. In 2014, Schneider suggested a number of modifications for the Dynamic Model in order to facilitate capturing linguistic realities in the non-postcolonial context. He suggested dropping the foundation and nativisation phases in this context and also suggested the concept of 'Transnational Attraction' to better understand the spread of English in today's globalised world (Schneider 2014). In her application of the model to English in the Netherlands, Edwards points out that 'the need to work around the colonial trappings of the model renders several of the phases and parameters drastically altered' (2016: 187). Edwards received Schneider's Transnational Attraction notion very positively.

The Extra- and Intra-territorial Forces (EIF) Model was first published in 2016, and it offered a 'unified framework' that would encompass PCEs and non-PCEs (Buschfeld and Kautzsch 2017: 10). The EIF Model's core principle is the 'notion of extra- and intra-territorial forces as constantly operating throughout the development of both PCEs and non-PCEs' (Buschfeld and Kautzsch 2017: 10). The EIF Model functions within the same five phases and four parameters of Schneider's Dynamic Model. Furthermore, the EIF Model suggests that apart from the colonial heritage, similar forces could be at play for both PCEs and non-PCEs (for a detailed description of the EIF Model, see Chapter 1).

As a result of its history and linguistic reality, the UAE has attracted the attention of a number of scholars. Addressing the status of English, Randall and Samimi stress the spread of English in the country and its essential role as a lingua franca there (2010). Additionally, Findlow points out the large spread of English in the higher educational system in the UAE (2006). With regard to World Englishes research, Boyle offers an application of Schneider's Dynamic Model to the case of the UAE (2012). According to Boyle, the STL strand includes 'native English speakers (including functional English speakers)' (2012: 314). The IDG strand is constituted by 'the Arabic speaking people of the UAE [. . .] while the South Asian immigrants form the "adstrate" strand of the population' (2012: 314). Boyle points out that the UAE is entering phase 3 of the Dynamic Model; he also sheds light on the fact that, unlike in many other varieties of English, the adstrate community in the UAE forms the largest strand. This study, however, argues that the IDG, STL and adstrate categories are rather inflexible and unable to fully capture the speech communities within the UAE. This study, however, argues that the STL strand is not exclusive to native speakers of English in the case of the Emirates. Since using English has become a necessity in almost all domains in the UAE, any expatriate living in the UAE could be considered a settler in the sense of the Dynamic Model. This way, each settler brings their variety of English and thus their own influence on language change in the UAE.

4.2 An Application of the Extra- and Intra-territorial Forces Model (EIF) to the Case of the UAE

As has been pointed out, the EIF Model is largely based on the notion that extra- and intra-territorial forces are the main drive for the development of a variety. The remainder of this section discusses a number of forces that mainly influence the development of English in the UAE both on the extra- and intra-territorial levels (for brevity, hereafter referred to as the intra and extra levels). This section also relies on evidence provided by sociolinguistic interviews conducted in 2017 (Sadek 2018).

4.2.1 Colonisation

The UAE was a British protectorate from 1820 to 1971. Within that period, the then Trucial States could be categorised as a subjection colony. Thus, in those years, the British had no significant settlements on land and came in contact with the native population mainly at the leadership level to manage and facilitate the various agreements reached by both parties. Thus, at the extra level, there was very limited contact between settlers and the native population. At the intra level, the country has a certain colonial baggage, but at the same time it has very little to almost no bearing on the country's image and situation today.

4.2.2 Discovery of oil

The exploration for oil began in the country in the 1930s. Beneficiary production of oil started approximately in the 1960s. By the time the UAE gained independence in 1971, oil production was at its highest, and the fresh Emirati government then capitalised on using the massive income brought in by oil in developing the country's infrastructure. At the extra level, the discovery and production of oil was possibly the main reason for more direct contact between the British and some of the local population in the last few decades of the Trucial years. At the intra level, the discovery of oil has been a game changer in Emirati history. Thanks to the booming oil industry and the investments that followed it, there has been a need for large numbers of expatriates who could keep up with the pace of the country's growth. Expatriates today are estimated to constitute over 90 per cent of the population. It could be argued that had it not been for the oil industry in its early years of independence and its after-effects, the UAE would be a different country and it would possibly not be as linguistically diverse as it is today.

4.2.3 Tourism

As has been noted already, the UAE is a world-famous tourist attraction. At the extra level, tourism attracts large numbers of tourists to the country. Despite their short visits, tourists contribute to the linguistic diversity in the country and increase the level of contact with numerous varieties of English. At the intra level, tourism allows the residents of the UAE's urban centres the chance to come in contact with a variety of speakers of different linguistic backgrounds and thus enlarge the language input to the Emirates even further. Tourism has also demanded a degree of linguistic accommodation to ensure a pleasant experience for tourists. Hence, the linguistic landscape in the country's major cities is very tourist-friendly and most public information is also available in English.

4.2.4 Social media and the internet

At the extra level, the internet offers a window into the Emirati social, political, economic and touristic realms. There are plenty of public and private websites and blogs that provide information about the UAE; whether seeking information on visa or work permit regulations, planning a vacation to the country, looking for a study programme or considering investing in the UAE, all the information is available online. At the intra level, social media and the internet have a particularly vital role in keeping the expatriate community in the UAE in contact with their families and friends in their countries of origin. Thus, the internet is another source of language input in the UAE.

4.2.5 Residency permits and visa regulations

Up until 2018, provided they had a job, expatriates in the UAE could obtain a three-year visa, which could be extended until the age of sixty. A new law which passed in 2018 allows up to ten-year visas for 'specialists working in medicine, science, research, and technical fields – plus their families' (Reynolds 2018). Then again, expatriates in the UAE have no means to apply for permanent stays. At the extra level, such regulations might pose a barrier for new groups of expatriates planning on working or living in the UAE. At the intra level, knowing they cannot obtain permanent residency status, expatriates in the Emirates may not be able to identify with the country as their home and may keep strong ties with their countries of origin. Thus, expatriates are less likely to accommodate to linguistic or social norms in the UAE.

4.2.6 Identity and religion

The UAE presents itself as a modern and moderate Muslim country. However, the local Emirati community might be relatively conservative in comparison to the expatriate communities in the country. Guéraiche believes that 'under the veneer, the Emirates have kept alive a conservative society' (2017: 9). This has an effect on the linguistic realities in the UAE. One could argue that this is reflected in the rhetoric that English, or other languages, could be a threat to the Arabic language and thus also to the Emirati identity. For instance, one headline in an Emirati newspaper read 'Special Report: Arabic at risk of becoming foreign language in UAE' (Pennington 2015). The report expresses a concern that Emirati students' competence in Arabic is on the decline in comparison to that in English.

Arabic remains less used in comparison to English or other languages in the Emirates. In fact, the UAE makes an effort to promote the Arabic language among expatriates. Then again, many expatriates do not see the need to learn Arabic since they can go about with English in all aspects of their lives; only some expats expressed an interest in learning Arabic, thinking it would help them better understand the Emirati community and to be part of it (Sadek 2018: 51–52). On the other hand, an Arabic-speaking expatriate who was born in the Emirates commented that using English is rather habitual; he further commented: 'Like, most of my thoughts are in English. So basically, when I wanna express myself like at the best of my ability [//] abilities, I would usually speak in English' (Sadek 2018: 52). This comment clearly shows that for some expatriates, using English is not only a matter of necessity; it also is part of the way they think and possibly part of their identity.

This study argues that the UAE is in the early stages of phase 3. The remainder of this section will discuss this argument by further applying the case of the UAE to the EIF Model in the light of the intra- and extra-territorial forces outlined above and while taking into consideration the historical and sociolinguistic background discussed in section 2 and section 3.

It is worth noting at this point that since English in the UAE is by no means a typical PCE, it is difficult to use the traditional notions of the STL and IDG strands in this case. While one could argue that expatriates in the UAE form the settler strand, they are however not there to settle. As long as expatriates cannot obtain permanent residency status or become naturalised citizens (discussed above under 'Residency permits and visa regulations'), their identities are very likely to be torn between their home countries and the UAE. Then again, this is not to deny the fact that many expats in the UAE identify with the country to a certain extent, that their linguistic and cultural repertoires are partly defined by their lives and experiences in the UAE, and that they in turn shape the country's cultural and linguistic identity. It is in fact for this very reason that the UAE is currently in phase 3, given that there are such a number of vibrant speech communities and widespread bilingualism and uses and functions of English in the country (see section 3 and sub-section 3.1). Thus, while forces such as globalisation, tourism, trade and the internet do constitute a part of the missing settler strand in the Emirati case, as is the case in typical non-PCEs (cf. Buschfeld and Kautzsch

2017: 18), expatriates constitute the remainder and the more significant part of the missing settler strand. The existence of large numbers of expatriates in the UAE is in effect a result of trade relations, globalisation and the country's need for an expatriate force and its policy in that regard; they are not the result of colonial settlements nor the country's colonial past. Hence, it could be argued that extra- and intra-territorial forces such as globalisation, trade and visa regulations in the Emirati case not only point to the variety's status in the UAE but also help one better understand the structure and complexity of the country's speech communities.

It has been pointed out that the local Emirati community could be considered conservative in comparison to many expatriate communities in the country. However, the social divide in the UAE is not restricted to Emiratis versus non-Emiratis. A Russian living in Dubai describes the city as segregated; they commented that the city has housing clusters where South Asians, westerners, Arabs, Emiratis and other groups happen to live in separate parts of the city (Sadek 2018: 45). Kantaria describes this phenomenon in Dubai as 'expat bubbles', where expatriates in Dubai mostly live within similar cultural or speech communities and have very little contact with Emiratis (2016). Yet again, according to Sadek, some expatriates also reported having regular social contact with Emiratis in Dubai (2018: 45). There is evidence to suggest that expatriates and locals are merging, which would be typical of phase 3 (Schneider 2007: 41). However, there is also an indication of a certain degree of social separation between locals and non-locals and between different groups of expatriates. This social separation could be interpreted as a reason why English in the UAE is likely not to develop past phase 3, which is typically the case for non-PCEs.

What remains largely unanswered and under-researched is the question of whether English in the UAE has developed its own linguistic features. This study has not investigated the development of potential features distinct to the variety; rather, it has focused on language attitude, functions and forms. Then again, this study suggests that the grounds for an endonormative linguistic behaviour are there, especially due to the widespread use of English in schools, higher education, inter-ethnic communication, everyday life and in the media. However, because there seems to be a degree of social separation, it is hard to speculate that one variety would be able to reflect the various speech communities in question (Emiratis, South East Asians, westerners, Arabic-speaking expatriates, etc.). An observation has been made that a number of westerners in the UAE reported using numerous Arabic words to describe food, local traditions or places (Sadek 2018).

5. CONCLUSION

This study has overviewed the history of the UAE with a special focus on the colonial aspects it entails. The point was made that the Emirates represents a borderline case between a PCE and a non-PCE. After discussing some of the main functions of English in the UAE, this study also stressed the vital role of English across the country and its spread in all domains. Based on that, it is argued that English in the UAE is closer to the ESL end on the EFL-ESL continuum. The study has also attempted an application of the EIF Model to the case of the UAE.

The EIF Model, in fact, proves to be a flexible tool in capturing a complex linguistic reality such as that of the Emirates. By being able to account for variables and forces which have a large effect on the development of English in the UAE, the model thus also helps one better understand and categorise the complexity of speech communities in the country. By accounting for forces such as globalisation, identity and religion, and visa regulations, the model offers the grounds for understanding speech communities in the UAE outside the traditional STL-IDG rhetoric. What sticks out in the case of the UAE is that while the expatriate community at large could easily be thought of as a settler strand in the traditional PCE context, doing that could misrepresent the reality of the situation. The expatriate strand in the Emirates, which constitutes the majority of the population by far, is an ever-changing group with new waves of expatriates due to extra-territorial forces such as trade and globalisation and intra-territorial forces such as visa regulations. Moreover, despite the fact that expatriates in the UAE might have strong relations with their home countries, and despite any social divides between locals and expatriates or between expatriate communities themselves, these speech communities shape the linguistic and cultural fabric of the UAE in the same manner that the local community does. This is one of the main reasons why English in the UAE is argued to be entering phase 3.

There are many aspects of English in the UAE which deserve deeper and more focused research. The complexity and diversity of the speech communities in the country, among other factors, indicate the development of linguistic markers of this variety. This study also concludes that

English in the UAE is set on a trajectory to become a far more complex variety of its own right. The future of this variety, however, will be highly influenced by whether expatriates in the UAE will one day be able to obtain permanent resident status and develop stronger ties with the country.

REFERENCES

Abdullah, Muhammad Morsy. 1978. *The United Arab Emirates*. London: Croom Helm.
About the UAE. 2018. *Gulf News*, https://gulfnews.com/news/uae/society/dubai-population-to-double-by-2027-1.2249245 (last accessed 16 September 2018).
Ahmed, Ashfaq. 2008. Expats make up to 99% of Private Sector Staff in UAE. *Gulf News*, https://gulfnews.com/business/sectors/employment/expats-make-up-99-of-private-sector-staff-in-uae-1.96744 (last accessed 25 March 2018).
Alittihad.ae. 2018. About Us, http://www.alittihad.ae/aboutus.php (last accessed 23 March 2018).
Badih, Samia. 2010. Gulf News No. 1 English online paper in Mena. *Gulf News*, https://gulfnews.com/news/uae/media/gulf-news-no-1-english-online-paper-in-mena-1.702961 (last accessed 24 March 2018).
Baldwin, Derek. 2018. Dubai population to double by 2027. *Gulf News*, https://gulfnews.com/news/uae/society/dubai-population-to-double-by-2027-1.2249245 (last accessed 10 August 2018).
Bassiouney, Reem. 2009. *Arabic Sociolinguistics*. Edinburgh: Edinburgh University Press.
Boyle, Ronald. 2012. Language contact in the United Arab Emirates. *World Englishes* 31.3: 312–330.
Buschfeld, Sarah. 2013. *English in Cyprus or Cyprus English*. Amsterdam: John Benjamins.
Buschfeld, Sarah and Alexander Kautzsch. 2017. Towards an integrated approach to postcolonial and non-postcolonial Englishes. *World Englishes* 36.1: 104–126.
Department of Culture and Tourism. 2018. Who we are, http://tcaabudhabi.ae/en/who.we.are.aspx (last accessed 22 March 2018).
Edwards, Alison. 2016. *English in the Netherlands: Functions, Forms and Attitudes*. Amsterdam: John Benjamins.

Federal Research Division. 2007. Country Profile: United Arab Emirates (UAE), https://www.loc.gov/rr/frd/cs/profiles/UAE.pdf (last accessed 25 March 2018).

Fenelon, K. G. 1976. *The United Arab Emirates: An Economic and Social Survey*. London: Longman.

Findlow, Sally. 2006. Higher education and linguistic dualism in the Arab Gulf. *British Journal of Sociology of Education* 27.1: 19–36.

Gaad, Eman, Mohammed Arif and Fentey Scott. 2006. Systems analysis of the UAE education system. *International Journal of Educational Management* 20.4: 291–303.

Guéraiche, William. 2017. *The UAE: Geopolitics, Modernity and Tradition*. London: I. B. Tauris.

Holes, Clive. 2004. *Modern Arabic: Structures, Functions, and Varieties*. Washington: Georgetown University Press.

Höselbarth, Frank. 2010. *The Education Revolution in the Gulf: A Guide*. Hildesheim: Georg Olms Verlag.

Ibrahim, Ali S. 2011. Education in the United Arab Emirates: A socio-cultural analysis. In Yong Zhao, ed. 2011, *Handbook of Asian Education: A Cultural Perspective*. New York: Routledge, 327–344.

Kachru, Braj B. 1992. *The Other Tongue: English Across Cultures*. Chicago: University of Illinois Press.

Kantaria, Annabel. 2016. Living in Dubai: Why don't expats integrate with Emiratis? *Telegraph*, https://www.telegraph.co.uk/expat/life/living-in-dubai-why-dont-expats-integrate-with-emiratis/ (last accessed 6 May 2018).

Kautzsch, Alexander. 2014. English in Germany: Spreading bilingualism, retracting exonormative orientation and incipient nativization? In Sarah Buschfeld, Thomas Hoffmann, Magnus Huber and Alexander Kautzsch, eds. 2014, *The Dynamic Model and Beyond*. Amsterdam: John Benjamins, 203–227.

Khaleej Times. 2018. About Us, https://www.khaleejtimes.com/about-us (last accessed 23 March 2018).

Khalifa, Ali Mohammed. 1979. *The United Arab Emirates: Unity in Fragmentation*. London: Westview Press.

Leith, Dick. 2007. English – Colonial to postcolonial. In David Graddol, Dick Leith, Joann Swann, Martin Rhys and Julia Gillen, eds. 2007, *Changing English*. London: Routledge, 117–152.

Maceda, Cleofe. 2018. 15.8 million people visited Dubai in 2017. *Gulf News*, https://gulfnews.com/business/sectors/tourism/15-8-million-people-visited-dubai-in-2017-1.2169807 (last accessed 12 March 2018).

MBC Group. 2018. About MBC GROUP, http://www.mbc.net/en/corporate/about-us.html (last accessed 3 March 2018).

Mollin, Sandra. 2006. *Euro-English: Assessing Variety Status*. Tübingen: Gunter Narr.

Peck, Malcom C. 1986. *The United Arab Emirates: A Venture in Unity*. London: Westview Press.

Pennington, Roberta. 2015. Special Report: Arabic 'at risk of becoming foreign language in UAE', https://www.thenational.ae/uae/education/special-report-arabic-at-risk-of-becoming-foreign-language-in-uae-1.21382 (last accessed 2 April 2018).

Platt, John, Heidi Weber and Ho Mian Lian. 1984. *The New Englishes*. London: Routledge and Kegan Paul.

Quirk, Randall, Sidney Greenbaum, Geoffrey Leech and Jan Svartvik. 1985. *A Comprehensive Grammar of the English Language*. New York: Longman.

Randall, Mick and Mohammad Amir Samimi. 2010. The status of English in Dubai. *English Today* 26.1: 43–50.

Reynolds, Rory. 2018. UAE's new visa regulations: What we know. *The National*, https://www.thenational.ae/uae/uae-s-new-visa-regulations-what-we-know-1.732407 (last accessed 22 May 2018).

Sadaqat, Rohma. 2018. Dubai is fourth most visited city globally, https://www.khaleejtimes.com/business/local/dubai-is-fourth-most-visited-city-globally (last accessed 3 March 2018).

Sadek, Saeb. 2016. The use of English articles in the writings of Emirati students. *10plus1: Living Linguistics* 2: 71–85.

Sadek, Saeb. 2018. English in the United Arab Emirates: Modelling the UAE–Functions and Identity. Unpublished Master's thesis, Universität Bielefeld.

Salem, Ola. 2014. Arabic must be main language of UAE, urge FNC Members, https://www.thenational.ae/uae/government/arabic-must-be-main-language-of-uae-urge-fnc-members-1.651886 (last accessed 27 March 2018).

Schneider, Edgar W. 2007. *Postcolonial English. Varieties Around the World*. Cambridge: Cambridge University Press.

Schneider, Edgar W. 2014. New reflections on the evolutionary dynamics of world Englishes. *World Englishes* 33.1: 9–32.

The Official Portal of the UAE Government. 2018. Media in the UAE, https://government.ae/en/media/media (last accessed 22 March 2018).

Ulrichsen, Kristian Coates. 2017. *The United Arab Emirates: Power, Politics, and Policymaking*. London: Routledge.

United Arab Emirates Ministry of Education. 2018. Reports and Statistics, https://www.moe.gov.ae/En/OpenData/Pages/ReportsAndStatistics.aspx (last accessed 24 March 2018).

Visit Abu Dhabi. 2018. Language & Useful Phrases, https://visitabudhabi.ae/en/travel/essential.info/language.and.useful.phrases.aspx (last accessed 20 March 2018).

Worldometers. 2018. United Arab Emirates Population (Live), http://www.worldometers.info/world-population/united-arab-emirates-population/ (last accessed 16 February 2018).

CHAPTER 5

English in India: Global Aspirations, Local Identities at the Grassroots

Sachin Labade, Claudia Lange and Sven Leuckert

1. INTRODUCTION

The global spread of English in new forms and functions has prompted several suggestions for updates on existing taxonomies or altogether new models of the evolution of Englishes. While most researchers would readily concur with the pronouncement that "recent realities seem to be rendering the ENL [English as a Native Language] – ESL [English as a Second Language] distinction increasingly obsolete" (Schneider 2007: 13), the debate about a similar blurring of the boundaries between ESL/Outer Circle and EFL (English as a Foreign Language)/Expanding Circle is still in full swing, as this volume testifies. The editors' own proposal, the Extra- and Intra-territorial Forces (EIF) Model, is designed to 'decolonise' (in the sense of Edwards [2016]) Schneider's Dynamic Model of the evolution of postcolonial Englishes (PCEs) in order to include "those types of traditionally Expanding Circle Englishes which appear to be developing into second-language varieties of English even without a (post)colonial history" (Buschfeld and Kautzsch 2017: 105). Schneider himself put forward the notion of 'Transnational Attraction' to come to terms with "English in emergent contexts" (Schneider 2014: 24) which do not fit readily into his original model. Yet another framework by Mair (2013) goes one step further in incorporating globalization and transnationalism as constitutive for the dynamics of 'the world system of Englishes'.

This chapter focuses on the first two models and attempts to tease out each proposal's explanatory potential with respect to speakers of English in India situated at both ends of the lectal continuum. For the young urban middle class, English is a natural part of their linguistic repertoire and arguably also an integral part of their identity. For the large majority of the less affluent, rural population, however, English is a foreign language and a much sought-after commodity for upward social mobility (cf. Uma et al. 2014). We will present the results from an attitude study carried out in and among Mumbai and other parts of Maharashtra, documenting the extent of English usage in different domains vis-à-vis the local languages, as well as Hindi as the overarching official language besides English (cf. Satyanath 2015). Another focus of the study is speakers' differential attitudes towards English as an identity carrier within their respective social contexts. The study thus targets both ESL and EFL speakers of English, allowing us to flesh out the merits of each model introduced above from the perspective of the Indian communicative space. In particular, our study zooms in on and contributes to the discussion of those aspects of the Dynamic Model and the EIF Model that relate to identity construction and language attitudes, with a focus on the interplay of the two. The chapter is structured as follows: section 2 will first summarize the scholarly discussion about the evolutionary trajectory of Indian English (IndE) within the Dynamic Model. We will also look beyond IndE and into the multilingual Indian communicative space. Section 3 is devoted to our case study, while section 4 evaluates its repercussions for Schneider's and Buschfeld and Kautzsch's model.

2. THEORIZING INDIAN ENGLISH

2.1 The Dynamic Model and Indian English

IndE, which has been characterized by Schneider as "a topic marked by never-ending paradoxes" (2007: 161), lends itself particularly well to a scrutiny of models. There are two partially overlapping accounts of the evolution of IndE which diverge notably when it comes to its current status. Both studies were published in 2007, but apparently independently of each other: Schneider's own account forms part of his book as one of the case studies illustrating the Dynamic Model, while Mukherjee (2007) refers to the Dynamic Model as first published in Schneider (2003), where IndE was not included, and sets out to apply the model to IndE. The earlier phases of IndE have been extensively described elsewhere (e.g. Lange 2020; Sharma 2012); what is of interest for our purposes is the current status of IndE which emerges from Schneider's and Mukherjee's perspectives and possible theoretical consequences for any further assessment of it.

The "never-ending paradoxes" envisaged by Schneider in 2007 largely hold true today: one part of the paradox is the fact that IndE constitutes one of the largest varieties of English in terms of speaker numbers, focusing on India but also taking the diaspora into account. IndE has broadened its home base both demographically and socially: the sheer population growth (from around 1 billion citizens according to the 2001 census to 1.2 billion in 2011) (Census India 2011) has added to the potential number of IndE speakers. The further spread of English education has made the language more accessible, the continuous growth of an urban middle class has led to an increase in speakers proficient in IndE.[1] Still, the other side of the paradox is also very evident. Schneider characterizes English in the Indian context as "essentially utilitarian" (2007: 173), largely confined to specific official domains and far from being or becoming a rallying-point for a unique pan-Indian identity. Given these tensions, Schneider sees IndE still in the nativization stage, beginning in 1905 with the *Swadeshi* movement following the partition of Bengal (2007: 166) and continuing even after independence in 1947.[2] Despite ongoing structural nativization and despite some indications of endonormative stabilization (e.g. literary creativity in IndE, positive [covert] attitudes towards IndE), Schneider points to two factors that impede any further move towards completion of the Dynamic Model's developmental cycle: "the strong position of Hindi and the small fraction of English speakers" (2007: 167). The Indian context even prompts him to limit the explanatory power of his model to a specific speech community rather than the nation as a whole, an important caveat that will be taken up in the next section:

> the application of the Dynamic Model to Indian English accounts for only that segment of society that has been infiltrated by English, even if this is a strongly visible and powerful cohort. *The majority of realities and lives of people on the subcontinent are untouched by the presence of English.* (2007: 161, our emphasis)

---

[1] One example for urbanization: the city of Pune in Maharashtra experienced population growth of more than 30 percent for each decade since 1991, with 9.4 million inhabitants in 2011 (Census India 2011).
[2] *Swadeshi*: lit. 'of one's own country,' a movement to boycott British products in favor of indigenous alternatives.

The position of English vis-à-vis Hindi and other indigenous languages also plays an important role for Mukherjee's account of the development of IndE in its later stages. He posits a nativization stage from around 1835, the date of Macaulay's *Minute on Education* which led to the establishment of English as the language of instruction in schools and later in universities, up to the 1960s. The language riots in South India in 1965 can be seen as an 'Event X' in Schneider's sense, bringing about a notable change in identity constructions: South Indians, that is, speakers of Dravidian languages, protested violently against the phasing out of English as co-official language, which would have left only Hindi (an Indo-Aryan language) as the sole language of the Union. The political unrest lasted for months, with the loss of many lives, and eventually resulted in legislation maintaining the status as second official language. Still, even though Mukherjee is much more decisive about IndE as an endonormatively stabilized variety, he shares Schneider's doubts about further progress along the cycle. In his analysis, IndE is a "semiautonomous" variety (2007: 182) "in which two conflicting forces are in equilibrium" (2007: 171), namely progressive and conservative forces. Both forces operate on three distinct but converging levels, the structural, functional, and attitudinal. Progressive forces endorse further nativization of the variety, embrace an extension of English to further domains of use, and support a positive attitude towards moving further along the cycle; conservative forces resist such change and propagate the exonormative norm. Despite acknowledging phase 4 rather than phase 3 for IndE, Mukherjee seconds Schneider's skepticism about the likelihood of any further development, for similar reasons: since English in India is and always will be in competition with indigenous languages, it "will always remain secondary in processes of Indian identity constructions" (2007: 174). Mukherjee already notes a contrast between settler varieties such as American English in the United States, which invariably complete the cycle, and PCEs in multilingual contexts, where English has to get in line with other languages when it comes to acquiring identity-marking functions. While this aspect is linked to colonization types as well (more on that below), this is where Schneider's and Mukherjee's views on the prospects of IndE as a variety in its own right converge: both doubt whether English can continue along the cycle if it is part of a multilingual repertoire rather than the only contestant for identity formation.

In principle, the Dynamic Model is also intended to cater for multilingual societies; it explicitly recognizes different contact scenarios and acknowledges systematic differences according to settlement types. To take the last point first: India would be a classic example of a trade colony, developing from the initial contact situation in the early seventeenth century onwards into an exploitation colony, with the typical hallmarks of a small settler (STL) strand and only restricted acquisition of English by select members of the indigenous (IDG) strand, giving rise to an indigenized form of English. Settlement colonies, on the other hand, are characterized by large STL groups arriving successively, paving the way for the widespread acceptance of the endonormatively stabilized variety in its final stages. Input from the IDG strand is obviously fairly limited, verging on the negligible, but still: "in the long run these settlement and transmission types, important as they are, are not prime determinants of the outcome of the process of new dialect emergence" (Schneider 2007: 25).

This is where Denis and d'Arcy (2018), in the same vein as Mukherjee (2007), beg to differ. They argue that what they call 'settler colonial Englishes' are not PCEs since decolonization has never happened: what we know as 'independence' in the context of, for example, the United States or Canada involves the status of the settlers with respect to their country of origin and never the indigenous population, who quite simply remain colonized. In the same vein, they reject Schneider's concept of identity rewritings as structurally untenable:

> [. . .] in settler colonial contexts, convergence between settlers and Indigenous populations, linguistic or otherwise, is predominantly a matter of hegemony and legislated attempts at forcible assimilation and coercive erasure. As a basic precondition of settler colonialism, the language-ecological conditions have never existed for mutual negotiation to take place. Thus, the development of English under settler colonialism is not a matter of convergence but of absorption. (2018: 10–11)

With regard to the issue of multilingualism as a potentially detrimental factor for the development of indigenized Englishes as identity carriers for the speech community, Schneider explicitly rejects any such link between monolingualism and a variety's prospects for completing the cycle (2007: 316). On the contrary, he asserts that in multilingual societies

> it has been observed that nativized and localized forms of English coexist alongside indigenous languages. If that is the case both

types of varieties can either share the functions of communicating within narrow social confines and of projecting group identities, or they can adopt complementary symbolic roles in a society. (2007: 316)

It is precisely this dynamic interplay of languages within a multilingual communicative space which will be in focus of our case study, outlined in section 3.

2.2 Modelling Indian English

We have seen that IndE is somewhat oddly poised within the Dynamic Model, even though it happens to be one of the largest and highly influential varieties across South Asia. In addition, it has been researched extensively before and especially after the publication of the Dynamic Model. The next section will briefly consider research on IndE over the last decade, informed by the premises of the Dynamic Model, and will discuss the implications of this research for our understanding of the Indian communicative space overall, as well as for different models as such. The question now is whether the EIF Model might be better able to accommodate the intricacies of the Indian case compared to previous models, in particular the Dynamic Model.

The EIF Model indeed allows for more internal differentiation by positing a range of extra- and intra-territorial factors (Figure 1.1; see the Introduction to this volume) and by explicitly incorporating variety-internal heterogeneity as a third dimension (Figure 1.2; see the Introduction to this volume). Our case study will present an opportunity to spell out whether, for example, 'language policies' or 'globalization' as extra-territorial forces vs. 'language policies/attitudes' and 'acceptance of globalization' as intra-territorial forces have explanatory power in the Indian context. The second aspect, the incorporation of heterogeneity, formalizes what so far every single model has acknowledged. The late Braj Kachru, who argued so relentlessly for acknowledging IndE as a 'non-native institutionalized variety,' also insisted that each such variety can be characterized as moving on a 'cline of bilingualism.' Fully proficient acrolectal speakers of English blur the line between 'genetic' and 'functional' nativeness; the other end of the scale is occupied by those who painstakingly acquire English as a Foreign Language. Sridhar and Sridhar (2018: 135–136) have recently reminded the World Englishes community that, thanks to Kachru, the notion of a cline of bilingualism has been around since the 1960s. Internal variation within the speech community is also recognized in the Dynamic Model (Schneider 2007: 32), and variation in the sense of 'superdiversity' (Vertovec 2007) is also nothing to write home about in the South Asian context: "extreme diversity and mixing have been the bread and butter of sociolinguistics in the so-called third world from time immemorial" (Sridhar and Sridhar 2018: 134).

2.3 The Indian Communicative Space

Our knowledge about IndE has been considerably increased by studies addressing a broad range of features (e.g. Balasubramanian 2009; Lange 2017; Sedlatschek 2009, etc.). IndE is represented by a textbook (Sailaja 2009), by usage guides (Nihalani et al. 1979), but not yet by its own reference grammar and dictionary, which would be a strong indicator for arrival in phase 4. Some studies have specifically looked for linguistic evidence for aligning IndE with a specific evolutionary stage within the Dynamic Model relative to other PCEs (e.g. Mukherjee and Gries 2009). All of these studies so far have targeted acrolectal IndE, for two main reasons. First, IndE as a variety in its own right is typically equated with/represented by its proficient speakers and not its learners – that is, while the distinction between ENL and ESL is more or less obsolete as already noted in the introduction (Schneider 2007: 13), the one between ENL/ESL and EFL is not for the purposes of Schneider's model. Second, all empirical studies of IndE rely on corpora which in turn rely on highly acrolectal IndE.[3] That is, learner varieties as well as grassroots Englishes in India have so far been left out of the picture, as have their speakers and their specific identity constructions within a highly multilingual, but also highly stratified, communicative space. Extremely relevant in this respect is Satyanath's synopsis (2015) of a number of case studies involving quite distinct linguistic scenarios within the Indian communicative space. The communicative interactions under scrutiny ranged from bidialectal to multilingual encounters, from rural to metropolitan contexts, from unscripted minority language to established

---

[3] The Kolhapur Corpus of IndE replicates the LOB/Brown corpora (1 million words of written [printed] language), the ICE corpora include standard(ized) varieties of English by definition, the South Asian Varieties of English (SAVE) corpus represents six South Asian varieties including IndE by 3 million words of newspaper language each.

literary language with high prestige. However, all case studies found that "there is no style shift" (Satyanath 2015: 114). Speakers fail to accommodate towards the more prestigious variety or variants, indicating that there is "no hierarchical evaluation of the standard and the vernacular" (Satyanath 2015: 114). This finding runs counter to the very foundation of the Labovian sociolinguistic enterprise which takes for granted that variation acquires social meaning, indexing social stratification. In such a scenario, the standard has overt prestige and typically induces speakers to accommodate to it in their more formal speech styles – a scenario whose validity has been confirmed in countless studies over the past decades. Satyanath (2015: 115) attributes the blatant absence of such a relation between social hierarchies mapping onto linguistic hierarchies to the Indian tradition of "pluralistic and inclusive practices" within the communicative space, "despite the presence of many inequalities on various levels" (2015: 116), notably caste.[4] That is, varieties and variation are multi-layered, partly domain-specific, and certainly markers of local and/or regional identities, but are not necessarily subject to the tidal pull of a standard variety.

The position of English within this dynamic communicative space deserves special attention in our context. Satyanath conceptualizes what she calls "new bilingualism" (2015: 108) in India as a row of concentric circles, progressing from the local to the national level. The innermost circle is reserved for "home and intra-community languages," the next comprises "local lingua francas," which may or may not be distinct from the next layer of "state languages," for example, Marathi in Maharashtra (Satyanath 2015: 108). The final circle includes the two official languages Hindi and English "which mainly serve as inter-state communication tools" (2015: 108). However, the place of English within this model is not confined to social and spatial distance: English may be the language of instruction in school even at a local level, and it invariably is the language of higher education; it has also become "a language of socialisation in urban areas" (2015: 108), thus making inroads from the outer rim to the inner core of Satyanath's model. Further, "[t]hough English has not replaced the local languages, it has replaced literacy in regional languages in major urban areas to a considerable extent due to rising English education" (2015: 108).

---

[4] Satyanath's claim that even caste in India is horizontal rather than vertical/hierarchical (2015: 116) is highly contentious, but a discussion of it goes far beyond the scope of this chapter.

Table 5.1 Schneider's original parameters of the Dynamic Model (2007) and their extension to the Expanding Circle

PCEs (Schneider 2007: 56)	Non-PCEs (Schneider 2014: 17–18)
History and politics	"language policy and English in education"
Identity construction	"attitudes to English (and possible impact on identities)"
Sociolinguistics of contact/use/attitudes	"sociolinguistic conditions of using and learning English"
Linguistics developments/structural effects	"structural consequences (features)"

Source: Schneider 2014.

The two preceding sub-sections have shown that multilingualism creates and sustains diversity and heterogeneity within the Indian communicative space, with – from a western perspective – unexpected results for language standardization and identity constructions. Table 5.1 captures Schneider's original parameters of the Dynamic Model (Schneider 2007) and his proposal for their extension to the Expanding Circle (Schneider 2014). Buschfeld and Kautzsch note that "we do not see an urgent need to differentiate between the parameter 'identity constructions' (as in the original version of the model) and 'attitudes to English' (Schneider's 2014: 17 reconception for non-PCEs) as the two concepts appear to be interlinked, especially in terms of language attitudes impacting identity constructions" (2017: 116).

In the case study to follow, we will highlight the interplay of identity constructions involving all languages within speakers' repertoires with their attitude to English. The data we present will allow us to test whether the concepts of 'identity' and 'attitudes' are converging or diverging. Evidence for the former would lend support to Buschfeld and Kautzsch's conflation of the two concepts and thus to a salient aspect of their model. Evidence for the latter, however, could be interpreted within the parameters of either model, as section 4 will show.

3. CASE STUDY: LANGUAGE USE AND LANGUAGE ATTITUDES IN AND AROUND MUMBAI

3.1 Rationale

For the present study, we focus on language use and language attitudes in and around Mumbai. Mumbai is the biggest city in the Western Indian state of Maharashtra and the second biggest city in India in terms of population, with 18.41 million inhabitants reported in 2011 (Census of India 2011). However, given the population dynamics of India overall with an increase of 17.64 percent in population since the last census of 2001, the current population is more likely to be closer to 22 million. The megacity of Mumbai is home to Bollywood millionaires, the stock market, and international corporations on the one hand and South Asia's largest slums on the other. The city attracts thousands of people daily from poorer rural areas within the state and from further afield, who are seeking a better life for themselves and their families. Linguistically, we would expect to see a stronger role for English as the language of the aspiring middle class, but also of Hindi as the lingua franca of the non-Marathi speaking poorer immigrants from other states. That is, the state language Marathi might find itself sandwiched in between both English and Hindi. Yet, despite these population dynamics, Marathi has not lost its appeal, if the extremely popular medium of film is any indication: Marathi films such as *Timepass* (2014) and *Sairat* (2016) were box office hits in Maharashtra, testifying to a renewed interest in regional language media.

While many different languages are spoken (as either L1 or L2) in Maharashtra, Marathi was mentioned most frequently as the mother tongue in the 2011 Census and also by the respondents in our questionnaire. The middle column in Table 5.2 indicates the speaker numbers for the most widely indicated mother tongues in Maharashtra in percentages and absolute figures; the right-hand column provides the frequency of mention (either as L1 or L2) in the questionnaires. Since several languages could be mentioned by one person, the total number of languages far exceeds the number of questionnaires.

We selected Maharashtra as our testing ground for the EIF Model for three reasons. First, the dynamic interplay between Marathi, English, Hindi, and the local languages has been politicized and also plays an important role in education. Maharashtra is home to the Shiv Sena, a right-wing political party which combines Hindu nationalism with an

Table 5.2 Languages indicated as mother tongues by Indians living in Maharashtra in descending order of speaker percentage (Census of India 2011) and speaker numbers in the questionnaires[a]

Language	Speaker numbers in Maharashtra	Speaker numbers in questionnaires
Marathi	77,461,172 (72.2%)	288 (31.61%)
Hindi	14,481,513 (13.5%)	277 (30.41%)
Urdu	7,540,324 (7.03%)	20 (2.19%)
Gujarati	2,371,743 (2.21%)	18 (1.98%)
Ahirani	1,616,730 (1.51%)	6 (0.66%)
Telugu	1,320,880 (1.23%)	5 (0.54%)
Kannada	1,000,463 (0.93%)	16 (1.76%)
Sindhi	723,748 (0.67%)	2 (0.21%)
Tamil	509,887 (0.48%)	4 (0.44%)
Bengali	442,090 (0.41%)	9 (0.99%)
Konkani	399,255 (0.37%)	11 (1.21%)
Malayalam	366,153 (0.34%)	10 (1.09%)
Punjabi	280,192 (0.26%)	4 (0.44%)
Odia	139,241 (0.13%)	2 (0.21%)
English	106,656 (0.09%)	237 (33.33%)
Sanskrit	3,802 (0.0035%)	2 (0.21%)

[a] Some respondents in the questionnaire named Banjari, Bhojpuri, Marwari, Rajasthani, or Surjapuri as L1 or L2; these languages are conflated with Hindi in the 2011 Census. Bilaspuri, in turn, is conflated with Punjabi in the Census data. No data are available on Jain (a religious rather than a linguistic label), which was also named both as L1 and L2 by different respondents. French, Italian, Spanish, and Russian were also named infrequently, but the Indian Census does not provide any data on these languages.

agenda of preferential treatment for everything Marathi, including the language. The Shiv Sena has been active in Maharashtra since the 1960s and currently forms the state government together with the equally Hindu-nationalist BJP (Bharatiya Janata Party). This appropriation of Marathi as a symbol of nationalist pride is counteracted by the all-Indian trend towards English-medium schools, which is also very much in evidence in Greater Mumbai. *The Indian Express* reported in May 2017 and again in March 2018 that Marathi-medium schools planned on introducing classes in English to raise student numbers (Sahoo 2018; Singh 2017). The report released in May 2017 also quotes the principal secretary of the school education department, Nand Kumar, with a statement on the perceived importance of English: "Today, even the poorest parents want their children to learn English. It is one of the major factors making students opt out of Marathi schools and join private English-medium schools" (Singh 2017). While newspaper reports are highly interesting sources in their own right, it is necessary to assess the language-related attitudes of the population within a sound sociolinguistic framework.

Another important reason for our focus on Maharashtra is that it is the Indian state with the second-highest population but, to the best of our knowledge, has not been the subject of a (sociolinguistic) attitudinal study.[5] Since Mumbai is one of India's biggest cities, the distinction between an urban and a rural upbringing and the related attitudes towards the different languages in the state are particularly interesting in the case of Maharashtra. Finally, the study was conducted as a cooperation between Mumbai in India and Dresden in Germany, which means that a diverse group of people in and around Mumbai could be consulted.

Overall, identifying the attitudes of different strata of the population represents an important step towards classifying the role of English in a given region. The attitudes of a population towards an indigenized variety (or indigenized varieties) have previously been noted as a crucial factor in the development of the respective variety (Bernaisch and Koch 2015: 119; Schneider 2007: 49). However, the multilingual nature of India and, accordingly, Maharashtra, as well as the varying accessibility of (higher) education, suggest complex and differing attitudes depending on factors such as the educational level of the parents. In the following, we present our study design and the first results of our case study.

3.2 Study Design

Due to the uncomplicated procedure of digital distribution, questionnaires represent the ideal tool in order to study questions related to language identity and language attitudes. Thus, we created and distributed a questionnaire using the Google Forms tool. The questions featured in the questionnaire are based on similar questionnaires used in previous studies (see Buschfeld 2011; Buschfeld and Kautzsch 2014; Edwards 2016), which means that the pre-testing of the questionnaire was largely accounted for. Nevertheless, the questionnaire was initially presented to a select number of respondents and slightly modified according to

---

[5] Pandurang (2018) is, to our knowledge, the only exception, albeit with a narrower focus on school pupils only.

potential difficulties identified on the basis of this test run. Since giving personal information online or elsewhere is potentially face-threatening (see Krug and Sell 2013: 79), we stated at the beginning of the questionnaire that all responses would be fully anonymous. The questionnaire itself has been divided into four sections which will be explained one by one in the following paragraphs.

3.2.1 Section 1: General information

The first section of the questionnaire was designed to gather general information and metadata about the respondents. This included questions on age, education, occupation, and years of residence in Maharashtra as well as questions related to proficiency and education in English, Marathi, and Hindi. The questionnaire also enquired about the place of birth, which represents an important variable in this study since it might be a valuable predictor for a more locally- or more globally-oriented attitude towards English. Instead of directly referring to the places indicated by respondents, we identified each given place of birth as rural or urban, depending on whether (a) it lies in the periphery or the center of a big city or (b) it is a village or small town.

3.2.2 Section 2: Usage contexts

The second section featured nineteen questions and was designed to identify usage contexts of languages; more precisely, the section aimed at identifying in which situations respondents prefer to use English, Marathi, Hindi, or another language. In this context, 'another language' corresponds to an additional language which speakers were asked to identify at the beginning of this section. This choice was made in order to accommodate the fact that many Indians have a further language in their inventory, and/or that they are speakers of a minority language. All usage-related questions in this section offered possible responses based on the frequency of language usage in a specific context, the possible answers being 'never,' 'sometimes,' 'often,' 'mostly,' and 'always.'

3.2.3 Section 3: Language identity

The third section featured four questions and had the purpose of investigating how the respondents viewed themselves and the major languages of Maharashtra with regard to prestige and identity construction.

Respondents were to indicate what they would call themselves with regard to language and culture (e.g. 'Indian' or 'Maharashtrian'), which language they prefer to use in most situations whenever possible, which language they identify with the most, and which language has the highest prestige.

3.2.4 Section 4: Language attitudes

The fourth and last section of the questionnaire comprised ten questions and investigated language attitudes towards Marathi, Hindi, English, and local languages. In this section, all responses were ordered on a 5-point Likert scale, with respondents being able to decide if they 'strongly disagree,' 'disagree,' are 'indifferent,' 'agree,' or 'strongly agree' to a statement. First, respondents had to decide if they considered knowledge of each of the four languages important for people living in Maharashtra. Second, respondents had to decide which of the four languages they considered advantageous or important in specific contexts such as finding a job or for personal advancement.

3.3 Dataset

Each respondent had the choice of answering the questionnaire in either English or Marathi. Some questions in the questionnaire were mandatory and others were optional. When the online questionnaire was closed, we checked for any duplicates and erased all lines with identical information. Table 5.3 shows the remaining number of questionnaires according to the gender of the respondents and the language of the chosen questionnaire.

Depending on the type of question, different methodological steps were employed. The majority of questions in the third and fourth sections on language use and attitudes were ordered based on a 5-point Likert scale, where 5 points indicates highest agreement or most fre-

Table 5.3 Number of questionnaires according to gender and language of the questionnaire

	English questionnaire	*Marathi questionnaire*
Female respondents	100	45
Male respondents	101	83
Total respondents	201	128

quent use and 1 point indicates lowest agreement or least frequent use (see Buschfeld and Kautzsch 2014). For these questions, mean and median ($\tilde{x}$) values were calculated in order to identify tendencies. For other questions, such as those relating to identity and prestige, we quantified the results by counting how often languages were mentioned and correlated them to other variables.

3.4 Selected Results

In the following, we present selected results from the case study. Instead of providing overviews of the responses to every question, we highlight certain questions and relate responses relevant to the EIF Model to each other.

3.4.1 Selection of questionnaire

In order to get a better idea of the potential reasons for why which language was indicated in different contexts, we considered the distinction between urban and rural and the education of the parents as potential factors. Both were specifically incorporated into the study to account for the whole range of speakers/users of English in India on the cline of bilingualism from EFL to ENL. In the Indian context, the urban-rural distinction overlaps with caste divisions and is often used as a euphemism for the latter. Further, standards of teaching and learning English are generally much higher in urban contexts. Our study also reached out to 'first generation learners', that is, respondents whose parents received very little (primary school) to no education, and thus had a long way to go to achieve educational success, and who definitely did not grow up with English as a home language. The Indian education system as well as the public sector in general operate with complex affirmative action policies and quotas in support of people from disadvantaged backgrounds; however, historical inequalities will take many generations to overcome.

A first aspect which we considered interesting in the present study is the choice given to respondents between filling in the questionnaire in either English or Marathi. As mentioned above, 201 respondents opted to fill in the questionnaire in English, while 128 respondents preferred to fill in the questionnaire in Marathi. In total, 145 (72.14 percent) of the respondents who chose the English-language questionnaire came from an urban background and 56 (27.86 percent) respondents came from a rural background. In the Marathi questionnaire, 55 (42.97 percent) respondents had an urban background and 73 (57.03 percent) respondents had a rural background. The difference between the two groups is highly statistically significant (x-squared = 26.707, df = 1, *p*-value = 2.368e-07), which is also evident in the much higher percentage of respondents with an urban background who selected the English questionnaire. The rural versus urban distinction was also taken into consideration in the analysis of the indicated language of identity and language of prestige, which we discuss in the following paragraphs.

3.4.2 *Language of identity and language of prestige*

A central aspect in the questionnaire relates to identity in the sense that speakers were asked to indicate with which language(s) they identify the most and which attitudes they have towards English, Hindi, Marathi, and other local languages. Answers to the question "With which language do you most strongly identify?" are visualized in Figure 5.1, with the black bars on the left indicating responses from the English questionnaire and the gray bars in the middle indicating responses from the Marathi questionnaire.[6] The light gray bars on

---

[6] The category 'Other' in this and the following figures includes other languages as well as responses such as 'all languages' or 'no languages'. These responses were conflated in order to avoid cramming the figures.

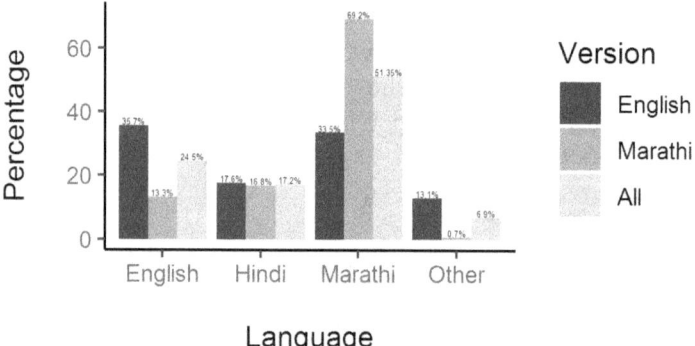

Figure 5.1 Language of identity indicated in the English and Marathi questionnaires

the right represent the average percentages across the two groups of questionnaires.[7]

In the English-language questionnaire, English and Marathi are mentioned almost equally frequently. However, in twenty-two cases, more than one language was listed, and in merely three of these cases English was not one of the mentioned languages. The Marathi questionnaire clearly shows a much stronger tendency towards Marathi, with English being named even less frequently than Hindi.

In terms of background in relation to the indicated language of identity, people with a rural background strongly favored Marathi (72.87 percent, $n=94$), while English (13.18 percent, $n=17$) and Hindi (13.95 percent, $n=18$) were indicated less frequently. For Indians with an urban background, Marathi is still the language they most strongly identify with (48 percent, $n=96$), but English is mentioned far more frequently in comparison to the previous group (33.5 percent, $n=67$). Hindi is named as the language of identification at an almost identical percentage (14.5 percent, $n=29$). Overall, the differences between the rural and the urban groups are highly significant (x-squared = 20.794, df = 2, p-value = 3.053e-05). The preliminary conclusion which can be drawn from this comparison is that an urban background leads to a stronger identification with English, while Maharashtrians with a rural background favor Marathi.

Figure 5.2 summarizes the responses to the identity question correlated with the educational level of the parents. Thus, we differentiated between 'high' education, which refers to an education at least to the secondary level, and 'low' education, which refers to no or only primary education.

Overall, the results clearly indicate that the participants' language of identity is Marathi, followed by English, with Hindi in third place. The loyalty towards Marathi is much stronger in rural settings, and respondents who grew up in households with little education show a very high identification with the state language Marathi. In all configurations, the first official language, Hindi, ranks behind the other two languages.

The next question under scrutiny considers what respondents deem the most prestigious language in general. Figure 5.3 shows the results for the indicated language of prestige in the English and Marathi questionnaires and provides the overall figures.

---

[7] All graphs presented in this chapter were created with R (R Development Core Team 2019) and the R package *ggplot2* (Wickham 2009).

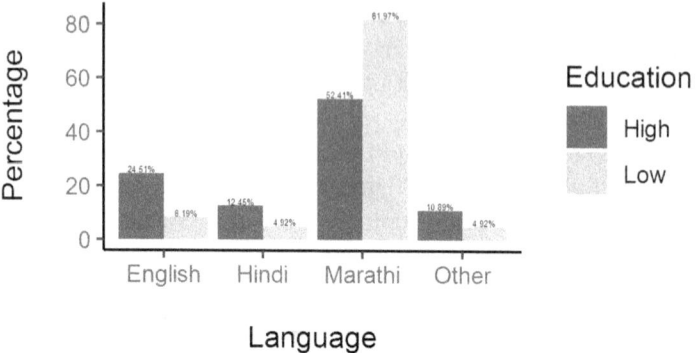

Figure 5.2 Educational level of the parents and language of identity

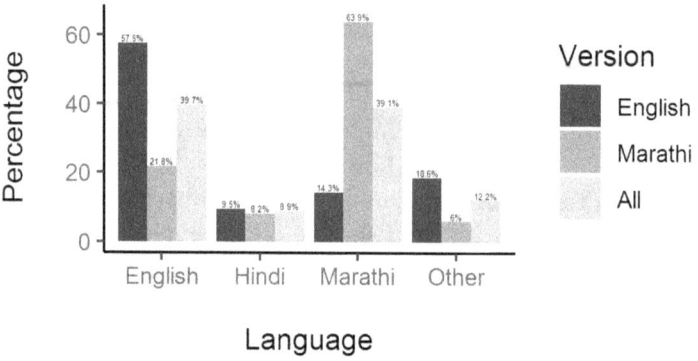

Figure 5.3 Indicated language of prestige in the English and Marathi questionnaires

Considering all questionnaires, English barely edges out Marathi as the most prestigious language. However, respondents who decided to work with the English questionnaire clearly consider English to be the more prestigious language, while respondents who opted to fill in the Marathi questionnaire strongly favor Marathi. For Hindi, the number of respondents is almost equal in both questionnaires; other options are mentioned far more frequently in the English questionnaire.

In terms of the rural versus urban background, it is interesting to compare if there is a difference with regard to what is considered the language of identity and the most prestigious language. The situation does not seem clear with regard to the question of prestige in particular – does a rural background automatically mean that English is considered a

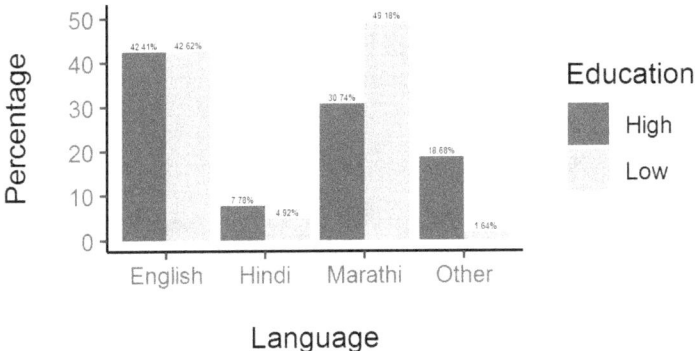

Figure 5.4 Educational level of the parents and most prestigious language

more prestigious language? Some answers given by respondents indicate that English is the key to success; others see all languages as equal. Quantitatively, Marathi is most frequently named as the most prestigious language by respondents with a rural background (52.71 percent, $n=68$), but English receives a noticeably higher score compared to the results indicated for language of identity (44.96 percent, $n=58$). Hindi, in turn, receives the lowest score by this group of respondents (9.3 percent, $n=12$).[8] The picture looks different for people from an urban background, since English is named as the most prestigious language (46.5 percent, $n=93$) over Marathi (28 percent, $n=56$) and Hindi (10.5 percent, $n=21$). Once again, the differences are significant, but they are less pronounced (x-squared = 8.4954, df = 2, p-value = 0.0143). Thus, English is considered a very prestigious language by people from either a rural or an urban background in our data, but it does not represent a language of identity for many people with a rural background. In this context, it is interesting to see if the education of the parents plays an important role in what respondents take to be the most prestigious language; the results for this question are presented in Figure 5.4.

It is noteworthy that English receives almost equally high results from both groups. In situations where parents have a lower education, Marathi is considered more prestigious at almost 50 percent, while other options are rated as much less important. Again, it is important to stress that the category 'Other' includes other languages as well as any other

---

[8] Please note that more than one language could be named, which is why the numbers do not have to add up to 100 percent.

possible response, such as 'All' languages. For both language of identity and language of prestige, higher levels of parental education result in English being named more frequently.

3.4.3 The importance of languages in different contexts

In addition to the questions discussed above, respondents were also asked to rate the level of importance assigned to Marathi, English, Hindi, and other local languages in general and in a variety of contexts. Table 5.4 indicates the answers given by respondents to the question of how important they consider knowing Marathi, English, Hindi, or another local language in general. The values in the table represent mean values of the Likert scale ratings from 1 to 5, which correspond to the most negative rating ('strongly disagree') and the most positive rating ('strongly agree'). For the added values across all questionnaires, we also indicate the median.

The results show that Marathi is considered to be more important than both English and Hindi; rather interestingly, English received the lowest score of all languages in the English questionnaires. While it received a slightly higher rating in the Marathi questionnaires, it is still seen as less important than Marathi, other local languages, and Hindi. Across all questionnaires, the local languages are considered the most important; however, all languages received a high rating with an identical median value. In the Marathi questionnaire, six people disagreed or strongly disagreed that knowing English is important. Only one of these respondents indicated having problems with their English proficiency, giving all four receptive and productive language skills a 'with difficulty' rating. However, only one out of six also considered English to be 'not important' in the job market, which highlights that, despite the lower ratings overall, its importance in the job market is widely acknowledged. In the English questionnaire, twenty-eight people disagree or strongly disagree that knowing English is important.

Table 5.4 Knowing ___ is important for people living in Maharashtra

	Marathi	English	Hindi	Other local language
English questionnaire	4.12	3.75	3.86	4.2
Marathi questionnaire	4.68	4.32	4.23	4.68
All questionnaires	4.40 ($\tilde{x} = 4$)	4.04 ($\tilde{x} = 4$)	4.05 ($\tilde{x} = 4$)	4.44 ($\tilde{x} = 4$)

Table 5.5 Knowing ___ is an advantage in the job market

	Marathi	English	Hindi	Other local language
English questionnaire	3.52	4.72	3.79	3.78
Marathi questionnaire	4.05	4.70	4.09	4.07
All questionnaires	3.79 ($\tilde{x}=4$)	4.71 ($\tilde{x}=5$)	3.94 ($\tilde{x}=4$)	3.93 ($\tilde{x}=4$)

Twenty-three of these respondents have a university degree but all of them have at least a high school diploma. Out of the 112 responses which were counted here, only six indicated a 'with difficulty' proficiency in English, which means that all respondents have at least an average command of English.

A highly interesting aspect is the importance respondents assign to different languages in the job market, that is, to finding a job when they are capable of speaking these languages. The opinions given in response to this question could be a good indicator of how at least a functional command of different languages may be seen by the population. Table 5.5 provides an overview of the mean and median values based on the Likert scale.

English received a higher rating in both the English and the Marathi questionnaires compared to the general question of which language is considered important. Marathi, Hindi, and the local languages, on the other hand, all received a lower rating in both questionnaires. These results indicate rather clearly that the importance of English is acknowledged with regard to the job market in particular. The high rating for English is compatible with the EIF Model's parameters of 'globalization' (extra-territorial force) as well as 'acceptance of globalization' (intra-territorial).

The final context which we would like to analyze is the school context, since the educational sector is affected by an increasing demand for English medium schools and English language teaching in general. Table 5.6 shows the results for the question 'Knowing ___ is an advantage at school.'

Respondents selected English and 'other local languages' as the most important languages in the school context. However, the differences between the four options are less pronounced than in the previously mentioned contexts: all four possible answers received particularly high ratings. Respondents almost uniformly seem to agree that Marathi, English, Hindi, and local languages are relevant in the school context,

Table 5.6 Knowing ___ is an advantage at school

	Marathi	English	Hindi	Other local language
English questionnaire	4.27	4.60	4.26	4.36
Marathi questionnaire	4.75	4.77	4.57	4.78
All questionnaires	4.51 ($\tilde{x} = 4$)	4.69 ($\tilde{x} = 5$)	4.42 ($\tilde{x} = 4$)	4.57 ($\tilde{x} = 5$)

which might be due to the mixture of languages spoken at school and the fact that different languages may be used by teachers.

4. DISCUSSION AND CONCLUSION

The preceding section has highlighted some of the results derived from our questionnaire. In this section, we will put these results into perspective. We will first offer a sketch of the Maharashtrian communicative space informed by our data. We will then consider the complex interplay of language identities and attitudes as expressed by the participants in our study and evaluate our results with reference to the Dynamic Model and the EIF Model.

4.1 The Multilingual Communicative Space in and around Mumbai

Table 5.2 in section 3.1 above contains a remarkable figure: a third of our respondents named English as (one of) their mother tongue(s). This is in stark contrast to all available estimates about the number of proficient speakers of English in India, which range from 1 percent to 20 percent (Bhattacharya 2017: 4). English is thus becoming a home language for a considerable portion of the population in and around Mumbai. However, the integration of English into speakers' communicative repertoires does not seem to occur at the expense of indigenous languages: Both the other official language Hindi and the state language Marathi are well represented as mother tongues. Interestingly, the ratings for the statement 'knowing (language X) is important for people living in Maharashtra' testify not only to the perceived importance of the state language Marathi, but also to the vitality of other local languages, which receive the highest positive ratings. Speakers further engage extensively in code-switching: 41.03 percent indicated that they mix languages always, often, or mostly; 48.63 percent said they do so sometimes; and only 10.33 percent stated that they never mix their languages.

The picture that emerges, then, is one of a vibrant multilingual communicative space with strong language loyalties to the regional language(s), with little regard for Hindi beyond the school context, and an acknowledgment of the prestige and utility of English, to be discussed in the next section.

4.2 Language Identities and Attitudes

The results presented in section 3.4.2 clearly show that English is considered to be the language of success and, to an extent, prestige, but not necessarily of identity, even though a third of the respondents name English as their mother tongue. This picture becomes even more pronounced for those speakers on the fringes of affluent metropolitan settings, who overwhelmingly express a high degree of language loyalty to Marathi. Therefore, we would argue that for Maharashtrians overall, regardless of their position on the cline of bilingualism, the two parameters of 'identity constructions' and 'language attitudes' need to be kept apart. Thus, there is no straightforward mapping of Schneider's identity parameter to 'attitudes to English' as suggested by Buschfeld and Kautzsch (see section 2.3). Maharashtrians in general and especially those living in rural areas lend ample support to Mukherjee's pronouncement quoted in section 2.1 above, namely that "English will always remain secondary in processes of Indian identity constructions" (Mukherjee 2007: 174).

Seen from the perspective of the Dynamic Model, such a disjunction between identity rewritings and language attitudes (however positive) would impede a variety's further development: The model sees the acceptance of local norms, with codification as indexical for endonormative stabilization, as a further act of identity for the speech community. Even if this process is driven by an educated minority, it still relies for its eventual acceptance on the speech community as a whole. If English has to become an identity carrier in order to develop further, then our data suggest that this is unlikely to happen at least in Maharashtra, and English in India will remain in stage 3 or 4 of the model, depending on one's point of view (see section 2.1 above).

Whether attitudes to English in India are still shaped by the colonial experience is a matter of debate (see Bhattacharya 2017: 3–6 for a brief overview). The largely positive attitudes towards English in and around Mumbai are driven by the recognition that English is essential for upward social mobility. This high regard for English is exemplified by comments made in the questionnaires when respondents were asked to name the most prestigious language, for example:

1. "The language which ensures one the stability in life. Of course, English."
2. "English (sadly for Indians, it's a measurement of intelligence)."

The three relevant intra-territorial forces related to linguistic prestige which are suggested by the EIF Model are 'attitudes towards colonizing power,' 'language policies/attitudes,' and '"acceptance" of globalization' (Buschfeld and Kautzsch 2017: 114). From the currently available descriptions of the model, it is not quite clear how the extra- and intra-linguistic forces are to be conceptualized – rather cumulative, descriptive, and open-ended, or as analytical categories with specific manifestations at specific stages of the model. 'Attitudes' are one among many forces in the EIF Model, while 'identity rewritings' are central to the Dynamic Model. Our data strongly suggest that linguistic 'identity' and language 'attitudes' are quite distinct, which, in turn, requires a closer look at speakers' attitudes, the cultural and linguistic consequences of such attitudes, as well as at the very notion and its theoretical status.

4.3 Outlook

Our findings so far do not allow for a grand showdown between the two models, but again we would like to emphasize for future research that, for multilingual societies in general, issues of identity and attitudes should be treated as separate categories. This realization points to the usefulness of the EIF Model for the current study: it provides us with an opportunity to revisit the impact and explanatory power of notions that are all too easily lumped together, with identity construction and language attitudes as cases in point. Further attitudinal studies across Indian speech communities will be an indispensable next step towards a more sustained view of the future trajectory of English in India.

REFERENCES

Balasubramanian, Chandrika. 2009. *Register Variation in Indian English*. Amsterdam: John Benjamins.

Bernaisch, Tobias and Christopher Koch. 2015. Attitudes towards Englishes in India. *World Englishes* 35.1: 118–132.

Bhattacharya, Usree. 2017. Colonization and English ideologies in India: A language policy perspective. *Language Policy* 16.1: 1–21.

Buschfeld, Sarah. 2011. The English Language in Cyprus: An Empirical Investigation of Variety Status. PhD dissertation, University of Cologne.

Buschfeld, Sarah and Alexander Kautzsch. 2014. English in Namibia: A first approach. *English World-Wide* 35.2: 121–160.

Buschfeld, Sarah and Alexander Kautzsch. 2017. Towards an integrated approach to postcolonial and non-postcolonial Englishes. *World Englishes* 36.1: 104–126.

Census India. 2011. http://www.censusindia.gov.in/2011census/PCA/A-2_Data_Tables/00%20A%202-India.pdf (last accessed November 14, 2018).

Denis, Derek and Alexandra d'Arcy. 2018. Settler Colonial Englishes are distinct from Postcolonial Englishes. *American Speech* 93.1: 3–31.

Edwards, Alison. 2016. *English in the Netherlands: Functions, Forms and Attitudes*. Amsterdam: John Benjamins.

Krug, Manfred and Katrin Sell. 2013. Designing and conducting interviews and questionnaires. In Manfred Krug and Julia Schlüter, eds. 2013, *Research Methods in Language Variation and Change*. Cambridge: Cambridge University Press, 69–98.

Kumar, T. Vijay, ed. 2018. *Peoples' Linguistic Survey of India Volume 37: English and Other International Languages*. Hyderabad: Orient Blackswan.

Lange, Claudia. 2017. Indian English or Indian Englishes? Accounting for speakers' multilingual repertoires in corpora of Postcolonial Englishes. In Arja Nurmi, Tanja Rütten and Päivi Pahta, eds. 2017, *Challenging the Myth of Monolingual Corpora*. Leiden: Brill, 16–38.

Lange, Claudia. 2020. English in South Asia. In Daniel Schreier, Marianne Hundt and Edgar W. Schneider, eds. 2020, *The Cambridge Handbook of World Englishes*. Cambridge: Cambridge University Press, 236-262.

Mair, Christian. 2013. The world system of Englishes: Accounting for the transnational importance of mobile and mediated vernaculars. *English World-Wide* 34.3: 253–278.

Mukherjee, Joybrato. 2007. Steady states in the evolution of New Englishes: Present-day Indian English as an equilibrium. *Journal of English Linguistics* 35.2: 157–187.

Mukherjee, Joybrato and Stefan Th. Gries. 2009. Collostructional nativisation in New Englishes. *English World-Wide* 30.1: 27–51.

Nihalani, Paroo, R. K. Tongue and Priya Hosali. 1979. *Indian and British English: A Handbook of Usage and Pronunciation*. New Delhi: Oxford University Press.

Pandurang, Mala. 2018. English as alienating language vs. empowering language: Student perceptions of English – A case study. In Kumar, ed. 2018, 58–61.

R Development Core Team. 2019. *The R Project for Statistical Computing*. Version 3.6.0., http://www.r-project.org/ (last accessed November 14, 2018).

Sahoo, Priyanka. 2018. English-medium schools most preferred in Mumbai, enrolment in vernacular schools drops. *The Indian Express*, https://indianexpress.com/article/education/english-medium-schools-most-preferred-enrolment-in-vernacular-schools-drops-5085136/ (last accessed November 14, 2018).

Sailaja, Pingali. 2009. *Indian English*. Edinburgh: Edinburgh University Press.

Satyanath, Shobha. 2015. Language variation and change: The Indian experience. In Dick Smakman and Patrick Heinrich, eds. 2015, *Globalising Sociolinguistics: Challenging and Expanding Theory*. London: Routledge, 107–122.

Schneider, Edgar W. 2007. *Postcolonial English. Varieties Around the World*. Cambridge: Cambridge University Press.

Schneider, Edgar W. 2014. New reflections on the evolutionary dynamics of world Englishes. *World Englishes* 33.1: 9–32.

Sedlatschek, Andreas. 2009. *Contemporary Indian English: Variation and Change*. Amsterdam: John Benjamins.

Sharma, Devyani. 2012. Second-language varieties: English in India. In Alexander Bergs and Laurel J. Brinton, eds. 2012, *Historical Linguistics of English*. Berlin: Mouton de Gruyter, 2077–2091.

Singh, Dipti. 2017. Maharashtra to introduce spoken English classes in Marathi schools. *The Indian Express*, https://indianexpress.com/article/education/maharashtra-to-introduce-spoken-english-classes-in-marathi-schools-4634940/ (last accessed November 14, 2018).

Sridhar, S. N. and Kamal K. Sridhar. 2018. Coda 2 A bridge half-built: Toward a holistic theory of Second Language Acquisition and World Englishes. *World Englishes* 37.1: 127–139.

Uma, Alladi, K. Suneetha Rani and D. Murali Manohar, eds. 2014. *English in the Dalit Context*. New Delhi: Orient Blackswan.

Vertovec, Steven. 2007. Super-diversity and its implications. *Ethnic and Racial Studies* 30.6: 1024–1054.

Wickham, Hadley. 2009. *ggplot2: Elegant Graphics for Data Analysis*. New York: Springer.

CHAPTER 6

English in Singapore: Two Issues for the EIF Model

Lionel Wee

1. INTRODUCTION

Schneider's (2007) Dynamic Model (DM), which aims to provide an account of the development of postcolonial Englishes (PCEs), has proven to be extremely influential. The DM has made it possible to situate the various PCEs in relation to the five phases that it posits (foundation, exonormative stabilisation, nativisation, endonormative stabilisation and differentiation), thus connecting the developments of PCEs to their colonial histories as well as their later sociopolitical conditions. This also opens up ways of comparing the sociolinguistic trajectories of different PCEs, and even possibly to make predictions about their future developments given that the phases are ordered in a linear manner.

Despite its success, the DM does face two key issues, one internal to the model and the other external to it. The internal issue is this. There are developments in PCEs which go beyond the fifth phase of differentiation, such as the global mobility of peoples as well as cultural – including linguistic – products. The DM needs to address this issue of mobility because one of the key principles behind the DM is its consistency with macro-sociolinguistic processes (Schneider 2007: 20). This means that the model has to be able to establish connections with ongoing macro-sociolinguistic changes since the history of PCEs clearly does not end with the fifth phase. As Schneider himself acknowledges, 'the glocalization of English will continue' (2007: 317).

The external issue is this. There are observed similarities between PCEs and non-PCEs. Non-PCEs have been observed to display some of the features associated with PCEs, such as nativisation and second-language status (e.g. Edwards 2016). Unless these similarities are accounted for, the DM is in the awkward position where they have to be treated as coincidences.

The Extra- and Intra-territorial Forces Model (EIFM) (Buschfeld and Kautzsch 2017) attempts to address the external issue though not the internal one. It aims to address the external issue by arguing that both PCEs and non-PCEs develop along similar lines; that is, non-PCEs, too, present many of the same five phases identified by the DM. According to the EIFM, the two kinds of Englishes, PCEs and non-PCEs, differ mainly in whether their foundation phases involved a period of colonisation. Under the EIFM, all other phases are either attested for in both PCEs and non-PCEs (e.g. foundation, stabilisation, nativisation), or hypothesised as possible developments (e.g. endonormative stabilisation and differentiation are attested for in PCEs but speculated as potentialities for non-PCEs).

Because the EIFM argues that non-PCEs go through similar phases as PCEs (Buschfeld and Kautzsch 2017: 117–118), it therefore can be described as adopting a strategy of parallel development by trying to integrate PCEs and non-PCEs. But unless there is some deeper explanation as to why both PCEs and non-PCEs develop along parallel lines, the EIFM, too, runs the risk of treating the similarities in the development of both kinds of Englishes as simply a remarkable concurrence of events. The explanation offered by the EIFM is that such similarities are the results of extra- and intra-territorial forces, which are claimed to apply to both PCEs and non-PCEs. This is an important insight. But rather than conceptualising these similarities in terms of parallel development, I suggest in the latter half of the chapter that this insight might be conceptualised in terms of convergence. Under convergence, both PCEs and non-PCEs can be acknowledged to have different development phases rather than the similar ones that the EIFM is committed to emphasising. Both PCEs and non-PCEs, however, converge in the era of late modernity given the effects of extra- and intra-territorial forces.

2. THE EIFM

In a discussion of the development of English in non-postcolonial contexts, such as Namibia and the Netherlands, Buschfeld and Kautzsch (2017: 105) argue that there is a need for 'an enhanced analysis and stronger integration of Expanding Circle Englishes, that is, non-postcolonial Englishes (non-PCEs), and any other type of English developing beyond national boundaries'. They note that, in the case of Namibia, for example, English has been gaining in importance since the country's independence in 1990, and there are linguistic signs of nativisation emerging which, should these continue, would firmly place the variety of English there as a second-language rather than a foreign language variety (2017: 109).

But neither Namibia nor the Netherlands is easily incorporated into the DM because neither has a history of colonisation, and, therefore, the kinds of interactions between the settler and indigenous communities that were the foci of the DM are missing:

> ... a lack of (post)colonial background entails the following consequences: first of all English was 'transplanted' to non-postcolonial regions *in a completely different way* than to postcolonial territories, to which it was brought by a group of settlers and was thus truly transplanted. For non-postcolonial contexts *it is questionable whether the term 'transplanted' holds at all* ...
>
> Second, non-postcolonial societies lack both a settler strand and an external colonizing power governing and influencing the colony from the outside. Third, and as a consequence of the missing settler strand, the type(s) of language contact and the development of identity constructions and consequently linguistic accommodation between the two strands as observed in postcolonial societies do not emerge in non-postcolonial scenarios. Language contact in the latter type is more indirect and, depending on the country, does mainly evolve through international business transactions, tourism, formal instruction in the classroom, and, in more recent times, electronic media. (Buschfeld and Kautzsch 2017: 110, our emphasis)

Buschfeld and Kautzsch then suggest that it is possible to think of non-PCEs as evolving along the same lines as PCEs, that is, in much the same way that has been articulated by the DM: 'PCEs evolve along the developmental route and parameters suggested by Schneider's Dynamic Model. Non-PCEs follow a similar route, even if the initial forces operating on their development are *fundamentally different*' (2017: 118, our emphasis). For this suggestion to hold, however, it becomes necessary to claim that even non-PCEs manifest the first phase of foundation (2017: 118):

Still, we decided to maintain the label 'foundation' for the first phase in the development of non-PCEs, basically because the term 'foundation' appears to be wide enough to also cover the starting point of Englishes without colonizing influence, no matter what exact driving forces were behind this development. Nevertheless, we use inverted commas . . . to account for the differences observed for the two types of foundation.

Non-PCEs are also said to manifest the second phase of stabilisation. Whereas the DM specifically posits a second phase of exonormative stabilisation (given the colonial experience), the EIFM suggests that stabilisation in the case of non-PCEs need not occur via the intervention of external, that is, colonial, forces since 'intra-territorial forces like internal language policy decisions, access to English via the media, and attitudes on the side of the local population may play an equally important role in their developments' (Buschfeld and Kautzsch 2017: 118).

Both PCEs and non-PCEs are also said to undergo the third phase of nativisation:

> Despite the observed differences between PCEs and non-PCEs, phase 3 does not require any major modification for characterizing the development of non-PCEs. We assume that for non-PCEs, too, it is 'the most interesting and important, the most vibrant one, the central phase of both cultural and linguistic transformation' (Schneider 2007: 40), *even though the cultural transformations are certainly of a different nature, again since there is no classical settler strand involved in the development of non-PCEs.* Yet we assume that the issue of identity rewritings also plays an important role in the development of non-PCEs since absorbing a 'foreign' language to such a high degree, that is, making it part of one's individual language repertoire, becoming highly proficient and fully bilingual, as well as speaking a nativized form of English that is characterized by local features, does certainly not come without a rewriting of identity constructions, most likely in the form of a 'local-cum-English' identity (following Schneider's 2007: 37 notion of a 'British-cum-local' identity, which the settler strand prototypically starts to develop in phase 2 of the Dynamic Model). Buschfeld and Kautzsch 2017: 118, our emphasis)

Finally, since the fourth and fifth phases of, respectively, endonormative stabilisation and differentiation have yet to be empirically attested,

Buschfeld and Kautzsch (2017: 119) leave their applicability to non-PCEs as possible scenarios:

> Not knowing if and under what exact circumstances non-postcolonial territories might reach Phase 4 and not knowing of any country having reached Phase 5, it is subject to future research to keep track of the further development of non-PCEs. Since no hard facts stand against such a development, we suggest retaining both phases as possible developmental steps for non-PCEs.

There are a number of observations that we can make about the EIFM's attempt to use the DM as a conceptual point of departure for unifying PCEs and non-PCEs.

2.1 What about the Development of PCEs Beyond Phase 5?

The DM needs to address the question of what happens to PCEs beyond phase 5, and since the EIFM incorporates the DM, it also is obligated to address this question. This is the internal issue mentioned above. The key feature of the DM's phase 5 is 'internal differentiation' where 'differences within a society and between individuals . . . can be given greater prominence' (Schneider 2007: 53). According to Schneider:

> New varieties of the formerly new variety emerge, as carriers of new group identities *within the overall community*: regional and social dialects, linguistic markers (accents, lexical expressions, and structural patterns) which carry a diagnostic function only *within the new country* emerge. (2007: 54, our emphasis)

The end point of the DM thus tends to emphasise internal social differentiation (internal to the nation state and marked by the emergence of multiple speech communities along social, regional and other lines) and internal linguistic differentiation (marked by the emergence of dialects). However, the factors which need to be accommodated when we move to look at PCEs beyond phase 5 are different. Consider as an example the case of Singlish, the nativised variety of English found in Singapore. Schneider (2007: 153) suggests that 'the evolution of English [in Singapore] . . . is far advanced . . . and appears likely to go all the way along the cycle, given the linguistic dynamics that can be observed'. Schneider (2007: 160, citing Rubdy 2001: 347) also suggests that Singlish is likely to flourish, despite the official attempts to discourage its use:

> ... the willingness of the population to defend and stick to Singlish is remarkable, especially so in the light of the government's stern rejection of this speech variety... 'and observes that there is considerable pride in Singlish, with many Singaporeans seeing it as 'an icon of national identity'.

Singlish is not simply limited to being used *within* Singapore and by *only* Singaporeans (Wee 2014, 2018). Many Singaporeans working and living overseas use Singlish to express their national identity and to create a sense of community. In the DM, the interaction between the settler and indigenous communities essentially boils down to a relationship between the colonisers and the colonised, and the main sociolinguistic factor derives from an acceptance by both groups that they are going to be together for the long term (Schneider 2007: 26). Moreover, Schneider (2007: 31–32) likens the settler and indigenous capacities for English to the distinction between 'ENL' and 'ESL', 'given that typically the immigrants were native speakers of English and the indigenous population acquired it as a second language'. The migrant professional's relationship to the host society is significantly different, since migrant professionals are patently not the colonisers and members of the host society are certainly not the colonised. The relationship is more that of equals, between professional colleagues, all of whom – whether migrants or members of the host society – are well educated, relatively affluent and successful. This more equal relationship does not apply, of course, to other kinds of migrants, such as economic, political or environmental refugees.

Another aspect of the evolution of Singlish that is not widely discussed is its commodification. Singlish is becoming increasingly commodified as a cultural product that is exportable. A number of Singaporean films and theatre productions have been relatively well received internationally. Singlish lessons are offered to non-Singaporeans, skits prominently highlighting the use of Singlish are available on YouTube, and Singaporean-made films that feature Singlish speaking characters are gaining international recognition. In this regard, it is worth noting that the Netflix series *Orange Is The New Black* has even had one of its characters, a black American female, speaking Singlish in order to promote the series to a Singaporean audience. The issue of commodification therefore lends a different dynamic to language practices (Agha 2011; Budach et al. 2003). It can inform and influence the relationship between language and identity in interesting ways so that the impetus for retaining and expanding the use of a language variety becomes less reliant on solidarity considerations. Together with the issue of migration, the commodification of Singlish adds to the increasingly global scale at which Singlish might be seen to operate.

The migration of Singlish-speaking Singaporean professionals and its commodification are not easily accounted for under the DM's fifth and final phase, differentiation. These developments are relevant to our understanding of PCEs because, as the Singlish case demonstrates, they are possible aspects of their ongoing and future development.

The EIFM, having taken on board the DM in its entirety, also inherits this issue.

2.2 Can PCEs and Non-PCEs be Integrated as Part of the Same Conceptual Framework?

This is the external issue mentioned earlier, and it is the focus of the EIFM, which, as we have seen, adopts a strategy that argues that non-PCEs undergo the same parallel developmental phases as PCEs. To make the case that both PCEs and non-PCEs develop along parallel lines, the phases identified under the DM have had to be reinterpreted more broadly so that similarities with non-PCEs can be justified.

This is not an easy move given the earlier statements (Buschfeld and Kautzsch 2017: 110, see above) which noted that (1) compared to colonial contexts, English was 'transplanted' to non-postcolonial contexts in 'a completely different way' so that 'it is questionable whether the term "transplanted" holds at all'; and (2) that the cultural factors involved in the nativisation of non-PCEs are 'certainly of a different nature'. That is, by adopting a strategy of parallel development, things that were initially characterised as being 'completely different' and 'certainly of a different nature' now have to be treated as being actually quite similar.

For example, under the DM, the foundation phase has a very specific meaning. It refers to the initial phase where a settler community comes into contact with the indigenous community as result of colonisation (Schneider 2007: 33). The identity and interactional dynamics in the DM's foundation phase are therefore created by the specific attitudes that are the concomitants of the relationship between coloniser and colonised. Under the EIFM, however, 'foundation' has been reconceptualised to include the internet, popular culture and media (Buschfeld and Kautzsch 2017: 115, references omitted):

> Even though this does not normally take place in the form of a direct, spoken encounter and the linguistic effects in such language contact scenarios are certainly less strong, varieties influence each other and interact in many different respects . . . By way of example, we [would] here like to point to two such scenarios: (1) it has repeatedly been shown how American English, especially via the global media, exerts an ever increasing influence on the development of different PCEs . . . and there is no reason to assume that this is not taking place for non-PCEs as well. (2) The Internet and other modern communication devices provide situations and platforms for language contact all around the globe on a twenty-four-seven basis as, for example, in computer-mediated discourse such as text messaging or fanfiction writing . . . Both settings involve 'native' and 'non-native' speakers from both postcolonial and non-postcolonial territories alike, who interact with each other in electronically-mediated ways.

Once the concept of foundation has been broadened in this way so that an actual history of colonisation is just one way in which the foundation phase can be manifested, then we should also be able to speak of a foundation phase in the cases of other languages, such as the spread of Korean through K-Pop and Korean dramas, or the spread of Hindi via Bollywood. There is no reason why such cases should be dismissed as lacking a foundation phase.

The same considerations also apply to the use of 'stabilization' for the second phase of non-PCEs. Under the DM, this second phase is specifically one of 'exornormative stabilization' since the presence of external colonial forces is a factor of major interest. The EIFM wants to retain the term 'stabilization' for non-PCEs, but since the external colonial forces are absent, the modifier 'exornormative' has had to be dropped (Buschfeld and Kautzsch 2017: 118):

> In a second step, non-PCEs also undergo stabilization, but not necessarily by means of mainly external forces as was prototypically the case for PCEs. Intra-territorial forces like internal language policy decisions, access to English via the media, and attitudes on

the side of the local population may play an equally important role in their developments [. . .].

The specificity of 'exonormative stabilization' is now lost because 'exonormative stabilization' is now just one particular manifestation of 'stabilization'. As with the case of 'foundation', the result of this broadening is that the distinctiveness of the EIFM (and by extension, that of the DM) in accounting for the development and spread of English is lost. If internal policy issues and the role of the media are factors in stabilisation, then it is hard to see why this second phase (as in the case of the foundation phase) should not also apply to other languages than English.

By way of illustration, we can consider the matter historically by looking at the transplantation of Malayalam from Kerala, India, to Singapore. Pillai and Arumugam (2017: 17–18) point out that there are early records dating back to 1844 of Malayalee immigrants coming to Singapore to look for jobs. By the 1930s, many returned to India because the jobs were not as plentiful as had been assumed initially. But by the 1950s, the Immigration Ordinance prompted many to once again consider coming to Singapore by passing a bill intended to attract highly skilled professionals. And though Malayalam was not formally recognised or taught, informal language classes were organised by local community members and associations. The language also came to be used in general meetings, religious ceremonies, creative writings and radio programmes (Pillai and Arumugam 2017: 42–49). And by 2010 it was noted that while proficiency in the language was declining among the younger generation, those families in Singapore that retained some contact with relatives in Kerala spoke 'a hybrid variety of Malayalam' (2017: 51–53).

In the case of Malayalam's arrival in Singapore, we are looking at a foundation phase that actually cleaves more closely to Schneider's original definition in that there is some face-to-face contact between the immigrants and the indigenous population. Although this is by no means a case of colonisation, there is a more concrete sense in which the immigrants from Kerala might be characterised as a 'settler community' than in the case of the internet. The subsequent attempts by the Malayalee community in Singapore to preserve their language, such as using the language for various ceremonies and in the media, can be described as a phase of stabilisation. Here, parts of this phase may even be described as 'exonormative stabilization', especially if those in

Singapore start looking to the variety spoken in Kerala for normative guidance.

The point is that if we accept the broadened definitions of the DM's phases as proposed under the EIFM, then we have no reason not to categorise the Malayalee case as one that also involves (at the very least) the phases of foundation and stabilisation. In trying to absorb non-PCEs under the same framework as PCEs via the strategy of parallel development, it seems that the EIFM might now be opening up the framework so broadly that it cannot exclude cases of other languages that may or may not involve colonial histories. This, however, is not necessarily a bad thing, as I discuss below.

3. THE PARALLEL ARCHITECTURE OF THE EIFM

To account for why PCEs and non-PCEs go through the 'same' phases, the EIFM posits that there are extra- and intra-territorial forces that operate on both kinds of Englishes. The argument here is that because the same sets of forces are involved, we should not be surprised that the same phases are also observable (Buschfeld and Kautzsch 2017: 113):

> To that end, we here introduce the notion of extra- and intra-territorial forces as constantly operating throughout the development of both PCEs and non-PCEs . . . In general, we assume that such forces operate both on the national level, but also on the different groups of speakers within and ultimately also across particular countries, be they ethnic, social, or stratified by any other secondary variable like proficiency level or age.

The authors specify five categories of what such forces might be (Buschfeld and Kautzsch 2017: 113–114), which I reproduce in full despite the length, because doing so helps us better appreciate the problems involved in appealing to such extra- and intra-territorial forces:

> . . . namely, colonization (extra)/ attitudes towards colonization (intra), language policies (both extra and intra), globalization (extra)/'acceptance' of globalization (intra), foreign policies (both extra and intra), and the sociodemographic background of a country (mostly extraterritorial but with clear intra-territorial dimensions). How and in what ways colonization works as extra-territorial force

does not require any further explanation at this point, since this is explicitly addressed in the Dynamic Model. As intra-territorial side to this force, we suggest 'attitudes towards colonization', entailing aspects such as national pride, resistance against foreign rule, acceptance of foreign rule, but also the resulting differences in interaction and assimilation of the parties involved (that is, STL, IDG, and adstrate groups).

Turning towards how language policies might influence the development of English in a certain region, we again suggest an extra- as well as intra-territorial perspective. External forces might come from institutions like the British Council or the implementation of the TOEFL or any other outside factor influencing linguistic choices and norm orientations, for example, by prescribing rules of correctness. And again, such external factors turn into internal forces, namely, when it comes to how a country either accepts or rejects them. The intra-territorial side includes factors such as the development of teaching curricula, decisions on when to start which foreign language as school subject, the introduction of bilingual school programs or the introduction of English as a medium of instruction, and, of course, decisions on how to deal with extra-territorial influences like the ones mentioned above. With respect to globalization, the extra-territorial side mainly finds expression in, for example, linguistic and also cultural influences coming from the Internet, US popular culture, and modern media as well as trading relations between countries. However, this also has an intra-territorial side since territories differ with respect to whether and to what extend they accept or even admit these facets of globalization. The strict control or even restriction of Internet access as to be found in countries such as North Korea, Turkey, or China serves as an example to illustrate how this intra-territorial force might at least implicitly curb linguistic influence from the outside.

The next aspect we suggest as potential force influencing the development of English is foreign policies. The extra-territorial side of this force manifests itself in decisions on war, allies and opponents, but also treaties and diplomatic relations as coming from outside the country under investigation, the main idea being that such decisions influence cultural and linguistic affinities and consequently the popularity of a certain culture or language in a country. The intra-territorial side finds expression in exactly the same decisions being made by the country itself.

Our last set of factors that might have an influence on the linguistic development, more precisely the spread and use of English in a country, are of sociodemographic nature: these include the demographic developments in a country, for example the overall number of inhabitants, the overall number and ethnic distribution of immigrants, as well as the age distribution of the overall society.

This is intended to be a fairly eclectic set of forces. Also, one of the key concepts, territory, actually undergoes significant shifts over the course of a non-PCEs development, making it difficult to sustain the distinction between extra-territorial and intra-territorial forces. The term 'territory' is intended to serve as the boundary by which the extra-territorial forces can be demarcated from the intra-territorial ones. Territory here seems to be understood as 'the country' since there is reference to national pride and resistance against foreign rule. As the authors explain:

> In this respect, the group of extra-territorial forces includes any factor entering the country from the outside and intra-territorial forces are such that mainly operate on a local, that is, national or regional, level and therefore influence the cultural and linguistic development from within. (Buschfeld and Kautzsch 2017: 113)

But 'the country' is not an entity that remains constant throughout the five phases. Whether or not 'the country' refers to the nation state or simply to a physically bounded territory, these are entities that shift and change. For example, the fact that various communities may come to see themselves as belonging to the same nation state is itself a historically emergent phenomenon, as is the possibility of post-national communities. Therefore, the distinction between extra- and intra-territorial forces changes and shifts as different notions of 'territory' or 'the country' become relevant. The various social constructions which these entities undergo do have impacts on the ways in which various kinds of Englishes develop. Indeed, that is one of the key points that the DM makes. To illustrate, the possibility of varieties such as Singlish or Standard Singapore English emerging in Singapore is not unrelated to its maturation as a nation state. Prior to such maturation, when the 'territory' or 'the country' was either in the grip of a colonial power or a member of the Federation of Malaysia, it is doubtful if such varieties would have been attributed any kind of sociolinguistic reality.

While the distinction between forces that are extra-territorial and intra-territorial will still be relevant in some cases, there will also be situations where the distinction may have to be suspended in favour of a more trans-territorial perspective. For example, the internet is already part of the material infrastructure of many countries, and so treating this as 'extra-territorial' may be controversial. As many scholars of globalisation have argued, the phenomenon is not reducible to an 'out there' versus 'in here' distinction. Globalisation involves a rearranging of social relations at multiple levels (Giddens 1990), and because of this, globalisation is already 'in here' as well as 'out there'. Held et al. (1999: 16) describe globalisation as embodying 'a transformation in the spatial organization of social relations and transactions – assessed in terms of their extensivity, velocity and impact – generating transcontinental or interregional flows and networks of activity, interaction and exercise of power'. The views of globalisation presented by Giddens et al. are summarily described by Scholte (2000: 46) as affecting 'the nature of social space'. This way of thinking about globalisation, one that avoids the 'in' versus 'out' dichotomy, also undergirds Sassen's (2006) analysis of how globalisation is destabilising the traditional state assemblage of territory, authority and rights.

In the next section, I explore an alternative to parallel development, that of convergence. My remarks on this convergence possibility will of necessity be brief since it is not my intention to present a fully-fleshed out model but to simply outline an alternative for consideration.

4. AN ALTERNATIVE TO THE STRATEGY OF PARALLEL DEVELOPMENT: CONVERGENCE

Consider the fact that there are numerous rankings of English language competence involving countries or cities. For example, according to Yahoo! Finance (2013), the GlobalEnglish Corporation releases an annual Business English Index (BEI), where industries and countries with the highest and lowest BEI scores are ranked.

The 2013 BEI results are shown below:

Top 5 industries	Bottom 5 industries
Aerospace/Defence 6.63	Real Estate/Construction 2.82
Professional Services 6.22	Govt/Ed/Non-profit 3.18
Technology 5.72	Media/Comm/Entertainment 3.20

Financial Services 4.93   Energy/Utilities 3.96
Retail 4.92   Auto/Transportation 3.99

Top 5 countries   Bottom 5 countries
Philippines 7.95   Honduras 2.92
Norway 7.06   Columbia 3.05
Netherlands 7.03   Saudi Arabia 3.14
United Kingdom 6.81   Mexico 3.14
Australia 6.78   El Salvador & Chile 3.24

As a company, GlobalEnglish undoubtedly has a vested interest in stoking the desire for improving English language skills since it is in the business of providing business English to help 'improve the way your business communicates, collaborates and operates' (Pearson English, n.d.). Nevertheless, this desire for improving English is a very real one that exists independently of the company. Thus, in the 2012 BEI, the Philippines was also ranked highest, and this led to a clear sense of national pride (Mendoza 2012):

> Well, people will now have to think twice before mocking Pinoys' use of the English language. The Philippines was named the world's best country in business English proficiency, even beating the United States, according to a recent study by GlobalEnglish Corporation . . . For 2012, results showed that from 76 represented countries worldwide, only the Philippines attained a score above 7.0, 'a BEI level within range of a high proficiency that indicates an ability to take an active role in business discussions and perform relatively complex tasks.'

As another example, consider that when Sweden was named a high English proficiency country, this, too, led to a boosting of national pride (The Local 2013, Sweden's News in English):

> It's time to stop teasing the Swedes for their *Swenglish*, as they've yet again topped English Proficiency Index from language education company Education First (EF), which was founded in Sweden.
> 'It's the second time in a row, so I guess we're a bit used to it, but of course it's really neat that we are the world leaders when it comes to speaking English,' Sine Ejsing, Country Manager of EF Sweden, told The Local.

> The language test quizzed 750,000 people from 60 countries around the world, and the Nordic nations scored prominently, with Norway placing second, followed by the Netherlands, Estonia, Denmark, Austria and Finland.

This sense of competitive pride is particularly clear in the following report (Tan 2013), which describes Malaysia as 'edging out Singapore' in an English skills test:

> Malaysia took top marks in an English skills test given to Asian nations, narrowly edging out Singapore, where English is one of the official national languages.
> The Philippines, where English is also spoken as a national language, was excluded from the 60 countries and regions whose English skills were measured by international education company EF Education First for the 2013 English Proficiency Index.

In the examples presented above, the competition involves different countries – and to a lesser extent, different industries – being gauged on their relative competencies vis-à-vis English. While there are clear economic motivations behind the desire to do well in these rankings, there is also the matter of pride in doing better than other countries/cities.

These various rankings are clear demonstrations of Foucauldian surveillance technologies at work. A central monitoring institution creates awareness among the entities that are being ranked (Wee 2011: 45). Especially in the case of rankings which are updated and published publicly on a regular basis such as annually or biannually, this provides a means for tracking and comparing the performance of the ranked entities over time. As the peer entities monitor each other's progress (or lack thereof), those who manage to 'outdo' their competitors evince pride in their achievement should they manage to move up the rankings to improve their positioning. This creates a strong reflexive awareness among the entities that they are being monitored for their ability to demonstrate those specific attributes prized by the rankings. This effectively exerts a pressure towards convergence since the competing entities are being measured in terms of whatever set of criteria is being used to assign rankings. As Harvey (2012: 104–105) observes in his own discussion of competition among cities for symbolic capital, there are claims to local distinction and uniqueness even though, somewhat contradictorily, the result of such competition, more often than not, tends to be an increased homogenisation.

Another factor which contributes to convergence is the fact that policies themselves are increasingly mobile, as a result of the fact that policymakers are increasingly engaged in looking outward to learn from the recommendations of other policymakers while also sharing their own experiences. As Peck and Theodore (2015: xvi) point out:

> Learning from, and 'referencing', distant models and practices is now commonplace, even as literal replication never really happens. And learning curves can be shortened – sometimes dramatically – if local reform efforts are framed, from the get-go, by a reading of the best-practice literature, by borrowing from a well-known model, or by the importation of authorized designs, expertise, and formulations. It is a widely acknowledged feature of policymaking common sense, in many parts of the world today, that shorthand processes like these, and the various forms of 'speed-up' they imply, have become normalized.

Peck and Theodore (2015) discuss the example of New York City's experiment with Conditional Cash Transfers (CCTs) to address the problem of urban poverty. After a review of over sixty anti-poverty strategies as well as a scheme from Latin America where payouts to poor families were conditional to 'the maintenance of human-capital building behaviors like school attendance and regular health screening', Mayor Bloomberg announced that 'Conditional cash transfer programs have proven effective in countries around the world and, frankly, we need some new ideas here in New York City to fight poverty' (2015: 46).

In the case of the English language, the outward desire to learn from established designs and best practices has also resulted in policy mobility with tweaks that facilitate local adaptation (DeCosta, Park and Wee 2019). Consider the Common European Framework of Reference for Languages: Learning, teaching, assessment (CEFR), which is a framework 'designed to provide a transparent, coherent and comprehensive basis for the elaboration of language syllabuses and curriculum guidelines, the design of teaching and learning materials, and the assessment of foreign language proficiency' (Council of Europe). While originally intended for Europe, the CEFR has also been adopted in Taiwan, Japan and China, where the predominant interest has been in how it can be used to improve upon English language proficiency (Read 2014; Zheng et al.; though see Zhang and Song 2008).'Since the influence of the CEFR cannot be ignored, instead of building an original framework, we decided to consider the implementation of the CEFR into Japanese contexts, and how to do it scientifically.' A large-scale survey of more than 7,000 'business persons', 100 'Super English Learning High schools', textbooks used in Korea, China and Taiwan, and 'major English grammar items in the NICT JLE (spoken Japanese EFL learner corpus)' resulted in a 2008 report of more than 500 pages. A later report of over 300 pages on the implementation of a Beta version for 'major empirical validation' was produced in 2010. A finalised version was produced in 2012, after a series of studies were conducted, which included examinations of the correlations between 'what learners think they can do and what they actually can do', and a school pilot.

The CEFR and its adaptations to Asian contexts are thus aimed primarily at evaluating the effectiveness of proposed syllabi for English language education, associated teaching materials, and assessment procedures. In the parlance of audit culture, these serve to assess the assessors. That is, whereas learners are taught and examined by institutions, the CEFR and its variants provide a framework within which the institutions' effectiveness in serving their learners can be gauged. This framework is intended to facilitate and, indeed, encourage, self-examination on the part of the educational institutions. The CEFR 'is offered to users as a descriptive tool that allows them to reflect on their decisions and practice, and to situate and co-ordinate their efforts, as appropriate, for the benefit of language learners in their specific contexts'. In the case of the CEFR's adaptation in Japan, for instance, the CEFR-J version as it is called, is free to download for academic as well as commercial uses in the hope that 'it will be useful for developing teaching materials and syllabuses as well as assessment of English in Japan'.

Yet another case that is relevant to convergence is that both PCEs and non-PCEs continue, for various reasons, to privilege the traditional native speaker as the reference point for 'proper/good' English. In India and the Philippines, call centres (Mirchandani 2012; Tupas and Salonga 2016) have long been known to train workers to sound as American or British as possible, usually with the goal of convincing callers from these countries that they are speaking to a fellow native speaker. Here, the business process of outsourcing and PCEs converge to generate a labour market for call centre work. In the call centre industry, older ideologies of authenticity and standardisation are observable when the call centre workers are under pressure to accommodate to the ways of speaking of their customers. In China, Gao (2012, 2014) describes how a small neighbourhood in rural China, West Street in Yangshuo County, has become a so-called 'global village' for domestic tourists, that is, Chinese nationals who want to learn English from 'native speakers'. The influx of international travellers has resulted in many of the locals starting businesses intended to cater to this clientele, such as western food restaurants, small family hotels, and shops specialising in carving, painting and calligraphy (Gao: 2012: 340–341). West Street since acquired a reputation within China as a place popular with westerners and where businesses transactions are completed using English. What is particularly interesting from a World Englishes perspective is the secondary wave of domestic tourists, who flocked to West Street in order to seek opportunities to improve their English by hoping to strike up conversations and thus interacted with the international travellers (Gao 2012: 342–344). The result is that non-PCEs, too, are ideologically aiming to approximate what they assume are native speaker norms for speaking English. While there are obvious differences between a call centre and the domestic tourism of West Street, the fundamental similarities are that the acquisition of both PCEs and non-PCEs are propelled by the commodification of English and moreover by the belief that it is the native speaker variety that has the greatest commodity value. A strategy of convergence would allow for the DM to be treated as a model that accounts for PCEs, as originally intended. There would not be any need to reinterpret its five phases in order to absorb non-PCEs. The latter would stay outside the DM. Instead, we can address both the internal issue (i.e. what happens to PCEs beyond phase 5) and the external issues (i.e. the similarities between PCEs and non-PCEs) in one fell swoop – by suggesting that after phase 5, there are forces that lead to a convergence between PCEs and non-PCEs. This is where the EIFM can come in. It would not need to postulate that non-PCEs undergo the same phases as PCEs. Rather, its major insight and contribution will be to draw attention to the various forces that lead to non-PCEs and PCEs converging in the era of late modernity. Such a convergence may itself be amenable to an analysis in terms of phases. But there is no need to assume that these will have to be those same phases that were operative under the DM. The EIFM would be free to identify newer kinds of phases.

5. CONCLUSION

It remains a significant challenge to try to come up with a model that accounts for the global spread of English. A model with a narrower scope, such as the DM, leaves out of its ambit other Englishes such as non-PCEs. On the other hand, one with a broader scope, such as the EIFM, risks losing the possibility of saying anything distinctive about English. This possible risk exists regardless of whether a strategy of convergence is adopted or not.

This is because the kinds of forces identified by the EIFM can be argued to be operative to varying degrees across different languages, and not just English or its sub-varieties. This is actually an advantage since a model of the spread of English ought to be, in principle, applicable to other languages (Bruthiaux 2003). The emphasis that the EIFM places on forces such as colonisation, attitudes, policies, globalisation and demographics will be key to understanding how English and other languages rise, fall and, indeed, compete with one another for global dominance.

REFERENCES

Agha, Asif. 2011. Commodity registers. *Journal of Linguistic Anthropology* 21.1: 22–53.

Bruthiaux, Paul. 2003. Squaring the circles: Issues in modelling English worldwide. *International Journal of Applied Linguistics* 13.2: 159–178.

Budach, Gabriele. Sylvie Roy and Monica Heller. 2003. Community and commodity in French Ontario. *Language in Society* 32.5: 603–627.

Buschfeld, Sarah and Alexander Kautzsch. 2017. Towards an integrated approach to postcolonial and non-postocolonial Englishes. *World Englishes* 36.1: 104–126.

Council of Europe. Common European Framework of Reference for Languages: Learning, Teaching, Assessment (CEFR), http://www.coe.int/t/dg4/linguistic/cadre1_en.asp (last accessed 1 July 2019).

DeCosta, Peter, Joseph Park and Lionel Wee. 2019. Language entrepreneurship as affective regime: Organizations, audit culture, and Second/Foreign Language Education Policy. *Language Policy* 18.3: 387–406.

Edwards, Alison. 2016. *English in the Netherlands: Functions, Forms and Attitudes.* Amsterdam: John Benjamins.

Gao, Shuang. 2012. Commodification of place, consumption of identity: The sociolinguistic construction of a 'global village' in rural China. *Journal of Sociolinguistics* 16.3: 336–357.

Gao, Shuang. 2014. Aspiring to be Global: Language, Mobilities, and Social Change in a Tourism Village in China. PhD Dissertation, National University of Singapore and King's College, London.

Giddens, Anthony. 1990. *The Consequences of Modernity*. Cambridge: Polity.
Harvey, David. 2012. *Rebel Cities: From the Right to the City to the Urban Revolution*. London: Verso.
Held, David and Anthony McGrew. 2003. The great globalization debate: An introduction. In David Held and Anthony McGrew, eds. 2003, *The Global Transformations Reader*. Cambridge: Polity, 1–50.
Held, David, Anthony McGrew, David Goldblatt and Jonathan Perraton. 1999. *Global Transformations*. Stanford, CA: Stanford University Press.
Mendoza, Shielo. 2012. PH: World's best country in business English. *Yahoo! News Philippines*, https://ph.news.yahoo.com/ph--world-s-best-country-in-business-english.html (last accessed 16 September 2014).
Mirchandani, Kiran. 2012. *Phone Clones: Authenticity Work in the Transnational Service Economy*. Ithaca, NY: ILR Press.
Pearson English. N.d. http://www.globalenglish.com/purchase/busi ness (last accessed 16 September 2014).
Peck, Jamie and Nick Theodore. 2015. *Fast Policy: Experimental Statecraft at the Thresholds of Neoliberalism*. Minneapolis: University of Minnesota Press.
Pillai, Anitha Devi and Puva Arumugam. 2017. *From Kerala to Singapore*. Singapore: Marshall Cavendish.
Read, J. (2014). The influence of the Common European Framework of Reference (CEFR) in the Asia-Pacific region. *LEARN Journal*, Special issue, 33–39.
Rubdy, Rani. 2001. Creative destruction: Singapore's Speak Good English Movement. *World Englishes* 20.3: 341–355.
Sassen, Saskia. 2006. *Territory, Authority, Rights: From Medieval to Global Assemblages*. Princeton, NJ: Princeton University Press.
Schneider, Edgar W. 2007. *Postcolonial English: Varieties Around the World*. Cambridge: Cambridge University Press.
Scholte, Jan Aart. 2000. *Globalization: A Critical Introduction*. Basingstoke: Palgrave.
Singlish videos, https://www.youtube.com/watch?v=wOo-hvXc9kY (last accessed 7 August 2016).
Tan, Yi Liang. 2013. Study: Malaysia has best English language speakers in Asia. *The Star Online*, https://www.thestar.com.my/news/nation/2013/11/07/msia-best-english-asia-study (last accessed 31 August 2019).

The Local. 2013. Swedes 'best in the world' at English – again, http://www.thelocal.se/20131107/swedes-ranked-again-best-world-english (last accessed 16 September 2014).
Tupas, Ruanni and Aileen Salonga. 2016. Unequal Englishes in the Philippines. *Journal of Sociolinguistics* 20.3: 367–381.
Wee, Lionel. 2011. The ranked list as panopticon in enterprise culture. *Pragmatics & Society* 2.1: 37–56.
Wee. Lionel. 2014. Evolution of Singlish in late modernity: Beyond phase 5? In Sarah Buschfeld, Thomas Hoffman, Magnus Huber and Alexander Kautzsch, eds. 2014, *The Evolution of Englishes*. Amsterdam: John Benjamins, 126–141.
Wee, Lionel. 2018. *The Singlish Controversy: Language, Culture and Identity in a Globalizing World*. Cambridge: Cambridge University Press.
Yahoo! Finance. 2013. http://finance.yahoo.com/news/globalenglish-releases-business-english-index-12-300860.html (last accessed 16 September 2014).
Zhang, G. and L. Y. Song. 2008. Benchmarking Chinese language, http://eacea.ec.europa.eu/LLp/projects/public_parts/documents/languages/lan_mp_511644_EBCLfinal.pdf (last accessed 5 January 2018).
Zheng, Y., Y. Y. Zhang and Y. Y. Yan. 2016. Investigating the practice of The Common European Framework of Reference for Languages (CEFR) outside Europe: A case study on the assessment of writing in English in China. *ELT Research Papers* 16.01. London: British Council.

CHAPTER 7

English in the Philippines: A Case of Rootedness and Routedness

Bejay Villaflores Bolivar

1. INTRODUCTION

While English in the Philippine context is a widely documented and studied area, it remains a curious case conflated with issues of socio-economic mobility, politics, and ethnicity among others. This chapter takes the position that an understanding of English in the Philippines necessitates more than just the description or codification of what has often been asserted as a clear-cut national variety, a Philippine English. To capture the fragmented sociolinguistic reality of the country, I take into consideration the existence of dynamic language practices attributed to various factors including but not limited to regional differences. Enlightened by Buschfeld and Kautzsch's (2017) contention that the development of Englishes, both in postcolonial and non-postcolonial contexts, is influenced by extra- and intra- territorial forces, I look into the dynamic make-up of the country's sociolinguistic soil, one which has been and continues to be configured by past and present forces; namely, its history of colonization and its present postcolonial situation, deep-seated ethnic tensions, and the globalizing movement. While there is much to be explored in an archipelagic country of 7,107 islands, my focus will be on the Cebuano context, specifically in identified online spaces where speakers negotiate their regional identity while seeking to connect and build networks in a global environment. Extra and intra-territorial forces, such as those mentioned above, create a fertile ground for the languaging dubbed as Bislish (Bisaya + English), an instance of what Schneider (2016: 341) refers to as unfixed hybrid forms that emerge from a contact between English and another language.

Like the extensively documented mixed variety called Taglish (Schneider 2016: 345; Thompson 2003: 40–41), Bislish is an unmarked behavior in various domains including media, education, and informal talk. Unlike Taglish, however, Bislish has a regional dimension worth looking into. It is prominent among speakers whose language practices may be affected, if not defined, by (1) their underlying collective resistance to Tagalog as the national language and (2) their strong affinity with English as the language of social and economic mobility in a globalizing world.

I argue that Bislish is propelled by the extra- and intra-territorial forces; namely, history, politics, and globalization. These can be summed up in terms of two attitudes: a sense of "rootedness" and a sense of "routedness." While the Cebuano-Bisaya speaker endeavors to remain rooted in his or her ethnic/regional identity while resisting what is perceived as a Tagalog-centric national identity, he or she simultaneously endeavors to surpass geographic boundaries and pursues promising routes within a global scope.[1] Bisaya is employed as the language of rootedness as opposed to the constitutionally mandated national language; English, on the other hand, takes the position as the language of routedness.

In this chapter, I will refer to utterances in online interactions as examples of linguistic hybridity involving English and Bisaya. It is, however, important to address a conceptual trap before exploring the extra- and intra-territorial forces behind the said hybrid. In an exploratory survey on linguistic hybridity involving the English language, Schneider (2016: 340) observes that "the presence and utility of English in many bilingual and multilingual countries and contexts has produced new types of hybrid linguistic usage." But would it be safe to refer to these utterances as instances of hybridity rather than mere incidents of language mixing? Schneider (2016: 342) recognizes the absence of a general consensus on how to distinguish between central terms and categories that touch on the mixing phenomena of languages. He notes that terms such as *borrowing*, *code-switching*, and *code-mixing* seem to overlap. While it is beyond the scope of this chapter to contribute to a resolution to this conceptual puzzle, I take the position that Bislish, like other linguistic hybrids, may include the aforementioned processes altogether. Furthermore, Bislish

---

[1] Cebuano or Cebuano-Bisaya is just one of the Bisaya varieties spoken in the country. Many Cebuano speakers interchangeably refer to their language as *Bisaya*, hence the colloquial term "Bislish," which we adopt in this chapter.

is not a fixed variety in itself but a varied way of using a repertoire of linguistic resources. I take Schneider's proposition that hybridity is viewed not as a fixed form but rather as an instance of what Canagarajah (2013: 11) describes as "a realization of translingual practice." Assuming this perspective, the Bislish speaker is not merely using a language or a set of languages; rather, he or she is involved in a process of languaging that takes advantage of linguistic and, at some point, non-linguistic resources available. I find that the concept of translanguaging more aptly captures the dynamic realities of language use, particularly the prominence of hybridity in informal communicative settings where identities are in constant negotiation. Such is the case in my selected online communities involving speakers sharing a regional ethos coupled with a global mindset.

2. "NATION" IN SEARCH OF A LANGUAGE

As an archipelagic country consisting of about 7,641 islands with 183 active languages (Eberhard et al. 2019), Filipinos are engaged in a constant debate over which language should take center stage in cultural, political, educational, and professional domains.

When viewed against Schneider's Dynamic Model, English in the Philippines remains in the stage of nativization. Despite claims that English has reached the dawn of endonormative stabilization, as evidenced by the homogenization of phonological and grammatical features and literary productivity in the Philippine variety (Borlongan 2016: 238), the lack of a general positive attitude towards or a unified acceptance of the said "national variety" confines it to the stage of nativization. However, I observe that this attitudinal ambivalence, while hindering a traversal into endonormative stabilization, may have its own productive outcome. My aim in this chapter, then, is not to build the case of a developed Philippine English variety; it is to embrace the fragmented reality of the country's linguistic situation by exploring the language practices of the Cebuano-speaking region.[2] This fragmentation is manifest in unfixed forms emerging from the constant linguistic contact between English as a global resource and prominent local languages. These are

---

[2] I thank Professor Isabel Martin for helping build the direction of this chapter with her valuable insights on the sociolinguistic situation of the Philippines.

hybrid forms such as the documented Taglish, a linguistic phenomenon characterized by the liberal meshing of English and Tagalog, observed to be an unmarked behavior in various social settings (Schneider 2016: 345; Thompson 2003: 40–41). However, while recognizing Taglish as a manifestation of the country's ambivalent linguistic situation, this study takes interest in another mixed form. Bislish is a combination of English and Cebuano-Bisaya, another prominent language spoken by about a quarter of the Filipino population. The emergence of Bislish and its prominence in interactive domains such as internet forums and vlogs (video blogs) reveals its prominence as a social language in communities of practice comprised of Filipinos residing in or originating from particular areas of Visayas and Mindanao. Unlike Taglish, which is a product of the contact between two politically powerful languages – English as the official language and Filipino as the national language – the Bislish hybrid combines English with Cebuano. While Cebuano is recognized as the statutory language of provincial identity in the Cebu province and four other areas in the country (Eberhard et al. 2019), it does not carry the same symbolic status and prestige as the Tagalog-based counterpart.

3. HYBRIDITY AND THE EIF MODEL

Bislish does not fit the mold of a national variety and as such does not follow the diachronic path pictured in Schneider's (2014: 11–12) Dynamic Model of postcolonial Englishes. Because of its unique nature as a hybrid and its position as a language of regional instead of national identification, it warrants a new lens. While still situating Bislish within its postcolonial context, which means recognizing the history of colonial "transplantation" of English by the American settler population and its acceptance and appropriation by the indigenous community, I feel the need to look into contemporary forces that are involved in the emergence of this hybrid under question. For this, I assume the perspective of extra and intra-territorial forces (Buschfeld and Kautzsch 2017). In their attempt to develop an integrated approach to postcolonial and non-postcolonial Englishes, Buschfeld and Kautzsch (2017) found (1) colonization, (2) language policies, (3) globalization, (4) foreign policies, and (5) sociodemographic background to be among the most common forces in various PCE and non-PCE contexts. These forces are either reinforced or resisted by the internal forces at play. The capacity of colonization, language policies, and globalization to shape or affect a community's linguistic landscape is also highly dependent on the "attitudes" towards the said forces. The integrated approach to PCE and non-PCE will enable an unpacking of Bislish, not only as a product of its history of colonization and regional rifts but also as an expression of present forces constantly at work. An approach that departs from a focus on language varieties shall enable us to study the forces behind the emergence of hybrid forms such as Bislish. Recognizing the fragmentation of the country's physical and linguistic landscapes, this exploration leaves behind the notion of a unified national variety and a shared attitude towards English. While I also point to the "sociolinguistics of globalization" (Blommaert 2010) as a force behind the emergence of the Bislish hybrid, particularly in the online domain, I am especially interested in looking into Cebu's climate of resistance to Tagalog's political and symbolic status. I explore how the mobilizing promise of English is coupled with a resistance to Tagalog as the language of the national agenda to foster the hybrid languaging in two online platforms utilized by Cebuanos.

The EIF framework captures what Schneider's Dynamic Model leaves out. It accounts for both PCE and non-PCE contexts addressing "not only the problem of a lacking foundation phase but also the missing settler strand as well as the external colonizing power" (Buschfeld and Kautzsch 2017: 12). Considering that the Bislish hybrid is neither a prototypical PCE (that is, it cannot be considered a national variety in the same sense as the concept of Philippine English) nor a non-PCE (while its existence owes from various contact sources such as the internet and media, its postcolonial context cannot be discounted), it would be interesting to see if the EIF framework can be put to use in order to understand the mechanisms behind it. This is an attempt to test the model's ability to account for a linguistic reality that waits for further exploration.

4. FORCES BEHIND ONLINE BISLISH

The viability of the internet as a platform to build or reinforce communities based on shared practices, cultural and political beliefs, geographies, interests, and the like, makes it a fertile soil for distinct languaging behaviors to thrive. My objective is to unearth the extra- and intra-territorial forces behind the said languaging.

4.1 Methodology

The study involved two different modes of online communication – spoken and written. The first domain is a platform that has enabled informal written exchanges among Bislish speakers. While no longer popular at present, I still recognize the said platform's value as a depository of hybrid utterances. In other words, I find that the selected platform provides a tangible imprint of the translanguaging practice in focus.

The exploration of the first domain involved a qualitative discourse analysis of selected entries from the "humor" category. This choice was based on the assumption that humor provides an avenue for creative wordplay without confining the speakers to specific rules of languaging. True to its nature as a product of translanguaging practice (Canagarajah 2013), the Bislish hybrid cannot be pinned down in terms of precise grammatical features and form. While I am interested in identifying the patterns of hybridity in the texts selected, I do not aim at a detailed description of the phenomenon.

The qualitative analysis of the data was followed by a sociodemographic exploration of the motivating forces behind the Bislish hybrid. I took advantage of entries from the online platform (regardless of category) to partially determine the language attitudes of the members. Unstructured interviews were then conducted with seven respondents whose names are withheld for privacy. The interviews were designed to elicit information on the respondents' social and educational background and their perceptions towards language.[3] This information contributes to an unearthing of the extra- and intra-territorial forces behind Bislish.

The second subject is a talk show aired through a social networking site's live streaming feature. The video chosen provides an instance of spontaneous hybrid languaging in the spoken mode. I have taken interest in both the languaging practice in the content and the content itself (particularly, the side notes revealing the participants' attitudes towards language). I chose the video for its ability to illustrate the Bislish phenomenon in casual and spontaneous communicative situations. An unstructured focused group discussion with the talk show participants (real nicknames identified as consented) was conducted to elicit information on the extra- and intra-territorial forces behind their languaging.

---

[3] Participants of this part of the study are selected according to convenience. They are either personal contacts or friends of personal contacts.

4.2 Bislish in Two Online Platforms

Istorya.net is an online community of practice where Cebuanos come together in a virtual tryst to "talk" about mundane as well as specialized topics. Linguistic hybridity is especially apparent in the "humor" section where playful and often deliberate use of Bislish takes a significant role in the concoction of what speakers refer to as *hugot*. The Bislish emerging from *hugot* posts are characterized by liberal inter-sentential and intra-sentential mixing of codes. While some shifts appear to be motivated by a creative objective – for instance, the deliberate shift to English to incorporate election-related parlance or formulaic expressions to enhance the dramatic or comedic element – other shifts may have been done undeliberately. Furthermore, while most of the intra-sentential code-mixing occurs at the clause level, it also takes place word internally. Cebuano-Bisayan affixes are used to conjugate words in English (constructions such as *mafall* to mean *will fall*). Another apparent trend is the incorporation of English formulaic expressions and use of culture-specific words (for example, *seen zone* and proper names referring to celebrities, movies, etc.) and domain-specific words and expression in English (for example, language used in electronic products' warranty). This could be attributed to the speakers' exposure to the English language, not only through school but also through other domains, such as popular culture, news and current affairs, and the online world. Moreover, in a majority of cases, the mixing of English and Cebuano-Bisaya plays an essential role in language play, enabling the speaker to integrate into the space of cultural affinity through emotionally relevant wit and humor.

Istorya, like other thriving virtual communities in the digital age, may be seen as an example of what Blommaert (2017: 8) refers to as a web-based peer network, a type of light social group (as opposed to "thick" groups, such as nation, religion, and family). While it is not premised on experiences of face-to-face interaction and physical space-time co-presence, it is a community with "thick" social practices and whose cohesion is based on the shared interest towards virtual interaction. It operates within a framework of social integration. While the prominence of *Istorya.net* may have declined in the midst of competing social media platforms, the fact that it used to host Cebu's biggest and first online community with users from the southern part of the Philippines (Cebuano-Bisaya-speaking regions), mostly ranging between twenty to forty years old, makes it a valuable resource to understand the emergence of Bislish. I am interested in the fact that this online community builds its solidarity based upon its sharedness of an ethnic identity among other things and as such may be telling of a collective regional ethos. In fact, in a thread titled "Do Cebuanos prefer English than Tagalog?", Istoryans (members of the online community) expressed their preference for English over Filipino, the constitutionally mandated national language of the Philippines. In the statement below, the member uses Bislish to express his or her relationship with English and Filipino:

> English is like a defence mechanism to us Cebuanos, maybe because 1) Weird ta mu tagalog *[we have a weird way of using Tagalog]* which is natural raman gyud *[which is really just natural]* since dili man ta native speakers sa dialect *[since we are not native speakers of the dialect]* 2) Mahadlok ta masayop *[we fear committing mistakes]* on how we speak the words or 3) Naanad lang gyud ta mag iningles kay mas na impose ang English sa schools nato *[or we are just more accustomed to English because it was the language more strongly imposed in schools]*. (Istorya.net)

The speaker does not identify himself/herself as a "native speaker" of Tagalog; instead, he/she expresses a strained relationship with the supposed language of national identity (that is, the fear of committing mistakes) and a preference for English being the more comfortable option. However, it is noticeable that despite his/her confidence in the English language, the speaker opts to word his/her testimony in Bislish. This statement can be viewed as an instance of a how the speaker's political and cultural attitudes (in this case a regional consciousness evident in the non-identification with the national language) and other forces such as education (in the above case, English is the strongly imposed language in school) may have influenced his/her language behavior.

Other *Istorya* members share an affinity for Cebuano and English over Filipino. In the unstructured interviews conducted with participants aged twenty-seven to thirty-eight, six out of seven speak Cebuano as their mother tongue. Mary spoke Tagalog growing up but learned Cebuano-Bisaya from her mother who is from Cebu. Like the other four, she chooses to interact in *Istorya.net* in Cebuano, English, or in a combination of Cebuano and English (respondent 1, personal communication, February 5, 2017). Lyn, a forum moderator, owes her ability to use English proficiently to her schools' reading program and English-only policy (respondent 2, personal communication, February 5,

2017). Most of the respondents received primary education in Cebu or in other Cebuano-Bisaya areas and have been taught English in school. The majority of the respondents feel that their proficiency in English enables them to communicate with ease, having learned it as a second language in school, or by watching television, reading magazines, and interacting online. There is, however, a common preference for using a mixed variety of English and Bisaya in order to better express themselves. Rick feels that mixing Cebuano and English in one utterance helps him connect better with others (respondent 3, personal communication, February 5, 2017). Roy does not feel comfortable speaking in "pure" English and only does so in certain situations. His "pure" English is reserved for the workplace, where he has to interact with non-Filipino colleagues and/or use work-related parlance. Paul draws from English when he finds no word equivalent in Cebuano and vice versa. They all describe the general language of *Istorya* as hybrid and dynamic in that it integrates English and Cebuano without regarding them as two separate languages. They treat English, Cebuano, and the mixed variety Bisaya-English as resources that help them in achieving social cohesion with the rest of the community across topics of talk. While all the respondents went through lessons in Tagalog as part of their education requirement (in Mary's case, Tagalog is the language she grew up with) and had access to national television where news and entertainment are often in the national language, they neither think of Tagalog nor Taglish as their default languages for their social interactions, especially within the *Istorya* community, except when communicating with individuals from Luzon and other Tagalog-speaking areas. While these members do not express a distaste for Tagalog, they do not identify easily with the national language in the same way that they identify with Cebuano, English, or the hybrid form.

Bislish has a strong presence not only in online in-groups such as *Istorya.net*, where there is an implied element of exclusivity. It is also felt in platforms meant for "reaching out" and expanding networks. Such is the case with C3 Live, an online talk show series produced and hosted by an interest group called Cebu Content Creators, a "multi-platform, multi-channel network of Cebu digital content creators utilizing blog, video, and social media content." With a mission to *create, connect*, and *collaborate*, C3 envisions to "become the leading organization of highly-skilled digital content creators and influencers in Cebu that encourages the community to improve their craft and maintain quality output, promotes advocacies to improve the society, and helps businesses improve their digital presence" (cebucontentcreators.com).

In an episode of C3 Live, content creators Dannea and Vernon facilitate a casual interview with Cyka, a make-up artist and vlogger (video blogger), to discuss tips and tricks on the beauty and lifestyle niche. The video was first shown through Facebook's live streaming feature, which enabled the audience to interact through the comments section. The three participants, unconstrained by a production script or an elaborate direction, engaged each other and their audience in an informal conversation. Aside from the fact that the video provides a very apparent instance where Bislish is used in the spoken mode in the social setting, it gives us a glimpse of the participants' linguistic attitudes. In the following excerpt, the participants draw attention to their language choice during the start of the show:

> Vernon: Yeah, are you ready?
> Cyka: Ay ko ninyo igrill ha kay di ko maayo anang grill grill. (Don't you grill me, okay, 'cos I'm not good at being grilled.) *laughs*
> Vernon: So, as what you guys have heard, Dannea introduced her, ah Cyka, what she does, so let's hear from Cyka herself. How do you want to be known? What is your branding as a makeup and beauty vlogger?
> Cyka: Bloopers. Pwede magbisaya? (May I speak Bisaya?) *laughs*
> Dannea: Sige go! (Alright, go ahead!)
> Cyka: Kapoya'g English oi. (It sure is taxing to speak English.) *laughs*
> Dannea: Ok ra na, multilingual man tang mga Filipino. (That's fine, we Filipinos are multilingual.) *laughs*

The participants engage in a Bislish banter, but when Cyka is asked about her identity as a vlogger, she jokingly asks permission to speak in Cebuano, referring to the said interruption as a "blooper." She may be concerned about not being understood by the audience who may include non-Cebuano-speaking viewers or about retaining a sense of formality in the show, but Dannea, reasoning that Filipinos are naturally multilingual, is quick to assure her that any language is appropriate. Here, the host opens the floor to spontaneous language behaviors. As the interview progresses, Cyka reverts to Bislish. Another interesting part of the conversation is where Dannea, one of the hosts, apologizes for defaulting in "English":

Dannea: Uhm, pasensya kay murag English sad ang akoang default.
(Uhm, my apologies but it seems like English is my default.)
laughs Pero masabot ra man, no? (But I'm being understood, right?)

Conscious that she may be alienating the participant and the viewers for using English, Dannea apologizes for her language choice and proceeds with Bislish. These interruptions enable the participants to set the tone and mood of the rest of the episode where Bislish is used for the most part. What is worth noting is the fact that although the topic of the discussion is "Beauty and Lifestyle" as a niche in online content creation, language still comes in as an issue. The participants' concerns towards intelligibility, formality, and acceptability make them conscious of their medium. Their shared repertoire of English and Cebuano may have caused this ambiguity at first, but they resolved to use Bislish, which proved to be an effective choice in that it made the participants less conscious and more at home. But where is Filipino/Tagalog in this scenario?

All three participants were born and raised in Cebu by Cebuano-speaking parents. Their educational, professional (both past and current), and social experience made them accustomed to English and Cebuano just the same. Cyka, who grew up with Cebuano as the language of the home and English as one of the languages in school (the other one being Tagalog), became further exposed to English because of her professional experience. Her stint as an agent in a call center with an American clientele and her current involvement with online English language teaching where she deals with students from Japan and other parts of Asia made English part of her everyday repertoire. She shares that she even battles between English and Cebuano when it comes to raising her own children. Cyka claims that she used to communicate with her first daughter in English but realized this choice later hindered the child from fully integrating into her social environment. She has since exposed both her children to Cebuano in the household to make sure that they are able to relate not only with school lessons and other resources integral to their development but also with their immediate physical communities (e.g. their cousins and playmates). Despite the prominence of Filipino as the national language and as a mandated course throughout the educational curriculum, Cyka's choice has always been between English and Cebuano. Like the first participant, Dannea grew up in a home of Cebuano speakers, but she later developed a strong relationship with English when she entered a private high school, which strictly imposed an English-only policy. Having excelled in her English classes, she was often sent to join composition contests. As a writer, Dannea's proficiency was not limited to English as she also dabbled in Filipino-based writing competitions. However, when she started an online job as a content writer where she had to deal with international clients and a global market, she was prompted to write in English. This would be her primary medium throughout her career in content creation. Vernon also spent his childhood years in Cebu where he acquired what he refers to as a "mixed" repertoire of English and Cebuano. Having developed an awareness of the varieties within his own local language through his travels within the Cebu province and in other Cebuano-speaking areas, he tends to adjust his languaging according to place and people. Bislish, he said, comes out mostly when talking to friends and acquaintances from within the city. For Vernon, Tagalog is more of a language of necessity than a personal preference, stating that it is only because "it's in the curriculum" that he needed to learn it. While his Tagalog has helped him in comprehending others during his visits to Manila, he still feels more comfortable engaging in English. This is despite the fact that Vernon's father has a considerable amount of Tagalog in his daily repertoire. Vernon fondly talked about a comical language tension within his home:

> [my mom] is very regionalistic, you know, but my Dad was an OFW [Overseas Filipino Worker] so he's exposed to his colleagues who are from Luzon so when he speaks there's also a mixture of . . . his accent is Bisaya . . . but there's a mixture of Tagalog words. Mao na mag-away na sila. *(That's why they fight.)* (Interview transcript)

As a content creator, Vernon oscillates between Cebuano and English (e.g. when writing blog entries), but whenever the circumstances allow, he defaults to his everyday Bislish (personal communication, July 2, 2018).

In all three cases, Tagalog does not surface as a top-of-mind language. While it is recognized as a helpful resource in social networking, the participants do not necessarily identify with it on a personal level. When asked whether she is conscious of her proficiency in the national language, Dannea is quick to point out: "I think, as a Cebuano or Bisaya . . . when you speak Tagalog . . . you just have to accept that you will not speak as they [the Tagalog speakers] do . . . the point is communication anyway" (interview transcript). Cyka, for instance, feels that her proficiency in Tagalog has helped her launch her career as a beauty and lifestyle vlogger. She also admits that incorporating Tagalog in her videos has helped her attract and retain national viewership (personal communication, July 2, 2018).

English, on the other hand, is strongly enmeshed in their personal lives and career. To the participants, English is not someone else's language, unlike Filipino/Tagalog, which is often referred to as "their" [the Tagalog's] language and not their own. This bias towards English over Filipino puts into question the prominence of Filipino in the regional setting.

National language policies elevating the status of Filipino and English (for instance, the imposition of English as medium of instruction and the inclusion of Filipino as a mandatory discipline in school) are noteworthy forces propelling the participants' languaging. But where should national policies be situated in the EIF framework? To determine whether these are extra- or intra-territorial requires a consideration of which perspective is taken. From a national viewpoint, language policies elevating the status of English can be seen as the intra-territorial dimension to an extra-territorial force (that is, the colonizing power of the Americans). However, in the case of Bislish, it is important to consider a regional vantage point in which national language policies are seen as extra-territorial, their intra-territorial dimension being the speakers' general attitude towards said policies. It can be gleaned from the sociodemographic exploration that the participants connect with Cebuano as their language of identity and English as their language of social and economic mobility.

5. ENGLISH VS. FILIPINO: THE CEBUANO SENTIMENT

Thompson (2003: 69) recognizes that English has occupied a significant place in the Philippines for 100 years as a force that would enrich, ennoble, and empower. However, the switch to bilingual education in 1974 changed the linguistic landscape. Scholars predicted that Tagalog would soon displace English especially in urban areas, citing the following reasons: (1) the abundance of opportunities for informal acquisition of Tagalog-based Filipino provided by the media; (2) the fact that "Tagalog is so closely related to the other languages spoken in the Philippines," making "street Tagalog" fairly easy to acquire (Sibayan

1978: 310); and (3) the "extensive internal migration and the rapid urbanization" resulting in the collapse of traditional bonds with local languages (Gonzales 1977, in Thompson 2003: 69). Sibayan (1978) projects that while English would continue to thrive in Metro Manila, the rise of Tagalog in the provinces, including the Cebuano-speaking areas, could result in the decline of English proficiency where there is limited social support outside the classroom. The predictions may not have been correct.

It cannot be denied that English continues to be "the essential language for social and economic mobility" in the Philippine context, enabling full participation in economics, culture, and politics (Thompson 2003: 74). But whether or not there are equal motivations all over the country is worth looking into. Thompson (2003: 75) notes that while "the best opportunities for learning English are in Metro Manila" (where there is a large concentration of educational institutions), "it is also the driving force for the spread of Tagalog" as the media capital. He recognizes that "the most positive attitude for maintaining English lies in the Visayas" where there is strong political opposition to Tagalog-based Filipino as the national language (Thompson 2003: 75).

When Tagalog (later renamed Filipino), the language attributed to the political center, was declared the national language of the country as part of a decolonizing movement in the 1930s, speakers of Cebuano-Bisaya, then the most widely spoken language in the country, disapproved (Tupas 2009: 25). For Gonzales (1991: 117), a better understanding of the anti-Tagalog sentiment among Cebuanos should be seen in the light of history. The land-locked Tagalogs of Central Luzon and the sea-bound Cebuanos of the south were two of the three tribal groups who have been aggressive migrants and settlers. While the Tagalogs displaced only inhabitants of the lowlands, with whom they have been in cultural and linguistic contact, the Cebuanos erected settlements in Dumaguete, Negros Oriental, Southern Leyte, and then in different parts of Mindanao, including the southernmost group of islands of the archipelago, Jolo (Gonzales 1991: 117). This "pattern of dispersal" could explain why Cebuano and related Bisayan languages are found in various parts of the country. What may have elevated the Tagalogs into prominence? Despite the fact that Manila was founded by the Spanish colonizers only six years after they set up a settlement in Cebu, it became prominent as an intermediary center of trade and transhipment between Manila and Acapulco from the late sixteenth to the late eighteenth centuries. Gonzales (1991: 118) notes that as with all capital cities, the prominence of the Tagalogs which began with the founding of the city of Manila by the Spaniards was an accidental confluence of colonial policy and geographical location resulting in economic and eventually political and cultural dominance.

Despite the fact that Cebu was the oldest See of the Roman Church, Manila soon rose up to prominence.

While the first two decades of the American colonial period were dominated by a Cebuano leader as the first speaker of the Philippine Assembly, the rest of the period saw the rise in power of a Tagalog who served as Senate President of the newly established bicameral legislature in 1916. In 1923, the Cebuano Osmeña took a secondary role to the Tagalog Quezon as the Senate President pro tempore (Gonzales 1991: 118). He further points out that "the pattern set by Quezon and Osmeña . . . resulted in a balancing of North and South among presidential and vice-presidential candidates as well as among senators." This balance in terms of political representation remained until the reign of Corazon Aquino as President and Salvador Laurel as Vice-President, both of whom are Tagalogs. However, the deep-seated rivalry may have been aggravated by much greater forces. Gonzales surmises:

> [W]hat the Cebuanos want is more autonomy under a Federal model, liberation from the seeming bureaucratic imperialism in Manila which is dominated by Tagalogs, and freedom to develop as an island not saddled with the drawbacks which have impeded rapid growth in Manila, the center of the country's stormy political wrangling and seeming ineptitude in terms of public results as well as the fruitless investigations of the legislature instead of creative initiatives to hasten the country's socio-economic growth in the region. (Gonzales 1991: 119)

The desire for political and economic autonomy may have caused the renewed assertion of ethnic identity among Cebuanos "symbolized by an assertion of linguistic rights" (Gonzales 1991: 119). Such is reflected in the "anti-imperialist Manila" discourse of some regional language advocates. In an article published in a national newspaper, Mansueto faults the elevation of the Tagalog-based Filipino as the national language and official language of communication in government offices and school bolstered by its wide use in the mass media for the decline of more than

100 languages spoken in the Philippines, including Cebuano (Mansueto 2013). To Mansueto, celebrating National Language Month, an annual celebration which has its precursor in Executive Order No. 335 enjoining the use of Filipino in official communication, remains meaningless until the government honors all the other local languages in the country. "Otherwise," Mansueto concludes, "it will be merely a celebration of a victorious imperialist language rammed down everyone else's throat."

At present, the desire to elevate the Cebuano identity in the midst of the nationalist agenda is felt in the literary and creative sphere. In an interview with Erlinda Alburo, a creative writer and academic from Cebu, she claims that her reasons for using either English or Cebuano Bisaya and not Tagalog for her creative and critical works are both practical and political:

> I'm not confident with my Tagalog/Filipino ... I know both Cebuano and English as reader and writer so it's a practical choice. However, my poems are in Cebuano as a political statement because I want Cebuano to prosper as a literary medium. (E. Alburo, personal communication, June 15, 2018)

Alburo is aware that the "language wars" have not yet fully resolved, opining that although some Cebuano writers have become more open to writing in or translating into Tagalog, "[t]here is still a psychological resistance ... because of the superior attitude of the Tagalogs" (E. Alburo, personal communication, June 15, 2018). Despite this perceived "superiority" complex, however, Alburo believes there is no use contesting Tagalog's position as the national language. "Writers will still write in the language they know best," she says. What the Cebuanos have is the "advantage of knowing another Philippine language compared to the NCR people" (E. Alburo, personal communication, June 15, 2018). While she believes an aggressive resistance to Tagalog is no longer necessary, she asserts the need to maintain and preserve the zeal for Cebuano through literary production.

The Cebuanos' relationship with English seems to be different. For Alburo, like many Cebuanos, English is not perceived as a threat. As multilinguals, Cebuanos "owe English a lot and [are] comfortable with it" even if it is not an integral part of their identity in the same way that the Cebuano language is (E. Alburo, personal communication, June 15, 2018). Alburo believes that a typical Cebuano is trilingual, capable of Cebuano, English, and Tagalog, "in descending order of competence"

(E. Alburo, personal communication, June 15, 2018). It is worth noting that while she believes that the Cebuano language is tied to the Cebuano identity, she does not subscribe to a "purist" perspective, stating that "whatever works for communication purposes is OK" (E. Alburo, personal communication, June 15, 2018). To Alburo, Bislish is not only permissible but necessary.

This attitude of acceptance can be felt in Cebuano literary and popular culture. Although more common in conversational, everyday situations, there is also an observable presence of hybrid languaging in Cebuano poetry, fiction, and music. The utilization of Bislish usually functions to create a realistic conversational tone and/or dramatize communicative situations involving the Cebuano persona. In what seems to be a commentary on the penetrative force of hybrid languaging into the Cebuano's daily repertoire, a popular song by the Bisrock (Bisayan rock) band Missing Filemon makes use of Bislish to dramatize the speaker's sentiment of his lover whom he notices has slowly influenced his own language. The speaker quips: *Nausab na ang akong sinultian / May sagol nang eninglish like* whatever *and* well */ Sukad na nakaila tika* (My language has changed / It's starting to mix in English like *whatever and well* / Since I have known you). The rest of the song makes use of a languaging typical of colloquial communicative situations involving the Cebuano speaker, as evident in the line: *Giingnan ko sa imong friends / Na you find kuno badoy kung bisaya ang pinulungan* (Your friends told me / That you find the Bisaya language unfashionable) (Missing Filemon 2005). A suite of poems by the Cebuano literary artist Michael Obenieta, called *Teknolohibat* (a playful combination of two terms: *technology* or *teknolohiya* and the Bisaya *hibat*, an adjective describing something crooked, unsymmetrical, or malposed), which won first prize in a Cebuano-Bisaya writing contest in 2006, provides a witty illustration of how English is enmeshed into the Cebuano repertoire, specifically in the language of everyday mobile and online technology. The poem *Ngadto sa Tikasan Nakong Textmate* (To my Deceitful Textmate) makes use of Bislish "textspeak," as in the line *"coz of u pwrte pamakak nako ni mam"* ("coz of u I had to lie to mam") (Obenieta 2007), to capture the tone and register of the situation dramatized. I assume that conventions of literariness as opposed to the conditions of spontaneity found in casual conversation spaces may be a limiting factor to the presence of hybrid languaging in Cebuano literary tradition. However, with some authors' aim to capture the reality of human conditions, the choice of Bislish becomes an artistic device in itself.

6. TAGALOG RESISTANCE AND A GLOBAL MINDSET AS INTRA-TERRITORIAL FORCES

Bislish may be propelled by a deep-seated resistance to an extra-territorial force – that is the nationalist agenda manifesting in language policies among others. This is symbolized by an assertion of ethnolinguistic rights resulting in an indifference to, if not a distancing from, Tagalog as the constitutionally mandated national language. Another apparent extra-territorial force behind Bislish is globalization. Its intra-territorial dimension is the perceived mobilizing potential of English, which may have contributed to what seems to be the equal valuing of Cebuano and English.

What I picture is a Cebuano that is both *rooted and routed*: strongly bound to one's ethnic roots, yet at once aiming for social, economic, and political mobility. This is the case of the Bislish speakers in the online sphere – the Istoryans who have managed to build an exclusive, coherent community partly defined by their shared Bisaya-English repertoire and the content creators (C_3 members) who have attained social and financial mobility through their proficiency in both English and Bisaya.

The Bislish hybrid is a melding of a local language and a global language motivated by socio-economic forces. But the stronger force at play is a resistance to what is supposedly the language of national unification. I surmise that the surge of globalization, which reinforces the role of English as an enabling language of mobility, makes its way into the indigenous community (illustrated by the Cebuano communities of practice explored) without much resistance. As to how much colonial history, economics, policies, education, and other factors contribute to the positive attitude towards globalization may be difficult to quantify given the limits of my research. What I find significant is what happens to English when it enters the Cebuano territory. Unlike the national variety that is pictured in Schneider's Dynamic Model of Postcolonial Englishes, it does not just nativize, stabilize in an endonormative sense, and differentiate as a distinct variety. What happens, particularly in the case of the Cebuano communities of practice in focus, is that English comes in contact with Cebuano, which is prominent for being the language of ethnic identity. The product of this constant contact is a hybrid languaging that enables the Cebuano to participate in globalizing practices and at the same time assert a separate ethnic identity that is not defined by what is perceived as a Tagalog-centric nationalist agenda.

7. CONCLUSION

One notable attribute of the EIF Model is its ability to unify PCE and non-PCE contexts without falling into the trap of universalizing. By suggesting that "extra- and intra-territorial forces are the driving mechanisms behind the development of PCEs and non-PCEs at all times, namely in their foundation phases but also throughout their further developments" (Buschfeld and Kautzsch 2017: 14), their model enables a way of seeing a commonality between contexts "without obscuring the obvious differences between the two types" (Buschfeld and Kautzsch 2017: 18). The model emphasizes that not all forces "are equally at work in all countries at all times"; rather, "the presence and impact of the forces depend on the respective context and development phase of the country" (Buschfeld and Kautzsch 2017: 14). It is important to note, however, that hybrid forms, being products of translingual processes rather than actual varieties, may not fit the mold of PCE and non-PCEs. The EIF Model accommodates the unique nature of hybrids.

While Bislish is an offshoot of the English transplanted through colonization, it does not possess the nation-building qualities and the structural and institutional stability. Aiming to codify it, in the same manner that scholars have attempted to define Philippine English as a national variety, may prove to be counter-intuitive. Tracking its development against the phases suggested by Schneider in his Dynamic Model (2007) may also prove difficult, hence the need for a framework that could account for the nature of the Bislish hybrid, which is neither a PCE nor a non-PCE. Aside from the fact that Bislish has a regional, almost antinational, dimension, it may be difficult to conceive of it as a nativized version of the English transplanted by the settler population during the American colonial period. While it may be safe to say that its colonial foundation is essential to its current existence, the nature and currency of Bislish owes much to dynamic and constant forces, namely the ethnically rooted resistance to a national language and the strong, globalizing forces of internet and media.

In the field of English language research, there is a dearth of available conceptual frameworks that may enable a better understanding of the mechanisms behind linguistic hybridity. This is despite the prevalence of such mixed forms in various communities of practice all over the world (for example, Taglish in the Philippines and Singlish in Singapore) as documented by Schneider (2016: 339–351) in his exploratory survey. Looking into hybrids such as Bislish is necessary if one desires to understand the dynamic sociolinguistic situation of multilingual contexts without the presumption of national homogeneity. Bislish, for instance, provides a peek into the fragmented linguistic situation of the Philippines tied to political and ethnic tensions. Furthermore, hybridity may not be considered a deviation, but part of the natural course of how Englishes may develop in different soils. I find that the EIF Model provides a useful framework in explaining the unique mechanisms behind each case of hybridity as a manifestation of the melding of extra- and intra-territorial forces, whether in PCE or non-PCE settings. In this particular exploration, the framework has provided an opportunity to capture the uniqueness of the Cebuano linguistic context characterized by its resistance to the perceived hegemonizing force of the national agenda melding with a strong global mindset. I recommend that other cases of hybridity be studied under the EIF lens as a way of unearthing forces that may have significant social and political implications.

REFERENCES

Blommaert, Jan. 2010. *The Sociolinguistics of Globalization*. Cambridge: Cambridge University Press.

Blommaert, Jan. 2017. Society through the lens of language: A new look at social groups and integration. *Working Papers in Urban Language and Literacies*. London: Kings College London, 1–20.

Borlongan, Ariane M. 2016. Relocating Philippine English in Schneider's Dynamic Model. *Asian Englishes* 18.3: 232–241.

Buschfeld, Sarah and Alexander Kautzsch. 2017. Towards an integrated approach to postcolonial and non-postcolonial Englishes. *World Englishes* 36.1: 104–126.

Canagarajah, Suresh. 2013. *Translingual Practice: Global Englishes and Cosmopolitan Relations*. London: Routledge.

cebucontentcreators.com, http://cebucontentcreators.com/ (last accessed October 16, 2019).

Eberhard, David M., Gary Simons and Charles D. Fennig, eds. 2019. *Ethnologue: Languages of the World*. 22nd edn. Dallas, TX: SIL International.

Gonzales, Andrew. 1991. Cebuano and Tagalog: Ethnic rivalry redivivus. In James R. Dow, ed. 1991, *Focus on Language and Ethnicity: Essays in Honor of Joshua A. Fishman*. Amsterdam: John Benjamins Publishing, 111–129.

Istorya.net, https://www.istorya.net/ (last accessed May 16, 2019).

Mansueto, Trizer. 2013. Preserving Cebuano and other languages. *Inquirer Visayas*, https://newsinfo.inquirer.net/479137/preserving-cebuano-and-other-languages-2 (last accessed May 16, 2019).

Missing Filemon. 2005. Englisera. ICO Music.

Obenieta, Michael. 2007. Teknolohibat. *Bisaya Magazine*, http://bismag.pbworks.com/w/page/9015667/Bismag%2006-27-07 (last accessed May 16, 2019).

Schneider, Edgar W. 2007. *Postcolonial English. Varieties Around the World*. Cambridge: Cambridge University Press.

Schneider, Edgar W. 2014. New reflections on the evolutionary dynamics of world Englishes. *World Englishes* 33.1: 9–32.

Schneider, Edgar W. 2016. Hybrid Englishes: An exploratory survey. *World Englishes* 35.3: 339–354.

Sibayan, Bonifacio. 1978. Bilingual education in the Philippines: Strategy and structure. In James E. Alatis, ed. 1978, *International Dimensions of Bilingual Education. Georgetown University Round Table on Languages and Linguistics*. Washington, DC: Georgetown University, 302–329.

Thompson, Roger. 2003. *Filipino English and Taglish. Language Switching from Multiple Perspectives*. Amsterdam: John Benjamins.

Tupas, Ruanni. 2009. Language as a problem of development. *AILA Review* 22.1: 23.

CHAPTER 8

English in South Korea: Applying the EIF Model

Sofia Rüdiger

1. INTRODUCTION

These ambiguities, redundancies, and deficiencies recall those attributed by Dr. Franz Kuhn to a certain Chinese encyclopedia called the *Heavenly Emporium of Benevolent Knowledge*. In its distant pages it is written that animals are divided into (a) those that belong to the emperor; (b) embalmed ones; (c) those that are trained; (d) suckling pigs; (e) mermaids; (f) fabulous ones; (g) stray dogs; (h) those that are included in this classification; (i) those that tremble as if they were mad; (j) innumerable ones; (k) those drawn with a very fine camel's-hair brush; (l) etcetera; (m) those that have just broken the flower vase; (n) those that at a distance resemble flies. (Borges [1942] 1999: 231; emphasis in original)

Classification, be it of objects, behaviors, characteristics, or processes (or anything else that is remotely classifiable), is part of our human drive to understand the world and to generate knowledge. Just as the *Heavenly Emporium of Benevolent Knowledge* referenced above classifies animals, linguists organize and label phonemes and morphemes, distinguish between sentence types, and categorize speech acts. Variationist linguists, particularly scholars of World Englishes, identify and classify different types of Englishes. World Englishes modeling started in the 1970s with a straightforward triad paradigm model distinguishing between A-speakers (ENL), B-speakers (ESL), and C-speakers (EFL) (Strang 1970: 17–18) and has since then become so productive that it is possible to classify models of World Englishes into different types themselves. Thus, there are models based on the notion of a central member, not coincidentally the biggest grouping of models (e.g. Kachru 1985; McArthur 1987; Görlach 1990; Mair 2013), developmental models (Schneider 2003, 2007), communicative models (Meierkord 2012), or contact-based models (Onysko 2016).

With the EIF Model by Buschfeld and Kautzsch (2017), a new method of classifying Englishes has entered the scene. This model combines the advantages of the developmental models with the contact-based and communicative ones, as contextual factors (i.e. the forces) play an essential role in the make-up of the model. This has been a long overdue advancement in the field and the edited volume at hand presents a wealth of applications to different contexts. The one introduced in this chapter is South Korea (variably referenced as Korea/South Korea in the following text), which in the past was often overlooked or classified without too much in-depth consideration (but see Rüdiger 2019 for a first comprehensive account).

First, I will give a short overview and an evaluation of how previous World Englishes modeling has been applied to or is applicable to the South Korean context. The subsequent section will demonstrate the implementation of the EIF Model for South Korea by going through a selection of the extra- and intra-territorial forces one by one. After having thus shed light on aspects of colonization and attitudes towards colonizing power, language policies and language attitudes, globalization and attitudes towards globalization, foreign policies, and sociodemographic background, the discussion will propose to add "cultural phenomena" and the "presence of English in the linguistic landscape and in the native language (L1)" as amendments to the EIF Model. In the end, I will use the evidence given in this chapter to place South Korea between the stabilization (phase 2) and nativization phase (phase 3) of the EIF Model.

2. WORLD ENGLISHES MODELING AND ENGLISH IN SOUTH KOREA

Previous models of World Englishes usually found South Korea a clear case for categorization. It is outside of the scope of this chapter to review the application of these models to the Korean context in detail, but I will shortly consider how three of these models have been applied to Korea in the past. As English does not have official status within the country and is learned as a foreign language within the official education system, categorization seemed to be a rather straightforward process. South Korea is thus easily classified as an EFL (English as a Foreign Language) context (using the triad ENL – ESL – EFL Model) or as member of the *Expanding Circle* (as posited by Kachru 1985). Besides the nowadays much-criticized staticity of these models (see, e.g., Buschfeld 2013; Edwards 2016), this pigeon-holing is somewhat unsatisfactory when it comes to English in South Korea as it neither considers the rich, dynamic, and innovative uses of English by South Koreans, nor does it take account of the particular socio-historical background and current demographic developments in the region. Schneider's (2003, 2007) Dynamic Model devised as a representation of the evolution and dynamic nature of postcolonial Englishes, a priori excludes an application to the Korean context as it does not fulfill the (post)colonial prerequisite. An attempt to, nevertheless, apply the Dynamic Model to non-postcolonial contexts (i.e. China, Korea, and Japan) undertaken by Schneider (2014) himself failed, as the Dynamic Model is not suitable for capturing the realities of language use within those countries.

The EIF Model, developed by Buschfeld and Kautzsch (2017) as a further development of Schneider's Dynamic Model, is not only dynamic in nature and applicable to both post- and non-postcolonial Englishes, it also allows a fine-grained description of the context(s) of use for the variety of English it is applied to. Besides categorization into the five phases known from the Dynamic Model (i.e., foundation, exonormative stabilization, nativization, endonormative stabilization, and differentiation), the EIF framework provides a means to accurately and systematically describe the factors relevant to language use within the specified context. Some forces might be similar in many, if not most, regions (but by no means exactly the same), such as influences of the internet or American pop culture, while others might be truly unique to particular locales. Applying the EIF Model to a specific context, researchers can then focus on the forces that are most relevant while keeping the overall bigger picture in mind.

3. APPLYING THE EIF MODEL TO SOUTH KOREA

In the following sections, I apply the extra- and intra-territorial forces as originally proposed by Buschfeld and Kautzsch (2017) to the Korean context. By no means does this represent an exhaustive list of all forces at work on the southern part of the peninsula; rather, it focuses on a selection of both those deemed to be most important and those that have not been considered or mentioned yet for the South Korean context. Of course, this selective focus is biased to a certain degree by my own experiences, both as a scholar of English in the Korean context as well as by my own exposure to life in South Korea. This in no way means that the description of forces presented here is anecdotal, however, as it is based on an extensive review of previous literature as well as statistical information provided through official channels (e.g. KOSTAT – Statistics Korea, an institution which is part of the Korean Ministry of Strategy and Finance). An overview of the forces described in this chapter can be found in the appendix to the chapter.

3.1 Colonization and Attitudes towards the Colonizing Power

Despite a long history of invasion by foreign powers, South Korea has never been colonized by an anglophone nation. Recent Korean history (since the 1900s) is characterized by caesura and turmoil: a thirty-five-year-long colonization by the Japanese from 1910 to 1945 was succeeded by a brief period of interim government by the United States and was followed by the Korean War (1950–1953), which officially has not ended yet, despite an armistice having been in effect since 1953 and renewed political peace efforts currently underway (for a detailed overview of ancient and modern Korean history see, e.g., Seth 2016).

I claim that despite the lack of colonization by an English-speaking force, the extra- and intra-territorial forces of colonization and attitudes towards the colonizing power are of high relevance for the South Korean context, though in modified form. The United States Army Military Government in Korea (USAMGIK) ruled Korea as an interim government from 1945 to 1948. This must have been particularly formative in the Korean context as it superseded the Japanese occupation of Korea during which the Japanese actively tried to 'Japanize' the Korean population and their identity. One of the targets in erasing Korean identity formation was the Korean language. In addition to "making Japanese the sole official language, liquidating the Korean language by prohibiting all publications in Korean, forcing all Koreans to adopt Japanese names, and using Japanese as the sole medium of instruction" (Yim 2007: 42), the use of English was also forbidden during the latter part of the occupation as it was considered to be the language of the enemy. These measures of forced language management might well have contributed to the strong connection that exists between Korean identity and the Korean language at the present time. In other words, being Korean means speaking Korean. This has also been noted, for example, by Song (2012: 10), who identified a "correlation between Koreans and the Korean language."

The governance of the USAMGIK was relatively short, only three years, but led to a presence of American forces within the country. Even more drastic, however, was the placement of American soldiers into the country during the outbreak of the Korean War. Hayes (2012: 139) reports that 328,000 American soldiers had been sent to the country by 1953. Interestingly, a short-lived Korean English pidgin called Bamboo English developed during the peak time of American involvement in the Korean War (see, e.g., Algeo 1960; Duke 1970).[1] Most of the American forces were withdrawn with the armistice (which was also the point at which Bamboo English faded into oblivion again), but the United States continues to deploy American soldiers to South Korea in order to protect the country from its northern neighbor. Even though the number of American soldiers has continuously decreased over the last few decades, sizable numbers of armed forces are still stationed in Korea; Hayes (2012: 139) reports 28,500 for 2010.

The American involvement in Korea explains the influence the United States holds on the southern part of the peninsula, not only on politics but also in terms of language. With the USAMGIK, English was firmly established as an obligatory subject from middle school onwards in the Korean education system (see Kim 2011 for more information on English educational policies during and after the USAMGIK). American English is thus the input variety in the education system and the presence of American military personnel contributes to the high visibility of the language in the country. Additionally, this has led to an extremely interesting contact situation on the American army bases in Korean territory. The Korean Augmentation to the United States Army program (KATUSA), for example, places some Korean conscripts into the American bases for the duration of their military service (see Kwak

---

[1] According to Webster (1960: 261–262), Korean Bamboo English was mainly used between American and Korean soldiers, but also for oral communication between American soldiers and Korean non-military personnel such as "houseboys, barbers, kitchen help, interpreters, and the like." It should be noted that the term Bamboo English is also used to refer to the linguistic outcome of other contact situations involving American soldiers, for example in Japan or in Vietnam (see Duke 1970).

2006: 89), thus providing a very intense language contact situation within the national boundary of South Korea. Attitudes towards the United States of America are dichotomous, and both positive as well as anti-American sentiments have been reported in a range of studies and papers (see, e.g., Moon 2003 and the contributions in Steinberg 2005). How far the Trump administration, in combination with very recent political developments (often connected to North Korea; e.g. Donald Trump's meeting with Kim Jong-un in Singapore in 2018), influences this picture is, at the time of writing, still unknown.

The establishment of the USAMGIK after World War II does not justify contextualizing Korea as a postcolonial setting. I argue, however, that this can, nevertheless, be interpreted as the onset of the foundation phase in which English became a fixed part of the Korean language ecology. In addition to this, foundation was further established by what Edwards (2016) terms "foundation-through-globalisation." This reflects the global influences of the United States via cultural phenomena (such as pop music, movies, TV shows, and computer games) and the internet.[2]

This section has shown how, despite not falling into the category of postcolonial settings per se, issues which can approximate the notion of "colonization" and "attitudes towards colonizing power" are important for placing Korea in terms of the EIF Model. For the Korean context, I suggest relabeling these forces, in order to reflect the non-colonial nature of the United States Army Military Government in Korea, to "foreign government and military involvement" and "attitudes toward foreign government and military involvement." Despite being of a non-colonial nature, these forces can stand in for the forces present in colonial contexts. This does not mean that the effects are necessarily comparable and of the same nature, but in the Korean context the USAMGIK and its consequences are of utmost importance for the evolution of "English in Korea" and should thus receive prominent attention in applying the EIF Model to South Korea. The next section will now turn to more general notions of language policies and language attitudes which can be found in the Korean context.

---

[2] South Korean internet access is famous for being fast and reliable; free access to the internet should by no means be considered a given in every regional context (cf. the situation in North Korea).

3.2 Language Policies and Language Attitudes

3.2.1 *Language policies*

Currently, the sole official and national language of South Korea is Korean. English is, in most cases, acquired as a foreign language in school. In 1997, English was "upgraded," from being an obligatory middle and high school subject only, to being taught from grade 3 of elementary school. In 2001, the Korean Ministry of Education adopted an English-teaching-in-English-only policy, which means that nowadays the language of instruction in all English classes in Korean schools is English (at least theoretically). The popular English Program in Korea (EPIK), founded in 1995 and officially affiliated with the Korean Ministry of Education, places English native speakers into Korean schools (EPIK 2013). It needs to be kept in mind, however, that private language education often starts earlier than third grade and Koreans are notorious for spending large sums of their income on private English-language education (see Song 2012: 56). This has greatly contributed to the "English divide" between those who can and those who cannot afford private English education (Jeon 2012; Song 2012). Indeed, the desire for English education and basically English itself is so great that scholars have referred to this extreme form of orientation towards the English language as "English Fever" (J.-K. Park 2009).

Interestingly, there has been a debate in Korea on making English an official language (also referred to as the "Official English Debate"; Song 2011). This idea was first brought up in a book by Bok Geo-il published in 1998, called *Ethnic Languages in the Age of an International Language* (국제어 시대의 민족어; *Gukjeeo Sidaeui Minjokeo* in Korean), and was subsequently fiercely discussed by the media, politicians, and the public (see Yoo 2005). The interest in this issue waxes and wanes and it is doubtful whether such an artificial change in official language policy will ever be realized in Korea. However, the mere fact that this is part of a public and seriously undertaken discussion within the country shows how conflicted Koreans are towards issues of language policy and further illustrates that "English is unquestionably the most important foreign language in South Korea" (Song 2012: 56).

3.2.2 Language attitudes and ideologies

Relatively few studies have explored language attitudes in the South Korean context. McTague's (1990) research of the language attitudes of university students and employees of major Korean corporations taking English evening classes found dichotomous attitudes. Participants wanted to harness the power of English but, at the same time, feared its overuse in the Korean context (McTague 1990: 191). Ahn (2014, 2017) surveyed attitudes to World Englishes (including Korean English) by English teachers in South Korea. According to Ahn's research, English teachers in Korea experience an internal conflict; on the one hand, they prefer American English (over a local Korean English variety) due to a (perceived) obligation to fulfill their students' needs (e.g. for English testing), but they also generally value a Korean form of English as fitting their cultural and linguistic needs (Ahn 2014: 215–216).[3] English test preparation, job assurance, and communication with foreigners were identified as important reasons for studying English in Korea (Ahn 2017: 116). For English-Korean translators and interpreters, English represents cultural, economic, political, social, and symbolic capital (Cho 2017: 170). The drive to become "the perfect English speaker," which is propagated by the media, is found to have particular leverage among ambitious Korean women (Cho 2017: 171).

A thorough exploration of mediatized and/or naturally occurring metalinguistic commentaries on the English language across a range of Korean discursive sites – i.e. written debates on language policy, humor in spoken, online, and mediatized language, and face-to-face interactions between Koreans – has identified three overarching ideologies pertaining to English in modern day Korean society: necessitation, externalization, and self-deprecation (J. S.-Y. Park 2009). English is commonly viewed as a "language one must acquire and secure in order to survive and flourish in the globalizing world"; it is therefore both "valuable and indispensable" for Koreans to know English (J. S.-Y. Park 2009: 26). Even elderly Korean women report pressure to learn

---

[3] The attitudes towards British English reported in Ahn (2017: 78–82) are generally positive, but participants also expressed the perception that Korean teachers of English do not know British English well enough to teach it. Additionally, British English is "not considered as a useful English variety for exams in South Korea" (Ahn 2017: 78). These notions again underline the status of American English as the target variety in the South Korean context.

English or further their English skills, as they feel continually excluded and outdistanced by English use in localized Korean contexts, such as in conversations with younger family members and the linguistic land- and audioscape (Lee 2016). At the same time, English is considered a language not "at home" in the Korean context; it is, after all, "the language of an Other" (J. S.-Y. Park 2009: 26). The mixing of English and Korean, for example, by using English loan words when speaking Korean is therefore not always received positively (Rüdiger 2018). Last but not least, the self-deprecation ideology constructs Koreans as not able to use English competently. This erases the "variation in the level of English skills that actually exists among Koreans," constructs Koreans as one national group as "hopelessly incapable of mastering English" (J. S.-Y. Park 2009: 80), and demonstrates the native speaker hegemony persisting in the country.

3.3 Globalization and Attitudes Towards Globalization

A full overview of Korean political developments and their relationship to globalization is outside of the scope of this chapter, as a wide range of historical and political aspects would need to be covered in order to give just a first impression of the complexities involved here. A few points can be considered of particular relevance, however, and shall be mentioned in the following.

With a transition to a fully democratic system starting in 1987–1988 and the first election of a civilian president in 1992, The Republic of Korea (ROK) belongs to the third-wave democracies (Kim 2003: 3) and is a rather recent addition to democratic societies worldwide. The change from military dictatorship to democracy in South Korea has been described as a "remarkable success in democratization" (Shin 1999: xxiii) and undoubtedly constitutes the starting point of global aspirations in the country. The Olympic Games held in Seoul in 1988 are often portrayed as a turning point in recent Korean history which "changed the Korean social mood, forcing people to try harder to understand other people, to open their borders wider, and to consider Korea as a part of the world" (Duk 2005: 11).

President Kim Young-sam (1993–1998) and President Kim Dae-jung (1998–2003) have been subsequent key figures in the development of the *segyehwa* (globalization) drive (Kihl 2005: 152–157), which is connected to a mindset that views globalization in terms of its opportunities rather than its perils (Kihl 2005: 163). As a "trading state [. . .], with an extremely high trade/gross national product ratio, the extent of its openness and transparency and the degree of its global competitiveness" (Kim 2003: 9) is particularly important for Korea's economic success. South Korean *chaebol*, "family-owned and -managed business conglomerates, which have dominated the South Korean economy since the 1960s" (Kim 2000: 103), such as Samsung, Hyundai, and LG, nowadays operate around the world. The globalization of these businesses and their outward foreign investments have not only contributed to Korea's global visibility but also provide important contact points between Korea and the rest of the world. As Kim (2000: 103) argues, the globalization of *chaebol* businesses also comes with inward foreign investment and constitutes a mutual relationship between outward and inward foreign economic processes. Of course, globalization and economic success have not always been straightforward, and setbacks – such as the Southeast Asian financial crisis in late 1997, during which several *chaebol* companies went bankrupt – have occurred as well (Kong 2000: 144; see also Sikorski 2004 on the Asian financial crisis and global economy).

From an economic point of view, globalization and the *segyehwa* drive in South Korea are constrained by nationalist sentiment (Lee and Lee 2015). A similar point has been observed by Joseph Sung-Yul Park (2009: 26) regarding the language ideology of externalization, which views English as a language of an "Other," constructed purposefully as non-inherent part of Korean cultural identity (see section 3.2). Many of the notions mentioned in this chapter, particularly those related to economic policy, go hand in hand with the foreign policies that we will consider next.

3.4 Foreign Policies

In terms of foreign policies and economic development in general, South Korea has performed an astounding 180-degree turn from "insular orientation" (Mimiko 2005: 61) and "isolationist past" (Seol 2013: 214) to global player. Economic relations, particularly with the United States, have also changed drastically; while South Korea was on the receiving end of financial help until the mid-1960s, it is now a major trading partner for not only the United States but for many other countries worldwide (Song 2003: 238–241). Korea also joined the Organisation for Economic Co-Operation and Development (OECD) in 1996 (OECD 2018) and since 1997 has been connected to the Association of Southeast Asian Nations (ASEAN) via the ASEAN+3 forum, an association that links the original member states of ASEAN (Brunei, Indonesia, Malaysia, the Philippines, Singapore, Thailand, Myanmar, Cambodia, Laos, Vietnam) with China, Japan, and South Korea. The working languages of the OECD are English and French and the sole working language of ASEAN is English. As Schneider (2014: 251) points out regarding membership of ASEAN but which is equally applicable to the OECD, "it is absolutely clear that this situation [that is, being part of ASEAN] generates and further increases a huge demand for English – both in formal schooling and in a process of grassroots diffusion."

3.5 Sociodemographic Background

South Korea, a peninsula in the East Asian region, has a total population of circa 51,069,000 vis-à-vis 1,363,000 foreign nationals (data for 2015 from the Korean Statistical Information Service 2017) and has been described as a currently young but rapidly aging society (Howe et al. 2007). Manifold aspects are relevant for describing the sociodemographic background as a whole, particularly including both an extra- and intra-territorial perspective, but I will focus on three elements that are of notable relevance for the linguistic situation in Korea: urbanization, the higher education sector, and incoming and outgoing travel.

3.5.1 Urbanization

"[C]ities have always been extraordinary places" (Smakman and Heinrich 2018: 2) and urbanization is an important factor to be considered in describing sociolinguistic context. In cities, people "come into daily contact with strangers having different belief systems, behavioral norms, day-to-day rituals and linguistic practices, and they must somehow learn 'to get along' for the city to function" (Smakman and Heinrich 2018: 2). Despite having been generally described as a homogeneous country, cities play an important role in the Korean sociolinguistic ecology as well, as these urban contexts provide the most points of contact between Koreans and non-Koreans and thus also between the Korean and English languages. Urbanization, therefore, plays an influential role in facilitating language contact and in creating opportunities for English use. In this vein, it is important to know that Korea is an extremely urbanized country, as nearly 10 million (i.e. approximately a fifth) of its total population (51 million) live in Seoul (CIA The World Factbook 2016). Altogether, 25 million people live in the designated Seoul Capital Area, which includes cities and territory surrounding Seoul. With 85 percent of Korea's population living in the seven major cities of the country (Song 2012: 3), urbanization can indeed be classified as high. Living in an urban context is thus not an exception but the norm in Korea, and, in particular, the mobility between rural and urban areas and the resulting changes regarding encounters between different languages, including English, might be of high relevance for future studies of the linguistic situation in Korea.

3.5.2 Growth of the higher education sector

Over the last decades, the number of higher education institutions has grown considerably in Korea, from four universities in 1948 to 200 in 2005 (K. H. Lee 2007: 29). According to Kyu Hwan Lee (2007: 29), 70 percent of the relevant age group attended tertiary educational institutes by 2005; the permeability between high school and tertiary education is thus relatively high. Important here is that English is one of the subjects in the notorious Korean university entrance exam, *suneung*. This provides high impetus for the respective parts of the population in the attendance of after-school language institutes and cram schools. English clearly has a gatekeeping function in Korea, which is also attested to by the importance of English proficiency tests (e.g. the Test of English as a Foreign Language also known as TOEFL and the Test of English for International Communication also known as TOEIC) within Korean education and work settings. English test results, for example, are used to "determine employability but also benefits awarded and future promotion" (Yim 2007: 41). Interestingly, English proficiency tests are not only imported from outside Korea. The "home-grown" Test of English Proficiency (TEPS) was developed by Seoul National University and launched in 1999 (Test of English Proficiency by Seoul National University 2018).

Hand in hand with the growth of the higher education sector in South Korea, English-medium education in universities has been continually expanded (see, e.g., Lee 2010 on English-medium chemistry lectures in Korean universities). Kang (2012: 30) reports that "[u]niversity administrators have encouraged or mandated their faculty to use English exclusively in delivering lectures and interacting with students across different academic areas, ranging from humanities and social sciences to engineering and hard sciences." The expansion of English-medium university education has been received controversially and has also been heavily criticized by the media and other stakeholders (Cho 2012).

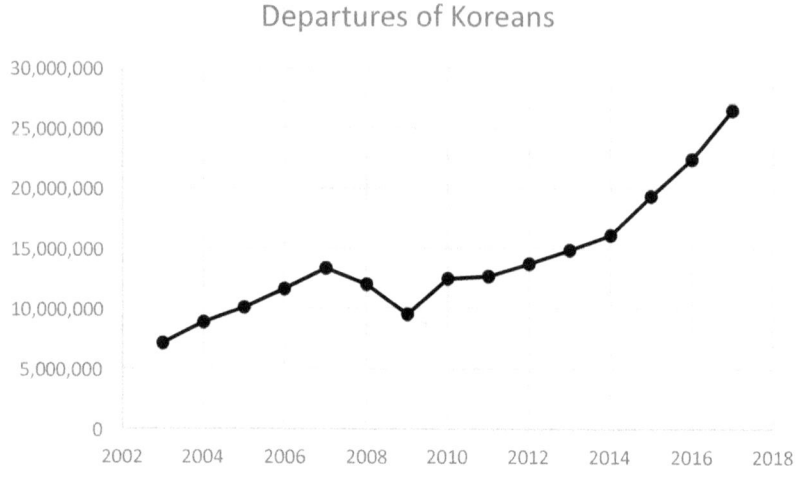

Figure 8.1 Departures of Koreans from Korea 2003–2017
Source: data from Korea Tourism Organization –
Departures of Koreans/Visitor Arrivals, n.d.

3.5.3 Incoming and outgoing mobility

Koreans go abroad in record numbers; in 2017, more than 26 million departures by Koreans were recorded by the Korea Tourism Organization. As can be seen in Figure 8.1, this follows a general trend of South Koreans being increasingly internationally mobile.

The number of arrivals by visitors has also been on a steady rise since 1997, with a particularly high peak in 2016. More than 13 million visits to Korea were recorded by the Korea Tourism Organization in 2017 – more than triple the visits recorded in 1997. The numbers in Figure 8.2 are an aggregate of tourism, business, official, and "other" reasons to visit Korea.

The numbers in Figure 8.2 also include visits by overseas Koreans. Despite detailed information on visitor nationalities available via the Korea Tourism Organization website, I have not analyzed these numbers at this point as we are still ignorant about language choices in specific intercultural encounters taking place in Korea. We do not know, for example, which language(s) is/are chosen in encounters between Japanese (who are among the most numerous visitors) and Korean people – Korean, Japanese, Chinese, and English

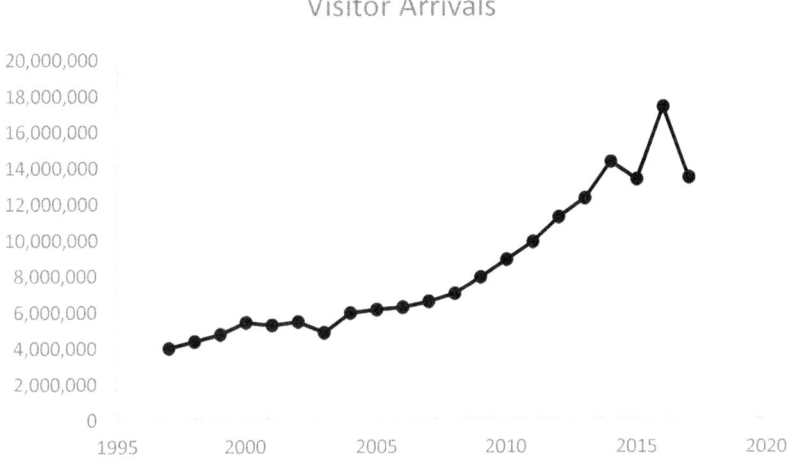

Figure 8.2 Visitor Arrivals in Korea 1997–2017
Source: data from Korea Tourism Organization –
Departures of Koreans/Visitor Arrivals, n.d.

are just the most obvious possible language choices. We do know, however, that this increase in mobility, both incoming and outgoing, constitutes a clear expansion of potential and actual language contact situations.

4. DISCUSSION

The intra- and extra-territorial forces interweave and are at times difficult to unravel clearly, particularly when it comes to globalization, language ideologies and attitudes, as well as language and foreign policies. Nevertheless, it is clearly advantageous for linguists to conceptualize these notions for different contexts. In the following, I propose to add yet another two factors which are of considerable importance to describe the Korean context (and potentially other contexts, too):

1. The presence of English in the linguistic landscape and the L1 (i.e. the Korean language).
2. *Hallyu* (i.e. the 'Korean Wave') as a network of cultural phenomena.

Presence of English in the Linguistic Landscape and the L1

Linguistic landscapes are only mentioned once and in passing in the original article on the EIF Model when the effect of language policies on the linguistic landscape of Scandinavian countries and France are mentioned as illustrating the effect (and power) of language policies (Buschfeld and Kautzsch 2017: 115). I argue that linguistic landscapes are an important instantiation of the intra-territorial side of language policies and attitudes and should therefore receive more attention. In Korea, substantial English use has been reported for signage in general (Lawrence 2012; Tan and Tan 2015). English thus often seems omnipresent, as one of Lee's elderly research participants stated: "Everywhere you go, you see English!" (2016: 332). In the case of shop signs, this can be related to market forces, albeit from within the country. Tan and Tan additionally observe that, in Korea, the use of English on shop signs serves indexical and symbolic, instead of informative, functions (2015: 77). English is thus a tool to sell a certain image and to brand the shop as well as its customers as modern and of high social standing (Tan and Tan 2015: 77).

Moreover, English is not only very visible on the streets (i.e. the linguistic landscape) but also in the Korean language itself. Despite evidence that Koreans themselves at times perceive the influx of English loan words as worrying (Rüdiger 2018), English loan words are very pervasive in Korean. In the 1990s, Sohn (1999: 118) reported that "the total number of current loan words [in Korean] is estimated at over 20,000, of which English occupies over 90%." Unfortunately, we lack more current numbers, but with increasing global mobility, pop culture, and political developments, the number of English loan words in Korea can be expected to have increased considerably since then. This means not only that even monolingual Koreans come into contact with English on a regular basis, but also that English is a part of mundane, everyday life. In the case of South Korea, we are urgently in need of more research on English loanwords, their use, and their pervasiveness, so we can more accurately consider the effects this has on the linguistic ecology within the country.

Cultural Phenomena: *Hallyu* – The Korean Wave

The term *Hallyu* (which translates as "Korean wave") refers to "the current impact of products specific to South Korean popular culture (films, music, games, fashion)" around the world (Marinescu 2014a:

2). The Korean wave first spread throughout Asia (e.g. China, Japan, Taiwan, see Yang 2012; Indonesia, see Nugroho 2014), then to diasporic Asian communities around the world (see, e.g., Park 2013), and is now a global phenomenon (see many of the contributions in Marinescu 2014b). In the early 2000s, Dator and Seo were still wondering whether this "fascination with Korea could be nothing more than a passing fad that has no special meaning at all" (2004: 34). At the time of writing this chapter (2018), however, the Korean wave has not only clearly outlived the status of a "passing fad" but has also entered a new evolutionary stage related to different patterns of spread due to social media: *Hallyu 2.0* (Lee and Nornes 2015) or the *New Korean Wave* (Jin 2016).

The remainder of this section focuses on one part of the *Hallyu* wave, K-pop and K-pop lyrics as both a linguistic phenomenon and a particular case in point illustrating the role of English in Korea. Even though English was virtually absent from the Korean music scene until the 1990s (Lee 2004: 429), a high presence of English in choruses, intros, and titles of K-pop songs (the 2012 hit song *Gangnam Style* by Psy serves as an excellent example) has been attested for more recent musical releases (Lawrence 2010: 42).[4] Several reasons for the use of English across Korean pop music have been proposed: English can be used to challenge authority and serves as a form of resistance and self-assertion in an otherwise hierarchical and at times rather conservative society (Lee 2004: 446); English lexical items are also employed for euphemism (Lawrence 2010: 49); and, last but not least, English is creatively and playfully used for verbal art, rhythm, and rhyming (Lawrence 2010: 49, 51, 55). Interestingly, different Englishes have thus found their way into Korean lyrics. Jamie Shinhee Lee (2006, 2007), for example, observed the use of African American Vernacular English, "Standard English," and Koreanized English.

These uses of English seem, at first sight, to be an intra-territorial force which is at work in the Korean context: the use of English by Korean artists leads to English consumption by Koreans who listen to the music and perpetuates the status of English as a global language. I argue, however, that this can be related to reciprocal effects of both an intra- and extra-territorial nature. The global success of K-pop has led to a "commercial imperative" (Jin and Ryoo 2014: 129) for many K-pop artists to also address the American and international music market. One way of doing this is to use English. Thus, this "commercial imperative" enters

---

[4] An observation which is not without exception, of course.

the Korean context from the outside, that is, as an extra-territorial force, as if the *Hallyu* wave has hit a physical object and is now swashing back.

The market forces at play here can be illustrated with one of the most recent K-pop success stories, BTS. BTS is a South Korean boy band with seven members which has been extremely successful globally and particularly in the United States. BTS is an acronym for **Bangtan Sonyeondan** (in the Korean alphabet, Hangul: 방탄소년단) which translates to "Bulletproof Boy Scouts." In 2017, the group changed its brand image and announced that the acronym from now on would also stand for "Beyond the Scene." The acquisition of an additional English language resolution to the acronym (which did not work for the band's translated name, cf. "Bulletproof Boy Scouts" resulting rather in BBS but not BTS), reflects the expansion of the target audience of Korean pop music and can be related to external market forces influencing the branding of the group (for a similar phenomenon, see the notion of commodification as addressed by Wee, Chapter 6 this volume).

Sophisticated language strategies in adaptation to target markets are nothing new in the South Korean music business and, it should be mentioned, are not always concerned with the English language. For example, the K-pop band Exo, formed in 2011, temporarily split up into two sub-groups: Exo-K and Exo-M (Wikipedia – Exo (band) 2018), with Exo-K performing and releasing songs in Korean and Exo-M doing so in Mandarin. (Pop) cultural phenomena such as the ones described in this section are hence an important factor in the linguistic ecology of specific contexts and particularly large-scale phenomena such as *Hallyu* should be treated with the amount of attention that they deserve. Therefore, I propose that aspects related to popular culture should have a fixed place in the EIF Model and should be included regularly in the description of varieties in specific contexts.

5. CONCLUSION

As this chapter has shown, applying the EIF Model to South Korea is indeed a very productive undertaking. The overview of extra- and intra-territorial forces has provided evidence that English has become a fixed part of the linguistic ecology in Korea. Some factors, such as the establishment of a US interim military government in the 1940s as well as the extreme orientation towards the English language (known as 'English Fever'), may constitute particularly important characteristics to be considered here. Several studies into Korean English forms additionally indicate that localized features have developed or are currently developing on different levels of language (see Jung and Min 1999; Shim 1999; Hadikin 2014; Rüdiger 2017, 2019). Combining this with the evidence from the EIF analysis (see also the appendix for a succinct overview), I therefore propose to place South Korea between the stabilization phase (phase 2) and nativization phase (phase 3) of the EIF Model.

Applying the EIF Model as has been done in this chapter also shows quite plainly in which areas further research is most urgently needed. In the case of South Korea, these are the areas of language attitudes, English loan words within the Korean language, and in-depth studies of the connection between pop-cultural and linguistic phenomena. It would also be extremely insightful and fruitful to dig deeper into what happened during and shortly after the interim US government as a very incisive and formative event in recent Korean history, and the effect this had on linguistic features, language attitudes, and language ideologies. Here, it is sensible to follow the call by Brato (Chapter 17 this volume) for more rigor in the investigation of historical demographic backgrounds.

Appendix 8.1: Extra- and Intra-Territorial Forces Pertaining to the Korean Context – Overview

Type of force	Force	Application to the Korean context
Extra-territorial force	1) colonization	• N/A (but: US Military Government in Korea for three years after World War II and current deployment of American soldiers to Korea)
	2) language policies	• TOEFL (Test of English as a Foreign Language) and TOEIC (Test of English for International Communication) as widely used proficiency tests
	3) globalization	• modern media accessible via the internet • American and other western pop culture and movies • cultural phenomena (particularly *Hallyu* and related market forces) • bilateral economic relations between the United States and South Korea (free trade agreement); global trade relationships, free trade agreement with the EU • popularity of study and work-abroad programs • South Korea as member of ASEAN+3 and OECD

Appendix 8.1: (*continued*)

Type of force	Force	Application to the Korean context
	4) foreign policies	• extensive relations between Korea and the United States starting after World War II (due to American support in the Korean War against North Korea) • deployment of American soldiers to Korea as part of a military alliance
	5) socio-demographic background	• tourism from other countries • returnees from Korean migrant communities abroad
Intra-territorial force	1) attitudes towards colonizing power	• N/A (but: acceptance of American presence in Korea vis-à-vis flares of anti-American sentiments)
	2) language attitudes/ language policies	• EPIK (English Program in Korea) → hegemony of native speaker teachers • English mandatory subject in school starting in grade 3 • official education policy: English education in English • public discussion of English as (co-)official language • English as subject in the university entrance exam • tremendous demand for private English education; "English Fever" • Test of English Proficiency (TEPS) developed by Seoul National University • presence of English in the linguistic landscape and the L1 • English as status symbol • ideologies of necessitation, externalization, and self-deprecation
	3) attitudes towards globalization	• active promotion of globalization via the government • unrestricted access to modern media via the internet
	4) foreign policies	• military alliance with the United States
	5) socio-demographic background	• c. 1,363,000 foreign nationals residing in Korea vis-à-vis a total population of c. 51,069,000 • currently a young but rapidly aging society • Korean tourism around the world

REFERENCES

Ahn, Hyejeong. 2014. Teachers' attitudes towards Korean English in South Korea. *World Englishes* 33.2: 195–222.

Ahn, Hyejeong. 2017. *Attitudes to World Englishes: Implications for Teaching English in South Korea*. Abingdon and New York: Routledge.

Algeo, John T. 1960. Korean Bamboo English. *American Speech* 35.2: 117–123.

Borges, Jorge Luis. 1999. *Selected Non-Fiction*. In Eliot Weinberger, ed. 1999. New York and London: Viking (translated by Esther Allen, Suzanne Jill Levine and Eliot Weinberger).

Buschfeld, Sarah. 2013. *English in Cyprus or Cyprus English: An Empirical Investigation of Variety Status*. Amsterdam and Philadelphia: John Benjamins.

Buschfeld, Sarah and Kautzsch, Alexander. 2017. Towards an integrated approach to postcolonial and non-postcolonial Englishes. *World Englishes* 36.1: 104–126.

Cho, Jinhyun. 2012. Campus in English or campus in shock? Korean students hit hard by English-medium lectures. *English Today* 28.2: 18–25.

Cho, Jinhyun. 2017. *English Language Ideologies in Korea: Interpreting the Past and Present*. Cham: Springer.

CIA The World Factbook. Korea, South. 2016, https://www.cia.gov/library/publications/the-world-factbook/geos/ks.html (last accessed December 19, 2016).

Dator, Jim and Yongseok Seo. 2004. Korea as the wave of a future: The emerging dream society of icons and aesthetic experience. *Journal of Futures Studies* 9.1: 31–44.

Duk, Yi Jeong. 2005. Globalization and recent changes to daily life in the Republic of Korea. In James Lewis and Amadu Sesay, eds. 2005, *Korean and Globalization – Politics, Economics and Culture*. Abingdon: Routledge Curzon, 10–35.

Duke, Charles R. 1970. The Bamboo style of English. *College Composition and Communication* 21.2: 170–172.

Edwards, Alison. 2016. *English in the Netherlands: Functions, Forms and Attitudes*. Amsterdam and Philadelphia: John Benjamins.

EPIK. 2013. EPIK (English Program in Korea), http://www.epik.go.kr/index.do (last accessed September 9, 2018).

Görlach, Manfred. 1990. *Studies in the History of the English Language*. Heidelberg: Winter.

Hadikin, Glenn S. 2014. *Korean English: A Corpus-Driven Study of a New English*. Amsterdam and Philadelphia: John Benjamins.

Hayes, Louis D. 2012. *Political Systems of East Asia: China, Korea, and Japan*. New York and London: M. E. Sharpe.

Howe, Neil, Richard Jackson and Keisuke Nakashima. 2007. The aging of Korea: Demographics and retirement policy in the land of the morning calm. *Center for Strategic and International Studies*, https://csis-prod.s3.amazonaws.com/s3fs-public/.../070321_gai_aging korea_eng.pdf (last accessed February 15, 2017).

Jeon, Mihyon. 2012. English immersion and educational inequality in South Korea. *Journal of Multilingual and Multicultural Development* 33.4: 395–408.

Jin, Dal Yong. 2016. *New Korean Wave – Transnational Cultural Power in the Age of Social Media*. Urbana/Chicago/Springfield: University of Illinois Press.

Jin, Dal Yong and Woongjae Ryoo. 2014. Critical interpretation of hybrid K-Pop: The global-local paradigm of English mixing in lyrics. *Popular Music and Society* 37.2: 113–131.

Jung, Kyutae and Su J. Min. 1999. Some lexico-grammatical features of Korean English newspapers. *World Englishes* 18.1: 23–37.

Kachru, Braj B. 1985. Standards, codification and sociolinguistic realism: The English language in the Outer Circle. In Randolph Quirk and Henry G. Widdowson, eds. 1985, *English in the World: Teaching and Learning the Language and Literatures*. Cambridge: Cambridge University Press, 11–30.

Kang, Hyun-Sook. 2012. English-only instruction at Korean universities: Help or hindrance to higher learning? *English Today* 28.1: 29–34.

Kihl, Young Whan. 2005. *Transforming Korean Politics – Democracy, Reform, and Culture*. New York and London: M. E. Sharpe.

Kim, Eun Gyong. 2011. English educational policies of the U.S. Army Military Government in Korea from 1945 to 1948 and their effects on the development of English language teaching in Korea. *Language Policy* 10.3: 193–220.

Kim, Eun Mee. 2000. Globalization of the South Korean *Chaebol*. In Samuel S. Kim, ed. 2000, *Korea's Globalization*. Cambridge: Cambridge University Press, 102–125.

Kim, Samuel S. 2003. Korea's democratization in the global-local nexus. In Samuel S. Kim, ed. 2003, *Korea's Democratization*. Cambridge: Cambridge University Press, 3–44.

Kong, Tat Yan. 2000. *The Politics of Economic Reform in South Korea: A Fragile Miracle*. London and New York: Routledge.
Korea Tourism Organization – Departures of Koreans/Visitor Arrivals, https://kto.visitkorea.or.kr/eng/tourismStatics/keyFacts/KoreaMonthlyStatistics/eng/inout/inout.kto (last accessed July 31, 2018).
Korean Statistical Information Service. 2017. Statistical database: Population, households and housing units, http://kosis.kr/eng/statisticsList/statisticsList_01List.jsp?vwcd= MT_ETITLE&parentId =A#SubCont (last accessed February 15, 2017).
Kwak, Kwang S. 2006. The US-ROK Alliance, 1953–2004: Alliance Institutionalization. PhD Dissertation, Southern Illinois University Carbondale.
Lawrence, Bruce C. 2010. The verbal art of borrowing: Analysis of English borrowing in Korean pop songs. *Asian Englishes* 13.2: 42–63.
Lawrence, Bruce C. 2012. The Korean English linguistic landscape. *World Englishes* 31.1: 70–92.
Lee, Jae-seung. 2010. Offering English-mediated chemistry classes in South Korea: A note on this nationwide experiment. *Journal of Chemical Education* 87.5: 470–471.
Lee, Jamie S. 2004. Linguistic hybridization in K-Pop: Discourse of self-assertion and resistance. *World Englishes* 23.3: 429–450.
Lee, Jamie S. 2006. *Crossing* and *crossers* in East Asian pop music: Korea and Japan. *World Englishes* 25.2: 235–250.
Lee, Jamie S. 2007. *I'm the illest fucka*: An analysis of African American English in South Korean hip hop. *English Today* 23.2: 54–60.
Lee, Jamie S. 2016. "Everywhere you go, you see English!" Elderly women's perspective on globalization and English. *Critical Inquiry in Language Studies* 14.4: 319–350.
Lee, Kyu Hwan. 2007. Changing higher education reform policy in South Korea and the idea of the university. *Bildung und Erziehung* 60.1: 21–37.
Lee, Sangjoon and Abé Mark Nornes, eds. 2015. *Hallyu 2.0 – The Korean Wave in the Age of Social Media*. Ann Arbor: University of Michigan Press.
Lee, You-il and Kyung Tae Lee. 2015. Economic nationalism and globalization in South Korea: A critical insight. *Asian Perspective* 39.1: 125–151.
McArthur, Tom. 1987. The English languages? *English Today* 3.3: 9–13.

McTague, Mark J. 1990. A Sociolinguistic Description of Attitudes to and Usage of English by Adult Korean Employees of Major Korean Corporations in Seoul. PhD dissertation, University of Texas at Austin.

Mair, Christian. 2013. The World System of Englishes: Accounting for the transnational importance of mobile and mediated vernaculars. *English World-Wide* 34.3: 253–278.

Marinescu, Valentina. 2014a. Many faces of *Hallyu* in the global world. In Valentina Marinescu, ed. 2014, *The Global Impact of South Korean Popular Culture – Hallyu Unbound*. Lanham/Boulder/New York/London: Lexington Books, 1–4.

Marinescu, Valentina, ed. 2014b. *The Global Impact of South Korean Popular Culture – Hallyu Unbound*. Lanham/Boulder/New York/London: Lexington Books.

Meierkord, Christiane. 2012. *Interactions Across Englishes: Linguistic Choices in Local and International Contact Situations*. Cambridge: Cambridge University Press.

Mimiko, Nahzeem Oluwafemi. 2005. From insularity to Segyehwa: The political economy of globalization in Korea. In James Lewis and Amadu Sesay, eds. 2005, *Korean and Globalization – Politics, Economics and Culture*. Abingdon: Routledge Curzon, 61–78.

Moon, Katharine H. S. 2003. Korean nationalism, anti-Americanism, and democratic consolidation. In Samuel S. Kim, ed. 2003, *Korea's Democratization*. Cambridge: Cambridge University Press, 135–157.

Nugroho, Suray Agung. 2014. *Hallyu* in Indonesia. In Valentina Marinescu, ed. 2014, 19–32.

OECD. 2018. Korea and the OECD, http://www.oecd.org/korea/korea-and-the-oecd.htm (last accessed September 13, 2018).

Onysko, Alexander. 2016. Modeling World Englishes from the perspective of language contact. *World Englishes* 35.2: 196–220.

Park, Jin-Kyu. 2009. 'English Fever' in South Korea: Its history and symptoms. *English Today* 25.1: 50–57.

Park, Joseph Sung-Yul. 2009. *The Local Construction of a Global Language: Ideologies of English in South Korea*. Berlin and New York: Mouton de Gruyter.

Park, Jung-Sun. 2013. Negotiating identity and power in transnational cultural consumption: Korean American youths and the Korean Wave. In Youna Kim, ed. 2013, *The Korean Wave – Korean Media Go Global*. London and New York: Routledge, 120–134.

Rüdiger, Sofia. 2017. Spoken English in Korea: An Expanding Circle English revisited. In Christopher J. Jenks and Jerry Won Lee, eds. 2017, *Korean Englishes in Transnational Contexts*. Cham: Palgrave Macmillan, 75–92.

Rüdiger, Sofia. 2018. Mixed feelings: Attitudes towards English loanwords and their use in South Korea. *Open Linguistics* 4.1: 184–198.

Rüdiger, Sofia. 2019. *Morpho-Syntactic Patterns in Spoken Korean English*. Amsterdam and Philadelphia: John Benjamins.

Schneider, Edgar W. 2003. The dynamics of New Englishes: From identity construction to dialect birth. *Language* 79.2: 233–281.

Schneider, Edgar W. 2007. *Postcolonial English: Varieties Around the World*. Cambridge: Cambridge University Press.

Schneider, Edgar W. 2014. Asian Englishes – Into the future: A bird's eye view. *Asian Englishes* 16.3: 249–256.

Seol, Dong-Hoon. 2013. Mobilizing public opinion for/against foreign labor policies in Korea, 1995–2005: NGOs, trade unions, and employers' association in contested terrain. In Hee-Yeon Cho, Lawrence Surendra and Hyo-Je Cho, eds. 2013, *Contemporary South Korean Society – A Critical Perspective*. London: Routledge, 209–220.

Seth, Michael J. 2016. *A Concise History of Korea – From Antiquity to the Present*. 2nd edn. Lanham, MD: Rowman & Littlefield.

Shim, Rosa J. 1999. Codified Korean English: Process, characteristics and consequence. *World Englishes* 18.2: 247–258.

Shin, Doh C. 1999. *Mass Politics and Culture in Democratizing Korea*. Cambridge: Cambridge University Press.

Sikorski, Douglas J. 2004. Global capitalism and the Asian financial crisis. In John A. Turner and Young-Chan Kim, eds. 2004, *Globalisation and Korean Foreign Investment*. Aldershot and Burlington, VT: Ashgate Publishing, 60–80.

Smakman, Dick and Patrick Heinrich. 2018. Introduction: Why cities matter for a globalising sociolinguistics. In Dick Smakman and Patrick Heinrich, eds. 2018, *Urban Sociolinguistics – The City as a Linguistic Process and Experience*. London and New York: Routledge, 1–11.

Sohn, Ho-Min. 1999. *The Korean Language*. Cambridge: Cambridge University Press.

Song, Byung-nak. 2003. *The Rise of the Korean Economy*. 3rd edn. Oxford: Oxford University Press.

Song, Jae J. 2011. English as an official language in South Korea: Global English or social malady? *Language Problems & Language Planning* 35.1: 35–55.

Song, Jae J. 2012. South Korea: Language policy and planning in the making. *Current Issues in Language Planning* 13.1: 1–68.

Steinberg, David I., ed. 2005. *Korean Attitudes Toward the United States: Changing Dynamics*. New York and London: M. E. Sharpe.

Strang, Barbara M. H. 1970. *A History of English*. London: Methuen & Co Ltd.

Tan, Shanna X.-W. and Ying-Ying Tan. 2015. Examining the functions and identities associated with English and Korean in South Korea: A linguistic landscape study. *Asian Englishes* 17.1: 59–79.

Test of English Proficiency by Seoul National University. 2018. About TEPS, http://en.teps.or.kr/about_teps.html (last accessed September 26, 2018).

Webster, Grant. 1960. Korean Bamboo English once more. *American Speech* 35.4: 261–265.

Wikipedia – Exo (band). 2018, https://en.wikipedia.org/wiki/Exo_(band) (last accessed June 5, 2018).

Yang, Jonghoe. 2012. The Korean Wave (Hallyu) in East Asia: A comparison of Chinese, Japanese, and Taiwanese audiences who watch Korean TV dramas. *Development and Society* 41.1: 103–147.

Yim, Sungwon. 2007. Globalization and language policy in South Korea. In Amy B. M. Tsui and James W. Tollefson, eds. 2007, *Language Policy, Culture, and Identity in Asian Contexts*. Mahwah, NJ: Lawrence Erlbaum Associates, 37–53.

Yoo, Ok Kyoon. 2005. Discourses of English as an official language in a monolingual society: The case of South Korea. *Second Language Studies* 23.2: 1–44.

CHAPTER 9

English in Japan: The Applicability of the EIF Model

Saya Ike and James D'Angelo

1. INTRODUCTION[1]

Since its first configuration in the mid-1980s, the world Englishes (WE) paradigm (Kachru 1985) has been of significant use in helping scholars to understand the differences in English varieties viewed from a historico-political lens and has fostered an appreciation for the diversity and pluricentricity of English today. The paradigm was further strengthened by the work of Schneider (2007) which helped to account for the dynamic and ongoing process of varietal development and change. Yet these models have been called into question (e.g. Seidlhofer 2001; Bruthiaux 2003; D'Angelo 2008, 2013; Seargeant and Tagg 2011) for their perhaps excessive focus on describing varieties of English and their lack of accounting for the mushrooming use of English in non-postcolonial settings of the Expanding Circle. The EIF Model, as proposed by Buschfeld and Kautzsch (2017), addresses these concerns and can make an important contribution by providing new ways of looking at varieties, while at the same time accounting for the complex use of English in the ever-shifting speech communities of the twenty-first century. This chapter considers the case of Japan and its historical involvement with English from the point of earliest contact and analyzes the subsequent development of Japanese English to the present day. It presents a careful discussion of applying Buschfeld and Kautzsch's EIF Model to Japan, both from the viewpoint of Schneider's original

---

[1] We are deeply indebted to Jean Mulder for most helpful and insightful comments on an earlier draft of this chapter.

model, and the enhanced perspective offered by the EIF Model. Finally, the chapter investigates possible advantages of – and points that need further definition in – developing the EIF Model and its theoretical contribution to the field.

2. Issues with the Dynamic Model

Buschfeld and Kautzsch (this volume) thoroughly outline Schneider's Dynamic Model (2003, 2007). This section highlights essential parameters of the model which are especially pertinent to our discussion of the Japan context and discusses issues with applying the Dynamic Model to non-PCE settings.

In the Dynamic Model, the analysis of each of the five phases (foundation through differentiation) is framed within four key parameters. These are: (1) extra-linguistic factors (e.g. the historical and political development of the country), (2) characteristic identity constructions (e.g. factors which change the population's concept of their own identity), (3) sociolinguistic determinants of the contact situation (e.g. conditions of language contact, language attitudes, and use), and (4) structural effects (e.g. the development of lexical, phonological, and grammatical characteristics). In addition, Schneider (2003, 2007) claims that an "Event X" is crucial in identity construction development.

There have been several attempts to analyze Expanding Circle Englishes from a Dynamic Model perspective (M. Ike 1995; S. Ike 2012, 2014; Schneider 2014), but none seems to have succeeded thus far. As discussed in the Introduction to this volume by Buschfeld and Kautzsch, the main problems are the settler strand (STL) and Event X. In the case of Japan, there is evidence of linguistic contact, various political and sociolinguistic aspects of variety development, and a range of domains of English use, but as Japan has never been formally colonized, there is no settler strand that develops a sense of locally based identity after an Event X. In other words, Japan, too, lacks a necessary STL element for English variety development as proposed in Schneider's model (with regard to postcolonial settings); thus, the Dynamic Model is difficult to fully adopt in analyzing the Japanese context.

It does not mean, however, that variety development does not exist in Japan; rather, the introduction of English in non-PCE settings is quite different to that in PCE settings (Buschfeld and Kautzsch, Introduction to this volume), and the spread of English to the Expanding Circle is the spread of the English language, not of English speakers (Mesthrie and Bhatt 2008). Although it has been observed that attitudes towards their own English are at times highly negative (e.g. Chiba et al. 1995; McKenzie 2008a), and Japanese people do not seem to claim ownership of English (e.g. S. Ike 2012), studies indicate gradual attitude changes in educational settings as well as distinctiveness of English in Japan (e.g. Fujiwara 2012; S. Ike 2012). This too argues for a new model that accounts for the growing use of English in the Expanding Circle.

Schneider himself acknowledges the weakness of the Dynamic Model and has coined the term "transnational attraction" to account for the global boom of English in such contexts as East Asia or Continental Europe (Schneider 2014). Meanwhile, to substitute for the missing colonization factor in the foundation phase, Edwards (2016) suggests that worldwide globalization may trigger its start. Globalization in Japan today is evident in countless aspects, such as the growth of incoming tourism, a steadily increasing number of international businesses, and widespread use of the internet and social networking services (SNS). Inevitably, these affect the decisions by Japan's language policymakers (such as to steadily introduce English into lower levels of primary education), which then affect English education, the status of English in various domains, and language services for both tourists and local non-Japanese residents. However, as discussed in section 3.1, Japan seems to have experienced a form of foundation phase in the 1800s, whereby the forced "opening" of the country by Commodore Perry's Black Ships clearly marked the start of globalization for Japan.

Buschfeld and Kautzsch go on to stress that a more worked-out conceptualization which takes into account phenomena such as the above-mentioned transnational attraction, is needed, and hence propose their EIF Model. This model maintains the five phases of the Dynamic Model, both for postcolonial (PCE) and non-postcolonial (non-PCE) contexts. It does, however, add question marks for phases four and five in the non-PCE column. There are also minor changes to terminology, such as phase 2 simply being named "stabilization" rather than "exonormative stabilization" for the non-PCE strand. The model presents the phases as moving vertically along a timeline, with foundation at the bottom. The sequencing of this timeline is an issue for the Japanese context which is addressed in the following sections. We should also note that the EIF Model introduces the designation "EFL," "ESL," and "ENL" to the side of foundation, nativization, and differentiation phases, although ENL may not be relevant for non-PCE contexts, since a differentiation phase in non-PCE contexts is yet to be seen. Unlike the timeline, these designations are presented with bi-directional arrows, indicating that a context could possibly regress in some way to an earlier phase. Finally, one can also see extra- and intra-territorial forces impacting/influencing the phases from both sides as well as the bottom. Although still included in the figure, the four parameters are not explicitly addressed in the EIF Model. We discuss below areas where the parameters could be of use in analyzing the case of Japan.

In addition to the globalization trend, the EIF Model illustrates possible forces – both extra- and intra-territorial. Regarding the specifics of the all-important extra- and intra-territorial forces (which provide the main enhancement to the Dynamic Model), two forces ("sociodemographic background" and "foreign policies") are given the same title in both the extra- and intra-territorial columns, but three other forces are slightly modified: "attitudes towards colonizing power" is used rather than simply "colonization," "language attitudes" is added to "language policies," and "acceptance of globalization" is used rather than just "globalization." It can also be seen that colonization is neither an extra- nor an intra-territorial force in non-PCE contexts. A consideration of the relevance and usefulness of these forces is the main focus of the following section.

3. TESTING THE EIF MODEL: THE CASE OF JAPAN

The EIF Model is designed to identify factors that contribute to the development of an English variety in both PCE and non-PCE (Expanding Circle) settings. Thus, here we test the model with Japanese English as a case study, starting with a brief history of English in Japan.

3.1 Historical Review of English in Japan

It is said that the first contact with English in Japan was in 1603, and English was briefly used for trading purposes with Britain before Japan prohibited international trading (with the exception of China and Holland) and closed the country in 1639 (Takanashi and Ohmura 1975). There is some extant evidence to tell us that a few people attempted to learn or study English around that time, but there were no institutions for systematic English education (Tajima 2001; Koscielecki 2006), and, linguistically, there is no record of any emergence of loanwords (Loveday 1996). The need for English arose again in 1808 when a British battleship (HMS *Phaeton*) came and stole supplies at Nagasaki, one of the two main trading ports open only for China and Holland. Thus, it can be argued that this incident was an extra-territorial force which triggered the Shogunate to reconsider its defense plan, and to order state interpreters to learn English (Takanashi and Ohmura 1975; Loveday 1996; Stanlaw 2004). However, the need for English and exposure to it was highly limited since Japan remained closed and isolated (Saito 2001). In 1853, an American commodore Matthew Calbraith Perry came to Japan and Japan finally opened its doors to international trading in 1858, resulting in the first major contact with English (McKenzie 2008a). Both Perry's arrival and the subsequent opening of the country can be taken as influential extra-territorial forces. Although Japan was never colonized and thus English was not introduced as the language of power, the introduction of English is clearly traceable, and it is safe to say that the foundation phase began in the mid-nineteenth century.

There were also a number of sociolinguistic factors (both extra- and intra-territorial) which contributed to the spread of English in Japan. Since there were no English-Japanese interpreters at the time, the Convention of Kanagawa (Kanagawa Treaty) was first translated from English to Dutch by an American, and then from Dutch to Japanese, causing some confusion and leaving Japan at a disadvantage in the trade agreement (Oda 2000; Stanlaw 2004). English became an urgent necessity for the government in terms of foreign policy and international relations. In the early Meiji period, which began in 1868, almost all higher education, including subjects such as English literature and history, were taught by L1 English-speaking teachers in English (Takanashi and Ohmura 1975; Ohta 1981; Butler 2007b). Ohta (1981) also states that even Japanese teachers used English as a means of instruction in this period. English was an absolute necessity for those elites who wished to study any specific subject, and learning English meant gaining advanced western knowledge in order to "catch up with" those advanced countries, especially Britain. In fact, Takanashi and Ohmura (1975) state that students had to graduate from Tokyo English School, one of the English conversation schools at the time, in order to enter university. Furthermore, it is reported that there were seven national English schools and more than 1,000 private English schools in the Tokyo area alone in 1873 (Saito 2001), and that most of the language institutions had

L1 English-speaking teachers and used American textbooks (Takanashi and Ohmura 1975). Not only has this state of affairs been described as semi-colonization (e.g. Takanashi and Ohmura 1975; Ohta 1981; Imura 2003), but it can also be argued that English possessed a certain political power, as Arinori Mori – a later Japanese minister of education – suggested that Japan needed to consider English as an official language. Mori claimed that the Japanese language lacked communication ability without the help of Chinese elements, predicting that English would inundate Japanese when Japan took in western culture (Mori and Ohkubo 1972). This shows that there were strong extra- and intra-territorial forces for the development of Japanese English, leading it to the second phase of stabilization.

Meanwhile, as Yokohama opened as one of the main ports, there was another domain for English use among traders, resulting in the emergence and development of pidgin varieties of both Japanese and English (Kodama and Kodama 1979; Ohta 1981). Thus, there were mainly two domains for English use, one on the street for international business and day-to-day interactions, and the other within educational institutions for the purpose of higher-stake international relations, with both working as intra-territorial forces. The modified EIF Model (Buschfeld et al. 2018) works particularly well in describing these two domains, as it shows both the idiolectal and abstract level in the model (English through formal education and English pidgins through trading), and contact between the two languages, as well as the two groups of people (i.e. elites and traders), can be traced.

In terms of linguistic development, English was used not only in street signs, but also in books for the public. This is where loanword usage started, with semantic shift, broadening, and narrowing, evident in publications from this period. For example, Saito (2001) and Ohta (1981) show code-mixing examples in Japanese comical poetry (*Dodoitsu*) where many English words were used but not necessarily with the same meaning. Also, in an effort to integrate English into Japanese, English words (loanwords) were written in Japanese characters, although often they were pronounced quite differently (Honna 1995, 2008; McArthur 2003; Stanlaw 2004). By the late Meiji period (around 1900), more and more ordinary people were becoming familiar with English. Arakawa's dictionary was published in 1931, with 5,018 entries of "Japanized English" (Loveday 1996), indicating English nativization in Japan. This suggests that there was some innovative use of English in the Japanese context, functioning not only as an intra-territorial force but also to some extent as an extra-territorial force since the primary motivation for using English was communicating with non-Japanese. Such linguistic development can be seen as leading to the next phase of variety development.

Nevertheless, when the Meiji civilization came to an end, English lost its role as a means of gaining western knowledge (Imura 2003). Moreover, in part as a reaction to the westernization of the early Meiji period, nationalism emerged and gradually gained support (Saito 2007). A national education system was implemented in 1872 and, in the following years, educated Japanese people started to become teachers at higher educational institutions. Tokyo University changed its medium of instruction to Japanese in 1863, and in 1877 five of the seven national English schools were closed (Ohta 1981; Saito 2001). Even in the remaining two national English schools, only two out of twenty-eight teachers were L1 English speakers (Ohta 1981). In 1886, the first Minister of Education, Arinori Mori, declared Japanese to be the medium of instruction (Imura 2003), and the need for English decreased considerably. The number of foreign teachers decreased from 503 in 1872 to 77 in 1896 (Imura 2003), reflecting the nationalistic movement in Japan at the time. At this point, the status of English changed from a practical communication skill to merely a subject. Saito (2001) observes that the learning of English was framed as the study of English literature and linguistics, creating controversy over "practical English" and "educational English." This period of Japanese nationalism continued throughout the ensuing war period, which started with the First Sino-Japanese War (1894–1895) and the Russo–Japanese War (1904–1905). Overall, the nationalistic movement can be assessed as a counter-intra-territorial force that arrested English variety development in Japan. Importantly, the bi-directional arrows in the EIF Model nicely account for this type of event.

Moreover, nationalism led to setting up a standard Japanese language from 1902 to 1916, along with the unification of the written and spoken language (*genbun itchi undō*) (Carroll 2000). In 1939, names of foreign countries were changed into Chinese characters in the press, and the amount of new English borrowing significantly declined (Loveday 1996). When Japan entered World War II and England and America became enemies in 1941, there was yet another strong nationalistic movement and almost all English words disappeared both from written signs and spoken conversations, with directly translated Japanese words being substituted (Ohta 1981; Loveday 1996; Saito 2001). However, English did remain as a subject in school education throughout the war period (M. Ike 1995; Imura 2003; Erikawa 2008). This demonstrates that political and sociolinguistic circumstances, both acting as counter-forces, prevented steady varietal development, resulting in Japan remaining in the early stabilization phase until the end of World War II.

Political and sociolinguistic factors dramatically changed between 1945 and 1952 while the US General Headquarters (GHQ) briefly occupied Japan. English was no longer the enemy's language but a means of survival. Loveday (1996) notes that there were as many as 500,000 American troops stationed in Japan at the time, and people all over Japan, including children and ordinary citizens, used English during the post-war period to ask for food (Ohta 1981). As the contexts for English use expanded, once again pidginized varieties of English appeared, which were different from the earlier ones used in Yokohama (Loveday 1996; Stanlaw 2004). This period can be viewed as a new era of globalization for Japan, shifting its foreign and language policies outwards again. Language restrictions no longer existed, and the education system underwent a major reformation. Nine years of compulsory education began in 1947, and a greater number of people started receiving formal English education in grade 7. However, there were significantly fewer L1 English speakers in Japan after the end of the occupation, providing much fewer opportunities for interaction. This contributed to the disappearance of pidginized varieties, and the remaining English education focused on reading and writing abilities (Saito 2001). In short, the GHQ occupation was a strong extra-territorial force, and the following educational reformation was a strong intra-territorial force in reaction to it; but the GHQ occupation only remained influential for a short period of time. Nonetheless, English words (loanwords) reappeared to a greater extent in the streets and in publications, especially in the 1960s and 1970s (Hashimoto 2006). Conversational English textbooks became bestsellers and English education programs were broadcast, attracting a large number of people (Loveday 1996; Saito 2001, 2007).

In post-war Japan, intra-territorial forces such as education policy and sociodemographic factors were present, yet were remarkably weaker compared to some earlier periods. However, it should be noted that general attitudes towards English were positive, and citizens became increasingly attracted to English and its accompanying globalization.

3.2 Japan in Modern Days

In modern days, with ever-increasing globalization, the need for English continues to grow, and the motivation for learning English has transmuted from that of survival to economic success and local interaction. Extra attention is paid in this section to identifying each force.

3.2.1 Language policies

A proposal for introducing English as an official language was brought up again by Prime Minister Keizo Obuchi in 2000. Although the proposal was rejected, an increasing number of companies have given English official status for intra-business communication in recent years. One of the earliest companies to do so was the major electronics component maker Sumida Corporation, which made English an official language as early as 1999 (Yoshihara et al. 2001). In 2010, a Japanese electronic commerce and internet company Rakuten, with more than 20 million customers worldwide, announced that English would be used for all communication, triggering nationwide controversy. International retail company Fast Retailing (known for its fashion brand UNIQLO), with over 1,000 branches overseas, introduced English as an official language for all internal meetings in Japan in 2012 (cf. Kim 2017).

In educational settings, the movement is even stronger with the government's support (MEXT 2011, 2014; also see Murata et al. 2018), and some universities have introduced English as a medium of instruction (EMI) again. Kojima (2016) notes that the number of universities which employ EMI increased from seven (eight departments) in 2008 to nineteen (thirty-eight departments) in 2013. If partial EMI programs are included, the number accounts for 36 percent of all the courses available in Japan in 2013 (Kojima 2016).

English education policy, proposed by the Ministry of Education, Culture, Sports, Science, and Technology (MEXT), has been changing too, with English introduced in primary schools in 2013 (starting in grade 5). From 2020, the introduction of English began earlier, in grade 3, and English became a compulsory subject in grade 5 (MEXT 2003, 2008). Prior to this, MEXT proposed its Action Plan in 2002 (MEXT 2002), to "acquire communication skills in English as a common international language," which includes sending an assistant language teacher (ALT) to every junior high school and high school at least once a week. An early statement by MEXT included norm-dependent terms such as "a native speaker of English" in describing the nature of ALTs and the motivation of English learning being "[t]o have one's English understood by a native speaker" (MEXT 2003). A more recent statement by MEXT (2013) has dropped the word "native," simply stating "English speakers" and puts emphasis on "what they can do" instead of "how well they can do." This indicates greater awareness of English as a Lingua Franca (ELF) and its application, such as in the Common European Framework (CEFR). In short, evaluating one's communicative ability instead of assessing proficiency against a native norm represents a small step towards nativization.

However, as Murata et al. (2018) point out, EMI and English education in Japan are still highly norm-dependent, which suggests that Japan remains in the stabilization phase today. The concern, moreover, is that MEXT is pushing more and more schools to focus on English education geared for standardized tests such as TOEIC and TOEFL. This can be considered as an intra-territorial force, due to institutional pressure on students to perform well, but at the same time as an extra-territorial force, since those wishing to study overseas are often required to present scores of such tests. Also, the demands of overseas trading partners accelerate corporate needs for English-proficient staff. Thus, it is argued that in many cases the intra- and extra-territorial forces can be viewed as flip sides of the same coin.

3.2.2 Domains of English

Linguistic forces – a reflection of language attitudes – are stronger than ever in present-day Japan. In the Japanese language, Loveday (1996) states that more than 7 percent of the total lexicon is English-derived loanwords, while the total proportion of loanwords in the Japanese language is approximately 10 percent. According to research in 1956 (published in 1962–1964) initiated by The National Language Research Institute (NLRI), 9.8 percent of the words used in ninety different magazines were loanwords, of which 80.8 percent were English words. A more recent survey (Hashimoto 2006) shows that almost 90 percent of loanwords used in newspapers are English. Here, we see the possibility of further English development in the Japanese context. In fact, Honna (2008) notes that those Japanized English words have gone through semantic nativization including semantic broadening, narrowing, and shifting, and S. Ike (2014) argues that these nativized expressions are then used in Japanese English, gaining more recognition over the years and making their way into English reference works. For example, words that were once heavily criticized as "incorrect," such as salaryman (a white-collar worker) and office lady (a woman working in an office) are now included in the *Oxford Living Dictionary* as well as the *Oxford Learner's Dictionaries*, both produced by Oxford University Press.

Linguistic landscapes in Japan also show evidence of sociodemographic forces. The annual number of visitors to Japan was approximately 350,000 in 1964 and reached one million in 1977. However, the growth rate of visitors was not particularly high until the 2000s. Since the Japanese government launched the Visit Japan Campaign (VJP) in 2003 to increase the number of tourists (Japan National Tourism Organization 2003), the annual number of visitors has significantly increased from just under five million in 2000 to more than 28 million in 2017 (Japan National Tourism Organization 2018). Buschfeld et al. (2018) see increasing tourism as an extra-territorial force, and there were indeed a number of other external factors such as the depreciation of the Japanese yen in the early 2010s (Andonian et al. 2016) that contributed to the government's involvement in such tourism-related promotions. However, tourism is, in fact, an intra-territorial force for Japan as well, as the government's promotion is not only in response to external globalization factors but was also formed as part of an internal financial plan. The resulting rise in the number of tourists then functions as an extra-territorial force in terms of their linguistic influence on English in Japan. Thus, tourism needs to be viewed both as an intra- and extra-territorial force.

In reaction, more and more tourist spots and shopping areas are providing multilingual signage and language services (e.g. Backhaus 2006; Iwata 2010). Backhaus (2005, 2007) reports that English is often used as the sole language to pass information to non-Japanese readers in the Tokyo area, suggesting that Japan now has prominent domains in which English functions as a communication tool. He has also studied linguistic landscapes diachronically and illustrates the increase of official English signage in the last twenty years in Japan, as well as the increase of Chinese and Korean in the last ten years (Backhaus 2005). Similarly, S. Ike (2016b, 2017a), based on a survey of signage at two major stations in Japan (Kyoto and Nagoya), reports that more than two-thirds of signage regarding location and direction at Japan Railway (JR) platforms are provided bilingually in English and Japanese. More recently, a major typhoon that swept the full length of Japan on September 30, 2018 was accompanied by extensive instructions on the NHK television network that targeted foreign residents and advised about proper precautions via easy-to-read enlarged English text visuals from their homepage. Such actions not only address short-term travelers but demonstrate the reality of international mobility and small-scale immigration.

Meanwhile, there is also natural growth at the grassroots level of those using English through electronic media to interact with friends and associates from around the world. As highlighted by D'Angelo (2016) and Seargeant and Tagg (2011), the explosion of internet use and SNS in particular greatly expands the possibilities for increased use of English. It is not clear as yet to what extent these ELF-like interactions by Japanese users of English with those from a variety of NS and NNS backgrounds may engender further development of Japanese English, but it is sure to have an impact. Recent data indicates that 47.54 million Japanese were users of SNS in 2015, reaching 54.99 million in 2018, and the number is expected to be 63.63 million in 2022 (Statista 2018). Clearly, this is both an intra- and extra-territorial force of globalization, which will have an impact on English and multilingual language use in Japan.

Partly due to the limited domains of English use in Japan and partly because of English education still largely being focused on reading/writing activities (Hino 2018), functional bilingualism in Japan is not common, and general English proficiency remains low. Honna and Takeshita's (2000) study shows that most university students who have had at least six years of formal English instruction are unhappy with their proficiency, and the average score on the Test of English as a Foreign Language (TOEFL) ranked Japan 149th of 162 countries in 1993 (ETS 2018a). As of 2017, the TOEIC mean score in Japan is 516, compared to 679 in Korea, 644 in Malaysia, and 586 in China (ETS 2018a). Similarly, Japan's mean TOEFL score is ranked 27th among 29 Asian regions (ETS 2018b). Some caution should be taken in using this data since Japan as an affluent country is widely known to have a large percentage of high school and university students taking these tests, many of whom may not be serious about their future need for English. Nevertheless, the figures may indicate some lack of an adequate intra-territorial force to strongly promote English proficiency across wider swaths of Japanese society. Japan is also a dynamo for translation of English fiction and academic/scientific works into Japanese, with over 50,000 works translated annually (Higuchi 2007), and has produced products such as the professional translation software TRADOS (SDL 2018). TRADOS is a computer-assisted translation tool which allows for a high degree of accuracy by giving translators a range of options at the phrasal level that reflect the complex variety of usages and idioms inherent in language. The extent to which such technological AI-type breakthroughs may impact variety development remains to be seen, but it demonstrates that to some extent Japanese learners of English may deem such developments as a way to make "an end run" around actually working towards higher levels of English proficiency, which in turn facilitates variety development.

In sum, the statistics reported here suggest that English has not fully spread in all domains in Japan, and there are several counter-forces inhibiting English variety development. In fact, even at large Japanese corporations, only about 10 percent of employees can be considered to need English for their work (Honna 2008). Overall, the use of English is generally limited to communication in English-speaking communities in Japan and communication between Japanese and the outside world (Makarova and Rodgers 2004). Thus, in terms of linguistic development, Japan can be assessed as being in a late phase of stabilization or a very early phase of nativization, but whether it develops further given the range of counter-forces remains to be seen.

3.2.3 Language attitudes

Finally, language attitudes need to be examined. The assumption that English is used between Japanese and "native" English speakers, which was held by the very top government policymakers in the early 2000s, is reflected in teachers' and students' attitudes towards English. Surveys reveal that over half of elementary school teachers think English is best taught by native speakers (Butler 2007a), and almost half of the students either in English teaching courses or majoring in English at university believe that native speakers – viewed as ideal and authentic – are more successful in teaching English than non-native speakers (Nakai 2003). Greisamer (2006) provides comments by university students such as "real English is better" and "native speakers have better pronunciation," in support of native English-speaking instructors. The assumption behind these results is that English spoken by native speakers is "real" and "authentic" but English spoken by Japanese or other non-native speakers is not, arguing that in terms of language attitudes in education, Japan is still in an early stabilization phase.

Similarly, students' lower awareness and tolerance of Outer and Expanding Circle varieties have been reported. McKenzie's studies (2008a, 2008b) show that Japanese university students evaluated Japanese English speakers lower than American or British English speakers in terms of language competence. Most students believe that they learn English in order to communicate with native English speakers, and very few have non-native English speakers in mind (Honna and Takeshita 2000). Also, Adachi (2007) observes that while more than 80 percent of students strongly agreed with the statement that they would like to be able to communicate with native English speakers, only 36 percent showed strong agreement to the statement that they would like to be able to communicate with people whose mother tongue is not English. Adachi argues that this is due to a lack of awareness of ELF and WE perspectives among Japanese learners of English.

More recent surveys, however, show that an increasing number of students in Japan are familiar with the concept of WE, and although still small in number more and more Japanese are in support of Japanese English as a variety, recognizing its function as ELF (Hino 2012; Murata et al. 2018). Based on data from ten years of graduates and their actual English needs, D'Angelo (2016, 2018) indicates that students exposed to pluralistic models of English truly see the value of such approaches once out in the working world. He proposes that WE, ELF, and English as an International Language (EIL) can work in harmony in Japan, under the term "The World Englishes Enterprise." There have been various attempts among educators and scholars to integrate the notion of World Englishes into English teaching in the recent years, such as the inclusion of characters with various language/cultural backgrounds in English textbooks (cf. Kanata 2005; Yamanaka 2006) and specific WE courses at tertiary education (Yoshikawa 2005). On the academic level, WE is actively discussed in a number of societies such as The Japan Association of College English Teachers (JACET), The Japan Association for Language Teaching (JALT), and The Japan Association for Asian Englishes (JAFAE).

The importance of recognition and acceptance of Japanese English as a legitimate new variety has been argued for by a number of scholars (Hino 1989, 2008, 2012; Honna 1999, 2002, 2003, 2006a, 2006b, 2008; Honna and Meinhof 1999; Morrow 2004; S. Ike 2010, 2012, 2014), and features and distinctiveness of Japanese English have been discussed (e.g. Fujiwara 2012; S. Ike 2012, 2016a, 2017b). Furthermore, studies (S. Ike 2012; Miyake and Tsushima 2012) suggest that Japanese English is viewed as intelligible and acceptable (at least to some extent) in ELF communication, and non-Japanese participants have mostly positive attitudes, although Japanese participants still hold fairly negative attitudes towards the variety (S. Ike 2012). Thus, in terms of social identity, the ownership of English remains Inner Circle-oriented, with only a limited amount of language evolution observable. Taken together, however, current language attitudes suggest that Japan is slowly moving forward to the nativization phase.

Over the course of this section, we have considered the history of English in Japan, using the EIF Model with its flexibility and use of extra- and intra-territorial forces as an analytical approach for capturing and evaluating the factors that have contributed to, as well as arrested, the development of English as a variety in Japan. The richness of the discussion and resulting insights not only give us a better understanding of the place of English in Japan but, as we explore in more detail in the next section, argue for further development of the EIF Model.

4. DISCUSSION AND CONCLUDING REMARKS

As mentioned earlier, there is a clear need for a new model with inclusivity for (and concrete analysis of) non-PCEs, since it is common knowledge today that non-PCE users of English outnumber native and PCE users. While the synopsis presented in the previous section suggests that the EIF Model works well in cases of the Expanding Circle, we contend that it still needs improvement in some areas. In this section, we review the significance of the model and discuss possible modifications.

In looking at Japan, the identification of forces in the EIF Model helps justify the existence of the foundation phase, and this can help scholars look at factors influencing variety development. In testing the model, we find that there are not only factors that facilitate variety development, but there are also factors that act as counter-forces. For example, technological developments such as increasingly sophisticated translation software (e.g. Google translation, TRADOS) may make variety development in non-PCE contexts a less pressing matter, since the need for English is served through technology rather than an individual user's proficiency. Second, we find that the time factor in the development of English in Japan (and probably many other Expanding Circle contexts in this volume) is quite "compressed" – with rapid development occurring over a much shorter timeframe – as compared with a classic PCE such as Singapore, where changes in English happened more gradually. Moreover, the gestation/incubation period appears to be less important, whereas forces such as language policy, attitudes, and globalization play a much larger role. The EIF Model enables us to analyze not only what motivates the variety development, but also to identify what inhibits the development. Identified forces in the model are quite useful in evaluating the status of English in a given context, and having a set of forces to look for enables scholars to examine and compare English variety development across both nations and regions as well as smaller speech communities.

At the same time, our case study indicates that certain aspects of the model need to be developed further. First, the distinction between extra-territorial and intra-territorial forces needs additional clarification. We find that often the same forces in EIF simultaneously act externally and internally. However, if one realizes that the international roles and use of English are more important for non-PCEs, as well as increasingly in PCE contexts such as India, then one need not be overly concerned about the interplay of the same force on both levels. As shown above, tourism in Japan, for example, can be both an extra- and intra-territorial force. Listing this force individually as an extra-territorial force and as an intra-territorial force may mislead the audience to view tourism as two separate forces. Instead, it is suggested that once the triggers for variety development are identified and listed, the interconnected and dynamic nature of each of the intra- and extra-territorial forces needs to be carefully analyzed.

Second, we argue that the term "exonormative" should remain as in the Dynamic Model. In many Expanding Circle cases – Asian countries in particular – there remains a clear preference for "native" English as a learning model. This means that English has not just been stabilized in a given context, but that it retains its attribution of ownership to L1 users. Therefore, English is recognized as the language of "others" instead of "ours," and this phase needs to be clearly demonstrated in the model.

Third, while the EIF Model contains the same five phases as the Dynamic Model, clear identification of these developmental phases is yet to be explored. As outlined in this chapter, Schneider's four parameters (especially identity re-settings and linguistic developments) are not clearly defined in the EIF Model, yet these are important considerations in variety development. The sociolinguistic parameters and linguistic parameters do not necessarily correspond, especially with regard to attitudes and features. The EIF Model may indicate that identity construction and attitudes towards English are intertwined in one category or force, but identity construction as an "English speaker" and as "Japanese speaker" are still two different concepts in early phases, and thus need to be accounted for separately. While the EIF Model seems to work well in analyzing the sociolinguistic condition of the variety in any given phase, it needs further consideration in capturing the sequence of variety development. Obviously, other forces not yet identified in the EIF Model need to be sought and considered, with testing and applying the model in more cases. The multiple case studies will then help identify particular forces uniquely tied to certain phases. In so doing, we will be able to establish a more concrete framework for discussing the developmental process in addition to assessing the status of English. It is hoped that through this chapter, and others in this volume, progress will be made towards this end.

In conclusion, our case study of Japan broadly supports the validity of the EIF Model, as it allows us to consider variety developments in non-PCE settings as well as in PCE settings. The model also considers idiolectal use of English (as speech communities become more dynamic), beyond the consideration of national varieties, and demonstrates the ongoing importance of revising our models to meet the changing conditions of global English use (D'Angelo 2018). The model shows some compatibility between the two settings, especially in identifying the foundation phase, although modification such as integrating the continuum-like nature of intra-extra forces and clearer description of each phase in terms of the four parameters seems to be necessary. Clearly, the EIF Model needs more testing in specific non-PCE settings, but we hope the proposed modifications in this chapter will strengthen the applicability of it to a wider range of contexts.

REFERENCES

Adachi, Masayuki. 2007. "International English" and English education in Japan. *Obirin Studies in English Language and Literature* 47: 1–15.

Andonian, André, Tasuku Kuwabara, Naomi Yamakawa and Ryo Ishida. 2016. The Future of Japan's tourism: Path for sustainable growth towards 2020, https://www.mckinsey.com/~/media/mckinsey/industries/travel%20transport%20and%20logistics/our%20insights/can%20inbound%20tourism%20fuel%20japans%20economic%20growth/the%20future%20of%20japans%20tourism%20full%20report.ashx (last accessed September 30, 2018).

Backhaus, Peter. 2005. Signs of multilingualism in Tokyo: A diachronic look at the linguistic landscape. *International Journal of the Sociology of Language* 175/176: 103–121.

Backhaus, Peter. 2006. Multilingualism in Tokyo: A look into the linguistic landscape. *International Journal of Multilingualism* 3.1: 52–66.

Backhaus, Peter. 2007. *Linguistic Landscapes: A Comparative Study of Urban Multilingualism in Tokyo*. Clevedon and Buffalo: Multilingual Matters.

Bruthiaux, Paul. 2003. Squaring the circles: Issues in modeling English worldwide. *International Journal of Applied Linguistics* 13.2: 159–178.

Buschfeld, Sarah and Alexander Kautzsch. 2017. Towards an integrated approach to postcolonial and non-postcolonial Englishes. *World Englishes* 36.1: 104–126.

Buschfeld, Sarah, Alexander Kautzsch and Edgar W. Schneider. 2018. From colonial dynamism to current transnationalism: A unified view on postcolonial and non-postcolonial Englishes. In Sandra C. Deshors, ed. 2018, *Modelling World Englishes in the 21st Century: Assessing the Interplay of Emancipation and Globalization of ESL Varieties*. Amsterdam: John Benjamins, 15–44.

Butler, Yuko Goto. 2007a. Factors associated with the notion that native speakers are the ideal language teachers: An examination of elementary school teachers in Japan. *JALT Journal* 29.1: 7–40.

Butler, Yuko Goto. 2007b. Foreign language education at elementary schools in Japan: Searching for solutions amidst growing diversification. *Current Issues in Language Planning* 8.2: 129–147.

Carroll, Tessa. 2000. *Language Planning and Language Change in Japan*. Richmond: Curzon.

Chiba, Reiko, Hiroko Matsuura and Asako Yamamoto. 1995. Japanese attitudes toward English accents. *World Englishes* 14.1: 77–86.

D'Angelo, James. 2008. The Japan context and the expanding circle: A Kachruvian response to Debbie Ho. *Asian Englishes* 11.2: 64–74.

D'Angelo, James. 2013. Japanese English?: Refocusing the discussion. *Asian English Studies* 15: 99–124.

D'Angelo, James. 2016. A Broader Concept of World Englishes for Educational Contexts: Applying the 'WE Enterprise' to Japanese Higher Education Curriculum. PhD dissertation, North-West University.

D'Angelo, James. 2018. Editorial. *Asian Englishes* 20.3: 1.

Edwards, Alison. 2016. *English in the Netherlands: Functions, Forms and Attitudes*. Amsterdam: John Benjamins.

Erikawa, Haruo. 2008. *Nihonjin wa Eigo wo dou manande kitaka: Eigo kyoiku no Shakai-bunka-shi* [How have Japanese learned English: Sociocultural history of English education]. Tokyo: Kenkyusha.

ETS. 2018a. 2017 TOEIC report on test takers worldwide, https://www.ets.org/s/toeic/pdf/2017-report-on-test-takers-worldwide.pdf (last accessed September 30, 2018).

ETS. 2018b. Test and score data summary for TOEFL iBT® tests: January 2017–December 2017 test data, https://www.ets.org/s/toefl/pdf/94227_unlweb.pdf (last accessed September 30, 2018).

Fujiwara, Yasuhiro. 2012. Identifying trends of English lexical borrowings from Japanese. *Asian English Studies* 14: 21–42.

Greisamer, Michael. 2006. Attitudes of Japanese university ESL learners: A contextual motivation survey. *Kobe Shinwa Studies in English Linguistics and Literature* 25: 94–112.

Hashimoto, Waka. 2006. Asahi Shimbun shasetsu no gairaigo: Shutsujibetsu suii o chushin ni [Loanwords in Asahi Shimbun: focus on changes in resources]. *Doshisha Kokubungaku* 64: 178–186.

Higuchi, Seiichi. 2007. The Book Market of Japan. Paper presented at the Breakfast Meeting, Frankfurt, Germany.

Hino, Nobuyuki. 1989. Nihonshiki-eigo no kanosei [The possibility of Japanese English]. *Modern English Teaching* 26.9: 8–9.

Hino, Nobuyuki. 2008. Kokusai-eigo [English as an international language]. In Shigeaki Kotera and Haruyo Yoshida, eds. 2008, *Supesharisuto ni yoru eigo-kyoiku no riron to oyo* [Theories and Practice of English Language Teaching by Specialists]. Tokyo: Shohakusha, 15–32.

Hino, Nobuyuki. 2012. Endonormative models of EIL for the Expanding Circle. In Aya Matsuda, ed. 2012, *Principles and Practices of Teaching English as an International Language*. Bristol: Multilingual Matters, 28–43.

Hino, Nobuyuki. 2018. English as an international language for Japan: Historical contexts and future prospects. *Asian Englishes* 20.1: 27–40.

Honna, Nobuyuki. 1995. English in Japanese society: Language within language. *Journal of Multilingual and Multicultural Development* 16.1–16.2: 45–62.

Honna, Nobuyuki. 1999. *Asia wo tsunagu Eigo* [English that unites Asia]. Tokyo: Alc press inc.

Honna, Nobuyuki. 2002. *Jiten Asia no saishin eigo jijo* [Encyclopedia of Latest Englishes in Asia]. Tokyo: Taishukan.

Honna, Nobuyuki. 2003. *Sekai no Eigo wo aruku* [Walking through Englishes in the World]. Tokyo: Shueisha.

Honna, Nobuyuki. 2006a. East Asian Englishes. In Braj B. Kachru, Yamuna Kachru and Cecil L. Nelson, eds. 2006, *The Handbook of World Englishes*. Oxford: Blackwell Publisher, 114–129.

Honna, Nobuyuki. 2006b. *Eigo wa Asia wo musubu* [English brings Asia together]. Tokyo: Tamagawa University Press.

Honna, Nobuyuki. 2008. *English as a Multicultural Language in Asian Contexts: Issues and Ideas*. Tokyo: Kuroshio Publishers.

Honna, Nobuyuki and Ulrike Hanna Meinhof. 1999. English in Japanese society: Reactions and directions. In David Graddol and Ulrike H. Meinhof, eds. 1999, *English in a Changing World – L'anglais dans un monde changeant*. Oxford: AILA, 48–56.

Honna, Nobuyuki and Yuko Takeshita. 2000. English language teaching for international understanding in Japan. *English Australia Journal* 18.1: 60–78.

Ike, Minoru. 1995. A historical review of English in Japan (1600–1880). *World Englishes* 14.1: 3–11.

Ike, Saya. 2010. Backchannel: A feature of Japanese English. *JALT 2009 Conference Proceedings*, 205–215.

Ike, Saya. 2012. Japanese English as a Variety: Features and Intelligibility of an Emerging Variety of English. PhD dissertation, University of Melbourne.

Ike, Saya. 2014. Variety development in the Expanding-Circle: Variety for EIL communication. In Raqib Chowdhury and Roby Marlina, eds. 2014, *Enacting English Across Borders: Critical Studies in the Asia Pacific*. Cambridge: Cambridge Scholars Publishing, 104–122.

Ike, Saya. 2016a. The interactional basis of backchannel behaviour in Japanese English. *Journal of Sugiyama Jogakuen Universit: Humanities* 47: 129–138.

Ike, Saya. 2016b. Planning Multilingual Linguistic Landscapes: A Case in Japan. Paper presented at the 9th International Conference of English as a Lingua Franca (ELF9), Lieda, Spain.

Ike, Saya. 2017a. ELF in Linguistic Landscapes of Japan: Multilingual Services. Paper presented at the 10th Anniversary Conference of English as a Lingua Franca, ELF 10, Helsinki, Finland.

Ike, Saya. 2017b. Negotiating backchannel behaviour: Challenges in ELF communication. *Journal of Sugiyama Jogakuen University Humanities* 48: 21–32.

Imura, Motomichi. 2003. *Nihon no Eigo kyouiku 200nen* [200 Years of English education in Japan]. Tokyo: Taishukan.

Iwata, Kazunari. 2010. The preference for English in linguistic services: 'Japanese for living: Countrywide survey' and Hiroshima. *The Japanese Journal of Language in Society* 13.1: 81–94.

Japan National Tourism Organization (JNTO). 2003. JAPAN launches the Visit Japan Campaign!!, https://us.jnto.go.jp/press/press_item.php?past=0&prid=11 (last accessed September 30, 2018).

Japan National Tourism Organization (JNTO). 2018. Trends in visitor arrivals to Japan, https://statistics.jnto.go.jp/en/graph/#graph--inbound--travelers--transition (last accessed September 30, 2018).

Kachru, Braj B. 1985. Standards, codification and sociolinguistic realm: The English language in the outer circle. In Randolph Quirk and Henry G. Widdowson, eds. 1985, *English In the World*. Cambridge: Cambridge University Press, 11–30.

Kanata, Naoko. 2005. Understanding different cultures in junior high school English textbooks of Japan: An analysis from a viewpoint of subject matters. *The Graduate School Review of the English Language and Literature* 33: 129–149.

Kim, Heejin. 2017. Language strategy and knowledge transfer. *Organizational Science* 50.4: 13–20.

Kodama, Koichi and Toshiko Kodama. 1979. *Eigo/Kirisutokyo bungaku: Meiji no Yokohama* [English and Christian literature: Yokohama in Meiji era]. Tokyo: Sasama Shoin.

Kojima, Naoko. 2016. Eigo ni yoru gakushu (EMI) no genjo: EMI junbi ko-za no do-kizuke chosa kara [Current status of English Medium Instruction (EMI): Survey of motivation in EMI preparation courses]. *Doshisha University Annual Report of Center for Learning Support and Faculty Development* 7: 25–41.

Koscielecki, Marek. 2006. Japanized English, its context and socio-historical background. *English Today* 22.4: 25–31.

Loveday, Leo J. 1996. *Language Contact in Japan: A Socio-linguistic History*. Oxford: Clarendon Press.

McArthur, Tom. 2003. *The Oxford Guide to World English*. Oxford: Oxford University Press.

McKenzie, Robert M. 2008a. The role of variety recognition in japanese university students' attitudes towards english speech varieties. *Journal of Multilingual and Multicultural Development* 29.2: 139–153.

McKenzie, Robert M. 2008b. Social factors and non-native attitudes towards varieties of spoken English: A Japanese case study. *International Journal of Applied Linguistics* 18.1: 63–88.

Makarova, Veronika and Theodore Rodgers. 2004. *English Language Teaching: The Case of Japan*. Munich: LINCOM.

Mesthrie, Rajend and Rakesh M. Bhatt. 2008. *World Englishes: The Study of New Linguistic Varieties*. Cambridge: Cambridge University Press.
MEXT. 2002. Developing a strategic plan to cultivate "Japanese with English abilities", http://www.mext.go.jp/english/news/2002/07/020901.htm (last accessed September 30, 2018).
MEXT. 2003. Regarding the establishment of an action plan to cultivate "Japanese with English abilities", http://www.mext.go.jp/english/topics/03072801.htm (last accessed September 30, 2018).
MEXT. 2008. The new course of study guidelines: Foreign language activities, http://www.mext.go.jp/a_menu/shotou/gaikokugo/kanren/index.htm (last accessed September 30, 2018).
MEXT. 2011. Five proposals and specific measures for developing proficiency in English for international communication, http://www.mext.go.jp/component/english/__icsFiles/afieldfile/2012/07/09/1319707_1.pdf (last accessed September 30, 2018).
MEXT. 2013. Global-ka ni taio shita Eigo kyouiku kaikaku jisshi keikaku [Action plans for English education improvement for Globalisation], http://www.mext.go.jp/a_menu/kokusai/gaikokugo/__icsFiles/afieldfile/2014/01/31/1343704_01.pdf (last accessed September 30, 2018).
MEXT. 2014. Press release. Selection for the FY 2014 top Global University Project, http://www.mext.go.jp/b_menu/houdou/26/09/__icsFiles/afieldfile/2014/10/07/1352218_02.pdf (last accessed September 30, 2018).
Miyake, Hiroko and Teruaki Tsushima. 2012. Three constructions used by Japanese speakers of English: Their linguistic features and acceptability. *Asian Englishes* 15.1: 46–67.
Mori, Arinori and Toshiaki Ohkubo, eds. 1972, *Mori Arinori Zenshu*. Vol. 3. Tokyo: Senbundo Shoten.
Morrow, Phillip R. 2004. English in Japan: The World Englishes perspective. *JALT Journal* 26.1: 79–100.
Murata, Kumiko, Mayu Konakahara, Masakazu Iino and Noboru Toyoshima. 2018. An investigation into attitudes towards English as a Lingua Franca (ELF) in English-medium instruction (EMI) and business settings and its implications for English language pedagogy institute for advanced studies in education. *Waseda Kyouiku Hyoron* 32.1: 55–75.
Nakai, Motohiro. 2003. EFL students' perceptions of native and non-native speaking teachers. *Gogakukyoiku Kenkyuronshu* 20: 159–177.

Oda, Minoru. 2000. *Kotoba no kenkyu to Eigo kyouiku: Kyouka to shite no kakuritsu wo motomete* [Language studies and English education: Aiming for English as a subject]. Suita: Kansai University Press.

Ohta, Yuzo. 1981. *Eigo to Nihonjin* [English language and Japanese people]. Tokyo: TBS Buritanika.

Saito, Yoshifumi. 2001. *Eigo shurai to Nihonjin: Egeresugo kotohajime* [The English arrival and Japanese: The begining). Tokyo: Kodansha.

Saito, Yoshifumi. 2007. *Nihonjin to Eigo: mouhitotsu no Eigo Hyakunen-shi* [Japanese people and English: Another 100-year history of English]. Tokyo: Kenkyusha.

Schneider, Edgar W. 2003. The dynamics of New Englishes: From identity construction to dialect birth. *Language* 79.2: 233–281.

Schneider, Edgar W. 2007. *Postcolonial English: Varieties Around the World*. Cambridge: Cambridge University Press.

Schneider, Edgar W. 2014. New reflections on the evolutionary dynamics of world Englishes. *World Englishes* 1: 9–32.

SDL. 2018. SDL Trados Studio, https://www.sdltrados.com/ (last accessed September 30, 2018).

Seargeant, Philip and Caroline Tagg. 2011. English on the internet and a 'post-varieties' approach to language. *World Englishes* 30.4: 496–514.

Seidlhofer, Barbara. 2001. Closing a conceptual gap: The case for a description of English as a Lingua Franca. *International Journal of Applied Linguistics* 11.2: 133–158.

Stanlaw, James. 2004. *Japanese English: Language and Culture Contact*. Hong Kong: Hong Kong University Press.

Statista. 2018. Number of social network users in Japan, 2015–2022, https://www.statista.com/statistics/278994/number-of-social-network-users-in-japan/ (last accessed September 30, 2018).

Tajima, Matsuji. 2001. *Wagakuni no Eigogaku 100nen: Kaiko to Tenbo* [100 years of English linguistics in our country: Reflection and future]. Tokyo: Nanundo.

Takanashi, Kenkichi and Kiyoshi Ohmura. 1975. *Nihon no Eigo kyouikushi* [The history of English education in Japan]. Tokyo: Taishukan.

Yamanaka, Nobuko. 2006. An evaluation of English textbooks in Japan from the viewpoint of nations in the inner, outer, and expanding circles. *JALT Journal* 28.1: 57–76.

Yoshihara, Hideki, Yoko Okabe and Seiko Sawaki. 2001. *Eigo de keiei suru jidai* [The era where we use English to manage]. Tokyo: Yuhikaku.

Yoshikawa, Hiroshi. 2005. Recognition of world Englishes: Changes in Chukyo University students' attitudes. *World Englishes* 24.3: 351–360.

CHAPTER 10

English in Australia – Extra-territorial Influences

Kate Burridge and Pam Peters

1. INTRODUCTION

This chapter discusses the extra-territorial influence of American English (AmE) on Australian English (AusE), in comparison with other varieties within the spectrum of World Englishes. Its aim is to compare the different orientations to AmE in Australia that can be observed using qualitative and quantitative methods, and so to illuminate the different ways in which extra- and intra-territorial influences can impact on individual varieties.

Within the EIF Model, the range of varieties included within the World English paradigm is enlarged with those that have no Anglo-colonial background (Buschfeld and Kautzsch 2017), and where English has no official or auxiliary status, and can only be typologised as 'supplementary' English (ESuppL), a language of convenience used for various reasons in multilingual contexts.[1] New models of World English need to be capable of embracing ESuppL varieties alongside those in the established Inner/Outer/Expanding Circle Model (Kachru 1992). Recently identified external forces in the development of varieties – extra-territorial influences – include 'transnational attraction' (Schneider 2014), which operates independently of the languages in contact within any regional context. But whether the transnational attraction of AmE works in the same way for all speakers across the ENL/ESL/EFL/

---

[1] Supplementary English (ESuppL) is used here for the various types of English used for business (as in the Netherlands, Korea, Thailand), and international tourism (Schneider 2013).

ESuppL spectrum should not be taken for granted. A further question to be explored is whether extra-territorial influence operates equally at all linguistic levels from phonology and orthography to lexical semantics.

Recent research on the extent to which English- and non-English-speaking countries are adopting AmE spellings and heteronyms over British English (BrE), is the subject of a major study by Gonçalves et al. (2018). Its data consists of a corpus of more than 30 million tweets extracted from geolocated Twitter (2010–2016), and two massive corpora consisting of several billion words from Google English-language books published in the United Kingdom and the United States (1800–2010). The latter serves as a foil to the Twitter corpus in being edited works representing Standard English and showing trends and gradual changes in the norms over time. The Twitter corpus includes data from thirty countries including six where English is the native language, four where it is an official second or auxiliary language, and twenty where it has no official status but serves as a supplementary language. In all these contexts the transnational attraction of AmE in non-English-speaking countries can be seen and heard, and extra-territorial influence is evident but dispersed. The Twitter data provide a solid concentration of it in written form, allowing the researchers to quantify the usage of AmE variants in spelling and lexical choices, and compare them across different geographical locations. Using multidimensional statistical analysis of a set of sixty-six spellings and ninety-one alternative word choices, Gonçalves et al. found ample support in their data for the notion of AmE as an extra-territorial influence on world languages including English. However, they found marked differences in the take-up of AmE variants in ENL countries, such as Australia, New Zealand, Ireland (with a more discernible British influence), in comparison with ESL/EFL and ESuppL contexts such as India, Turkey, Japan (showing strong American influence). Regional differences in the extent of this influence therefore seem to correlate with the different uses of English in traditional English-speaking bases in comparison with post- and non-postcolonial contexts.

This chapter takes up the question of extra-territorial influence (specifically AmE) on an established ENL variety of English, AusE. In section 2, it explores how that influence could be exercised on various Australian institutions; and section 3 explores how Australians position themselves in relation to it. Are they resistant to AmE, as indeed Gonçalves et al.'s (2018) results suggest? As we show, there is certainly a well-established complaint tradition against AmE infiltration at various levels of language, which is continually expressed in the public arena.

Yet AusE continually embraced new lexical items from AmE during the twentieth century (Peters 2001), in a tradition of lexical borrowing which continues into the twenty-first century. Data from GloWbE 2012 will be brought to bear on this in section 4, to quantify the various AmE loans current in AusE as a measure of the depth of their usage. Sections 5 and 6 discuss how extra-territorial influences play out for AusE with its traditional British colonial base, in a country where English is still the only official language. The implications are then extrapolated for American extra-territorial influence in multilingual countries, where English is used as a second, auxiliary or supplementary language.

2. AMERICAN INFLUENCE ON AUSTRALIAN INSTITUTIONS

Any discussion of linguistic influence needs to be able to identify the socio-historical context(s) in which language elements were or could have been transferred from donor to recipient; in other words, the times and scenarios for intensified levels of contact between speakers of the donor and recipient varieties in common enterprises, prompting the exchange of language.

Australia's contact with the United States was facilitated in the early nineteenth century by sharing a common ocean (the Pacific) for whaling and other oceanic trades, and a backdrop of similar settlement phases on the east coast of Australia and the west coast of the United States. Australian terms for the subdivision of land are those of the opening up of North America, using *block*, *location* and *township* (Ramson 1966: 135), as well as names for those with dubious claims to land: *squatter*, *land-shark*. Goldmining terms crossed the Pacific with miners moving from the Californian rush in 1849 to the first Australian gold rush in 1851, bringing *digger*, *prospector* and the miners' use of *dirt* for the medium in which gold may be found, among other terms (147–149). The wording of Australia's constitution is aligned with that of the American constitution federal system (e.g. adoption of the term *state* for its main regional sectors; Thompson 1998:120).

Reliable shipping across the Pacific from the 1870s brought American entertainments to Australia, including minstrel shows, vaudeville and melodrama, often displacing Australian theatre shows (Waterhouse 1998: 48–49). From 1918, American movies dominated Australian cinemas, and Australian commercial radio stations drew much of their content from American popular music. After World War II (WWII), American musical comedies enjoyed great popularity, with television serials, family dramas and westerns becoming the mainstay of the numerous Australian commercial channels (Bell 1998: 194–195). As a vernacular medium, television embedded colloquial American speech in Australian homes (in 1959, the 'top ten' programmes originated in the US).

By what we have seen so far, AmE was not unfamiliar to Australians from its settlement phase on through the nineteenth century, with continued exposure to it through co-participation in WWI and especially WWII, during the war in the Pacific. American soldiers were stationed in Australia and continued to visit for 'rest and recreation' after the war. In 1951, Australia entered into the ANZUS (Australia, New Zealand, United States Security) Treaty, a strategic alliance which served to strengthen defence with the United States, and paved the way for wide-ranging trade agreements and major changes in Australia's foreign policy after Britain joined the European Economic Community (now the European Union).

Thus, in war and peace during the twentieth century, Australians were continually exposed to AmE speech via the entertainment industry and visiting Americans. Linguistic commentators such as Baker (1966), Taylor (1989) and Sussex (1995) draw attention to the numbers of AmE words and expressions that were being taken up. Many of these have become assimilated so that Australians are hardly aware of their American origins, for example AmE *boss*, *cinch*, *dago*, *lay off* ('to dismiss a worker'), *okay*, and so on. Alternative forms of verbs associated with AmE, such as *gotten* now have widespread use in Australia. The *Macquarie Dictionary* has progressively recognised this assimilation of AmE forms from one edition to the next. Thus, the label attached to entries has gradually adjusted from ('US') to ('chiefly US') to ('originally US') and then omitted entirely, from the first to the later editions. Lexical evidence of ordinary AmE forms becoming steadily assimilated in AusE are symptoms of sustained extra-territorial influence from the United States over more than two centuries.

3. AUSTRALIAN ATTITUDES TO AMERICAN INFLUENCE

3.1 Preliminaries

Waterhouse (1998: 45) maintains that '[b]efore World War I, concern that Australian culture was becoming Americanised was voiced only intermittently'. This is certainly born out by linguistic commentary at this time. People were aware of AmE, but little was made of its influence on the home-grown variety – certainly, there was nothing of the intensive fearmongering that characterises public opinion today. A. Richards, writing to the editor of the Melbourne *Argus* (4 January 1894), had this to say on the pronunciation he was hearing in the state of Victoria:[2]

> Take class for class, the Victorians speak English more correctly, as I said before, than the Canadians, Americans, or the Englishmen born and bred. The Rev. Mark Guy Pearse, when on a visit to these colonies a few years ago, expressed this opinion also. No doubt the Victorians of the next generation or two will speak worse English than they do now, but I very much doubt if the English tongue will 'Americanise' itself judging from the present. –Yours, &c.,

This opinion from a senior Australian citizen captures the perennial critique of younger people's speech, without making American extraterritorial influence the agency of deterioration. It is worth foregrounding here that colonial Australia was used to thinking of itself (and being thought of) as a 'young society'. The use of 'young' contrasted with 'old' in 'the Old Country' (as Britain was commonly referred to), and also foregrounded the high percentage of young people in society: in the 1850s, at the height of immigration, the proportion of non-indigenous Australians aged 65 or more was around 1 per cent (Benczes et al. 2017). It was a time of experimentation, innovation and discovery – no one seemed much fussed by any transgressions of the defining boundaries of the AusE that was emerging.

As documented by Damousi (2010), disparaging commentary around American influence was not apparent until American cultural products had well and truly embedded themselves and become a way of life in Australia. It seems to have taken off with the 'talkies' (talking films) of the 1920s.

> It must be already apparent to many thinking people that since the introduction of the American talking films . . . we are in grave danger of the Americanisation of our speech . . . I do hope that this matter will be taken up by all those possessing the true Australian

---

[2] Our thanks to Lee Murray for generously allowing us access to her corpus of early letters on Victorian speech.

spirit, and help to save their country from this wholesale invasion and exploitation by a foreign Power. (*Sydney Morning Herald*, 23 June 1930: 5)

Nothing much has changed since then. In personal correspondence we receive, Australians continue to denounce 'this wholesale invasion and exploitation'; vehement objections are made to 'American infiltration into our lingo' and 'annoying American habits . . . spreading to Australia' – blame is laid squarely on 'the invidious impact of American TV' and 'the Microsoft spell-checker'. While all aspects of the structure of English are felt to be under siege, a running theme throughout the complaints is a perceived threat of American influence, specifically on spelling, pronunciation and word choice – it's these features that appear high on people's linguistic radar.

Australians' preoccupation with the more superficial aspects of speaking and writing reflects the fact that, as predicted by Labov's (1993) 'sociolinguistic monitor', phonological and lexical knowledge is more socially salient and therefore open to attracting more evaluative attention; by comparison, syntactic knowledge is less observable and largely flies under the radar. Also, relevant here is the English education received in schools (Severin and Burridge in press). The move away from the explicit teaching of linguistic awareness in the latter half of the twentieth century left the general public with a limited knowledge of the complexities of grammar. Just as Curzan (2014:73) has described for AmE, the Australian school system, especially in the early years, targets punctuation and spelling – those most standardised elements. Spelling bees, spelling tests, dictionaries and computer spell-checkers reinforce the notion that variation in spelling is unacceptable, and where it exists (as in UK *honour* versus US *honor*) students are usually instructed that one of these forms is 'correct' and the other is 'American' (i.e. 'incorrect').

In the next section, we briefly examine people's reactions to the impact of AmE, drawing on a selection (2006–2011) of the personal letters, emails and general feedback we have received during our long involvement with various radio and television programmes.[3] We also include the results of two surveys carried out by our students, one focusing on

---

[3] These include language-focused radio programmes for both commercial and national broadcasters and the ABC TV series *Can We Help* (http://www.abc.net.au/tv/canwehelp/); in them, listeners/viewers offer their observations on language and pose queries about usage.

attitudes to spelling and the other on student impressions of AmE influence (Wren 2009 and Ferguson 2008 respectively). All examples given here illustrate the Americanisms that attract most media commentary and censure.

3.2 Spelling

In the following email (dated 9 May 2008), FW queries the correct spelling of the word meaning 'to send out goods':[4]

> is it *dispatch* or *despatch*? All my googling is suggesting that one is an English term and the other is American. I loathe Americanising of English words and would rather like to be able to write 'The Queens English' with confidence.

When spelling shows variation in this way, Americans are typically held responsible. In an email (10 September 2011), PC wonders about *enquiry* and *inquiry*. 'Is one just American?', he asks, and 'If so, why do the yanks do that??? Can't they get their own language to mess with?'

Without doubt, the high visibility of spelling has intensified the widespread perception of American influence over the years. Although Australia's spelling conventions derive traditionally from the British, the technological presence of America means this is an area of rapidly growing American influence. On a discussion forum website, Coyourh (2018) points to changes in spelling that have been altered over time 'without our control. Even spelling is an issue, programs such as word are set to default to American spelling, leaving out our precious U's, and I've noticed even at University, lecture slides will commonly spell words the American way [. . .].' Ferguson (2008) surveyed ninety-three first-year linguistics undergraduates at Monash University to determine how often they used Americanisms and how they felt about AmE influence on AusE generally. Spelling came across as the hottest topic, with the following being typical of the replies 'I can't stand it how Australians are now beginning to use "ize" rather than the traditional "ise"' (p. 90).[5] Even those who expressed 'neutral' or 'positive' atti-

---

[4] Here and elsewhere below, the initials represent the particular correspondent to the radio or television programme.
[5] Even though prestigious British publications, including the London *Times* and Daniel Jones's *English Pronouncing Dictionary*, promote *-ize* spellings like *legalize*, most Australians reject them outright because they smack of AmE.

tudes towards AmE influence often gave spelling as the one exception: 'Neutral – good aspects – interesting variation from trad Brit English pronunciation BUT spelling sometimes is annoying when it departs from the trad eng' (p. 82). Spelling highlights the complex and often unclear role that AmE has played in many AusE developments. Since the early 1850s *-or* spellings (such as *color*) have been commonplace in Australia – *The Age* newspaper in Melbourne was using these from the beginning of its publication in 1854. While an unlikely inheritance from America, as Baker points out (1966: 403), people went on to perceive this convention as endorsing 'American' *-or* spellings in place of English *-our*. When, in 1969, the State of Victoria also advocated spellings such as *color* and *honor*, writers ignored the edict, one complaining to *The Age* (9 October 1969):[6] 'What right has the Victorian Department of Education to change the spelling of 1349 words in the English language? We speak English in this country therefore [sic] why should our spelling be changed to follow the American pattern.' People's beliefs about their language world are powerful – in 2001 public pressure persuaded *The Age* to instate the *-our* spelling.

3.3 Pronunciation

In the following letter (4 September 2008), JP protests that while French and British English borrowings are acceptable, American additions are not. She also complains about the shift in the primary stress of the words *ceremony* and *hurricane* (*ceremony* from *ceremony* and *hurricane* from *hurricane*):

> I have just heard your discourse on the Americanisation of English. I am one of the population who is *very much against* this phenomenon, particularly on the Australian Broadcasting Corporation, because, after all, I am one part of the public who help to pay the ABC announcers wages. The words which particularly annoy me are 'cere moany' and 'hurri cane'. You made reference to many other words which have been integrated from the French or British language in relation to food, but these are accepted words to describe the article . . .
> If the offenders are so enamoured of the American language that they have to inflict these words on the Australian listeners, they

---

[6] Cited in Jernudd (1989: 15).

should be made redundant, emigrate to the United States of America, and go get paid by the American Broadcasting Commission.

Phonological developments such as this stress shift highlight again the difficulty of pinpointing AmE influence. Many features people denounce as Americanisms could well represent cases of independently motivated change rather than direct borrowing – with AmE accelerating trends that are immanent or already underway. The pronunciations *ceremony* and *hurricane* demonstrate a well-trodden path of phonological change; namely, the modern propensity for spelling pronunciations. Similarly, 'Americanisms' such as the yodless articulation of *stupid* [stupəd], the realisation of inter-vocalic /t/ as a flap or tap [ɾ] variant and the shift to antepenultimate stress in words such as *voluntarily* and *primarily* (still noted as 'chiefly US' in the *Macquarie Dictionary*) are part of long-term changes planted long ago and now affecting varieties around the English-speaking world. While Moore might be overstating the case when he writes 'the Australian accent has remained utterly unaffected by American accent' (2008: 163), it is true that American influence is shallow and has done little to shape the structure of AusE phonology. Even clear phonological transfers are largely limited to individual lexical items (e.g. *schedule* /ˈskedjul/, labelled 'chiefly US' in the third edition of the *Macquarie Dictionary*, and an alternative pronunciation alongside /ˈʃedjul/ in the fifth edition; Korhonen 2018: 48).

3.4 Lexicogrammatical Features

The fact that AmE expressions are high on people's radar is not surprising. Words are accessible and lexical influence is always conspicuous; words are also linked, more than other aspects of language, to the life and culture of speakers, and this gives them a special significance. In an email (25 September 2008) KC writes:

> . . . in the last 30 to 40 years we have dumped (not trashed!) most of our idiomatic language . . . This has all come about because of our constant exposure to American television which has seduced us into this wholesale and unfortunate change in our language. Most of these 'new' words have a long history, but that does not preclude the fact that they have come into our language direct from the American culture and at the expense of our own. I refer to this change as Australians becoming very good pseudo Americans!!

MM calls on 'Our Protective Aunty' (the nickname for the Australian Broadcasting Corporation) to step up and shield Australians from American date-formatting.

> What ever happened to the 'First of January' or the 'Third of March' or the 'Fifth of April'? We seem to be following the Yanks with their 'January one' or 'March three' or 'April five'. Is this some insidious plot by media moguls to convert us to American ways? And will the ABC 'Our protective Aunty' come to the rescue and challenge this trend by bringing back the 'Day first' as our official date order?

As this last case (date-formatting word order) illustrates, the sort of grammatical phenomena that come to speakers' attention and acquire social significance are essentially lexical. In the next example (17 March 2011), PB is complaining of the American usage *to impact*, one of many cases where verbs with direct objects (*to battle*) are in the process of replacing their prepositional verb counterparts (*to battle against*): 'When did impact cease to need its preposition as in "impact upon"? Now we just impact!' These new transitive verbs illustrate the flexibility of English word classes and the long tradition that has allowed nouns like *impact* to convert to verbs (and the long tradition of condemning such neologisms).

In the following email (15 October 2011), disgruntled MH declares his preference for *got* over *gotten*. This again is a more lexical than grammatical issue – that of choosing the right word rather than the correct form for past participle of *get*.

> ... we even see the American 'GOTTEN' metastasizing into our media (although I note that you do not seem to use either word). Am I a troglodyte unaware of the sunrise outside or is this something against which we should still fight?

The verb form *gotten* is one of the many conservative features of AmE, and there have always been vestiges of dialectal *gotten* users in Australia. As with the transitive verbs just mentioned, contact with AmE might well simply be fast-tracking the take-up of this form.

Even questions and complaints involving inflectional suffixes such as *-ed/-t* for the past forms of *earn*, *learn* and *burn* are not fundamentally grammatical. Most queries indicate that this is viewed as a spelling fluctuation (with many seeking guidance as to 'the correct spelling' of these words); for others, it might reflect a difference in pronunciation. GW (10 April 2010) asks the following:

> Earnt (earned), learnt (learned), burnt (burned) – my American friend and I had a rather interesting discussion about these words, she'd never heard of 'earnt' and thought it 'wrong'. Are there correct usages? And do you know the origin? Is this a US/Aussie English thing?

3.5 Demographics

The majority of people who go to the trouble of phoning in to radio stations and writing letters to the editor are middle-aged Australians or older. So what about younger English speakers today – those who have grown up with variation and change as facts of linguistic life? Earlier we mentioned Ferguson's (2008) survey of first-year linguistics students; this study revealed that these young speakers overwhelmingly showed intolerance towards language change, especially AmE influence. Of the ninety-three students surveyed, 81 per cent expressed the view that the incorporation of American elements into AusE was detrimental to the language. The following are typical of the explanations offered (Ferguson 2008: 81–91):

- Americans do not speak to the Australian identity.
- Why would we want to speak American English? I think 'they' are lazy with language.

One question in the orthography survey mentioned earlier (Wren 2009) specifically asked participants about the acceptability of alternative spellings. The following responses are representative of the mindset of the 20–30-year-old age group (curiously, Wren observed a greater tolerance of spelling variation among the over 50-year-olds; pp. 53–54):

> – I think it's important . . . not to fall for America's kind of childish bastardisation of a very old language;
> – I think most instances of this have come from American and since we are not American this should be avoided at all costs and never enter into school English programmes;

These respondents have all gone through the 'language in use' approach at school (emphasising variation and change) and, in the case of Ferguson's students, have also had one year of linguistics and have been immersed in the accepted wisdom of the discipline. Yet there is little evidence of any new open-mindedness in their linguistic thinking when it comes to perceived American influence. Clearly, it is not simply older and linguistically insecure listeners/viewers of Australia's national broadcaster who feel strongly about the threat that AmE usage poses to their language.

4. ASSIMILATION OF AME ELEMENTS IN AUSE

4.1 Examining the Evidence of Extra-territorial Influence

The responses of older and younger Australians to perceived American influence on AusE are typically negative, as illustrated in the previous section. They do not suggest a high degree of 'transnational attraction', as suggested by Schneider (2014), or of finding prestige value in elements of AmE, as postulated in earlier language contact models (Weinreich 1953: 59–60). Yet the historical and contemporary impact of US culture on Australia is unmistakable, as indicated in section 2, and the record of American words and terms assimilated into AusE is clear. Evidently, some kinds of American expression are readily assimilated, noted only briefly as foreignisms, and somehow neutralised within the matrix of AusE. A few remain stigmatised in the general conversation, a focus for continuing objections and sometimes erratic generalisations (as discussed in section 3).

This paradox suggests more and less conscious processes at work in the take-up of external elements. Those which become stigmatised are like the 'old chestnuts' of English usage commentary, the well-worn topics of language complaint, whereas others are quietly assimilated 'under the radar', and then spread as changes in AusE through social and geographical space. They secure their place in the variety by ordinary and apparently unmarked usage, starting as minor variants or alternatives in heteronymic pairs or sets, and not deposing the major incumbent in the variety – at least in the short run. Thus, AmE *movie* has taken its place in AusE alongside *documentary* as the terms for (non)-fiction categories of the established *film*, which retains its place as the superordinate.

Other examples of Americanisms which have become established in AusE are discussed in the four examples presented in the following section. We use data from large corpora of AmE, BrE, AusE and NZE as evidence of just how frequent the American innovations are, and whether they are actually displacing AusE alternatives, as complainants may claim. The corpora include the Corpus of Historical American (COHA, 400 million words from 1810–2000); the British National Corpus (BNC, 100 million words from 1975–1995), with large volumes of written and spoken data; and the Global Web-based English corpus (GloWbE 1.9 billion words), consisting of blogs and websites from twenty English-using countries including the United States, the United Kingdom, Australia and New Zealand. The data from these corpora help to put the targets of complaint into perspective.

4.2 Americanisms in Lexical Sets

The relative frequencies of *garbage*, *rubbish*, *junk*, *trash* in the later twentieth century and early twenty-first century show the shifting interrelationships among the set of terms relating to waste matter and material waste in different varieties. They help to provide a linguistic model for the integration of expressions attributable to extra-territorial influence from AmE. The earliest public notification in the United Kingdom of American influence in this semantic set (Strang 1970) was of *junk* as the American newcomer beginning to challenge the long-standing BrE *rubbish*. Its presence is registered in data from the BNC a decade or two later, where it is the most frequent of the three alternatives shown in Table 10.1, while *garbage* and *trash* were also gaining some currency. All three were far more common in late twentieth-century AmE than *rubbish*, which is the least used variant in the figures from COHA in Table 10.1. The most commonly used terms in AmE according to COHA were *garbage* and *trash*, which developed their general sense of material waste in the United States. The application of *trash* ('*spec.* in the U.S') to the sense of 'domestic refuse, garbage' is noted in the *Oxford English Dictionary*, and is paraphrased in a 1906 citation: 'Rubbish is discarded trash, composed principally of all kinds of paper, wood, rags, mattresses, bedding, boxes, ... tin cans, ... bottles, ... and the like'. Since then *trash* has increased its currency inside and outside the United S, especially since the digital revolution as the word for 'data to be discarded'.

In the normalised figures in COHA and GloWbE-US, the rankings of the four words in AmE before and after 2000 are much the same,

Table 10.1 Relative frequencies of *rubbish, garbage, trash* in corpora before and after 2000[a]

	BNC 1975–1995 100 m.	COHA 1990 28 m.	GloWbE US 2012 386 m.	GloWbE GB 2012 387 m.	GloWbE AUS 2012 148 m.	GloWbE NZ 2012 81 m.
rubbish	2186 (*21.86*)	59 (*2.11*)	1700 (*4.4*)	12199 (*31.42*)	4120 (*27.8*)	2003 (*24.61*)
junk	525 (*5.25*)	465 (*16.64*)	5640 (*14.58*)	3506 (*9.05*)	1941 (*13.10*)	741 (*9.10*)
garbage	276 (*2.76*)	779 (*27.88*)	7120 (*18.41*)	2643 (*6.82*)	1687 (*11.38*)	481 (*5.91*)
trash (*n*)	159 (*1.59*)	625 (*22.37*)	5847 (*15.42*)	1717 (*4.43*)	870 (*5.87*)	363 (*4.46*)

[a] The figures in italics in parentheses are normalisations per million words of the raw figures alongside, to help in comparing numerical data from corpora of different sizes, and the rankings within each regional set.

with *garbage* the most frequent and *trash* running second. Similarly, for BrE before and after 2000, the rankings of the words in the BNC and GloWbE-GB are similar, with *rubbish* still far more frequent than the others. Yet the proportional increases of *junk*, *garbage* and *trash* show more diversification within the British paradigm as the twenty-first century opens up and suggest ongoing extra-territorial influence on BrE from across the Atlantic. Meanwhile in the Antipodes, the rankings in AusE and NZE in the twenty-first century are like those of BrE, with *rubbish* dominant, and the three AmE alternatives represented in lesser proportions. This data aligns with the findings of Gonçalves et al. (2018), that ex-British colonial varieties maintain British preferences in lexical sets like these (and in numerous other sets beyond the fifty used in Gonçalves et al.'s research).

Interestingly, the ranking of the three AmE alternatives for *rubbish* are the same in the GloWbE data for both AusE and NZE and might reflect in apparent time the real-time phases of AmE influence from the nineteenth century on (see section 2). This aligns with the evidence of the *Oxford English Dictionary* online (2010), that the earliest uses of *junk* and *garbage* in the sense of 'material waste' were in AmE compounds: *junk cart* (1854), *garbage-box* (1882). *Trash* has been noted only relatively recently in AusE (Sussex 1995) and is still the object of some complaint in Australia (see section 3.4), though used by Baker (1966:72) in defining terms used in the sugar industry. The corpus evidence suggests all three are thriving as lesser players in the semantic field and have probably lost their AmE identity for many Australians. This example is thus paradoxical, in showing that AusE maintains its British identity against AmE influence at the highest level in the paradigm (in its preference for *rubbish*) but can accommodate AmE words as lesser alternatives within a convergent lexical set.

A second set of words shows less equal usage of its members over time. It includes four terms relating to residential units in a housing block: *apartment, flat, condominium, home unit*. Both *apartment* and *condominium* are North American in origin, while *flat* is British (originally Scottish), and *home unit* originated in the Antipodes. In Table 10.2 (as in Table 10.1), distinct patterns of preference are maintained in AmE and BrE before and after the year 2000, with *apartment* dominant in AmE and *flat* in BrE. Neither makes much use of *condominium*, first on record in the United States in 1962, or *home unit* dating from 1929 in Australia and 1987 in New Zealand, as shown by entries in the *Oxford English Dictionary* online, the *Australian*

Table 10.2 Relative frequencies of *apartment*, *flat*, *condominium*, *home unit* in corpora before and after 2000

	BNC 1975–1995 100 m.	COHA 1990 28 m.	GloWbE US 2012 386 m.	GloWbE GB 2012 387 m.	GloWbE AUS 2012 148 m.	GloWbE NZ 2012 81 m.
apartment	1221	2896	11379	7395	4328	1686
	(12.21)	(103.65)	(29.42)	(19.08)	(29.20)	(20.72)
flat (n)	4596	681	3518	10073	1984	1564
	(45.96)	(24.37)	(9.10)	(25.99)	(13.39)	(19.22)
condominium	13	57	305	109	65	43
	(0.13)	(2.04)	(0.79)	(0.28)	(0.44)	(0.53)
home unit	1	0	9	2	17	4
	(0.01)		(0.02)	(0.01)	(0.11)	(0.01)

National Dictionary (2016) and the *Dictionary of New Zealand English* (1997) respectively.

In this semantic field, the rankings and patterns of usage for GloWbE-Aus and -NZE depart from those of BrE: *apartment* rather than *flat* as the most frequent term in their respective sets. Neither the AmE *condominium* nor the home-grown *home unit* seems popular now. In AusE the usage of *apartment* is already markedly higher than *flat*, showing widespread acceptance of the AmE term. The crossover to it from *flat* is still happening in NZE, as it too responds to extra-territorial influence. *Apartment* seems to have been taken up in Australia without any conservative opposition, perhaps because it arrived during the 1980s (Sussex 1985), when relations with the United States were generally positive (see section 2).[7]

4.3 American Influence on Morpho-syntactic Patterns

The divergences between AmE and BrE verb morphology have been described in grammars and usage guides since the nineteenth century (Anderwald 2016). They show that BrE is typically more pluralistic than AmE (Peters 2012), for example in its acceptance of alternative forms of derivational suffixes, such as *-ize* and *-ise*, and inflectional suffixes such as *-ed/-t* for the past forms of *spell, spill, spoil* and *burn, dream, lean, leap*. While the BrE legacy gives Australians some latitude for variation, the extra-territorial influence of AmE here (and general levelling processes) would suggest the value of consistency, making *-ed* the regular spelling for both past tense and past participle. Some L1 users nevertheless prefer to deploy both according to whether they hear them pronounced with /d/ or /t/. Others differentiate *-ed* and *-t* according to grammar: past tense/past participle; intransitive/transitive; continuous/non-continuous action. The result is inconsistency in usage generally. Table 10.3 shows the variable past forms of two common verbs belonging to this set (*burn, dream*), as well as for *earn*.

The figures in Table 10.3 for the past of *burn* and *dream* show a large concentration of *-ed* in the GloWbE-US data, in keeping with the findings from late twentieth-century corpora (Peters 2004: 83, 165).

---

[7] This influence of realpolitik on regional spelling emerged in Heffernan et al. (2010), who noted that American spellings decreased dramatically during the Korean War, the Vietnam War and the first Gulf War, that is, periods when American foreign policy was viewed negatively by Canadians.

Table 10.3 Relative frequencies of *-ed* and *-t* for past tense/past participle in four GloWbE corpora

	GloWbE US 2012 386 m.	*GloWbE GB* 2012 387 m.	*GloWbE AUS* 2012 148 m.	*GloWbE NZ* 2012 81 m.
burned past tense	2367 *(6.12)*	1376 *(3.55)*	519 *(3.50)*	248 *(3.05)*
burned past participle	4380 *(11.32)*	2668 *(6.68)*	1006 *(6.79)*	554 *(6.81)*
burnt past tense	171 *(0.44)*	310 *(0.80)*	159 *(1.07)*	72 *(0.88)*
burnt past participle	1265 *(3.27)*	2173 *(5.61)*	1288 *(8.69)*	605 *(7.43)*
dreamed past tense	1209 *(3.13)*	897 *(2.31)*	335 *(2.26)*	212 *(2.60)*
dreamed past participle	1486 *(3.84)*	1279 *(3.30)*	546 *(3.68)*	308 *(3.78)*
dreamt past tense	385 *(1.00)*	620 *(1.60)*	199 *(1.33)*	66 *(0.81)*
dreamt past participle	158 *(0.41)*	457 *(1.18)*	149 *(1.01)*	67 *(0.82)*
earned past tense	6429 *(16.62)*	3797 *(9.80)*	1175 *(7.93)*	803 *(9.87)*
earned past participle	5628 *(14.55)*	4502 *(11.61)*	1483 *(10.01)*	997 *(12.25)*
earnt past tense	8 *(0.02)*	78 *(0.20)*	46 *(0.31)*	16 *(0.20)*
earnt past participle	20 *(0.05)*	152 *(0.39)*	64 *(0.43)*	28 *(0.35)*

The proportions of usage in the BrE data are similar, though with somewhat more use of the *-t* for the past participle. This trend is intensified in both AusE and NZE, which set themselves apart by their stronger use of the *-t* form in *burnt* as the past participle of *burn*. There are no marked regional differences for the *-t* forms associated with *dream*.

The usage of *earnt* shown in Table 10.3 comes as a surprise since both the unabridged *Webster's Dictionary* (1986) and the *Oxford English Dictionary* online have *earn* as a regular verb whose past forms are *earned* (though the latter has recently [2015] added *earnt* as 'nonstandard'). While the GloWbE data for AmE still show minimal use of *earnt*, there is more of it in the other three datasets for both past tense and past participle. If there is extra-territorial influence, it could only be from BrE. Yet the parallel variability among the three varieties suggests rather that it stems from the mixed paradigm they all share – except that the -*t* variant is more extensively used in AusE than either of the others. This provides an evidence-based answer to the Australian query about it, reported in section 3.4: *earnt* is not an Americanism. In the AusE and NZE data, we note also that the examples are frequently transitive, as in the adage 'respect must be earnt'. But since much of the GloWbE data comes from unedited blogs, we cannot assume the writers are referring to a grammatical rule here. Rather they may be spelling the word as they hear it – finishing with a devoiced dental. This accords with the finding that the -*t* forms with *burn* and so on were found more often in spoken than written data in the ICE corpora from Britain, Australia and New Zealand (Peters 2009: 24). It seems altogether unlikely that the southern hemisphere penchant for the -*t* spelling here is a sign of American extra-territorial influence.

The second paradigmatic example is the formulation of dates in AmE, another focus of Australian complaints (see section 3.4). The established AmE way of presenting dates is to put the month before the day, using *January 1* rather than *1 January* with the day before the month, as in standard British practice. Either order could be preferred in relation to three-part dates that include the year. The American order with year>month>day (or just month>day) is carefully documented by the *Chicago Manual of Style* (2010: 477), though it recognises that this differentiates it from other English-speaking countries, including Canada. The year>month>day system is in fact the ISO standard, and is widely used in data-based systems. Meanwhile the British order with day>month>year (from smaller to larger units) underwrites the conventional way of speaking dates. The order of items is of course just one dimension of difference in writing dates; the second is whether to use cardinal numbers (as already illustrated) or ordinal ones as in *January 1st, 1st January*. While the ordinals are often used in speaking dates, cardinal numbers are increasingly used in writing, and are recommended by the Australian Government *Style Manual* (2002: 170) because it requires fewer keystrokes and no internal punctuation.

Corpus data for four different dates in the calendar are shown in Table 10.4, to see how consistently dates are worded in the four varieties

Table 10.4 Relative frequencies for alternative expressions of dates from four regional corpora

	GloWbE US 2012 386 m.	*GloWbE GB* 2012 387 m.	*GloWbE AUS* 2012 148 m.	*GloWbE NZ* 2012 81 m.
1 January	134 (0.35)	908 (2.34)	977 (6.59)	343 (4.2)
January 1	1913 (4.95)	466 (1.20)	256 (1.73)	130 (1.60)
28 March	27 (0.07)	176 (0.45)	60 (0.40)	25 (0.31)
March 28	425 (1.01)	138 (0.36)	116 (0.78)	34 (0.42)
6 July	63 (0.16)	260 (0.67)	72 (0.49)	31 (0.38)
July 6	441 (1.14)	187 (0.48)	62 (0.42)	40 (0.49)
14 October	60 (0.16)	382 (0.99)	128 (0.86)	60 (0.74)
October 14	1556 (4.02)	280 (0.72)	169 (1.14)	93 (1.14)

of English, and whether any kind of extra-territorial influence can be detected from AmE.

The standard American way of expressing dates emerges clearly from the GloWbE-US data, with month>day order preferred for all four dates. Likewise, the British data from GloWbE-GB is consistent in preferring the day>month order, though the figures are less polarised. This is also in keeping with the greater pluralism allowed in BrE (Peters 2012), and the fact noted above that the GloWbE data contains large volumes of unedited prose (blogs). Clearly, some writers of BrE are not averse to expressing dates in the American order. The AusE and NZE data are even more mixed. Like the British, they prefer *1 January* over *January 1*, but their preferences go the opposite way for the second and fourth dates, and they go one each way with the third date. At any rate, there is no sign of the standard American pattern being adopted in AusE or NZE in formulating dates.

4.4 Summary of Corpus Findings

The four examples presented show differing configurations of AmE and traditional BrE elements in AusE. In the first two cases (4.1), AmE loan words have been integrated into well-known lexical fields, complementing existing vocabulary rather than eclipsing the AusE variants. It is telling that when asked to choose between *unit*, *flat* and *apartment*, the majority of Ferguson's (2008) participants circled all three, pointing out they attach different meanings to the forms (e.g. 'use all 3 – mean different things'; 'These are different things! All words in a different context'). In the third and fourth cases that involve morpho-syntactic paradigms (4.2), neither of the standard AmE patterns has taken root. In each case the AusE preferences may well be decided by reference to speech – how the past suffix is pronounced, or the conventional way of speaking dates with ordinal numbers. Those concerned about extra-territorial influence from AmE on these issues have little to fear.

5. DISCUSSION

Section 3 documented persistent vocal resistance to AmE since the arrival of and continual exposure to American films and television, and the perceived 'rising damp of Coca-Colonisation' (journalist FitzSimons's description of his 'irrits' [feelings of extreme irritation] at seeing 'so much of what is precious and unique being slowly swamped by, most particularly, American stories, expressions, and even accents'; FitzSimons 2018). Highly visible lexical incursions such as *trash*, *math* and *aluminum* are viewed as forming the thin end of a very undesirable wedge that will see the decline of Australian values and way of life. Furthermore, opposition to AmE usage shows no age watershed – all ages voice their 'irrits' at AmE influence, with 'loss of Australian identity' being a familiar refrain in the millennials' commentary at the end of Ferguson's (2008) survey.

But once we compare the themes of discontent emerging from section 3 with the corpus data in section 4, it is clear that people's sensitivity towards American influence is far greater than the reality. And here it is relevant to point out that the concerns Australians have about the well-being of their language go well beyond the complaint tradition observed in other ENL nations. (Lukač

2018: 8).⁸ Adding fuel to anti-American sentiments is the fact that many of the Americanisms in the cross-hairs of complainants today coincide with people's general linguistic bugbears, and are loathed because they might represent youth slang (*bro*, *chill out*), horrid redundancies (*gainfully employed*, *off of*), irritating workplace jargon (*going forward*, *game changer*), trendy noun conversions to verbs (*to impact*, *to protest*), and so on. However, named Americanisms are often not AmE, and misconceptions of this nature have been around since the disapproving media commentary began.

These branded forms contrast strikingly with all the Americanisms that have been able to sneak into AusE under the radar without detection, and there have been many over the years – around 10,000 (according to Sussex 1985, cited in Humphries 2011). Many everyday words relating to lifestyle and material culture, as well as a variety of discourse markers (as noted by Baker [1966], Taylor [1989], Sussex [1995]), assumed a position comfortably alongside the existing vocabulary without any conservative opposition. As discussed in section 4, extra-territorial linguistic influence may wax and wane with contemporary realpolitik, rather than remaining constant over time. It highlights once more the interplay between intra- and extra-territorial factors in American influence on AusE. Clearly, they are not equally at work in all countries at all times (Buschfeld and Kautzsch 2017: 117).

6. CONCLUSIONS

Two paradoxes have emerged from the contrasting data presented in sections 3 and 4. First, while AmE is firmly resisted in relation to the superficial and systematic aspects of language, it has nevertheless penetrated into the more 'porous' areas of language. Second, again despite the persistent vocal resistance to AmE influence, the bulk of this extra-territorial influence from AmE has gone unnoticed and unrecognised.

---

⁸ Severin and Burridge (in press) suggest this robust complaint tradition is also a hangover of *cultural cringe*, a distinctly Australian expression referring to 'the feeling that other (typically Anglophone) countries are better'. A convict past coupled with the nation's beginnings as a British colony has meant some Australian people have felt a need to prove the value of their country on the world stage, and a high standard of English encourages the notion that Australia is on par with other nations around the world.

Amid the pressures of globalisation, extra-territorial forces can be seen in linguistic and also cultural influences coming from the internet, US popular culture and modern media, as well as through international trading relations. However, these may be met by intra-territorial forces since territories differ with respect to whether and to what extent they accept or even admit these facets of globalisation (Buschfeld and Kautzsch 2017: 114).

Gonçalves et al. (2018) recorded that over the past two centuries, there has been a notable shift in vocabulary and spelling conventions from British to American around the world – '[n]aturally, the spread of the American culture is accompanied by the American linguistic variety, which ends up affecting (global) English' (Gonçalves et al. 2018: 12). However, their Twitter data also revealed some resistance against this global trend in ex-British colonies such as Australia (i.e. ENL varieties). So, as envisaged in the EIF Model, extra-territorial forces are not uniformly felt and can be offset by powerful intra-territorial forces operating at a local level, underscoring the benefits of a framework that integrates both forces in the linguistic development of a national variety.

In Australia, these forces coincided with nation-building and the forging of a national culture that then prompted fears of US practices putting Australian identity in jeopardy. By contrast, in contexts such as the Netherlands and other non-postcolonial countries, there is no comparable nation-making agenda attached to the use of English by EFL or ESuppL speakers, as pointed out by Edwards (2016: 184), and they do not experience such linguistic insecurities. Yet, in former colonies like Australia, which continue to be dominated by English, many speakers invest considerable national and personal identity in what is their only language. Whether this will change with Australia's increasing multilingual and multicultural population is an open question.

REFERENCES

Anderwald, Liselotte. 2016. *Language Between Description and Prescription: Verbs and Verb Categories in Nineteenth-Century Grammars*. Oxford: Oxford University Press.

Australian Government *Style Manual*. 6th edn. 2002, ed. Loma Snooks & Co. Brisbane: John Wiley.

Australian National Dictionary. 2016. 2 vols. Oxford: Oxford University Press.

Baker, Sidney. [1941] 1966. *The Australian Language.* Sydney: Currawong Press.
Bell, Philip. 1998. Television. In Bell and Bell, eds. 1998, 193–209.
Bell, Philip and Roger Bell, eds. 1998. *Americanization and Australia.* Sydney: UNSW Press.
Benczes, Réka, Kate Burridge, Keith Allan and Farzad Sharifian. 2017. Cultural linguistics and ageing: What naming practices can reveal about underlying cultural conceptualisation. In Farzad Sharifian, ed. 2017, *Advances in Cultural Linguistics.* New York: Springer, 607–624.
Buschfeld, Sarah and Alexander Kautzsch. 2017. Towards an integrated approach to postcolonial and non-postcolonial Englishes. *World Englishes* 36.1: 104–122.
Chicago Manual of Style. 16th edn. 2010. Chicago: Chicago University Press.
Coyourh. 2018. Is Australia being Americanised? *Reddit Political Post,* https://www.reddit.com/r/australia/comments/9n5l6n/is_australia_being_americanised/ (last accessed 3 August 2019).
Curzan, Anne. 2014. *Fixing English: Prescriptivism and Language History.* Cambridge: Cambridge University Press.
Damousi, Joy. 2010. *Colonial Voices: A Cultural History of English in Australia.* Cambridge: Cambridge University Press.
Dictionary of New Zealand English. 1997. ed. Harry Orsman. Oxford: Oxford University Press.
Edwards, Alison. 2016. *English in the Netherlands: Functions, Forms and Attitudes.* Amsterdam: John Benjamins.
Ferguson, Naomi. 2008. The Americanisation of Australian English: Attitudes, Perception and Usage. Monash University Honours thesis.
FitzSimons, Peter. 2018. Bring back these Aussie sayings. They're fresh, brilliant and ours. *The Sidney Morning Herald,* https://www.smh.com.au/national/fresh-and-brilliant-and-ours-bring-back-these-aussie-sayings-20180903-p501dp.html (last accessed 12 December 2018).
Gonçalves, Bruno, Lucía Loureiro-Porto, José J. Ramasco and David Sánchez. 2018. Mapping the Americanization of English in space and time. *PLoS ONE* 13.5: e0197741.
Heffernan, Kevin, Alison Borden, Alexandra Erath and Julie Yin Yang. 2010. Preserving Canada's 'honour': Ideology and diachronic change in Canadian spelling variants. *Written Language and Literacy* 13.1: 1–23.

Humphries, David. 2011. Let every new word bloom: Trying to keep Americanisms out of Australian speech ignores the way language works. *The Sydney Morning Herald* 1, https://www.smh.com.au/politics/federal/let-every-new-word-bloom-20110812-1iqtx.html (last accessed 7 December 2018).

Jernudd, Björn. 1989. The texture of language purism: An introduction. In Björn H. Jernudd and Michael J. Shapiro, eds. 1989, *The Politics of Language Purism*. Berlin: Mouton de Gruyter, 1–20.

Kachru, Braj. 1992. Models for non-native Englishes. In Braj Kachru, ed. 1992, *The Other Tongue: English Across Cultures (English in the Global Context)*. 2nd edn. Urbana, IL: University of Illinois Press, 48–74.

Korhonen, Minna. 2018. *Perspectives on the Americanisation of Australian English: A Sociolinguistic Study of Variation*. Helsinki: University of Helsinki.

Labov, William. 1993. The Unobservability of Structure and its Linguistic Consequences. Paper presented at NWAV 22, University of Ottawa, October 1993.

Lukač, Morana. 2018. Grassroots prescriptivism: An analysis of individual speakers' efforts at maintaining the standard language ideology. *English Today* 34.4: 5–12.

Macquarie Dictionary. 5th edn. 2009. Sydney: Macmillan.

Moore, Bruce. 2008. *Speaking Our Language: The Story of Australian English*. Melbourne: Oxford University Press.

Oxford English Dictionary. 2010. Oxford: Oxford University Press, https://www.oed.com (last accessed 3 August 2019).

Peters, Pam. 2001. Varietal effects: The influence of American English on British and Australian English. In Bruce Moore, ed. 2001, *Who's Centric Now?* Oxford: Oxford University Press, 296–309.

Peters, Pam. 2004. *Cambridge Guide to English Usage*. Cambridge: Cambridge University Press.

Peters, Pam. 2009. Irregular verbs: Regularization and ongoing variability. In Pam Peters, Peter Collins and Adam Smith, eds. 2009, *Comparative Studies of Australian and New Zealand English: Grammar and Beyond*. Amsterdam: John Benjamins, 13–29.

Peters, Pam. 2012. Standard British English. In Alexander Bergs and Laurel J. Brinton, eds. 2012, *English Historical Linguistics*. Berlin: De Gruyter.

Ramson, William. 1966. *Australian English: An Historical Study of the Vocabulary 1788–1898*. Canberra: Australia National University Press.

Schneider, Edgar. 2013. Leisure-activity ESP as a special case of ELF: The example of scuba diving English. *English Today* 29.3: 47–57.

Schneider, Edgar. 2014. New reflections on the evolutionary dynamics of World Englishes. *World Englishes* 33.1: 9–32.

Severin, Alyssa and Kate Burridge. In press. What do 'little Aussie sticklers' value most. In Don Chapman and Jacob D. Rawlins, eds. *Language Prescription: Values, Ideologies and Identity*. Bristol: Multilingual Matters.

Strang, Barbara. 1970. *A History of English*. London: Methuen.

Sussex, Roland. 1985. Linguistic evidence of the Americanisation of Australian English: Preliminary report. In J. E. Clark, ed. 1985, *The Cultivated Australian: Festschrift in Honour of Arthur Delbridge*. Hamburg: Helmut Buske Verlag.

Sussex, Roland. 1995. Americanisms roll into Australian English. *Australian Style* 3.2: 2–3.

Taylor, Brian. 1989. American, British and other influences on Australian English. In Peter Collins and David Blair, eds. 1989, *Australian English: The Language of a New Society*. St Lucia: University of Queensland Press, 225–254.

Thompson, Elaine. 1998. Political Culture. In Bell and Bell, eds. 1998, 106–122.

Waterhouse, Richard. 1998. Popular Culture. In Bell and Bell, eds. 1998, 45–60.

Webster's Third International Dictionary. 1986. Philippines: Merriam Webster.

Weinreich, U. 1953. *Languages in Contact*. New York: Linguistic Circle of New York Publication No. 2.

Wren, Melissa. 2009. Experiences and Attitudes Concerning English Spelling. Monash University Honours thesis.

CHAPTER 11

English in North America: Accounting for its Evolution

Edgar W. Schneider

1. INTRODUCTION

It is debatable whether American English (AmE) constitutes the cradle of World Englishes as the first of the new varieties growing outside of the British Isles. Strictly speaking, Indian English, going back to the foundation of the East India Company in 1600, antedates it slightly. In practice, however, for a long time English in India was used in limited trading contacts and in a small number of trading outposts only, while in North America English became rooted quickly by settler streams migrating there after 1607 in the South and 1620 in New England. This difference in colonization type, the migration of British settlers, in fact, constitutes one of the main differences between English as a Native Language (ENL) and English as a Second Language (ESL) in postcolonial countries in general, and, for that matter, between British colonization and the colonization strategies practiced by other European powers, notably the Spanish. The British came late in the European race for colonial possessions, but in the long run they were more successful and persistent, leaving stronger traces than the Dutch, the Portuguese, or the Spanish by having founded new English-speaking nations on other continents. The reason for this is the replenishment of overseas colonies, the fact that millions of settlers left the British Isles for good to build "clones" of the mother country in faraway lands (notably North America, Australia, New Zealand, and also but less strongly the Caribbean, South Africa, Kenya, and other locations; cf. Belich 2009; Schneider 2018, forthcoming 2020).

Given that American English branched off of its British parent varieties some 400 years ago, this variety can be observed over a substantial timeframe in hindsight which permits an extensive analysis and assessment of a major manifestation of postcolonial language evolution. Its overall development has been described in a wide range of sources, including Algeo (2001) and classics such as Krapp (1925) and Mencken ([1919] 1963). Schneider (2007) devotes an entire chapter to a comprehensive discussion of the history of American English viewed through the lens of his "Dynamic Model" (DM), which was proposed in Schneider (2003, 2007). The model has been widely accepted and found to explain evolutionary processes of postcolonial Englishes in a uniform framework. Schneider (2014) offers some stocktaking, surveying reactions and applications in the first decade after the model's publication; Seoane (2016: 4) states that this "groundbreaking ... Model ... fundamentally changed the way we approach World Englishes," and Deshors designates it "an improvement on Kachru's classification" (2018: 4). What is special about AmE in this perspective is the fact that it is the most advanced of all colonial offspring varieties, being the only one to have fully proceeded through the developmental cycle of five consecutive phases posited in the model. This includes a full manifestation of the final phase of "differentiation" which has not been reached to the same extent anywhere else, with different regional and social sub-varieties of American English having been associated with distinctive identities.

The massive growth of World Englishes as a scholarly discipline over the last few decades has produced extensive theorizing with the goal of identifying fundamental patterns such as variety types or evolutionary schemes. Kachru's "Three Circles" model (1985, 1992) and Schneider's "Dynamic Model of the evolution of Postcolonial Englishes" (2003, 2007) have been dominant (Deshors 2018), though other frameworks have also been proposed. In the present context there is no need to recapitulate these approaches and discussions, since in addition to being referred to in this volume's Introduction (Buschfeld and Kautzsch, this volume) plenty of accessible summaries are available, both of the Three Circles and the Dynamic Models and of recent theoretical discussions and advances in general (e.g. Schneider 2010, 2017; Buschfeld et al. 2014; Buschfeld and Schneider 2018; Deshors 2018). While the evolutionary trajectory spelled out in the Dynamic Model has been found to account well for the growth of postcolonial Englishes, it faces limitations when applied to non-postcolonial varieties (Schneider 2014; Edwards 2016), which have been undergoing a vibrant development in the very recent past (Schneider 2014; Buschfeld and Buschfeld, this volume). Buschfeld and Kautzsch's (2017) EIF ("Extra- and Intra-territorial Forces") Model attempts to bridge this gap by building upon the Dynamic Model but at the same time broadening this perspective to encompass non-postcolonial varieties as well. The question which explicitly underlies the present volume is whether, or to what extent, their framework is able to account for postcolonial and non-postcolonial contexts on a par.

The present chapter sets out to explore this question with respect to a long-established postcolonial variety, focusing on American English as a suitable model case. One core question is whether the perspective offered by the EIF Model adds anything of value to existing descriptions. Obviously, the historical account of the evolution of AmE in the light of the Dynamic Model as provided in chapter 6 of Schneider (2007) constitutes the natural backdrop for such a comparison. Hence, in this chapter I attempt to "translate" the components of the evolutionary stages described there, including extra-linguistic, historical conditions, the main agents' motivations, and other factors, into "forces," asking for the nature, systematicity, and comprehensiveness of the set of forces that can be identified.[1] The question, then, is whether the supplementary perspective offered by the EIF Model allows us to identify and assess differences which result from the varying frameworks.

By now two slightly different versions of the EIF Model have been published. The original one (Buschfeld and Kautzsch 2017) suggests five major sub-categories both of extra- and intra-territorial forces respectively, namely, colonization (extra)/attitudes towards colonization (intra), language policies (both extra and intra), globalization (extra)/'acceptance' of globalization (intra), foreign policies (both extra and intra), and the sociodemographic background of a country (mostly extra-territorial but with clear intra-territorial dimensions) (113), while retaining the five phases posited in the DM. Buschfeld et al. (2018: 25) add an important dimension of variability, namely a focus on internal heterogeneity, "zooming in to possible differences between speaker groups and – in its most detailed form – into the idiolects of individual speakers." This is visualized graphically by adding a second plane of an "idiolectal level" to the "abstract level" of the original representation form; both are connected by a triangle whose spread is taken to represent higher levels of internal linguistic variability (cf. the graph on p. 25 in Buschfeld et al.'s 2018 paper, reproduced in the Introduction to this

---

[1] In the subchapter titles I retain the contemporary "motto" statements from Schneider (2007), since they are nicely illustrative of prevailing attitudes in the respective periods.

volume, p. 7). This variability represents and is motivated by classic sociolinguistic parameters such as age, ethnicity, social class, gender, and so on (cf. Buschfeld et al. 2018: 25–26). Clearly this turns out to be relevant for AmE – so I take this version as my starting point of the discussion to follow.

2. EXTRA- AND INTRA-TERRITORIAL FORCES IN THE EVOLUTION OF NORTH AMERICAN ENGLISH

2.1 Foundation: "Assembled in America from Various Quarters" (1607–1670s)

Not surprisingly, Buschfeld and Kautzsch (2017) state that "colonization works as extra-territorial force" (113) – this applies to the foundation of AmE in the seventeenth century and also to later settlement waves by British and other migrants into the nineteenth century. Colonization itself, however, is driven by specific reasons, and these causes, the motivation for settlers to leave their homes and seek their fortune in a faraway land, constitute the ultimate "extra-territorial forces" behind societal and linguistic migration and re-rooting. While in other locations the social causes of settlement were more homogeneous (cf. the need to empty congested prisons to cause convicts to be shipped to Australia after 1788, or the relatively homogeneous and well-organized settler streams to New Zealand after 1840), in North America the reasons, and hence forces, were manifold and partly chaotic. Especially in the early foundation phase, religious motivations played a strong role: the Puritans who settled in New England and the Quakers who came to Pennsylvania later in the seventeenth century (and other groups as well) were religious unobstructed-by-state dissenters in England; they migrated in order to be able to practice their faith away from authorities without religious tolerance. The same applies to most of the so-called "Scotch-Irish" Presbyterians who resisted integration into the Church of England in the seventeenth century. A second force was political, fleeing oppression: many of the Cavaliers and Royalists who populated the South were driven out of England by the Civil War and Cromwell's reign in England. Similar constellations recur later in various forms and at different times – for example, Russian Jews fleeing pogroms or Germans leaving the country to avoid political persecution, such as after the mid-nineteenth century revolution. Third, of course, economic motives were important – the desire to improve one's lot, to gain land of one's own for farming, or, in extreme scenarios, to flee starvation (as in the case of the Great Famine in Ireland in the 1840s), or to accumulate wealth as quickly as possible (e.g. during the California gold rush of 1848–1849).

Buschfeld and Kautzsch's (2017) equivalent as an intra-territorial force is "attitudes towards colonization" (or, in their table 1, "attitudes towards the colonizing power"), more specifically defined as "aspects such as national pride, resistance against foreign rule, acceptance of foreign rule, but also the resulting differences in interaction and assimilation of the parties involved" (114). However, in the North American context these attitudes appear not to have strongly influenced language evolution for a long while. The indigenous people lost their lands and often resisted the colonizers, but their impact on the emerging AmE has remained marginal. White North Americans of the early period were the colonizers, so they did not experience "foreign rule" and had not yet developed a nation-based identity separate from the original British one. It was only much later, after phases 1 and 2, that their descendants, together with later immigrants, developed a local, American identity and started to view the British as an "other" group, as something like a "colonizing power" to which many of them came to develop a hostile attitude.

An intra-territorial force which did affect the population structure of North America significantly, however, was the demand for cheap labor, coupled with utter disrespect for the human rights of non-Caucasians – which caused the forced importation of millions of African slaves from the seventeenth through the nineteenth centuries. From the side of the white Americans this can be viewed as a variant of economic motives; their goal was not only to improve their economic situation but also to pursue the desire for wealth, at the expense of other humans.

While the "indigenous strand" remained rather insignificant in the evolution of North American English, one quality associated with the use of English turned into another intra-territorial force promoting it, namely its usefulness as a lingua franca, for inter-ethnic communication (similar to its status as an ethnically neutral variety in some Outer Circle countries). It is well known that an "Indian Pidgin" evolved fairly soon, and we have reports of it being used among Native Americans for internal communication, such as in a text from 1628: "a savage . . . who [was] talking with another savage, they were glad to use broken English to express their mind to each other, not being able to understand one another in their language" (Read 2002: 26). Similarly, so-called "linguisters," bilingual translators, were trained and employed for inter-ethnic communication (Romaine 2001: 58; cf. Schneider 2007: 259).

As elsewhere, another intra-territorial force which has shaped the development of North American English is, quite simply, the need to understand each other, that is, to downplay linguistic differences between interlocutors who come from different regions in the British Isles. Hence, the avoidance of rare or strongly localized linguistic forms and features, those which communication partners from other origins seem not to understand, produces koinéization, the growth of a relatively neutral intermediate dialect, observed historically twice in North America, in the seventeenth century along the east coast and in the nineteenth century during the westward expansion (Schneider 2007: 261, 270, 290).

2.2 Exonormative Stabilization: "English with Great Classical Purity" (1670s–1770s)

Is stability a "force"? Presumably so, an intra-territorial one in the form of prestige attributed to an external, in this case the British norm in manners and speech, since this strengthens the colonists' motivation, at least many of them, to behave and speak in a certain fashion. Algeo states that "the British standard ... exerted a powerful influence on Colonial English" (2001: 19), with cultural exchange going on (young prosperous men from the colonies seeking education in England, for instance), and prestige associated with east coast urban centers (such as Boston) which resembled a (presumably idealized) notion of English manners and speech, an attitude that upheld an English ideal even in more remote regions such as the Midwest (Mencken 1963: 57–61). The prestige attributed to British speech actually influenced American dialects quite significantly, causing, for instance, non-rhotic accents in New England and the traditional south or the "Boston broad a" (Schneider 2007: 271–272). The exonormative orientation also shows nicely in the fact that the growing local lexis, the use of early Americanisms, was branded as "improprieties and vulgarisms" (Mencken 1963: 6).

The cohesive social force of working towards increased social integration, or at least approximation to the people in one's environment, can also be seen to operate strongly during this period in all social cohorts. Among settlers, koinéization seems to be a continuously strong process which appears to have produced remarkably homogeneous speech forms despite great geographical distances. Contemporary travelers and commentators observed that "a striking similarity of speech universally prevails" (1770, quoted in Read 1933: 44), that "No County or Colonial dialect is to be distinguished here" (1777, quoted in Read 1933: 45), and "a perfect uniformity" (1777, quoted in Mencken 1963: 403). However, this should not be mistaken as complete speech homogeneity; due to differences in origins, regions, and social settings clearly some dialect differences persisted, as Montgomery (1996) showed.

In the indigenous (IDG) groups, an increasing number of Native Americans picked up some (possibly pidginized) English (Romaine 2001: 158). Especially in the early, "homestead" phase of slavery, African American slaves, the largest of the adstrate (ADS) groups, tended to live on small plantations (farming tobacco, predominantly) and in relatively close proximity to white owner families, a situation that apparently offered reasonably good conditions for natural second-language acquisition and some degree of linguistic adjustment, an approximation to settler dialects (Winford 1997; Mufwene 2000, 2003). It is noteworthy that these influences are likely to have been bi-directional, since, as is well known, white planters' children were given care by black "mammies" and often played with African American children during childhood, so it seems likely that their speech was also influenced by African American speech habits (Schneider 1989: 37). As to other ADS groups, this period saw increased immigration by non-British settlers, mainly Caucasians from other parts of Europe (again, often with religious or economic motives), and they obviously also strove to integrate into the social setting of their new environment by picking up the English language – mostly undergoing language shift by the third generation.

Of course, the intra-territorial force of demographic relations also played a substantial role during this period and in these processes. On small homestead farms along the Atlantic seaboard, the numerical relationship between whites and Africans tended to be roughly even – which supported reasonably good language and dialect acquisition among the latter, given that the former's speech was the target norm. In contrast, South Carolina, and in particular the state's southern part, was the only region with a strong black population majority, and consequently roughly the southern third of this state is the only region where strong contact effects or creole-like structures can be identified in the speech of local African Americans (Kautzsch and Schneider 2000). Other ADS immigrant groups tended to live together in ethnic neighborhoods, a habit which tended to preserve some degree of heritage language usage for a while, especially in ritual, such as religious, contexts. However, overall in society they were a clear minority, so their motivation to blend in and acquire English quickly must have been high.

2.3 Nativization: "That Torrent of Barbarous Phraseology" (1770s–1840s)

While the English used in North America showed a small but increasing set of peculiarities (new meanings associated with existing words, borrowings, or words used in innovative constructions) from the very beginning, it was the late eighteenth century and the period thereafter that produced a radical increase of usage patterns diverging from those of the inherited varieties and, in particular, an awareness and growing appreciation of such differences. Schneider (2007: 278–281) points out a number of innovations from that period.

The force which motivated these developments, clearly an intra-territorial one, can broadly be subsumed under the heading of "language policy," though in essence it was more a matter of social attitudes and identity rewritings on the side of the American colonists towards the British mother country. During the French and Indian War of 1754–1763, resentment grew between the "polished" British troops and their allies among the colonists, who were perceived as less civilized (Algeo 2001). Tensions grew over the issues of taxation and the lack of parliamentary representation of the colonies, leading to the "Boston Massacre" of 1770 (in which some colonists were killed by British troops) and the Boston Tea Party of 1773, a case of barely disguised rebellion (colonists dressed as Native Americans threw shiploads of tea into the Boston Harbor to resist taxation). Punitive measures and further debates and pamphlets ultimately led to the Declaration of Independence in 1776 (which clearly not all Americans supported). Hence, a sense of socio-political cleavage gradually manifested itself in a firm political stance which then triggered the move towards independence, manifested in the declaration and ensuing War of Independence.

As part of the separation movement, a perceived need for a distinct American version of the English language became a strong component of public discourse during the following years with some leading politicians, including John Adams, Benjamin Franklin, and Thomas Jefferson, involved (Krapp 1925 I: 10; Mencken 1963; Wolfram and Schilling-Estes 1998: 106; Schneider 2007: 276). The "great surge of linguistic and cultural patriotism" (Pyles 1952: 72) of that period resulted in several calls to become "entirely separated from Britain" linguistically also (Witherspoon in 1784, quoted from Krapp 1925 I: 47). The movement was then spearheaded by Noah Webster, who rather than creating a new "Federal English" was satisfied in the end with establishing some systematic spelling differences, which despite being relatively minor were perceived as "radical and revolutionary" (Krapp 1925 I: 328). The call for linguistic innovation also had a political dimension to it: the American version of the English language should be "fresh" and "honest," "free from all follies of unphilosophical fashion" (Thornton in 1793, quoted from Fisher 2001: 61), and access to it should be equally available to every citizen and "yeoman"; in the same vein, access to "eloquence" was perceived as a tool of individual freedom and as a genuinely democratic quality. So the force which promoted the growing split between the two main varieties of English in that decisive period was not a formally established language policy but, broadly similar in effect, a set of pertinent attitudes shared in and strengthened by public discourse and debates.

2.4 Endonormative Stabilization: "Our Honor Requires us to Have a System of our Own" (1840s–1898)

The nineteenth century was a period of transition and a lot of turmoil – the War of 1812 against Britain; President Jackson's removal of the Native Americans from the east, followed by the westward expansion and the Indian Wars; and the Civil War and Reconstruction period. In the end, however, it consolidated the United States as a nation and enabled her to enter the international scene for the first time as seen in the victory of the Spanish-American War of 1898. The nationalist orientation continued to thrive in matters of culture and linguistic orientation as well. Attitudes towards Americanisms changed in indicative ways: while they were originally branded as "incorrect," Bartlett's *Dictionary of Americanisms* of 1848 "gloried in the newly developing American diction" (Read 2002: 17). In fact, lexicographic coverage of American English was thriving, epitomized by Webster's *An American Dictionary of the English Language* of 1828 – an indicator of the move towards endonormativity. An internal norm orientation was also both mirrored and strongly promoted by Webster's most successful product, popularly known as the "Blue Backed Speller," estimated to have sold 100 million copies until the recent past (Algeo 2001: 34); it is significant that Webster deliberately changed the title of the first part of his "Grammatical Institute of the English Language" to "American Spelling Book." The same attitude also prevailed among and helped to integrate new immigrants, at least those whose complexion allowed them to blend into the mainstream of society: "nationalism encouraged newly arrived Europeans to think that they could participate fully in American life by adopting Anglo-Saxon virtues, including the English language" (Conklin and Lourie 1983: 70).

Interestingly enough, the nationalist linguistic orientation merged with ideas of moralism and democratization. An idea widely proclaimed was that "good usage" should become available to everyone, regardless of class differences, so following these linguistic models became a "patriotic duty" (Pyles 1952: 70). Similar to the literal acceptance of the message of the Bible, the literal adoption of grammar rules and lexical usage proposed by authorities "regardless of the discrepancies between grammatical rules and the actual language" was perceived as a moral obligation (McDavid Jr. 1958: 510–511). It is not a surprise, then, that a deeply rooted prescriptive attitude, the belief of many Americans in the importance of "proper English" as taught by the proverbial "schoolma'm" and registered in dictionaries as opposed to one's own inadequate usage acquired only "on the street," remains fundamentally entrenched into the American linguistic psyche. Cases in point illustrating this attitude include the public scorning of local dialect forms in a "Good Speech Week" in schools (R. Bailey 2006: 173–176; Schneider 2007: 288–289) or the heated debate on the very fact that the "unacceptable" word *ain't* was printed in *Webster's Third New International Dictionary* in 1961 (even if flagged as nonstandard) (Sledd and Ebbitt 1962). In addition, AmE is perceived and conceptualized as remarkably homogeneous, for example, "extensive as the country is, one uniform correctness obtains in speaking the English language" (Horton James in 1847; quoted from Read 2002: 64).

Where is all of this to be situated within the EIF Model? All the above-mentioned trends, viewed as forces, are intra-territorial, sociopsychological factors: attitudes and identity manifestations shared by a majority of the community. These are not official policies, linguistic or otherwise, but something similarly effective, effects of equally tuned mindsets in a society.

2.5 Differentiation: "We Know Who we Are by Our Language" (1898–)

In the twentieth century, the same types of factors, or intra-territorial forces, continue to drive the development of AmE, but the directionality and effects are different, strengthening no longer uniformity but differences. Interestingly enough, in an economically secure, socially stable, and powerful nation, speakers come to focus increasingly upon their immediate environment, deriving their identity from their regional, ethnic, or social group membership and sense of belonging – and these orientations are then symbolized by increasing speech differences. Read describes this tendency in very fundamental terms:

> Those of us whose memories go back several decades recall the time when the term melting pot represented a high ideal in American culture . . . [it] guided American thinking . . . Its tendency was toward uniformity . . . But in recent years our thinking has swung in a different direction, toward the recognition of diversity. (2002: 30–31)

Schneider (2007: 292–307) offers general observations, data, and further references for a number of case studies and contexts where identity-driven dialect diversification can be observed, where speakers (especially those with less education and a reduced supra-regional perspective) show pride in their ways of speaking as an indexical manifestation of their belonging to specific groups (cf. Wolfram and Schilling-Estes 1998: 20) – irrespective of the ongoing official promotion of "proper," Standard English. Labov's work on the centralization of the onsets of diphthongs on Martha's Vineyard (1972: 1–42) and the studies by Walt Wolfram and his associates (e.g. Wolfram and Schilling-Estes 1997) on /aɪ/-backing on Ocracoke show how specific, conservative dialect pronunciation features are being recycled and instilled with new life as symbolic representations of belonging to an island and hence claiming cultural authority against incoming new residents and tourists. More generally, the dialect of the American South has increasingly been seen as "a strong marker of regional identity and often as a source of cultural pride" (Wolfram and Schilling-Estes 1998: 115; cf. Nagle and Sanders 2003). Following Guy Bailey (1997) and Tillery and Bailey (2003), many of its distinctive features are remarkably young, going back to the Reconstruction and World War II periods, when regional identities were endangered or affected by social changes. Similarly, in the Great Lakes region the "Northern Cities Shift," a clockwise rotation of short vowels, has become regionally distinctive. Some European-American groups, for example, Italians, French, or Swedes, have selected small-scale pronunciation details to signal ethnolinguistic belonging. In line with the ongoing revitalization of cultural traditions, some Native Americans show distinctive speech features on the levels of pronunciation, grammar, or discourse organization which can be interpreted as transfer from tribal languages. Also mirroring movements instilling ethnic pride since the 1960s, African American English has clearly become an identity carrier for many blacks in the United States (Wolfram and Schilling-Estes 1998: 179–180) – and increasingly so, as the "divergence hypothesis" has claimed (Bailey and Maynor 1989). Many Mexican Americans in the Southwest have embraced a dialect called "Chicano English," a kind of English which sounds Spanish-influenced even if many of its speakers do not command Spanish at all. Similarly, a cultural renaissance of the Cajuns in Louisiana has produced a French-accented dialect called "Cajun English" (Dubois and Horvath 2004). On Hawai'i, the contact language locally called "Pidgin" has increasingly become "an important badge of local identity – that is, the language of people born and bred in Hawai'i, especially ethnic Hawaiians and descendants of plantation laborers" (Sakoda and Siegel 2003: 18). The basic pattern is essentially the same in all of these regions, groups, and contexts: people signal their regional, social, or ethnic belonging by specific speech forms, so group identities serve as a main intra-territorial force to establish and strengthen variety differences. In the light of the more recent version of the EIF Model mentioned initially (Buschfeld et al. 2018: 25), we have to locate these varieties somewhere away from the left-hand "abstract level" (presumably of "AmE" as such) further towards and up until the "idiolectal level," with increased internal linguistic variability.

Focusing upon the very recent past and the present situation, Tillery et al. (2004) explicitly identify forces which keep driving linguistic changes, and notably diversification, in AmE. These forces include ongoing urbanization, increased migration across regions, and ethnic diversification. The latter is associated with what they call "balkanization": in urban settings and also larger regions, residential patterns favor tightly-knit ethnic neighborhoods, often with African Americans populating the inner-city areas, whites living in certain suburbs, and so on. Hence, spatial reorganization contributes to ethnolinguistic fragmentation and increased diversification.

2.6 Observations on Canadian English

Canadian English (CanE), as described (among many others) by Avis (1973), Boberg (2011), or Schneider (2007: 238–250), has also been shaped by diverse forces that have become effective during different phases of its history. In the beginning, these forces were the same as those which produced AmE. Colonization brought English settler groups to Newfoundland (though this island has a different founder population and developmental trajectory from the rest of Canada, which it only joined in 1949), Nova Scotia, and Eastern Canada, mainly in the early eighteenth century. Subsequently, a sense of politically belonging to a nation (or not) became decisive, though with a different direction: a large number of American settlers who objected to the independence of the United States and wanted to remain loyal to the Crown left the thirteen colonies and moved north to Canada, which remained a colony. These "Loyalists," who arrived up until the early nineteenth century, are often considered the cradle of CanE, and responsible for the continuing impact of British English on this variety and remaining similarities. A force which strengthened the pro-British orientation of CanE was the Canadian government's immigration policy in the first half of the nineteenth century: out of distrust of all citizens with American roots, settlers directly from Britain were primarily attracted. The highlighted kinship with Britain and the desire to avoid "Yankee barbarisms" (Avis 1973: 42) on the one hand, balanced against the roots in and geographical proximity to AmE on the other, produced the intermediate character of CanE, between BrE and AmE. Thus, the forces effective in this process include the intra-territorial one of attitudes and identity as well as the extra-territorial one of contact and interaction.

The tension between these tendencies and forces has shaped CanE to the present day. The effect of the latter seems natural and unavoidable, given the simple fact that the vast majority of Canada's population lives in a relatively narrow (but thousands of miles long) band of land across the American border. The former manifested itself in deliberate policy decisions – for instance, the fact that when the western provinces of British Columbia, Alberta, Saskatchewan, and Manitoba were opened to settlement, provisions were made to attract Canadian, not American, settlers, and also after the establishment of the Dominion of Canada, which practically meant independence, in 1867. Similarly to the United States (though different in directionality), spelling assumed a remarkably high degree of symbolic importance, retaining British habits with some but not all forms, for example, *centre*. There are obviously conflicting forces operating here. An extra-territorial force is the ongoing proximity to, contact, and exchange with AmE, a strong external influence which is impossible to avoid. This stands in stark contrast, however, to the intra-territorial force of identity, the desire to remain distinct: "one thing that unites almost all Canadians is the desire to show to the world that they are most emphatically *not Americans!*" (Barber 2001: 293).

Similar to what had happened to the United States about one and a half centuries earlier, Canada went through a period of "rabid Canadian nationalism" (Chambers 1998: 270) roughly between 1920 and 1970, fueled by participation in two world wars. Steps towards and symbols of independent nationhood included the 1931 Statute of Westminster bestowing full legislative equality, Canadian (non-British) citizenship established in 1947, a national flag (1965), and a national anthem (1967). Also similar to the United States and elsewhere, linguistic usage became an essential component of this movement – not necessarily in real-life speech forms but in public discourse and attention to details with a growing focus on "a small but significant set of features that are uniquely Canadian" (Boberg 2004: 355). Other traits associated with endonormativity can be identified as well: codification via national dictionaries, for example, the *Dictionary of Canadianisms on Historical Principles* (Avis et al. 1967); the perception of great uniformity ("Canadian English is remarkably homogeneous from one end of the country to the other" [Boberg 2004: 352]); and the growth of a national literature using the local language variety. Nationalism clearly constitutes a strong intra-territorial force, a variant of attitudes and identity formation.

For the last few decades, CanE has also begun to diversify, slowly but steadily. The cause of this development, the force that has brought it about, again basically can be defined as a set of attitudinal factors: the self-definition as an immigrant country, respecting and retaining heritage languages so that ethnically indexical variation may result from contact with them; the growing recognition of indigenous peoples (with some linguistic consequences); the demise of older Briticisms; and the emergence of early regionalisms.

3. ASSESSING AND COMPARING THE TWO MODELS

Since the DM is focused explicitly upon postcolonial Englishes and both AmE and CanE constitute prototypical representatives of colonial settings and such variety types, the observation that the DM works very well for both varieties (Schneider 2007: 238–308) should not come as a surprise. It accounts for their evolution in a coherent and comprehensive fashion, integrating a wide range of political, social, sociolinguistic, and linguistic facts and observations. The core question in this chapter was what the EIF Model may add, or if there are any fundamental differences between the two approaches. In hindsight, I do not think the differences are great – which is also not a surprise given that the EIF Model was conceived and defined as an extension and follow-up development of the DM (Buschfeld and Kautzsch 2017: 122), although with a focus on non-postcolonial countries. As I see it, it adds a slightly different thematic focus, as worked out in the following sections.

In section 2 of this chapter I have strongly highlighted the notion of "forces" understood as causes for any specific linguistic developments at any given place and time, and I have attempted to identify these forces in specific historical circumstances. The notion of "forces" focuses very strongly upon socio-political causes of developments. With respect to ensuing consequences, like the sociolinguistic conditions of contact or the linguistic consequences, the EIF Model obviously builds upon and thus upholds the claims and descriptive statements made by the DM, including some (such as linguistic forms) that do not constitute "forces" but are, of course, important elements of the overall developmental patterns. The notion of forces is thus somewhat reductive and more concise, but it highlights causal relationships, which are not so prominent in the DM. The EIF Model thus offers a welcome additional perspective, a shift of emphasis highlighting motives and causes.

The above discussions have yielded essentially two major types of forces, in my view. One has to do with movements of and interactions between people, grasped in Buschfeld and Kautzsch's original list of forces (2017: 113) as "colonization" and "sociodemographic background" – which obviously includes patterns of migration. I agree that colonization is usually extra-territorial, while demography (and migration, for that matter) can be both extra-territorial (considering immigration of settlers) and intra-territorial (for example, internal relocation, such as the westward expansion in the US). A second set of forces, one which appears to have become effective and increasingly strong over the course of time and nation-internally, both in the United States and in Canada, can be broadly defined as socio-psychological: attitudes (towards other speaker groups, nationhood, or other languages and varieties) and identities (perceiving oneself strongly as a member of a nation or a specific social, ethnic, or other group, typically symbolized by specific dialects or linguistic forms). This, I think, significantly supplements the set of forces originally (and tentatively) suggested in Buschfeld and Kautzsch (2017). There we find internal factors such as "attitudes towards colonization" or "acceptance of globalization," so attitudinal forces are considered and covered, yet the identities and attitudes worked out above appear to be more fundamental and far-reaching, not constrained to colonization and globalization. Hence, I suggest that in an updated and elaborated set of forces, socio-psychological factors (broadly, "identities and attitudes") deserve a prominent place amongst intra-territorial forces!

Another generalization which can be tentatively culled from the above analyses of the evolution of English in the United States and in Canada is the observation that different types of forces appear to have been effective to varying degrees at different phases – not absolutely but to some extent, as envisaged in general terms by Buschfeld and Kautzsch (2017: 15). Specifically, the analysis of the evolution of Englishes in North America suggests that the extra-territorial forces (colonization, migration, demographic relations) clearly get the ball rolling initially and remain important during the early phases of foundation, exonormative stabilization, and also, with migration and contact continuing, nativization, while intra-territorial, socio-psychological factors seem to get stronger and clearly predominant later, certainly during the endonormative stabilization and differentiation phases.

In a wider perspective, I wonder whether it is justified to extrapolate from this observation the putatively stronger impact of extra-territorial forces early on as opposed to intra-territorial forces in later phases, to the relationship between postcolonial and non-postcolonial varieties. Such a speculative hypothesis cannot be informed by an analysis of AmE and CanE alone, of course, but needs to consider other ESL and EFL varieties as well (as in Schneider 2007, 2014), so it may be interesting to see whether other contributions in the present volume yield a similar picture. But intuitively, given what we know about many such contexts, would it make sense to hypothesize that there exists a correlation between the relative strength of specific types of forces and variety types such that extra-territorial forces (policy decisions, migration, globalization, etc.) have a relatively stronger effect in "younger," that is, EFL, varieties, whereas intra-territorial forces (such as attitudes and identities) play a relatively stronger role in more strongly established varieties (ESL and especially ENL)? After all, for internal, psychologically driven differentiation to set in external, political stability (say, in an established nation) is a prerequisite, while the motivation to acquire another language often tends to result from external influences (migration to a foreign territory, contact with immigrants on the side of the locals, exposure to English as a prestigious language in international contexts, etc.). Thus, is the growth of internal, identity-driven differentiation as described above for the United States and Canada possibly (more) typical of advanced developmental stages, so far reached mainly in settler strands? Note that this idea is not meant to perpetuate the traditional distinction between ESL and EFL: on the basis of broadly similar structural properties and increasingly comparable sociolinguistic settings, the difference between these two categories has rightly been characterized as a continuum rather than a dichotomy, and a possible increase of the impact of intra- over extra-territorial forces in the course of time, as suggested above, will certainly also proceed as a gradual change and flip of the balance (if at all). Clearly, at this stage, this is quite tentative and possibly speculative, but the hypothesis may be worth pursuing.

4. CONCLUSION

The present chapter has described and interpreted the historical evolution processes of both AmE and CanE in the light of both the DM and the EIF Model, trying, above all, to identify the forces that were effective in the shaping of these varieties. It has argued and attempted to show that extra-territorial forces such as migration and demographic proportions are decisive in early phases of variety emergence while intra-territorial forces, notably socio-psychological ones such as attitudes and identities, become increasingly important and influential towards the later developmental phases.

In conclusion, I wish to widen the perspective from the merely regional (if large) North American continental context to a global one, integrating the above questions and raising new ones. I introduce three ideas, partially related to each other, which may inspire further inquiries in future work.

First, in the EIF Model the notion of "territory" figures rather prominently and similarly to the role of the nation state in the DM; it may safely be assumed that a "territory" often (though not necessarily in principle) equals a nation state (as in Buschfeld and Kautzsch's 2017 example of Namibia). This raises the question of whether indirectly the nation state remains a yardstick unit – despite claims to the contrary arguing that many of today's dissemination forces are transnational, for example, the internet (Buschfeld and Kautzsch 2017:115; Buschfeld et al. 2018: 33–39). In other words, does the distinction between intra- and extra-territorial forces, useful as it clearly is, indirectly uphold or perhaps even perpetuate a territory- or nation-based line of thinking that seems to be losing importance in an age of global integration and information flow (Seargeant and Tagg 2011; Mair 2013: 265–275)?[2]

Second, Mair (2013) forcefully argues that today AmE is the only "hyper-central variety" or "hub" of his "world system of Englishes," a variety with major "transnational impact" and a "potential factor in the development of all others" (261). In the above examples we find a clear manifestation of this pull effect in the development of CanE (and, conversely, the variety's resistance to becoming too strongly Americanized). In line with Mair's claim, the American impact on various World Englishes has been widely observed (and often lamented on; cf. Taylor 2001; Trüb 2008; Hackert and Deuber 2015; Gilquin 2018). Thus, the status of AmE as (the arguably only) hyper-central variety clearly constitutes a strong force in the development of all other Englishes, one which should be recognized and integrated into World Englishes modeling.

Third, a new force has arisen in the western world over the last few years which may have the potential of threatening and possibly stopping globalization and, with it, the further spread of English, namely nationalism and isolationism. Strong indicators include the Brexit vote in the United Kingdom, the election of Donald Trump to the presidency of the United States, and growing internal and nationalist orientations in several countries (such as Poland, Hungary, Turkey, and others). The question is whether this tendency will have to be built into a model of forces that shape the development of English on a global scale. In principle, this force, or developmental trend, may not be entirely new – we find similar developments, preventing, stopping, or reversing the further spread of English in specific contexts, postulated in early cyclic models of the development of varieties of English, albeit in quite different political contexts and for different reasons. This applies to some of the precursors to the DM: Llamzon (1986) observes a "restriction phase" in Philippine English; Moag (1992) suggests that in Fiji after phases of "expansion" and "institutionalization" a phase of "restriction of use and function" is likely to follow; and, similarly, Schmied (1991: 194–197) envisages the possibility of ultimate "repression" or "deinstitutionalization" in African Englishes. Time will tell whether such trends will become stronger and threaten or even throttle globalization and the global role of English. Given that these days in many countries there is

---

[2] Buschfeld and Kautzsch (2017: 2) also propose to integrate "any other type of English developing beyond national boundaries."

a substantial cohort of globally oriented young people who are widely traveled, fluent in English, and multiculturally oriented, I think this is unlikely in the end – the flow of time cannot be reversed; but it is a force that needs to be considered and observed.

REFERENCES

Algeo, John. 2001. External history. In Algeo, ed. 2001, 1–58.
Algeo, John, ed. 2001. *The Cambridge History of the English Language*. Vol. VI: *English in North America*. Cambridge: Cambridge University Press.
Avis, Walter S. 1973. The English language in Canada. In Thomas A. Sebeok, ed. 1973, *Current Trends in Linguistics*. Vol. 10: *Linguistics in North America*. The Hague: Mouton, 40–74.
Avis, Walter S., Charles Crate, Patrick Drysdale, Douglas Leechman, Matthew H. Scargill and Charles J. Lovell, eds. 1967, *A Dictionary of Canadianisms on Historical Principles*. Toronto: Gage.
Bailey, Guy. 1997. When did Southern English begin? In Edgar W. Schneider, ed. 1997, *Englishes Around the World. Vol. 1: General Studies, British Isles, North America. Studies in Honour of Manfred Görlach*. Amsterdam and Philadelphia: Benjamins, 255–275.
Bailey, Guy and Nathalie Maynor. 1989. The divergence controversy. *American Speech* 64.1: 12–39.
Bailey, Richard W. 2006. Standardizing the Heartland. In Thomas Murray and Beth Lee Simon, eds. 2006, *Language Variation and Change in the American Midland: A New Look at "Heartland" English*. Amsterdam: John Benjamins, 165–178.
Barber, Katherine. 2001. Neither Uncle Sam nor John Bull: Canadian English comes of age. In Bruce Moore, ed. 2001, *"Who's Centric Now?" The Present State of Post-Colonial Englishes*. South Melbourne: Oxford University Press, 284–296.
Belich, James. 2009. *Replenishing the Earth: The Settler Revolution and the Rise of the Anglo-World, 1783–1939*. Oxford and New York: Oxford University Press.
Boberg, Charles. 2004. English in Canada: Phonology. In Schneider et al., eds. 2004, 351–365.
Boberg, Charles. 2011. *The English Language in Canada. Status, History, and Comparative Analysis*. Cambridge: Cambridge University Press.

Buschfeld, Sarah and Alexander Kautzsch. 2017. Towards an integrated approach to postcolonial and non-postcolonial Englishes. *World Englishes* 36.1: 104–126.
Buschfeld, Sarah and Edgar W. Schneider. 2018. World Englishes: Postcolonial Englishes and beyond. In Ee Ling Low and Anne Pakir, eds. 2018, *World Englishes: Re-Thinking Paradigms*. London: Routledge, 29–46.
Buschfeld, Sarah, Alexander Kautzsch and Edgar W. Schneider. 2018. From colonial dynamism to current transnationalism: A unified view on postcolonial and non-postcolonial Englishes. In Deshors, ed. 2018, 15–44.
Buschfeld, Sarah, Thomas Hoffmann, Magnus Huber and Alexander Kautzsch, eds. 2014. *The Evolution of Englishes: The Dynamic Model and Beyond*. Amsterdam: John Benjamins.
Chambers, J. K. 1998. Social embedding of changes in progress. *Journal of English Linguistics* 26.1: 5–36.
Conklin, Nancy Faires and Margaret A. Lourie. 1983. *A Host of Tongues. Language Communities in the United States*. New York: Free Press, Macmillan.
Deshors, Sandra C. 2018. Modeling World Englishes in the 21st century. A thematic introduction. In Deshors, ed. 2018, 1–14.
Deshors. Sandra C., ed. 2018. *Modelling World Englishes in the 21st Century: Assessing the Interplay of Emancipation and Globalization of ESL Varieties*. Amsterdam: John Benjamins.
Dubois, Sylvie and Barbara M. Horvath. 2004. Cajun Vernacular English: Phonology. In Schneider et al., eds. 2004, 407–416.
Edwards, Alison. 2016. *English in the Netherlands. Functions, Forms and Attitudes*. Amsterdam: John Benjamins.
Fisher, John Hurt. 2001. British and American, continuity and divergence. In John Algeo, ed. 2001, 59–85.
Gilquin, Gaetanelle. 2018. American and/or British influence on L2 Englishes – Does context tip the scale(s)? In Deshors, ed. 2018, 187–216.
Hackert, Stephanie and Dagmar Deuber. 2015. American influence on written Caribbean English: A diachronic analysis of newspaper reportage in the Bahamas and in Trinidad and Tobago. In Peter Collins, ed. 2015, *Grammatical Change in English World-Wide*. Amsterdam: John Benjamins, 389–410.
Kachru, Braj B. 1985. Standards, codification and sociolinguistic realism: The English language in the outer circle. In Randolph Quirk

and Henry G. Widdowson, eds. 1985, *English in the World. Teaching and Learning the Language and Literatures.* Cambridge: Cambridge University Press for The British Council, 11–30.

Kachru, Braj B., ed. 1992. *The Other Tongue: English Across Cultures.* 2nd edn. Urbana, Chicago: University of Illinois Press.

Kautzsch, Alexander and Edgar W. Schneider. 2000. Differential creolization: Some evidence from Earlier African American Vernacular English in South Carolina. In Ingrid Neumann-Holzschuh and Edgar W. Schneider, eds. 2000, *Degrees of Restructuring in Creole Languages.* Amsterdam: John Benjamins, 247–274.

Krapp, George P. 1925. *The English Language in America.* 2 vols. New York: Century.

Labov, William. 1972. *Sociolinguistic Patterns.* Oxford: Blackwell.

Llamzon, Teodoro A. 1986. Life cycle of New Englishes: Restriction phase of Filipino English. *English World-Wide* 7.1: 101–125.

McDavid Jr., Raven I. 1958. The dialects of American English. In W. Nelson Francis, ed. 1958, *The Structure of American English.* New York: Ronald, 480–543.

Mair, Christian. 2013. The world system of Englishes: Accounting for the transnational importance of mobile and mediated vernaculars. *English World-Wide* 34.3: 253–278.

Mencken, H. L. [1919] 1963. *The American Language. An Inquiry into the Development of English in the United States.* One-volume abridged edn. by Raven I. McDavid Jr. New York: Alfred Knopf (reprinted 1982).

Moag, Rodney F. 1992. The life cycle of non-native Englishes: A case study. In Kachru, ed. 1992, 233–252.

Montgomery, Michael. 1996. Was colonial American English a koiné? In Juhani Klemola, Merja Kytö and Matti Rissanen, eds. 1996, *Speech Past and Present: Studies in English Dialectology in Memory of Ossi Ihalainen.* Frankfurt a.M.: Peter Lang, 213–235.

Mufwene, Salikoko S. 2000. Some sociohistorical inferences about the development of African American English. In Poplack, ed. 2000, 233–263.

Mufwene, Salikoko S. 2003. The shared ancestry of African-American and American White Southern Englishes: Some speculations dictated by history. In Nagle and Sanders, eds. 2003, 64–81.

Nagle, Stephen J. and Sara L. Sanders, eds. 2003. *English in the Southern United States.* Cambridge: Cambridge University Press.

Poplack, Shana, ed. 2000. *The English History of African American English.* Malden and Oxford: Blackwell.

Pyles, Thomas. 1952. *Words and Ways of American English*. London: Melrose.
Read, Allen Walker. 1933. British recognition of American speech in the eighteenth century. *Dialect Notes* 6: 313–334. (Quoted from reprint in Read 2002: 37–54.)
Read, Allen Walker. 2002. *Milestones in the History of English in America*, ed. 2002, Richard W. Bailey. (PADS 86.) Durham, NC: Duke University Press for the American Dialect Society.
Romaine, Suzanne. 2001. Contact with other languages. In Algeo, ed. 2001, 154–183.
Sakoda, Kent and Jeff Siegel. 2003. *Pidgin Grammar. An Introduction to the Creole Language of Hawai'i*. Honolulu: Bess Press.
Schmied, Josef J. 1991. *English in Africa: An Introduction*. London and New York: Longman.
Schneider, Edgar W. 1989. *American Earlier Black English. Morphological and Syntactic Variables*. Tuscaloosa: University of Alabama Press.
Schneider, Edgar W. 2003. The dynamics of New Englishes: From identity construction to dialect birth. *Language* 79.2: 233–281.
Schneider, Edgar W. 2007. *Postcolonial English. Varieties Around the World*. Cambridge: Cambridge University Press.
Schneider, Edgar W. 2010. Developmental patterns of English: Similar or different? In Andy Kirkpatrick, ed. 2010, *The Routledge Handbook of World Englishes*. London: Routledge, 372–384.
Schneider, Edgar W. 2014. New reflections on the evolutionary dynamics of world Englishes. *World Englishes* 33.1: 9–32.
Schneider, Edgar W. 2017. Models of English in the World. In Juhani Klemola, Markku Filppula and Devyani Sharma, eds. 2017, *The Oxford Handbook of World Englishes*. Oxford: Oxford University Press, 35–57.
Schneider, Edgar W. 2018. English and colonialism. In Philip Seargeant, Ann Hewings and Stephen Pihlaja, eds. 2018, *The Routledge Handbook of English Language Studies*. Malden, MA and Oxford: Routledge, 42–58.
Schneider, Edgar W. Forthcoming. 2020. The emergence of global languages: Why English? In Marianne Hundt, Johannes Katabek, Daniel Schreier and Danae Perez, eds. 2020, *English and Spanish. World Languages in Interaction*. Cambridge: Cambridge University Press.
Schneider, Edgar W., Kate Burridge, Bernd Kortmann, Rajend Mesthrie and Clive Upton, eds. 2004, *A Handbook of Varieties of English*. Vol. 1: *Phonology*. Berlin, New York: Mouton de Gruyter.

Seargeant, Philip and Caroline Tagg. 2011. English on the internet and a 'post-varieties' approach to language. *World Englishes* 30.4: 496–514.
Seoane, Elena. 2016. World Englishes today. In Seoane and Suárez-Gómez, eds. 2016, 1–16.
Seoane, Elena and Cristina Suárez-Gómez, eds. 2016. *World Englishes. New Theoretical and Methodological Considerations*. Amsterdam: John Benjamins.
Sledd, James and Wilma R. Ebbitt, eds. 1962. *Dictionaries and That Dictionary*. Glenview, IL: Scott, Foresman & Co.
Taylor, Brian. 2001. Australian English in interaction with other Englishes. In David Blair and Peter Collins, eds. 2001, *English in Australia*. Amsterdam: Benjamins, 317–340.
Tillery, Jan and Guy Bailey. 2003. Urbanization and the evolution of Southern American English. In Nagle and Sanders, eds. 2003, 159–172.
Tillery, Jan, Guy Bailey and Tom Wikle. 2004. Demographic change and American dialectology in the twenty-first century. *American Speech* 79.3: 227–249.
Trüb, Regina. 2008. American English Impact on South African English. An Empirical Analysis of its Manifestations and Attitudes Towards It. PhD dissertation, University of Regensburg.
Winford, Donald. 1997. On the origins of African American Vernacular English – A creolist perspective. Part I: The sociohistorical background. *Diachronica* 14.2: 305–344.
Wolfram, Walt and Natalie Schilling-Estes. 1997. *Hoi Toide on the Outer Banks. The Story of the Ocracoke Brogue*. Chapel Hill and London: University of North Carolina Press.
Wolfram, Walt and Natalie Schilling-Estes. 1998. *American English. Dialects and Variation*. Malden, MA and Oxford: Blackwell.

CHAPTER 12

English in The Bahamas and Developmental Models of World Englishes: A Critical Analysis

Stephanie Hackert, Alexander Laube and Diana Wengler

1. INTRODUCTION

Modeling Englishes has enjoyed quite some popularity since the late 1980s, when the focus of research shifted from the description of individual varieties to attempts at explaining the entire "English Language Complex" (Mesthrie and Bhatt 2008: 3). One of the most influential models which has emerged in this context is Schneider's (2003, 2007) Dynamic Model, which, in essence, claims that "it is possible to identify a single, underlying, fundamentally uniform evolutionary process which can be observed, with modifications and adjustments to local circumstances, in the evolution of all postcolonial forms of English" (Schneider 2017: 47). The realities of the twenty-first century, and primarily globalization and web-based communication, have dramatically altered the ways English is used around the world and have accelerated the diversification of the language. Schneider himself (2014: 28) draws attention to the limitations of the Dynamic Model in accounting for "this new kind of dynamism of global Englishes."

It is the explicit aim of Buschfeld and Kautzsch's "Extra- and Intra-territorial Forces" (EIF) Model to account for these "complex linguistic realities" (2017: 104). The EIF Model's basic assumption is that all Englishes have been shaped by a set of "forces," which can be divided into external ("extra-territorial") and internal ("intra-territorial") ones. These forces are viewed as "general mechanisms" affecting the development of any specific variety, the difference lying in the "concrete form" that they assume (2017: 116). This permits a unified treatment not only of postcolonial and non-postcolonial Englishes but also of the colonial and postcolonial periods for the former: "intra- and extra-territorial forces have always been the driving forces behind the (socio)linguistic developments in the territories throughout the process of colonization but also in postcolonial times" (2017: 116). The EIF Model builds on the basic components and assumptions of the Dynamic Model but integrates them in a "higher-level framework" (2017: 111), so that "all aspects of the model, most importantly the five phases and the four parameters operating on them, can be explained in terms of such extra- and intra-territorial forces" (2017: 116).

A question that arises in this context is in what way the description and explanation of English in a postcolonial anglophone nation such as The Bahamas fits into this new approach. In order to answer it, section 2 of this chapter looks into The Bahamas' sociolinguistic and linguistic history. We adopt Schneider's (2007: chapter 5) "countries-along-the-cycle" method and outline the history, identity constructions, sociolinguistics, and structural effects (2003: 56) that have shaped the use of English in The Bahamas and then turn to the effects of globalization as the most important twenty-first-century force affecting language use in the country. The EIF Model appears to suggest precisely this kind of treatment, in that Buschfeld and Kautzsch describe colonization as one of five "major subcategories" of extra- and intra-territorial forces and explicitly refer back to the Dynamic Model to account for it (2017: 113). As will become apparent shortly, even fairly typical postcolonial situations, such as the one found in The Bahamas today, present problems in this respect. In its focus on general forces, however, the EIF Model appears more flexible than the Dynamic Model, permitting, for example, the easy integration of postcolonial developments such as globalization.

In section 3, we briefly summarize the advantages and disadvantages of the two models and offer some critical remarks on the developmental approach to World Englishes that are of a general nature. They are thus not specific to the application of either model to The Bahamas. They are also not necessarily original but have occurred, in one form or another, in previous publications dealing critically with theorizing in World Englishes, for example, Pennycook (2007), Blommaert (2010), Hackert (2012a, 2014), Seargeant (2012), Canagarajah (2013), or Saraceni (2015). In principle, what is at stake is that even recent models of English around the world are "tied to the linguistics and politics of the twentieth century" (Pennycook 2007: 12). More specifically, we discuss the following ideological complexes: that varieties are discrete entities which may be "transported" or "translocated" somewhere or even "travel" and "spread" themselves; that such varieties are describable in terms of a set of more or less consistent but clearly identifiable features; that a variety's most natural basis is the nation; and that all varieties of English undergo evolution, that is not just change but teleological development, whose designated end point is the coming-into-being of autonomous standard varieties.

2. THE BAHAMAS AS A POSTCOLONIAL ANGLOPHONE COUNTRY: FROM SETTLEMENT TO GLOBALIZATION

The Bahamas were a British colony for more than 300 years, with thousands of slaves imported between roughly the mid-seventeenth and early nineteenth centuries and a continuum of varieties spoken today, "ranging from a creole retaining the most influence of the grammar of African and other languages (the basilect) to a variety of English whose grammatical differences from the Standard English spoken elsewhere are negligible (the acrolect)" (Holm and Shilling 1982: ix). At first sight, The Bahamas appear to constitute an uncontroversial case of a postcolonial speech community, so the Dynamic Model should nicely account for the linguistic and sociolinguistic situation that obtained there at least until the early years of independence. As noted in section 1, Buschfeld and Kautzsch (2017: 113) also draw on Schneider (2003, 2007) to describe colonization as one of the forces that have shaped postcolonial Englishes.

Fundamental to the emergence of any postcolonial English is "the translocation of the English language to a new territory" (Buschfeld and Kautzsch 2017: 106). Having been raided and depopulated by the Spanish in the wake of Columbus's landfall in the archipelago in 1492, The Bahamas were first settled by English speakers when a group of religious dissenters from Bermuda came to the northern island of Eleuthera in 1648. In the following years, more settlers from Bermuda arrived in The Bahamas, but in 1670, when a joint colony with the Carolinas was established by Charles II, The Bahamas' "Bermudian connection [. . .] was gradually replaced by a Carolinian one" (Hackert 2004: 35). This established a new but eventually long-lasting link with the American mainland.

Regarding the "Eleutherian Adventurers" (cf. Craton 1962: 57), there is no evidence as to what languages or dialects they spoke when they arrived on Bahamian shores. In terms of sociodemographics, blacks were among the earliest settlers, but whites outnumbered them during the initial colonial phase, and both population groups worked together in close contact in subsistence farming, fishing, or other small-scale enterprises (1962: 70). In terms of linguistic effects, this suggests some cross-dialect contact among white settlers but certainly not massive linguistic restructuring, as blacks must have had ample access to the settlers' dialects. The black population grew steadily during the eighteenth century, however, and blacks came to outnumber whites around 1760 (Craton and Saunders 1992: 151). The once intense contact between the two groups became more restricted, and so did the blacks' access to the white dialects of English (cf. Hackert 2004: 37–38). Nevertheless, it is still unlikely that a full-fledged creole existed in The Bahamas at the time.

The late eighteenth century, then, saw the arrival of thousands of loyalists and their slaves, who migrated to the archipelago in the wake of the American Revolutionary War (1775–1783). As a result of this migration, the Bahamian population tripled, and the proportion of blacks rose from one-half to three-quarters (Craton and Saunders 1992: 179). Most of the immigrant blacks originated from the Gullah-speaking regions of South Carolina and Georgia or from the coastal areas of Virginia, where a creole was also spoken at the time (cf. Hackert and Huber 2007: 297). The imported creole flourished particularly on the southern islands, where large groups of slaves were left to fend for themselves soon after their arrival, because the Bahamian plantation economy had quickly failed on account of both economic and environmental reasons (Craton and Saunders 1992: 304).

In the decades following the abolition of the slave trade in 1807, immigration to The Bahamas was dominated by large numbers of "liberated Africans" seized from foreign slave ships by British naval patrols (Craton and Saunders 1998: 5–12). In general, the nineteenth century was characterized by racial segregation and poverty. When tourist arrivals increased at the turn of the twentieth century, the economic situation started to improve. The American Prohibition of the 1920s also resulted in new business opportunities. While Prohibition came to an end by 1933, the tourism sector continued to flourish, and wealth came to the islands. A major political milestone was the founding of the Progressive Liberal Party in 1953, which aimed at shifting the political power to the black majority and led to major changes in institutional structures and political ideology, the latter turning toward the "Bahamianization" of politics, education, and the media (cf. Storr 2000: 251–254; Minnis 2009: 106–107). In 1973, The Bahamas gained independence from

Britain. Nevertheless, they have remained in the Commonwealth of Nations, and the influence of the former colonial power is still visible in the country's institutional structure and traditions, such as school uniforms or wigs in court.

One immediately apparent problem in applying the Dynamic Model to the Bahamian situation is that it is difficult to structure the country's colonial and postcolonial history into five phases (Schneider 2007: 56). For one, it appears unclear as to what exactly should count as the foundation phase. Following Schneider (2007: 33), we would have to consider the years after the Bermudian settlement in 1648: "English is brought to a new territory by a significant group of settlers, and begins to be used on a regular basis in a country which was not English-speaking before." And in fact, we seem to be dealing with a fairly "normal" settlement colony initially, even though no indigenous (IDG) population strand was present. This is not untypical, either, in that most creole-speaking communities began exactly with the kind of "homestead" phase that is suggested by the sociodemographic make-up of the early Bahamian colony (cf. Chaudenson 2001). The missing IDG strand is also unproblematic; as suggested by Schneider (2007: 62), slaves

> took the role of an IDG group. Socially, they were the one important, erstwhile "other" group the STL [i.e., settler] strand speakers were faced with. Linguistically, [...] like IDG groups slaves approached and acquired the target language, English, and accommodated and restructured it to their own purposes.

As noted above, though, between 1783 and 1785 Gullah speakers swamped the black population segment. Their variety must have quickly replaced the settlers' dialects and early slaves' approximations to those dialects as the dominant community language; it must have also functioned as the target of acquisition to later arrivals, primarily those confiscated from slave ships. The "foundation" of contemporary Bahamian Creole, thus, was laid not with the first settlement of English speakers from Bermuda, but with the later, massive shift in demographic make-up brought about by the loyalist immigration. Should we, then, assume a delayed foundation phase? Or two separate foundation phases? Or should we abide by temporal sequence and count the 1648 founding of an English-speaking community in The Bahamas as decisive, despite the fact that this early settlement could not possibly have exerted the kind of strong linguistic "founder effect" that Schneider (2007: 23), following Mufwene (2001), ascribes to the earliest population in any language contact situation?

As regards the other periods of Bahamian colonial and postcolonial history, their dating in terms of the phases of the Dynamic Model involves the same difficulties as do those of other anglophone Caribbean countries, such as Barbados (Schneider 2007: 219–224) and Jamaica (2007: 227–234). In order to solve these difficulties, Schneider himself recognizes creole formation as a "very special instantiation of the Dynamic Model" (2007: 60), with "structural nativization [. . .] in the forms of partial language acquisition in language shift as well as creolization" beginning as early as phase 1 (2007: 62), and phases 2 and 3 becoming blurred, on account of the fact that "a core political feature of phase 2, a stable colonial status, coincides with the central linguistic component of phase 3, nativization, i.e. creolization" (2007: 227). If this is done and the temporal sequencing and presence of fundamental socio-political and structural parameters are waived, then The Bahamas, like other creole-speaking communities, can be integrated into the Dynamic Model, but such a move obviously obviates core aspects of the model. Phase 4, by contrast, is unproblematic. Schneider predicts "cultural self-reliance" following political independence (2007: 48) as a central component of this phase, involving not just the naming of a new variety – "X English" instead of "English in X" (2007: 50) – but also its codification in dictionaries and its use in literary works. We see all of this in The Bahamas, with the production of the *Dictionary of Bahamian English* (Holm and Shilling 1982) and of numerous poems, plays, novels, and short stories (e.g. College of The Bahamas 1983; cf. Dahl 1995) as well as with the collection of folk tales (e.g. Glinton-Meicholas 1994) flourishing from the 1970s onward.

Another challenge in the application of the Dynamic Model to the Bahamian context is that the "identity constructions" (Schneider 2007: 31) we find in the various phases of the country's history do not conform to the model's predictions. Most importantly, phase 3 (which, as noted above, is said to fall together with phase 2 in creole-speaking societies) is supposedly characterized by a reduction in the gap separating STL and IDG speakers: "Both population groups realize and accept the fact that they will have to get along with each other for good, and therefore, for the first time, the STL and IDG strands become closely and directly intertwined" (Schneider 2007: 41). The history of demographic and power relations in the colonial and early postcolonial Bahamas contradicts such assumptions (cf. Curry 2017: 120); in fact, it suggests the opposite.

A divergence in group identities must have already taken place in the eighteenth century, as more and more free blacks and slaves came to the islands and gradually outnumbered the white settlers. In the nineteenth century, increasing racial segregation and the arrival of more blacks from Africa, who claimed "a greater ethnic authenticity" (Craton and Saunders 1992: 359) and tremendously influenced social life, religion, and art in The Bahamas, led to a shift in self-consciousness and attitudes among the black population, so that "the Afro-Bahamian society developed an identity of its own" (Cash et al. 1991: 220). And even though the country's road to independence was markedly less violent than that of other anglophone Caribbean nations, such as Jamaica, there is no reason to assume that substantial socio-psychological accommodation between black and white Bahamians would have taken place during decolonization. Rather, there is evidence that the life- and speechways of the two groups remained separate, if not segregated, in the majority of situations (cf. Craton and Saunders 1998: 91).

More generally, it appears doubtful whether sociolinguistic identity formation in creole-speaking communities is best described in terms of "processes of convergence" between the colonizers and the colonized (Schneider 2003: 242). While Schneider emphasizes the "common language experience and communication ethnography" shared by the two population groups in advanced colonial contact situations, resulting eventually in "the emergence of an overarching language community with a set of shared norms" (2003: 243), numerous creolists have pointed out that creole formation is neither the coming-into-being of a linguistic compromise nor the more or less successful approximation to a linguistic target, such as the European settler dialects, by the socially subordinate population. It is just as well possible that the laborers did not actually seek to sound like the power holders but that the retention or augmentation of linguistic differences by the colonized served to mark both social distance from the colonizers and solidarity among themselves. In this way, nascent creoles would have functioned not only as indicators of a new, hybrid sociocultural identity but also – and maybe equally importantly – as a means of linguistic empowerment and resistance to hegemony (Jourdan 2008: 373).

Phase 4 in the formation of any postcolonial English, finally, is said to be characterized by an emphasis on ethnic and linguistic homogeneity (Schneider 2007: 49). Interestingly, with the exception of the Haitian immigrants and their "Bahaitian" offspring (cf. Léger and Armbrister 2009: 22, 27–29), ethnicity is not often commented on explicitly in The

Bahamas (cf. Bethel 2007). Black-white relations are not much of a public issue, but there is also no emphasis on ethnic unity. Regarding language, it is certainly true that in all anglophone Caribbean countries, "the newly achieved psychological independence and the acceptance of a new, indigenous identity" has resulted in "a new, locally rooted linguistic self-confidence" (Schneider 2007: 49), which has transformed the creoles into carriers of a particular cultural-historical heritage and has led to their encroachment on Standard English in domains such as education, politics, and the media (cf. Hackert 2004: 56–64). However, in The Bahamas, this has definitely not promoted an emphasis on linguistic homogeneity (Schneider 2007: 51), if one abstracts away from the frequent denial by creole speakers that they use anything but "the Queen's English" (cf. Hackert 2004: 31) – a form of self-deprecation common in such speech communities. Despite occasional claims concerning decreolization (cf. Shilling 1978: 178; Seymour 1995: 17–40, 55) and a limited amount of "bilateral accommodation historically and currently" (Childs et al. 2003: 26), black and white vernaculars have not only remained remarkably distinct in structural terms, but they are also consistently described as different by Bahamians themselves. Differences between black speech from different locations are also frequently noted, as in "Eleuthera people is talk more like Americans" or "Cat Island people does talk bad" (cf. Hackert 2004: 7). This self-description is in stark contrast with at least some linguistic treatments of the Bahamian situation, where "Bahamian English" is taken to subsume both black and white vernaculars (e.g. Childs and Wolfram 2004; Reaser and Torbert 2012), despite the same authors' own findings of a "constant ethnic divide between the communities with reference to salient features" (Childs et al. 2003: 26–27). In sum, the relationship between black and white speech in The Bahamas appears to be more accurately captured by Shilling's (1980) reference to a "non-continuum" (cf. the title of her paper) than by the term "Bahamian English."

Even Standard English in The Bahamas is remarkably non-uniform. The emergence of new norms in the anglophone Caribbean was first described for Jamaica by Shields-Brodber (1997) as a process of bifurcation, leading to the emergence of two forms of Standard English: a traditional, British one, more often professed than actually used, and a local, creole-influenced one, heard in the speech of prominent actors, politicians, and other public figures. Recent work on standards of English in the Caribbean context has shown, however, that things have become even more fluid than predicted, and this holds true not only for speech production but also for the perception of norms. Initial work on the three Caribbean subcomponents of the International Corpus of English (e.g. Deuber and Youssef 2007; Deuber 2009, 2010; Hackert 2012b; Laube forthcoming) reveals tremendous amounts of morpho-syntactic variation, particularly but not exclusively in the most informal of text types, that is conversations; studies on educated accents show the persistence of some but not all creole features even at the highest acrolectal levels (e.g. Irvine 2004) as well as considerable variation between British and American pronunciations (e.g. Deuber and Leung 2013); and sociolinguistic studies have shown a fluidity in language attitudes and use hitherto unimagined (e.g. Jamaican Language Unit 2005; Oenbring and Fielding 2014). Thus, "traditional attitudes to 'low' and 'high' language have become diluted" in the postcolonial Caribbean (Craig 2006: 108), in the sense that the use of English or creole is no longer determined exclusively by social status but often indicates choices of style and register (cf. Deuber 2014). Attitudes towards and the adoption of pronunciation or vocabulary features from different standard varieties are also much more variable than envisaged by the Dynamic Model. This has been shown for Trinidad and Tobago (e.g. Deuber and Leung 2013; Hänsel and Deuber 2013); as for The Bahamas, initial work (Kraus and Laube forthcoming) points in the same direction. In sum, with regard to standards of English, the anglophone Caribbean appears to be heading not towards endonormativity but towards a stable "multinormative" orientation (Meer and Deuber, Chapter 13 this volume). While the emergence of a homogenous, national standard is thus one of the crucial components of the Dynamic Model, this component appears to be highly problematic in the case of the anglophone Caribbean.

As for linguistic globalization effects, these are generally assumed to involve the worldwide spread of features of American English (cf. Schneider 2006: 67). As Buschfeld and Kautzsch (2017: 114) state, globalization "finds expression in, for example, linguistic and also cultural influences coming from the Internet, U.S. popular culture, and modern media as well as trading relations between countries." The Bahamas have long-standing ties with the North American mainland. As outlined above, there was, first, the early colonial Carolinian connection, followed by the mass immigration of loyalists in the wake of the American Revolutionary War. Bahamians have always been traveling to the North American mainland to visit relatives, obtain an education, find work, or – more recently – simply go shopping. Finally, there is tourism, which, in fact, is the most important economic sector in today's Bahamas, next to banking, and the vast majority of tourists have always come from the United States (cf. Bahamas Ministry of Tourism 2019).

A feature which might be taken as indicative of recent linguistic Americanization in The Bahamas is the growing number of radio and television newsreaders and hosts, particularly on private channels, whose accent is rhotic. Most Englishes in the Caribbean, including Bahamian varieties, are traditionally non-rhotic (cf. Wells 1982: 590), but rhoticity appears to be spreading in various forms of contemporary Bahamian speech (cf. Kraus 2017), which suggests that American accents now enjoy considerable prestige, at least in public contexts. Still, we would claim that what we are dealing with in The Bahamas is not primarily postcolonial Americanization qua globalization. A study of so-called "pseudo-titles" (Bell 1988: 326), that is, determiner-less descriptive structures in front of name NPs, as in *former US president Bill Clinton*, for example (Hackert 2015), found that these structures, which are generally said to have originated in *Time* magazine (cf. Quirk et al. 1985: 276) and thus clearly constitute a "diachronic Americanism" (Algeo 1992: 287), were used liberally in Bahamian newspapers even before independence and that Bahamian journalists have, in fact, been leading their American (and British) colleagues in their development, in terms of both length and complexity. In sum, American influence on Bahamian English is not a recent phenomenon but involves long-standing economic, cultural, and personal links.

3. DEVELOPMENTAL MODELS OF WORLD ENGLISHES AND THE BAHAMAS: SOME CRITICAL REMARKS

As shown in section 2, a close examination of three core components of Schneider's Dynamic Model – that is developmental phases, identity constructions, and structural effects – in the Bahamian context reveals difficulties in the application of the model. Some of these difficulties are specific to the Bahamian situation; as noted by Childs and Wolfram (2004: 436), "[o]ne question concerns the significance of different founder English varieties that range from British and American English dialects to Gullah [. . .] Another matter is the past and present relationship between Afro-Bahamian and Anglo-Bahamian varieties." Other issues, such as the blurring of phases and the continued lack of linguistic homogenization, appear to be of a more general nature, at least with respect to the anglophone Caribbean. While the EIF Model builds on the Dynamic Model's basic components and assumptions, it still appears to offer some advantages over the latter, even in the description of postcolonial Englishes.

Most importantly, it explicitly acknowledges the fact that colonial and postcolonial history cannot be separated from each other and that most sociolinguistic and linguistic developments that have affected English speakers around the world in postcolonial times are neither necessarily ascribable to the influence of the former colonial power nor truly endocentric but often owed to the rise of the United States to global superpower status in political, economic, and cultural terms. The Bahamian case is unusual in that American influence long predates independence, but the EIF Model describes "Americanization" not as a purely postcolonial phenomenon but as a general force operating on the development of different Englishes at different times (Buschfeld and Kautzsch 2017: 111). By turning to a flexible set of forces, thus, the EIF Model elegantly accounts for the long-standing regional and supra-regional ties linking The Bahamas with Britain and the United States and for how they have led to the sociolinguistic and linguistic complexity that characterizes the Bahamian situation today.

That said, the EIF Model's primary aim is not an improved theory of postcolonial Englishes but an attempt at a unified account of postcolonial and non-postcolonial Englishes, which is achieved through the integration of the Dynamic Model in a "higher-level framework" (Buschfeld and Kautzsch 2017: 113). In consequence, this means that the EIF Model does not fully emancipate itself from the Dynamic Model; rather, as Buschfeld and Kautzsch themselves note, the former is based on the latter's core components, in particular "the five phases and the four parameters operating on them" (2017: 116). In this way, the EIF Model "inherits" a number of problems affecting the Dynamic Model, two of which we would like to highlight now.

First, there is the focus on national varieties. Up to this point, we have been refraining from a discussion of what we mean by "X English" (Schneider 2007: 50) in the Bahamian case. What exactly is "Bahamian English"? Definitely, the major variety in the contemporary Bahamas is Bahamian Creole, the language of black Bahamians in private and/or informal interaction. As shown by Hackert (2004), however, even urban Bahamian Creole as used in Nassau today shows tremendous variation. Also, as noted in section 2 of this chapter, the life- and speechways of the various Bahamian islands have always displayed considerable differences. Then there are white vernaculars, which constitute a "non-continuum" with black Bahamian speech (Shilling 1980). Finally, there is Standard Bahamian English, which, as we have seen, does not appear to be heading towards uniformity, either, but continues to show a multinormative orientation. In sum, there really is no such thing as "Bahamian English," despite its repeated evocation in the linguistic literature (e.g. Childs and Wolfram 2004; Reaser and Torbert 2012).

The focus on national varieties has been underlying the World Englishes enterprise ever since its inception. One of the greatest achievements of the paradigm has been the wide recognition that contemporary English is a language of "pluricentricity and multi-identities" (Kachru 1991: 4) and no longer a monolithic entity that originated in England and therefore belongs to the "best" speakers, that is, educated British (or Americans) setting down their own speech patterns as those most widely "received" (cf. Hackert 2012a: 115–117). The ideological underpinnings to the pluricentric approach came from postcolonial writers such as Chinua Achebe, Raja Rao, Ngũgĩ wa Thiong'o, or Gabriel Okara, who had championed the use of localized versions of English as a way of appropriating the former colonial language and making it bear the weight of the postcolonial experience. For these writers, political decolonization necessitated linguistic decolonization, and the creation of new nations necessitated the establishment of new languages along exactly the lines Noah Webster had advocated for American English in the late eighteenth century. As Allsopp (1996: xix) sketches the Caribbean situation upon independence, "these territories include[d] twelve independent nations in their number, each with a linguistic entitlement to a national standard language."

In its focus on the tranformation of "English in X" into "X English" (Schneider 2007: 50) and the "countries-along-the-cycle" method that we also applied in section 2 in describing the Bahamian situation, the Dynamic Model does not really appear to question this traditional focus on national varieties. But as Saraceni (2015: 67) aptly puts it,

> the idea of many Englishes isn't fundamentally different from that of one English [. . .] the idea of plural Englishes entails the same principle: many ones. If there is one English for the English, there can be one for the Americans, one for the Singaporeans, one for the Ghanaians, one for the New Zealanders and so on. One plus one plus one plus one.

The World Englishes concern with national varieties has been exposed to a lot of criticism (cf. e.g. Schneider 2017: 37; Deshors 2018: 3), and, accordingly, Buschfeld and Kautzsch (2017) explicitly propose to implement the "post-varieties" approach called for by Seargeant and Tagg (2011). While much of their argument still revolves around territorially based varieties, albeit non-postcolonial ones as they appear to be emerging in Namibia, for example, they also take into account "any other type of English developing beyond national boundaries," particularly in web-based communication (Buschfeld and Kautzsch 2017: 105), and consider the forces affecting the use of English "both on the national level, but also on the different groups of speakers within and ultimately also across particular countries" (2017: 113), eventually "zooming in to [...] the idiolects of individual speakers" (Buschfeld et al. 2018: 25). These forces include the usual sociolinguistic suspects: age, ethnicity, social status, and gender. In a way, however, this World Englishes-cum-sociolinguistics approach may be said to be subject to exactly the criticism leveled above: "[o]ne plus one plus one plus one." While a proliferation of lects certainly permits more "granularity" (2018: 25), it remains to be demonstrated in what way such a move increases any model's explanatory power.

This is because, in principle, neither the inclusion of new, transnational variety types nor the increase in "granularity" down to the idiolect solves another fundamental problem in World Englishes theorizing: that of the conception of "varieties" as more or less homogenous, stable, bounded sets of features. This conception is not unique to varieties studies but still underlies much contemporary linguistic thought, following Saussure's famous dictum of language as "un système où tout se tient" (cf. Koerner 1996/1997). While such an approach may have been important in early twentieth-century linguistics to bring the discipline in line with theoretical and methodological advances in other sciences, it has become questionable in postmodern times, with language widely recognized as social practice crucially premised on speaker agency, mobility, and mixing. However, it still shines through the conception of English as a thing that can be "relocated" (Buschfeld et al. 2018: 18) or is seen as "moving, expanding and growing" independently (2018: 16).

That said, the identification of the characteristic features of any postcolonial or other English often has not even taken the perspective of the system as a whole but follows what Saraceni (2015: 80) calls the "spot the difference" approach: "phonological, lexical, grammatical and syntactic peculiarities are meticulously singled out and displayed as proofs of the ways in which new varieties of English have evolved" (2015: 81). The feature approach replaced an earlier focus on "errors" committed by non-native speakers of English and emphasized the systematicity and legitimacy of postcolonial varieties as well as their sociocultural contingency. While traditional descriptions of new varieties of English often proceeded in anecdotal fashion, the advent of corpus linguistics made large-scale, quantitative comparisons possible, based on the insight that varieties differ not only in basic rules and categorical qualities, but also in statistical preferences and co-occurrence patterns (cf. Schneider 2007: 46). The EIF Model, however, still appears to be premised on the idea of feature checklists, one of its primary aims being to determine whether a particular form of English found in a particular (national) context constitutes a variety or not, for which Buschfeld and Kautzsch suggest the employment of a criteria catalogue crucially based on "nativized linguistic features" (2017: 109). An interesting proposal for overcoming the limitations of the varieties-as-sets-of-features paradigm is Schneider's notion of "Transnational Attraction," which explicitly recognizes "the appropriation of (components of) English(es) for whatever communicative purposes at hand, unbounded by distinctions of norms, nations or varieties" (2014: 28). Even though Buschfeld and Kautzsch (2017: 113) describe it as "too simple" and its precise implications for theorizing World Englishes actually remain to be spelled out, this proposal may eventually turn out to be more suitable for capturing the linguistic and sociolinguistic dynamics of postmodern forms of English than feature checklists.

Second, given their shared diachronic focus, developmental stages constitute an integral part of both the Dynamic Model and the EIF Model. As has been shown in section 2, it is difficult to match Bahamian history with the Dynamic Model's five phases. A more fundamental problem in applying the latter to creole-speaking societies is the assumption of a gradual reduction in linguistic variability along the developmental path of any one variety. In creole studies, we encounter this assumption in the once-popular decreolization hypothesis; the Dynamic Model posits the emergence of a homogenous, national standard as the culmination phase in the development of any postcolonial English. This, as we have seen, is equally problematic in the case of the anglophone Caribbean. The EIF Model puts a question mark around endonormative stabilization (Buschfeld and Kautzsch 2017: 117), but whether this question mark indicates general doubts about the validity of the concept or simply that it has not yet been attested for any non-postcolonial English is not clear (2017: 118–119). That said, in their phasal structure, both models are premised on the idea that new varieties of English undergo not merely change but directional development, every phase having a predetermined end point or goal. Particularly two of these end points, that is, nativization and stabilization, are problematic concepts, at least with regard to anglophone Caribbean creoles.

As Schneider (2017: 46) himself observes, the idea that new languages pass through characteristic phases in their development is not original but has enjoyed popularity in contact linguistics ever since the publication of Hall's pidgin-creole life cycle (1962), and, in fact, the similarities between the two models are striking. Similar to pidgins, postcolonial Englishes start out as a basic means of intercommunication used by incipiently bilingual speakers. The nativization phase occupies center stage in both models. What is involved in the transition from pidgin to creole is nativization in a demographic sense, that is, the coming-into-being of a community of first-language speakers, with structural consequences following, but demographic nativization has been found to be much less important for creole formation than once assumed. In the Dynamic Model, by contrast, nativization is defined in a purely structural sense, that is, as the emergence of a new, recognizably distinct local dialect through "regular use of English" by adult bilingual speakers (Schneider 2017: 50). The term "nativization" is thus understood differently in creole studies and World Englishes, though this is not usually overtly stated. Just as creoles supposedly develop into more standard forms if they remain in or come into contact with their lexifier ("decreolization"), so postcolonial Englishes are said to inevitably undergo endonormative stabilization.

Other than indicated by Schneider (2017: 46), however, cyclical accounts of creole origins no longer "figure [. . .] prominently" in creole studies, simply because they have been found to be inconsistent with both socio-historical facts and diachronic linguistic evidence (cf. e.g. Kouwenberg and Singler 2008: 8–10). With regard to the anglophone Caribbean, it has been demonstrated convincingly, for example, that creole continua must have existed from the earliest period of language contact and that it is wrong to automatically associate the existence of a continuum with decreolization, as implied by the once-popular term "post-creole continuum." In other words, creole continua do not mark a transitional stage in the development of any creole from (more or less homogenous) basilect to (more or less homogenous) acrolect. Rather, in many speech communities, they appear to constitute highly variable but stable sets of linguistic resources from which users draw in order to index particular situational meanings and position themselves in social space.

That said, the idea of evolution has a much longer history in linguistics than suggested by Schneider's (2017: 46) reference to Hall; in fact, it has played a significant role in linguistic theorizing ever since Charles Darwin published his *On the Origin of Species* (1859). Unfortunately, linguistic evolution is not a neutral concept at all but carries a heavy ideological baggage (cf. Hackert 2014; Mufwene 2015). In the nineteenth century, an evolutionary account was thought to explain, among others, the global spread of English as well as its rise to world language status (cf. Bailey 1991: 106–117). The standard variety of any language was described as the "fittest," commanding the widest range of functions and understood by most members of the speech community (Paul 1891: 53). Viewed from this angle, neither accounts celebrating the "spread" of English and its worldwide "indigenization" nor the idea that postcolonial varieties of English undergo evolution (rather than just change), advancing towards a stage of endonormative stabilization, are entirely value free, and even though a hierarchization of varieties is explicitly rejected (cf. Buschfeld et al. 2018: 21), comparisons of varieties according to developmental stages attained are not, either.

4. CONCLUSION

Our task in this chapter was to apply the latest World Englishes model, Buschfeld and Kautzsch's Model of Extra- and Intra-territorial Forces (2017), to The Bahamas, thereby putting it to the test and comparing its suitability to that of other models. The Bahamas were a British colony for more than 300 years and as such would seem to fall squarely within the domain of Schneider's (2003, 2007) Dynamic Model, which is explicitly geared towards the description and explanation of postcolonial Englishes. Buschfeld and Kautzsch's primary concern, by contrast, is not with postcolonial Englishes but with integrating non-postcolonial Englishes into a unified framework of varieties of English around the world (2017: 122). Not surprisingly, the EIF Model does not have much to say about postcolonial Englishes that is new; in fact, colonization is treated as one of five categories of extra- and intra-territorial forces (2017: 113–114), together with language policies, globalization, foreign policies, and sociodemographic background. What is more, the "overall setup" of the Dynamic Model and its "major assumptions" are not challenged by the EIF Model. Rather, the Dynamic Model is "an integrative part" of the latter and provides the "major components of the overall conceptual framework" (2017: 121–122). For our test, therefore, we initially fell back on the Dynamic Model and examined the history, identity constructions, sociolinguistics, and structural effects (Schneider 2003: 56) that have shaped the use of English in The Bahamas in colonial and early postcolonial times. We then looked at the effects of globalization as the most important twenty-first-century force affecting language use in the country.

Our findings indicate that, in its fairly rigid "principles" and "parameters" approach (Schneider 2003: 234), the Dynamic Model ran into problems in accounting for the blurred phases, unusual identity constructions, and continued lack of linguistic homogenization that we observe in Bahamian history. In its focus on colonial developments, it also cannot explain more recent phenomena affecting speakers of English around the world, particularly in the form of American cultural and linguistic influences. By integrating colonial and postcolonial Englishes into a unified account, the EIF Model is able to do precisely this. In its focus on a flexible and interacting set of "extra- and intraterritorial forces as the general mechanisms behind the development" of any type of English (Buschfeld and Kautzsch 2017: 116), it also elegantly accounts for "Americanization" scenarios, such as we find in The Bahamas, where, on account of long-standing economic, cultural, and personal ties with the North American mainland, local forms of speech have long been shaped by American influences or must, in fact, be described as genuinely American-origin in the first place.

The EIF Model is an offshoot of the Dynamic Model and as such based on some fundamental components of the latter, most notably its focus on the identification of clearly definable (national) varieties and its teleological character, that is, the assumption of a particular set of developmental phases, each endowed with a specific end point or goal. These two theoretical conceptions have a long standing in linguistics but may not actually be entirely suitable to the description and explanation of contemporary English in all its variety and complexity. Nevertheless, in its emphasis on the general forces impacting on all users of English in both colonial and postcolonial times, the EIF Model has made an important contribution towards accounting for unity and diversity among forms of English around the world today.

REFERENCES

Algeo, John. 1992. What is a Briticism? In Joan H. Hall, Nick Doane and Dick Ringler, eds. 1992, *Old English and New: Studies in Language and Linguistics in Honor of Frederic G. Cassidy*. New York and London: Garland, 287–304.

Allsopp, Richard, ed. 1996. *Dictionary of Caribbean English Usage*. Oxford: Oxford University Press.

Bahamas Ministry of Tourism. 2019. Tourist demographics 1996–2015, http://www.tourismtoday.com/sites/default/files/all_bahamas_demographics_1996_to_2016.pdf (last accessed February 22, 2019).

Bailey, Richard W. 1991. *Images of English: A Cultural History of the Language*. Ann Arbor, MI: The University of Michigan Press.

Bell, Allan. 1988. The British base and the American connection in New Zealand media English. *American Speech* 63.4: 326–344.

Bethel, Nicolette. 2007. On why race matters. *Bahama Pundit*, https://www.bahamapundit.com/2007/05/on_why_race_mat.html (last accessed January 28, 2019).

Blommaert, Jan. 2010. *The Sociolinguistics of Globalization*. Cambridge: Cambridge University Press.

Buschfeld, Sarah and Alexander Kautzsch. 2017. Towards an integrated approach to postcolonial and non-postcolonial Englishes. *World Englishes* 36.1: 104–126.

Buschfeld, Sarah, Alexander Kautzsch and Edgar W. Schneider. 2018. From colonial dynamism to current transnationalism: A unified view on postcolonial and non-postcolonial Englishes. In Sandra C. Deshors, ed. 2018, *Modeling World Englishes: Assessing the Interplay of Emancipation and Globalization of ESL Varieties*. Amsterdam: John Benjamins, 15–44.

Canagarajah, Suresh. 2013. *Translingual Practice: Global Englishes and Cosmopolitan Relations*. London: Routledge.

Cash, Philip, Shirley Gordon and Gail Saunders. 1991. *Sources of Bahamian History*. London: Macmillan.

Chaudenson, Robert. 2001. *Creolization of Language and Culture*. Revised in collaboration with Salikoko S. Mufwene. London and New York: Routledge.

Childs, Becky and Walt Wolfram. 2004. Bahamian English: Phonology. In Edgar W. Schneider, Kate Burridge, Bernd Kortmann, Rajend Mesthrie and Clive Upton, eds. 2004, *A Handbook of Varieties of English, Vol. 1: Phonology*. Berlin and New York: de Gruyter, 435–449.

Childs, Becky, Jeffrey Reaser and Walt Wolfram. 2003. Defining ethnic varieties in the Bahamas: Phonological accomodation in black and white enclaves. In Michael Aceto and Jeffrey P. Williams, eds. 2003, *Contact Englishes of the Eastern Caribbean*. Amsterdam: John Benjamins, 1–28.

College of the Bahamas. 1983. *Bahamian Anthology*. Oxford: Macmillan.

Craig, Dennis. 2006. The use of the vernacular in West Indian education. In Hazel Simmons-McDonald and Ian Robertson, eds. 2006, *Exploring the Boundaries of Caribbean Creole Languages*. Mona: University of the West Indies Press, 99–117.

Craton, Michael. 1962. *A History of the Bahamas*. London: Collins.

Craton, Michael and Gail Saunders. 1992. *Islanders in the Stream: A History of the Bahamian People. Vol. 1: From Aboriginal Times to the End of Slavery*. Athens, GA: University of Georgia Press.

Craton, Michael and Gail Saunders. 1998. *Islanders in the Stream: A History of the Bahamian People. Vol. 2: From the Ending of Slavery to the Twenty-First Century*. Athens, GA: University of Georgia Press.

Curry, Christopher. 2017. *Freedom and Resistance: A Social History of Black Loyalists in the Bahamas*. Gainesville, FL: University Press of Florida.

Dahl, Anthony G. 1995. *Literature of the Bahamas 1724–1992: The March Towards National Identity*. Lanham, MD: University Press of America.

Darwin, Charles. 1859. *On the Origin of Species by Means of Natural Selection, Or the Preservations of Favoured Races in the Struggle for Life*. London: John Murray.

Deshors, Sandra C. 2018. Modeling World Englishes in the 21st century: A thematic introduction. In Sandra C. Deshors, ed. 2018, *Modeling World Englishes: Assessing the Interplay of Emancipation and Globalization of ESL Varieties*. Amsterdam: John Benjamins, 1–14.

Deuber, Dagmar. 2009. 'The English we speaking': Morphological and syntactic variation in educated Jamaican speech. *Journal of Pidgin and Creole Languages* 24.1: 1–52.

Deuber, Dagmar. 2010. Modal verb usage at the interface of English and a related Creole: A corpus-based study of can/could and will/would in Trinidadian English. *Journal of English Linguistics* 38.2: 105–142.

Deuber, Dagmar. 2014. *English in the Caribbean: Variation, Style and Standards in Jamaica and Trinidad*. Cambridge: Cambridge University Press.

Deuber, Dagmar and Glenda Leung. 2013. Investigating attitudes towards an emerging standard of English: Evaluations of newscasters' accents in Trinidad. *Multilingua* 32.3: 289–319.

Deuber, Dagmar and Valerie Youssef. 2007. Teacher language in Trinidad: A pilot corpus study of direct and direct creolisms in the verb phrase. In *Proceedings from the Corpus Linguistics 2007 Conference*.

Glinton-Meicholas, Patricia. 1994. *An Evening in Guanima: A Treasury of Folktales From the Bahamas*. Nassau: Guanima Press.

Hackert, Stephanie. 2004. *Urban Bahamian Creole: System and Variation*. Amsterdam: John Benjamins.

Hackert, Stephanie. 2012a. *The Emergence of the English Native Speaker: A Chapter in Nineteenth-Century Linguistic Thought*. Berlin: Mouton de Gruyter.

Hackert, Stephanie. 2012b. Variation in educated speech: The case of Bahamian English. In Monika Fludernik and Benjamin Kohlmann, eds. 2012b, *Anglistentag 2011 Freiburg: Proceedings*. Trier: WVT, 21–36.

Hackert, Stephanie. 2014. The evolution of English(es): Notes on the history of an idea. In Sarah Buschfeld, Thomas Hoffmann, Magnus Huber and Alexander Kautzsch, eds. 2014, *The Evolution of Englishes: The Dynamic Model and Beyond*. Amsterdam: John Benjamins, 282–300.

Hackert, Stephanie. 2015. Pseudotitles in Bahamian English: A case of Americanization? *Journal of English Linguistics* 43.2: 143–167.

Hackert, Stephanie and Magnus Huber. 2007. Gullah in the diaspora: Historical and linguistic evidence from the Bahamas. *Diachronica* 24.2: 279–325.

Hall, Robert A. 1962. The life cycle of pidgin languages. *Lingua* 11: 151–156.

Hänsel, Eva and Dagmar Deuber. 2013. Globalization, postcolonial Englishes, and the English language press in Kenya, Singapore, and Trinidad and Tobago. *World Englishes* 32.3: 338–357.

Holm, John and Alison Shilling. 1982. *Dictionary of Bahamian English*. Cold Spring, NY: Lexik House.

Irvine, Alison. 2004. A good command of the English language: Phonological variation in the Jamaican acrolect. *Journal of Pidgin and Creole Languages* 19.1: 41–76.

Jamaican Language Unit. 2005. The Language Attitude Survey of Jamaica, https://www.mona.uwi.edu/dllp/jlu/projects/Report%20

for%20Language%20Attitude%20Survey%20of%20Jamaica.pdf (last accessed February 22, 2019).
Jourdan, Christine. 2008. The cultural in pidgin genesis. In Silvia Kouwenberg and John V. Singler, eds. 2008, *The Handbook of Pidgin and Creole Studies*. Malden, MA: Wiley-Blackwell, 359–381.
Kachru, Braj B. 1991. Liberation linguistics and the Quirk Concern. *English Today* 7.1: 3–13.
Koerner, E. F. K. 1996/1997. Notes on the history of the concept of language as a system 'où tout se tient'. *Linguistica Atlantica* 18/19: 1–20.
Kouwenberg, Silvia and John V. Singler. 2008. Introduction. In Silvia Kouwenberg and John V. Singler, eds. 2008, *The Handbook of Pidgin and Creole Studies*. Malden, MA: Wiley-Blackwell, 1–16.
Kraus, Janina. 2017. A Sociophonetic Study of the Urban Bahamian Creole Vowel System. PhD dissertation, LMU Munich.
Kraus, Janina and Alexander Laube. Forthcoming. 'Broken English', 'Dialect' or 'Bahamianese'? Language attitudes and identity in The Bahamas.
Laube, Alexander. Forthcoming. Style and Variation in Bahamian English. PhD dissertation, Ludwig-Maximilians-Unversität München (LMU).
Léger, Frenand and A. Philip Armbrister. 2009. Factors affecting the teaching and learning of Haitian Creole in the Bahamas. *International Journal of Bahamian Studies* 15: 22–35.
Mesthrie, Rajend and Rakesh M. Bhatt. 2008. *World Englishes: The Study of New Varieties*. Cambridge: Cambridge University Press.
Minnis, Edward A. 2009. At the Intersection of Tourism, National Identity and Bad Service: The Case Study of *The Fergusons of Farm Road*. MA thesis, University of Carleton.
Mufwene, Salikoko S. 2001. *The Ecology of Language Evolution*. Cambridge: Cambridge University Press.
Mufwene, Salikoko S. 2015. Race, racialism, and the study of language evolution in America. In Michael D. Picone and Katherine Evans Davies, eds. 2015, *New Perspectives on Language Variety in the South: Historical and Contemporary Approaches*. Tuscaloosa: University of Alabama Press, 449–474.
Oenbring, Raymond and William Fielding. 2014. Young adults' attitudes to standard and nonstandard English in an English-Creole-speaking country: The case of The Bahamas. *Language, Discourse & Society* 3.1: 28–51.
Paul, Hermann. 1891. *Principles of the History of Language*. Translated

from the second edition of the original by H. A. Strong. New and revised edition (1890). London: Longmans, Green & Co., http://archive.org/stream/cu31924026442586#page/n5/mode/2up (last accessed February 26, 2019).

Pennycook, Alastair. 2007. *Global Englishes and Transcultural Flows*. London: Routledge.

Quirk, Randolph, Sidney Greenbaum, Geoffrey Leech and Jan Svartvik. 1985. *A Comprehensive Grammar of the English Language*. London: Longman.

Reaser, Jeffrey and Benjamin Torbert. 2012. English in the Bahamas. In Bernd Kortmann and Kerstin Lunkenheimer, eds. 2012, *The Mouton World Atlas of Variation in English*. Berlin: de Gruyter, 169–179.

Saraceni, Mario. 2015. *World Englishes: A Critical Analysis*. London: Bloomsbury.

Schneider, Edgar W. 2003. The dynamics of New Englishes: From identity construction to dialect birth. *Language* 79.2: 233–281.

Schneider, Edgar W. 2006. English in North America. In Braj B. Kachru, Yamuna Kachru and Cecil L. Nelson, eds. 2006, *The Handbook of World Englishes*. Oxford: Blackwell, 58–73.

Schneider, Edgar W. 2007. *Postcolonial English: Varieties Around the World*. Cambridge: Cambridge University Press.

Schneider, Edgar W. 2014. New reflections on the evolutionary dynamics of world Englishes. *World Englishes* 33.1: 9–32.

Schneider, Edgar W. 2017. Models of English in the World. In Juhani Klemola, Markku Filppula and Devyani Sharma, eds. 2017, *The Oxford Handbook of World Englishes*. Oxford: Oxford University Press, 35–57.

Seargeant, Philip. 2012. *Exploring World Englishes: Language in a Global Context*. London: Routledge.

Seargeant, Philip and Caroline Tagg. 2011. English on the internet and a 'post-varieties' approach to language. *World Englishes* 30.4: 496–514.

Seymour, Chanti. 1995. The Decreolisation of Bahamian English: A Sociolinguistic Study. MA thesis, Georgetown University.

Shields-Brodber, Kathryn. 1997. Requiem for English in an 'English-speaking' community: The case of Jamaica. In Edgar W. Schneider, ed. 1997, *Englishes Around the World: Studies in Honour of Manfred Görlach. Vol. 2: Caribbean, Africa, Asia, Australasia*. Amsterdam: John Benjamins, 57–67.

Shilling, Alison. 1978. Some Non-standard Features of Bahamian Dialect Syntax. PhD dissertation, University of Hawaii.
Shilling, Alison. 1980. Bahamian English – A non-continuum? In Richard R. Day, ed. 1980, *Issues in English Creoles: Papers from the 1975 Hawaii Conference*. Heidelberg: Groos, 133–145.
Storr, Juliette. 2000. Changes and Challenges: A History of the Development of Broadcasting in the Commonwealth of the Bahamas, 1930–1980. PhD dissertation, Ohio University.
Wells, John C. 1982. *Accents of English. Vol. 3: Beyond the British Isles*. Cambridge: Cambridge University Press.

CHAPTER 13

Standard English in Trinidad: Multinormativity, Translocality, and Implications for the Dynamic Model and the EIF Model[1]

Philipp Meer and Dagmar Deuber

1. INTRODUCTION

This chapter aims at testing and applying the Dynamic Model (Schneider 2007) and the recently introduced Extra- and Intra-territorial Forces (EIF) Model (Buschfeld and Kautzsch 2017; Buschfeld et al. 2018) to the Caribbean island of Trinidad. With a focus on Standard English (as opposed to Trinidadian English Creole [TEC]), the findings of a large-scale attitude study conducted in the Trinidadian education context are combined with discussions of World Englishes models; empirical investigations in which these models were explicitly put to test were also taken into account.

This study provides an instructive case for World Englishes theorizing and model making for a number of reasons: first, given the complexity and dynamics of English in Trinidad and the wider anglophone Caribbean, Trinidadian English (TrinE) may serve as a potential example of a less prototypical postcolonial variety of English whose developments the EIF Model explicitly claims to account for as well (Buschfeld and Kautzsch 2017: 121). That is, placing English(es) in the Caribbean within categories and models of World Englishes has always

[1] The research for this study was conducted in the framework of the project "Translocality in the anglophone Caribbean: Regional, global and transnational aspects in standards of English", funded by the German Research Foundation (DFG, grant number: DE 2324/1-1, principal investigator: Dagmar Deuber). It is part of the ongoing PhD project of the first author at the Faculty of Philology at the University of Muenster, Germany.

been somewhat challenging. Traditional notions of English as a Native (ENL), English as a Second (ESL), or English as a Foreign Language (EFL) do not apply to the multivarietal speech communities of the English-speaking Caribbean where emerging Englishes coexist with English-based creoles along a continuum of sociolinguistic variation (Deuber 2014: 11) and the use of English, its functions, and social meanings are context-dependent and variable (Westphal 2017: 204). Second, the study allows for discussions of processes of norm (re-)orientation and standardization in small postcolonial speech communities where different local, regional, and global forces and norms interact (e.g. Mair 2013: 258; Hackert 2016: 106) and where linguistic emancipation processes have been shown to manifest in complex and diverse ways that may go beyond the traditional developmental path often anticipated in World Englishes models (Hundt et al. 2015; Mair 2017: 8; Westphal 2017: 224). Third, language attitudes and ideologies are fundamentally important for examining standardization processes (Schreier 2012: 357), investigating variety status, situating emerging varieties within models of World Englishes (Hundt et al. 2015: 705; Buschfeld and Schneider 2018: 41), and, therefore, also for testing such models.

The remainder of this chapter is structured as follows. First, we present an overview of some previous models of World Englishes, outline general drawbacks of the models in question, and thus describe the rationale for the creation of more recent models, focusing on the Dynamic Model and, particularly, the EIF Model (section 2). Section 3 describes the methodology and results of the Trinidadian case study. Both models are then discussed against the backdrop of the case study and other empirical findings from different postcolonial speech communities, and a number of modifications are suggested (section 4). We conclude by pointing out the necessity for an understanding that language attitudes, language use, and structural nativization need not be homogenous within postcolonial speech communities (section 5).

2. BACKGROUND: MODELS OF WORLD ENGLISHES

Most models of World Englishes have been static in nature and mostly focused on standard varieties of English (see Buschfeld and Schneider 2018 for an overview). Of these models, Kachru's (1985) Three Circles Model is certainly the most adopted one. However, more recently, Kachru's and other static models have been criticized for being too simplistic and for not taking into account hierarchies, dependencies, interactions among and across different Englishes, and the fact that the ENL-ESL-EFL distinction may be better conceptualized as a continuum (Buschfeld 2013; Mair 2013). More recent static models take these points into account and offer more fine-grained classification systems (e.g. Mair 2013). While these models perform well at modeling World Englishes today, they essentially only provide a synchronous perspective of what is an increasingly dynamic process (see also Buschfeld et al. 2018: 21).

Trudgill's (2004) Deterministic Model focuses on the diachronic perspective and explains the emergence of new varieties of English as an outcome of a deterministic process of three different stages which results from extensive contact and mixture of those dialects of English transplanted into a new colony; other factors such as identity formation, language attitudes, and social prestige of varieties in contact play no role according to the model. Trudgill's model is based on his observations of variety formation at the level of phonology in former settler colonies in which such massive contact scenarios took place in what he assumes were *tabula rasa* contexts (Trudgill 2004: 26–27). However, certain problems have been identified as far as the model's explanatory power and applicability are concerned: "Trudgill's model does not lend itself to extension beyond the Inner Circle, and even there, the argument that social forces are not central to the stabilization of the very variable input is mistaken" (Van Rooy 2010: 16).

The Dynamic Model of the evolution of postcolonial Englishes (PCEs) (Schneider 2007) has strongly influenced World Englishes research for more than the last decade. In essence, the model understands the emergence of PCEs as a set of processes of linguistic convergence triggered by different stages of identity (re-)constructions in two groups in a (former) colony, namely the settler (STL) and indigenous (IDG) strands of the population (Schneider 2007: 29). That is, given the right set of circumstances (cp. 2007: 57), PCEs prototypically undergo a five-phase developmental process (foundation, exonormative orientation, foundation, endonormative stabilization, differentiation), with each of the phases governed by a "monodirectional causal relationship" (2007: 30–31) between four main factors: socio-political and historical background, identity construction processes, the sociolinguistic situation, and resulting linguistic effects. Along this linear developmental process, norm orientation shifts from being exo- to endocentric. Schneider (2007: 51) also proposes that, in the phase of endonormative stabilization, the newly emerging English will be quite homogenous or at least perceived as such. However, the model also acknowledges that there may be situations in which the development of English stops and does not progress into the more advanced stages of the developmental cycle (2007: 57–58).

In line with Schneider (2014: 27–28), Buschfeld and Kautzsch (2017) note that the Dynamic Model (and, in fact, other models of World Englishes) may not be able to sufficiently explain and predict the global linguistic complexities of English in late modernity. This includes (1) the increasing diffusion of English into new territories induced by globalization and what Schneider (2014) terms "transnational attraction" of and to English(es), and (2) the plurality, dynamism, and complexity in norm development and variety formation processes that can be observed in some speech communities. They emphasize that, despite some problems in applying the Dynamic Model (see section 4.1), PCEs often follow the developmental route envisaged by Schneider (Buschfeld and Kautzsch 2017: 118; Buschfeld et al. 2018: 19) and that even some non-postcolonial Englishes (non-PCEs) seem to follow this pathway (Buschfeld 2013). However, they conclude that additional factors and forces also need to be considered when examining PCEs, such as the notion of transnational attraction, foreign policies, and globalization (Buschfeld and Kautzsch 2017: 113; Buschfeld and Schneider 2018: 41), and that the original version of Schneider's model only offers limited explanatory potential for the evolution of non-PCEs due to the fact that it was originally not designed for such contexts (Buschfeld and Kautzsch 2017: 110–111; Buschfeld and Schneider 2018: 41).

Therefore, Buschfeld and Kautzsch (2017) have introduced the latest addition to models of World Englishes, the EIF Model. The model has five core assumptions and components (Buschfeld et al. 2018: 23–26; see also Buschfeld and Kautzsch 2017: 113–118). First, it provides an integrated descriptive and explanatory framework for the evolution of PCEs and non-PCEs alike. The model assumes that the emergence of all Englishes is the result of a considerable number of different extra- and intra-territorial forces operating, interacting, and competing in a given speech community, based on which the model also predicts the development of both PCEs and non-PCEs. These forces may be divided into different categories, namely (post-)colonialism, as in the Dynamic Model, globalization, language policies and attitudes, foreign policies, the sociodemographic background (Buschfeld and Kautzsch 2017: 114), and speaker mobility (Rüdiger, Chapter 8 this volume). Second, the model explains the current diffusion of English(es) by making use of Schneider's (2014) notion of transnational attraction. Third, the diachronic element of the model is strongly based on Schneider's Dynamic Model. As far as PCEs are concerned, the model assumes the same developmental pathway driven by the same parameters, but stresses that additional forces may be at play. Moreover, more room is provided for the possibility of phases being skipped or taken in an alternative sequence by less prototypical cases. Fourth, the different phases are associated with continuous but possibly also reverse developments from EFL (phase 1) to ESL (phase 3) and finally to ENL (phase 5). Fifth, the authors (Buschfeld et al. 2018: 24–26) further take variety-internal heterogeneity into consideration as an additional dimension of the model when moving away from the abstract level of the speech community and zeroing in on concrete linguistic realities. They integrate heterogeneity as internal linguistic variability into their model, which, as they suggest, is determined by sociolinguistic parameters, such as age, ethnicity, social status, and so on. In sum, the EIF Model, insofar as it builds on the Dynamic Model, envisages endonormativity as a prototypical outcome in the evolution of postcolonial varieties of English, but also emphasizes that such endonormative varieties need not be homogenous.

3. CASE STUDY

Our case study was conducted on the Caribbean island of Trinidad. Trinidad is the southernmost island of the Eastern Caribbean and, together with its smaller sister island Tobago, forms the twin-island nation of Trinidad and Tobago, a former British colony, which has been independent since 1962. With a population of 1.27 million (Republic of Trinidad and Tobago 2012: 5), Trinidad is the second largest island in the anglophone Caribbean after Jamaica.

Trinidad has had a complex and diverse (linguistic) history (Deuber 2014: 28–29). After being claimed by Columbus in 1498, Trinidad was first officially Spanish until 1797. During this period, following large waves of immigration from francophone Caribbean islands, French and French Creole were mostly spoken on the island. In the nineteenth century, after being taken over by the British in 1802 and with the arrival of English and English Creole-speaking people from Britain and the Lesser Antilles islands, especially Barbados, TEC emerged. From the mid-nineteenth century onwards, when large numbers of indentured laborers from India came to Trinidad to work on the island's sugar cane plantations, English/Creole in Trinidad developed under additional adstrate influence from Indian languages, particularly Bhojpuri. The nativization of English/Creole in Trinidad thus occurred under the diverse influence of many different languages and language varieties. Today, however, these languages have largely given way to English/Creole. Trinidad's sociolinguistic situation therefore is similar to those of other anglophone Caribbean islands: Standard English coexists with a (mesolectal) English-based creole along a continuum of variation (Deuber 2014: 11). Standard English is associated with formal contexts of language use, for example in education. TEC, on the other hand, is associated with less formal contexts, increasingly carries covert prestige, and functions as a marker of local identity (see Meer et al. 2019: 89 for a summary of attitude research on Caribbean Creoles).

In the following, we summarize the main findings of a large-scale accent attitude survey conducted in the Trinidadian education sector that aimed to investigate the perception of standardness in this domain and to shed light on the question of exo- or endonormativity and of an emerging Trinidadian standard of English (Meer et al. 2019). The context-specific covert language attitudes of 485 Trinidadian upper-level students from twelve geographically widespread secondary schools towards a range of different (standard) varieties of English were analyzed. In a verbal-guise experimental setting, which had previously been piloted via an online survey with Caribbean informants, respondents were asked to listen to and evaluate eight different female teachers: four from Trinidad, and one each from other anglophone Caribbean territories (Jamaica and Grenada), Britain, and the United States. This selection of different teachers was chosen so as to reflect accent variation in Trinidadian schools and the "forcefield of influences" (Hackert 2016: 106) typical of the Trinidadian sociolinguistic situation. The teachers were to be rated on six-point Likert-type agreement scales and on several items that were specifically contextualized to the school domain and that related to a teacher's aptitude in the school context with regard to notions of authority and prestige (*is likely to teach at a prestige school*, *could be a school principal*, *is likely to be an English language teacher*), standardness (*proper*, *standard*), teacher personality (*friendly*, *arrogant*, *fun*), and whether a teacher sounded *foreign*. Contextualized controlled free speech samples that students could relate to easily were used: the different teachers all gave tips on how to give a good oral presentation in class based on a pre-prepared list of keywords. All stimuli were between thirty and forty-four seconds long and controlled for loudness and, to the extent possible, other possibly confounding paralinguistic aspects. The British and American samples showed regionally unmarked pronunciation features generally associated with Standard American and Standard Southern British speech; the Caribbean ones were all acrolectal and largely avoided accent features traditionally associated with Caribbean Creoles, with the four from Trinidad showing a degree of variation in the use of local pronunciation features. One Trinidadian teacher stuck out due to her American-influenced accent. Administered separately and subsequent to the verbal-guise experiment, a nationality identification task was conducted to shed further light on the informants' perception of the different teacher voices (see Meer et al. 2019 for details on the methodological approach and the statistical analysis).

Principal component analysis was carried out to investigate in which ways the ratings of the teachers across the different items clustered and formed more meaningful, underlying, attitudinal dimensions, as is commonly done in language attitude research. In line with many previous attitude studies, the analysis revealed that the items clustered in the two latent attitudinal dimensions of social status, here in the educational domain (*is likely to teach at a prestige school, proper, is likely to be an English language teacher, standard, could be a school principal*) and social attractiveness (*friendly, fun, arrogant*). Socially attractive teachers were generally perceived as likable, while teachers with a high social status in the school domain were associated with prestige, standardness, and authority in school.

The evaluations of the teachers' voices across both attitudinal dimensions showed a degree of variation that was, despite being statistically significant, numerically small, especially for social status. The difference between the highest and lowest scoring teacher voice on the social status dimension was, on average, limited to only approximately one Likert-scale point; this difference was larger for social attractiveness with around two Likert scale points. There were, however, fine-grained differences in the perceptions of the different teachers: for social status, British English was preferred overall, but was closely followed by the American-influenced Trinidadian accent. The American and Jamaican voices received intermediate but relatively high ratings, while the remaining Trinidadian teachers received the comparably lowest but still generally positive or neutral ratings around the numerical midpoint of the rating scale. For social attractiveness, American English was judged most favorably, followed by British English. The Trinidadian and other

Caribbean voices were undifferentiated and received high or intermediate ratings (see Meer et al. 2019 for detailed results).

The ratings in conjunction with the nationality identification task provide several insights into normativity in Trinidadian secondary schools. First, all accents were generally considered appropriate for the education context, since none of the teacher voices received negative ratings. Second, in accordance with findings from attitude studies conducted in the context of choral singing in Trinidad (Wilson 2017) and in other small postcolonial speech communities, namely in Jamaica (Westphal 2017) and Fiji (Hundt et al. 2015), the norm orientation was neither clearly endocentric nor exocentric. Third, while the nationality of most teachers was identified correctly by the respondents, the Grenadian and the American-influenced Trinidadian teacher deserve special attention: the Grenadian teacher was consistently misidentified as Trinidadian, and the accent of the American-influenced Trinidadian teacher showed a hybrid profile, as far as its perception and accent recognition is concerned. While this teacher received a very low foreignness rating and was also identified as a native Trinidadian by a large majority of the informants in the identification task, the teacher was also recurrently considered to be from Barbados, Guyana, or especially the United States by a minority of informants. Given that the Englishes (and English Creoles) spoken in these territories are all (semi-)rhotic (Aceto 2008: 294), the identification pattern also suggests that the teacher's semi-rhotic accent was perceived as salient and somewhat exonormatively influenced.

In sum, normativity in the Trinidadian secondary school domain is multifaceted and integrates exo- and endocentric influences. First and most importantly, different standards coexist as far as the attitudinal level is concerned, since no standard emerged as a superordinate norm and differences in the evaluations were generally very small. Preferred accents are, moreover, linguistically heterogeneous overall and comprise both local and non-local accents. Second, distinctions between exo- and endonormative accents are not clear-cut from an attitudinal perspective. The rating and identification of the Grenadian teacher, for instance, indicates that not all non-local accents are necessarily perceived as such. The evaluation of the American-influenced Trinidadian accent, moreover, shows how the notions of endo- and exonormativity may be integrated attitudinally: the teacher's social status cannot be considered as attitudinal evidence for an endonormative orientation, considering that the teacher's hybrid accent profile was also perceived as such, as shown in the nationality identification task. At the same time, the rating cannot be interpreted as evidence of exonormative orientation since this teacher even received a more positive evaluation than the actual American voice for social status. The American-influenced Trinidadian accent was probably held high in regard because of the mix of local and foreign-influenced features.

4. DISCUSSION OF AND IMPLICATIONS FOR BOTH MODELS

4.1 The Dynamic Model and Standard English in Trinidad

4.1.1 Applying the Dynamic Model

Given that TrinE is a postcolonial variety, the Dynamic Model (Schneider 2007) provides the obvious explanatory framework to discuss the results of the case study. However, the Dynamic Model is only partially able to explain the findings at hand. That is, in line with what has been argued by Buschfeld and Kautzsch (2017), forces of (de-)colonization and processes of linguistic convergence between different strands alone are unlikely to have resulted in the norm diversity observed here.

More specifically, the findings provide a number of additional perspectives for the Dynamic Model. First, while the Dynamic Model focuses on the (decreasing) influence of British English in the evolution of PCEs in former British colonies, in particular in earlier stages, and emancipation processes away from their historical ancestor variety, the findings highlight that other varieties of English also exert considerable influence on (later) norm reorientation processes in Trinidad. British English certainly serves as an important norm, as shown by the social status ratings, but it is only one among several (outside) norms. Different external (and internal) influences have an impact on the respondents' norm orientation, as indicated by the high social status ratings of the American-influenced Trinidadian, American, and Jamaican teachers. Such findings are not implausible considering the multitude of (exocentric) linguistic norms and influences that Trinidadian students encounter and that shape the Trinidadian sociolinguistic situation in general (see Hackert 2016: 106). Second, while Trinidad – not only with regard to its native Creole but also the local standard variety – has recently been claimed to have reached phase 4 of the Dynamic Model (Wilson 2017: 27), the results do not, from an attitude perspective, clearly support the development of a distinctly national standard that the model proposes. Rather, they suggest that the regional and global level in addition to the national are influential factors in local norm developmental processes that need to be taken into account when attempting to model the evolution of English in Trinidad. Two patterns in the respondents' attitudes and in the nationality identification task are indicative of this: Grenadian English, that is, the English spoken in a small neighboring sovereign Caribbean island nation, was perceived as Trinidadian, suggesting that, for Trinidadians, Standard English in Trinidad and Grenada, possibly due to shared accent features, is perceptually similar. Moreover, despite the very positive status rating of the American-influenced Trinidadian accent, this evaluation cannot serve as attitudinal evidence for the emergence of a national standard per se. In fact, the norm orientation goes beyond the national level, given that respondents also seem to have positive attitudes towards other Caribbean Englishes, most notably Jamaican English. Third, the case study questions the assumed outcome of (perceived) homogeneity in linguistic emancipation processes of PCEs. On the attitudinal level, several foreign and local accents are accepted and receive positive evaluations.

4.1.2 *Implications for the Dynamic Model*

The results support recent advances in World Englishes model making that extend the Dynamic Model (e.g. Mair 2013; Schneider 2014; Buschfeld and Kautzsch 2017; Buschfeld et al. 2018). First, the attitudinal dispositions of the informants show that persistent outside influences need to be taken into account to describe the outcomes of norm reorientation processes in postcolonial speech communities, especially in those, perhaps, that are relatively small in terms of sociodemographic size, geographically close to a powerful English-speaking country, and in which different linguistic norms interact due to a high degree of migration, tourism, presence of different linguistic norms in (new) media, or outward mobility of (parts of) the population. Processes of norm stabilization in such speech communities in particular might not necessarily be a clear-cut transition towards one endocentric norm, but rather involve different norms in different contexts or domains (see also Westphal 2017: 221; Wilson 2017: 28). Second, this transition may not only be geared towards the development of new national standards but may go beyond national confines, encompass the (sub-)regional and transnational level (Allsopp 1996), and/or involve the development of different standards for different domains on the national level (cp. e.g. Kristiansen 2001). Third, while the Dynamic Model acknowledges that a high degree of uniformity is not always achieved (Schneider 2007: 32), heterogeneity needs to be further understood as an integral part of linguistic emancipation and standardization processes in postcolonial territories. Based on investigations in various postcolonial territories, many have already noted that variety-internal heterogeneity on the linguistic level usually persists during and after the emergence of PCEs (e.g. Westphal 2017: 104) and that homogeneity can usually only manifest on a quite abstract level (Kretzschmar 2014: 157). For Trinidad and other Caribbean speech communities specifically, Deuber (2014: 253) emphasizes that differentiation has, to varying degrees, co-occurred with both earlier and later developmental stages during the colonial and postcolonial period. The results at hand, in addition, show that such heterogeneity not only exists from a structural but also from an attitudinal perspective (see also section 4.2.2 below and Wilson 2017: 28). Moreover, Van Rooy (2014) notes that endonormativity and homogeneity may also develop independently from each other. Therefore, while differentiation and heterogeneity may be particularly strong in phase 5 of the Dynamic Model (Schneider 2007: 54), they essentially need to be further accounted for throughout the entire evolutionary process.

Furthermore, the findings at hand require a discussion of the model's assumption that an extended evolutionary process beyond phase 3 typically results in the development of endonormativity in postcolonial territories. Given that the EIF Model is based on the Dynamic Model in that respect and largely sticks to its predictions, questions related to endonormativity will be further discussed below (see section 4.2.2).

4.2 The Extra- and Intra-territorial Forces Model and Standard English in Trinidad

4.2.1 Applying the Extra- and Intra-territorial Forces Model

Building on the Dynamic Model but extending it by taking into consideration outside influences, different norms and forces, and variety-internal heterogeneity, the EIF Model (Buschfeld and Kautzsch 2017; Buschfeld et al. 2018) seems to be able to explain the multidimensional norm orientation prevalent among Trinidadian secondary school students today. That is, given the complexity of norms observed, it is likely that not only processes of linguistic convergence between different strands alone have been at play, but also that other factors have been affecting the norm emancipation and stabilization process in Trinidad. Kretzschmar (2014: 143) similarly notes that the forces of (de-)colonization alone cannot explain the coexistence of different varieties. Although Kretzschmar's argument is mostly concerned with coexisting varieties in terms of language use, the same holds true for the attitudinal level: an interplay of different forces is likely to have led to the coexistence of different standards. Moreover, it is reasonable to assume that factors such as Trinidad's complex sociolinguistic situation, its geographical and geopolitical location within the Caribbean, its economic and cultural interconnectedness with many other English-speaking countries, and many others have been influencing the evolution of TrinE, especially after independence. Along these lines, the multidimensionality and complexity of norms can then be understood as a result of a continuous interaction of various extra- and intra-territorial forces related to Trinidad's transnational links to Britain, the United States, other anglophone Caribbean islands, and supranational Caribbean institutions.

We discuss these forces below with particular regard to our example of the school domain. Solely focusing on the forces of (de-)colonization and postcolonial emancipation, one might expect overall tendencies of endonormative reorientation in Trinidad. When considering other forces potentially at play, however, it becomes evident that the situation is more complex: Trinidad has for a long time been substantially influenced by forces related to regional integration processes and globalization, both of which it always had to be invested in due to its status as a small island. On the extra-territorial side, in addition to remaining British influences, there has been constant cultural (and linguistic) influence of, for instance, the United States and Jamaica through music, film, other types of (new) media, and youth culture more generally. At the same time, on the intra-territorial side, such influences are also frequently accepted or even embraced by Trinidadian teenagers (personal communication with students and teachers at Trinidadian secondary schools, April/May 2016).

Forces related to Trinidad's sociodemographic background, foreign policies, and others may also play an important role in this context: the island's rather small size in terms of population and territory, its geographical proximity and close economic ties to the United States (see CIA The World Factbook 2018), and membership in the supranational institution CARICOM (Caribbean Community and Common Market), may make the island more susceptible to global and regional influences. Another case in point can be seen in the regional University of the West Indies (UWI) in Trinidad (and other campuses in Jamaica and Barbados), which also attracts many students from other Caribbean countries. The relatively high degree of outward mobility of tertiary students (UNESCO 2018) and general outward migration (UN 2018) to the United States, Canada, and the United Kingdom in particular may also be considered an influential force, since some of these mobile Trinidadians, possibly linguistically influenced by their time abroad, are likely to return to Trinidad and diversify the local interaction of linguistic norms.

At the same time, Trinidad is the second largest island within the English-official Caribbean and its strongest economic player: due to its predominantly oil-based economy, Trinidad (together with its much smaller sister island Tobago) has the highest gross domestic product (GDP) within the entire anglophone Caribbean and one of the highest GDPs per capita in Latin American (CIA The World Factbook 2018). This economic situation, that is, the island's economic independence, power, and prosperity, might serve as a marker of a local identity for Trinidadians.[2] Therefore, in line with Mair (2014), who stresses the influential role of market forces in explaining the emergence of varieties of English, these intra-territorial economic forces could potentially indirectly support linguistic emancipation processes.

Moreover, forces related to language policies can be cited as a potential influence on the norm developmental processes, especially in the education domain: on the one hand, the supranational Caribbean Examinations Council (CXC), of which Trinidad and Tobago is also a member state, recognizes Caribbean Standard English as the target variety for teaching communication studies at the advanced secondary school level (Deuber 2013: 122). On the other hand, the national language policy is more neutral, since national curricula for the language arts do not specify any national standard as the norm (Deuber 2013: 121; Republic of Trinidad and Tobago 2015).

In sum, the interaction of these forces can explain why normativity, at least in so far as it pertains to Standard English, is not simply exo- or endocentric but more multifaceted. Additionally, these effects may be indirectly reinforced by the status of TEC in the multivarietal speech community. Creole often functions as the (primary) marker of

---

[2] We thank Ryan Durgasingh for several discussions on this topic and his insights as a native Trinidadian linguist.

Trinidadian identity, albeit with covert prestige, and is also the target of identity-driven norm reorientation processes; this situation may leave Trinidadian Standard English more susceptible to the influence of different forces and overall more room for a coexistence of different norms (see Deuber and Leung 2013: 309–310 for similar observations in the news media domain).

4.2.2 Implications for the Extra- and Intra-territorial Forces Model

Although the EIF Model (Buschfeld and Kautzsch 2017; Buschfeld et al. 2018) is a useful tool to explain the norm complexities revealed by the case study, the findings also suggest some modifications and extensions of the model, particularly insofar as it builds on the Dynamic Model. First and most importantly, the findings at hand have implications for the development of endonormativity, which both models, in prototypical cases and given the right circumstances (see section 2; see also Schneider 2007: 55–68; Buschfeld et al. 2018: 34), assume to be the outcome of the evolutionary process. The attitudinal evidence presented here supports Mair's (2016: 33, 2017: 7, 22) recent hypothesis that endonormativity may not always be reached (see Van Rooy 2010: 16). Mair (2016: 33) provides two sets of reasons for his argument, which can essentially also be conceptualized in the form of extra- and intra-territorial forces. First, on the intra-territorial side, forces such as failing states and ineffective education systems which do not provide sufficient access to Standard English to the majority of the population in a postcolonial territory can hamper the emergence of endonormativity. Second, on the extra-territorial side, forces such as the continued power of the former colonial norm, growing American English influence, or strong neighboring Englishes may limit the development of endonormativity of local PCEs (see also Schreier 2012: 357). In light especially of the latter set of forces, Mair (2017: 8) as well as Westphal (2017: 224) argue that the attainment of full endonormativity is unlikely for small postcolonial territories such as those of the anglophone Caribbean, although evolution away from the colonial norm may still be observed.

In order to explain and predict the norm developmental process in Trinidad and in Trinidadian secondary schools specifically, it is helpful to take into consideration the argument put forward by Mukherjee (2007) that PCEs can possibly enter steady states, which are viewed as relatively stable equilibria of conflicting progressive and conservative forces in the development of PCEs. Mukherjee (2007: 170–171) understands progressive forces as those which make a variety develop further along the evolutionary pathway envisaged in the Dynamic Model and the EIF Model and conservative forces as those which hamper a variety's further development. These forces operate at different levels, namely at the level of structure, functions, and attitudes towards a particular variety (see Mukherjee [2007] for a further explanation and examples). However, while it is certainly important to incorporate the notion of variation in the directionality of different forces when modeling and predicting the development of English in Trinidad and other postcolonial speech communities, a binary distinction between conservative and progressive forces in this sense is problematic insofar as it suggests a rather unidimensional mapping of the evolutionary trajectories of PCEs. That is, the development of PCEs is largely viewed as occurring on a continuum between a conservative (exocentric British) and a progressive (endocentric local) pole; more diverse and multifaceted but also stable norm scenarios in which additional regional and/or global norms exert steady influence on the development of English in a given territory, such as in Trinidad, are not accounted for.

Therefore, and bearing in mind that the complex interplay of forces of different directionalities that has shaped the evolution of English in Trinidad so far will likely continue and become more influential in the future, we suggest that endonormativity should not be considered the only possible outcome of linguistic emancipation processes beyond phase 3. Rather, the findings of the case study show how an alternative form of norm development might look, which would also need to be accounted for in evolutionary models of World Englishes: postcolonial speech communities could potentially reach a phase of *multinormative* rather than endonormative stabilization if these multidirectional forces form an equilibrial steady state in which different forces are balanced out and simultaneously impact normativity. This means an overall relatively stable phase in which normativity is essentially multidimensional, that is, it involves the coexistence of different local, regional, or global standards; exo- and endonormative aspects may be incorporated in such a way that they cannot be clearly differentiated, and there may be fine-grained differences in status between varieties. The results show evidence for such a multinormative orientation on the attitudinal level, but the functional and structural sphere could be affected, as well. For instance, regarding the functional level, we may observe a stable allocation of English (and English-based varieties/languages) to certain domains, in which different outside and local varieties each play a context-specific role and carry specific social meanings (cp. e.g. Westphal 2017: 201–230). Multinormative stabilization may also be concerned with the structural level: different lexical, morpho-syntactic, or phonological features associated with different norms may be accepted and used depending on the context, the formality, the interlocutor, or genre. In their recent reflections on World Englishes model making, Deshors and Gilquin (2018) similarly argue that new models may profit from conceptualizing normativity in more complex and dynamic ways compared to approaches that traditionally envisaged normativity in relation to a single variety of English.

Such an extension of both models which allows for multinormative stabilization as an alternative pathway has explanatory value for many postcolonial Englishes whose evolutionary processes are otherwise not accounted for by the traditional notion of endonormativity. These do not only include contexts in the anglophone Caribbean but also many other postcolonial speech communities where (1) different norms coexist and the dichotomy between exo- and endonormativity is increasingly blurred (Hundt et al. 2015; Westphal 2017; Wilson 2017) and (2) other varieties and/or (creole) languages also function as targets of (endo-)normativity (Mukherjee 2007; Coetzee-Van Rooy 2014), such as Fiji, India, or South Africa. We thus suggest that investigations of norm complexities as observed in these contexts may profit from conceptualizing these complexities as manifestations of multinormative stabilization processes. Given that we understand multinormativity as referring to a stable and systematic multidimensional orientation involving several coexisting norms as described above, we explicitly view multinormative stabilization as different from earlier developmental stages in which norms in postcolonial territories may not yet have stabilized and are very dynamic; we assume that multinormative stabilization is an alternative and more stable developmental stage in phase 4 of the Dynamic Model and the postcolonial component of the EIF Model.

We further suggest that both endo- and multinormative stabilization processes could be considered possible in phase 4 depending on the constellation, continuity, directionality, and interaction of different sets of forces: endonormative stabilization is more likely when unidirectional forces that favor the development of a local norm dominate the transition from phase 3 to phase 4, while multinormative developments are more likely to take place if multidirectional forces that pull the evolution of a variety into different directions are balanced out. Multinormativity may be further catalyzed by forces that leave room for variation and different kinds of influence, such as national school curricula in Trinidad that do not specify that a particular form of Standard English be taught, or the status of coexisting local varieties and languages, that may (also) function as targets of (endo-)normativity. Moreover, endo- and multinormativity should not be seen as strictly dichotomous concepts but rather as poles of a continuum within stage 4. That is, shifts towards a rather multinormative or a more endonormative pole are possible and likely to take place if particular forces begin pushing the evolutionary process into a new direction. There may also be situations in which the norm orientation is neither strictly multinormative, that is, a coexistence of norms that are all accepted to the same degree, nor strictly endonormative, that is, a clear preference of local over outside norms, but something in-between. Furthermore, multinormativity itself may also take different shapes depending on the constellation of forces. Especially in Trinidad and other contexts where a range of different norms are at play, that is, not only British and local, but also American, strong neighboring, and other norms, the status and role of individual varieties (in different domains) could vary considerably over time while an overall multinormative orientation stays in place.

Second, the case study also has implications for the third dimension of the EIF Model, which was recently added and accounts for variety-internal heterogeneity (Buschfeld et al. 2018). The results at hand suggest that this heterogeneity may not only involve internal linguistic variability but may also manifest on a language attitudinal level. As also shown by previous studies, language attitudes in anglophone Caribbean and other sociolinguistically complex postcolonial territories may often be overall heterogeneous, domain specific, and not necessarily in favor of one homogenous norm only (Deuber 2013: 116; Hundt et al. 2015: 704; Westphal 2017: 198–199; Wilson 2017). An extended version of the EIF Model which also takes the attitudinal level into consideration can therefore account more comprehensively for developments in these territories. Moreover, this attitudinal variability can then not only be explained by sociolinguistic parameters, which the model currently incorporates to account for internal linguistic variability, but the interaction of various forces themselves is also likely to explain this kind of heterogeneity.

Third, the discussion of norm developments in Trinidad bears implications on the conceptualization of forces in the model: it becomes apparent that it is not always possible to clearly differentiate between intra- and extra-territorial forces. The influence of re-migration to Trinidad or the return of mobile tertiary students who received some of their education abroad go beyond the division into intra- and extra-territorial forces. Similarly, this dichotomy is problematic to apply to forces that relate to supranational institutions that Trinidad and Tobago is also a member state of and in which it is part of the decision-making process, such as the Caribbean Examinations Council or CARICOM. Moreover, non-local linguistic influences and norms may not always be perceived as such: they may, in fact, be perceived as natural and authentic parts of the local linguistic diversity rather than something external (see Westphal 2017: 214). Overall, conceptualizing these forces as strictly binary in nature is rather restrictive and is not fully able to represent the spatial and sociolinguistic dynamics in postcolonial speech communities in late modernity, given that forces are increasingly interrelated and operate in and between different localities. Schneider's (2014: 28) concept of transnational attraction acknowledges similar dynamic processes and provides a framework to explain the spread and appropriation of English(es) "unbounded by distinctions of norms, nations or varieties." As indicated by the term *transnational*, the primary concern of this concept is the transcending of national boundaries. However, even more complexities exist in the global diffusion and emergence of English(es); other kinds of boundary transcendence beyond the transnational level may also affect norm developmental processes, such as regional dynamics within and beyond nation states or state-internal migration (see Greiner and Sakdapolrak 2013: 374).

Translocality may be a useful alternative perspective for conceptualizing the forces that affect the development of different Englishes and the diffusion of English overall. In essence, the term *translocality* captures "complex socio-spatial interactions in a holistic, actor-oriented, and multi-dimensional understanding" (Greiner and Sakdapolrak 2013: 376). More specifically, translocality is concerned with the following: first, it focuses on socio-spatial dynamics that transcend all kinds of boundaries, that is, not only those of nation states (Greiner and Sakdapolrak 2013: 376). Second, it considers various kinds of mobility, that is, movements of people and goods as well as symbolic flows of, for instance, ideas, practices, and norms (Greiner and Sakdapolrak 2013: 376). Third, translocality emphasizes the interdependence of mobility, flows, and border transgressions, on the one hand, and situatedness on the local level, on the other hand (Freitag and von Oppen 2010: 7). In the case of Trinidad, translocality draws particular attention to socio-spatially diverse forces that for instance include, in addition to other non-local and local factors: (1) supranational, pan-Caribbean political, economic, and educational institutions; (2) the large degree of outward mobility of Trinidadian tertiary students; (3) emigration and remigration to Trinidad from other Caribbean islands (including Tobago), Great Britain, Canada, and the United States; and (4) members of large diasporic communities such as in New York City who reside abroad but also, for some time of the year, in Trinidad.

We therefore argue that there are a number of advantages in conceptualizing forces as *translocal* in nature: most importantly, difficulties in conceptualizing forces are overcome, given that the notions of the local and the non-local are integrated. Some forces may be operating more on the local level and others more at the regional or global level but essentially they transcend binary notions of socio-spatial structures. Moreover, transnational, regional, and global influences can all be understood as types of translocal effects (Freitag and von Oppen 2010: 13; Greiner and Sakdapolrak 2013: 375). Therefore, different spatial structures which are all relevant in postcolonial speech communities are considered in a joint fashion in the conceptualization of forces.

Figure 13.1 introduces an extended and modified version of the postcolonial component of the EIF Model that takes the above-discussed aspects into consideration: it allows for an alternative development in phase 4, namely multinormative stabilization, depending on the constellation, directionality, and continuity of different sets of forces, and for changes to take place from multinormative to more endonormative stabilization processes and vice versa. It explains the development of postcolonial Englishes as the result of an interaction of translocal forces, that is, forces that transcend boundaries while relating to local contexts. In addition, in line with Buschfeld et al. (2018: 24) and as stated above, we assume that, although differentiation and heterogeneity may be particularly strong in the last phase of Schneider's Dynamic Model, both should be reckoned with during the entire evolutionary process. Differentiation as a separate phase is therefore displayed in parentheses. While the proposed extensions could theoretically also apply to non-postcolonial Englishes, empirical evidence from such contexts would be needed to assess this.

5. CONCLUSION

This chapter has applied the Dynamic Model (Schneider 2007) and the EIF Model (Buschfeld and Kautzsch 2017; Buschfeld et al. 2018) to

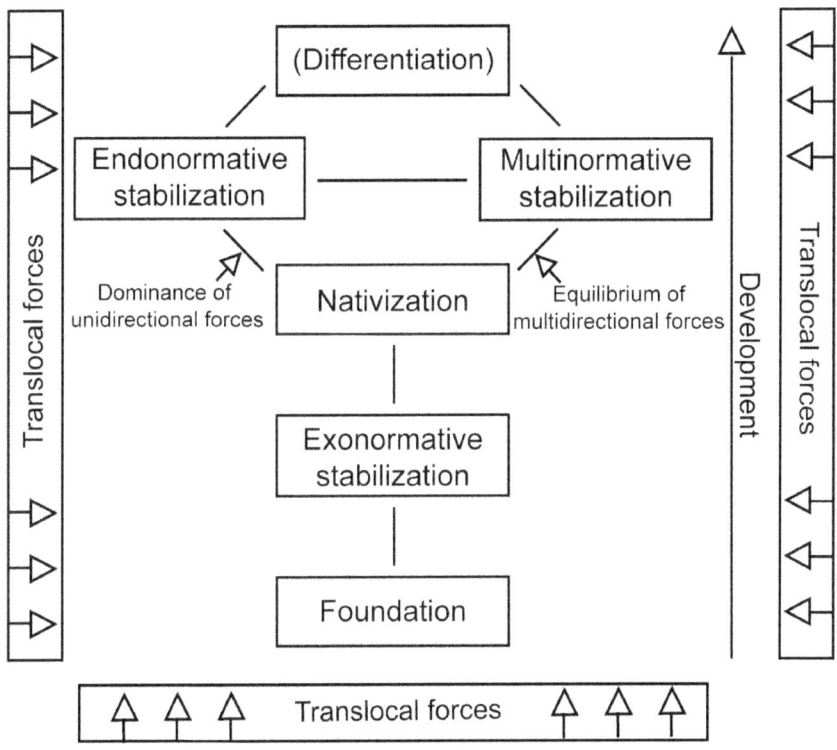

Figure 13.1 An extended and modified version of the postcolonial component of the EIF Model accounting for multinormative stabilization and translocality
Source: adapted from Buschfeld et al. (2018: 24).

Standard English in Trinidad with particular reference to the education context. The discussion of both models against the backdrop of the findings of the case study has shown that the norm complexities that were observed go beyond what the Dynamic Model predicts. The EIF Model can generally account for the findings, but the assumption underlying both models that, given a continued strong role for English combined with a fading orientation towards the former colonial power's norms, postcolonial Englishes are likely to achieve (full) endonormativity is problematic in view of the multidimensionality of norms prevalent in Trinidad and other sociolinguistically complex postcolonial speech communities. An extended and modified version of the EIF Model has been proposed which, depending on the interaction of different sets of forces, allows multinormative stabilization as an alternative outcome in the evolution of postcolonial Englishes. This extended model also allows for more complexities in the conceptualization of intra-varietal heterogeneity in that it considers manifestations of heterogeneity on the language attitudinal level. Finally, the modified model relies on the theoretical concept of translocality to better account for the forces that transcend traditional boundaries and operate in and between different localities.

Given the limited nature of our case study which dealt with context-specific covert attitudes only, more explicit language attitudes from the education realm and other contexts, such as the media or business domain, should also be considered in future research. Investigations of language use in such contexts are also needed to assess norm developmental processes in Trinidad more fully. Furthermore, it needs to be emphasized in conclusion that while this work has been concerned specifically with Standard English, a fuller picture of sociolinguistic norms and variation in Trinidad would, of course, have to incorporate TEC as well. What is important to bear in mind is that language use and structure and explicit and implicit language attitudes need not be homogeneous or harmonious. Rather, in sociolinguistically complex postcolonial territories like Trinidad, in which different sets of translocal forces may manifest in steady equilibrial states and differently so in different contexts, we should expect an overall heterogeneous norm orientation.

REFERENCES

Aceto, Michael. 2008. Eastern Caribbean English-derived language varieties: Phonology. In Edgar W. Schneider, ed. 2008, *Varieties of English: The Americas and the Caribbean*. Berlin: De Gruyter, 290–311.

Allsopp, Richard. 1996. *Dictionary of Caribbean English Usage*. Oxford: Oxford University Press.

Buschfeld, Sarah. 2013. *English in Cyprus or Cyprus English*. Amsterdam: John Benjamins.

Buschfeld, Sarah and Alexander Kautzsch. 2017. Towards an integrated approach to postcolonial and non-postcolonial Englishes. *World Englishes* 36.1: 104–126.

Buschfeld, Sarah and Edgar W. Schneider. 2018. World Englishes: Postcolonial Englishes and beyond. In Ee L. Low and Anne Pakir, eds. 2018, *World Englishes: Rethinking Paradigms*. London: Routledge, 29–46.

Buschfeld, Sarah, Alexander Kautzsch and Edgar W. Schneider. 2018. From colonial dynamism to current transnationalism: A unified view on postcolonial and non-postcolonial Englishes. In Deshors, ed. 2018, 15–44.

Buschfeld, Sarah, Thomas Hoffmann, Magnus Huber and Alexander Kautzsch, eds. 2014. *The Evolution of Englishes: The Dynamic Model and Beyond*. Amsterdam: John Benjamins.

CIA The World Factbook. Trinidad and Tobago. 2018, https://www.cia.gov/library/ publications/the-world-factbook/geos/td.html (last accessed February 20, 2018).

Coetzee-Van Rooy, Susan. 2014. The identity issue in bi- and multilingual repertoires in South Africa: Implications for Schneider's Dynamic Model. In Buschfeld, Hoffmann, Huber and Kautzsch, eds. 2014, 39–57.

Deshors, Sandra C, eds. 2018. *Modeling World Englishes: Assessing the Interplay of Emancipation and Globalization of ESL Varieties*. Amsterdam: John Benjamins.

Deshors, Sandra C. and Gaëtanelle Gilquin. 2018. Modeling World Englishes in the 21st century: New reflections on modeling-making. In Deshors, ed. 2018, 281–294.

Deuber, Dagmar. 2013. Towards endonormative standards of English in the Caribbean: A study of students' beliefs and school curricula. *Language, Culture and Curriculum* 26.2: 109–127.

Deuber, Dagmar. 2014. *English in the Caribbean: Variation, Style and Standards in Jamaica and Trinidad*. Cambridge: Cambridge University Press.

Deuber, Dagmar and Glenda-Alicia Leung. 2013. Investigating attitudes towards an emerging standard of English: Evaluations of newscasters' accents in Trinidad. *Multilingua* 32.3: 289–319.

Freitag, Ulrike and Achim v. Oppen. 2010. Introduction: 'Translocality': An approach to connection and transfer in area studies. In Ulrike Freitag and Achim v. Oppen, eds. 2010, *Translocality: The Study of Globalising Processes From a Southern Perspective*. Leiden: Brill, 1–21.

Greiner, Clemens and Patrick Sakdapolrak. 2013. Translocality: Concepts, applications and emerging research perspectives. *Geography Compass* 7.5: 373–384.

Hackert, Stephanie. 2016. Standards of English in the Caribbean: History, attitudes, functions, features. In Elena Seoane and Cristina Suárez-Gómez, eds. 2016, *World Englishes: New Theoretical and Methodological Considerations*. Amsterdam: John Benjamins, 85–111.

Hundt, Marianne, Lena Zipp and André Huber. 2015. Attitudes in Fiji towards varieties of English. *World Englishes* 34.4: 688–707.
Kachru, Braj B. 1985. Standards, codification and sociolinguistic realism: The English language in the outer circle. In Randolph Quirk and H. G. Widdowson, eds. 1985, *English in the World: Teaching and Learning the Language and Literatures*. Cambridge: Cambridge University Press, 11–30.
Kretzschmar, William A. Jr. 2014. Emergence of "new varieties" in speech as a complex system. In Buschfeld, Hoffmann, Huber and Kautzsch, eds. 2014, 142–159.
Kristiansen, Tore. 2001. Two standards: One for the media and one for the school. *Language Awareness* 10.1: 9–24.
Mair, Christian. 2013. The world system of Englishes: Accounting for the transnational importance of mobile and mediated vernaculars. *English World-Wide* 34.3: 253–278.
Mair, Christian. 2014. Does money talk, and do languages have price tags? Economic perspectives on English as a global language. In Buschfeld, Hoffmann, Huber and Kautzsch, eds. 2014, 249–266.
Mair, Christian. 2016. Beyond and between the three circles: World Englishes research in the age of globalization. In Elena Seoane and Cristina Suárez-Gómez, eds. 2016, *World Englishes: New Theoretical and Methodological Considerations*. Amsterdam: John Benjamins, 17–36.
Mair, Christian. 2017. Crisis of the "Outer Circle"? Globalisation, the weak nation state, and the need for new taxonomies in World Englishes research. In Markku Filppula, Juhani Klemola, Anna Mauranen and Svetlana Vetchinnikova, eds. 2017, *Changing English: Global and Local Perspectives*. Berlin: De Gruyter, 5–24.
Meer, Philipp, Michael Westphal, Eva C. Hänsel and Dagmar Deuber. 2019. Trinidadian secondary school students' attitudes toward accents of Standard English. *Journal of Pidgin and Creole Languages* 34.1: 83–125.
Mukherjee, Joybrato. 2007. Steady states in the evolution of New Englishes. *Journal of English Linguistics* 35.2: 157–187.
Republic of Trinidad and Tobago, Ministry of Education. 2015. *Secondary School Curriculum. English Language Arts. Forms 1–3. Draft*.
Republic of Trinidad and Tobago, Ministry of Planning and Sustainable Development, Central Statistical Office. 2012. Trinidad and Tobago 2011 Population and Housing Census. Demographic Report, https://www.guardian.co.tt/sites/default/files/story/2011_DemographicReport.pdf (last accessed September 2, 2018).

Schneider, Edgar W. 2007. *Postcolonial English: Varieties Around the World*. Cambridge: Cambridge University Press.

Schneider, Edgar W. 2014. New reflections on the evolutionary dynamics of world Englishes. *World Englishes* 33.1: 9–32.

Schreier, Daniel. 2012. Varieties resistant to standardization. In Raymond Hickey, ed. 2012, *Standards of English: Codified Varieties Around the World*. Cambridge: Cambridge University Press, 354–368.

Trudgill, Peter. 2004. *New-Dialect Formation: The Inevitability of Colonial Englishes*. Edinburgh: Edinburgh University Press.

UN. 2018. Migration Profiles: Trinidad and Tobago, https://esa.un.org/miggmgprofiles/ indicators/ files/TrinidadTobago.pdf (last accessed February 20, 2018).

UNESCO. 2018. Global flow of tertiary-level students, http://uis.unesco.org/en/uis-student-flow (last accessed February 20, 2018).

Van Rooy, Bertus. 2010. Social and linguistic perspectives on variability in World Englishes. *World Englishes* 29.1: 3–20.

Van Rooy, Bertus. 2014. Convergence and endonormativity at Phase 4 of the Dynamic Model. In Buschfeld, Hoffmann, Huber and Kautzsch, eds. 2014, 21–38.

Westphal, Michael. 2017. *Language Variation on Jamaican Radio*. Amsterdam: John Benjamins.

Wilson, Guyanne. 2017. Conflicting language ideologies in choral singing in Trinidad. *Language & Communication* 52: 19–30.

CHAPTER 14

Englishes in Tristan da Cunha, St Helena, Bermuda and the Falkland Islands: PCE, non-PCE or both? Blurred Boundaries in the Atlantic

Daniel Schreier

1. INTRODUCTION: FOUR SOCIOLINGUISTIC HISTORIES

This chapter looks at the interplay of extra- and intra-territorial forces that shaped the evolution and sociolinguistic characteristics of four varieties of English spoken in the Atlantic Ocean: Bermuda, St Helena, Tristan da Cunha and the Falkland Islands. Two of them are among the oldest colonial varieties (Bermudian and St Helenian English, established in the sixteenth and seventeenth centuries; Schreier 2008), those on the Falkland Islands and Tristan da Cunha are much younger. With reference to Buschfeld and Kautzsch (2017), I will single out and evaluate general and locally specific forces that operated in the formation of these varieties, with a focus on the nature of various coexisting dialects (ENL, ESL and EFL) in the early contact scenarios that straddle current dividing lines between social and ethnic communities in all four locations.

Crucially, all four involved an ENL founding stock of British founders, ESL-speaking settlers from Continental Europe (France, Scandinavia) and (with the exception of the Falkland Islands) slaves from various locations. Settler groups were small in size yet were characterized by division of labor and social segregation. Various population strands mixed to the extent that for St Helena, Governor Charles Elliot remarked in 1868 that "there can be no position on the face of the earth where it would be more difficult to discriminate between the various strains of blood of which the body of the population is composed than here in St. Helena."

Similarly, the Bermudian population was marked by extremely high mobility within and across the islands, so that qualitative differences are not community-diagnostic and there is now a tapestry of quantitative variation that links individual members and renders it difficult to outline pre-specified speech communities (cf. Eberle 2017). The question of particular interest is how such conditions lend themselves to theorizing and how they fit into current models of English as a world language, which will be explored in detail.

Though the Atlantic Ocean is not generally recognized as a prominent or influential area within the anglophone world, there is little doubt that it is characterized by sociolinguistic heterogeneity. The Caribbean, a vast and utterly complex conglomerate of English (and other) varieties, hosts some of the best-researched Creoles (Jamaican Creole English; Patrick 1999) as well as recently documented varieties (Dominican Kokoy; Aceto 2010). Further north, we find the equally diverse Bahamian Englishes, which are likely to have socio-historical connections with Gullah (Hackert and Huber 2007), spoken along the US American seaboard, as well as Bermudian English (BerE), "one of the most severely underresearched varieties of English" (Cutler et al. 2006: 2066). This is one of the least-documented varieties of English which has undergone full nativization, having been documented and studied only very recently (Eberle 2017). As for the South Atlantic, the three fully nativized varieties are St Helenian English (Schreier 2008), Tristan da Cunha English (Schreier 2003) and Falkland Islands English (Britain and Sudbury 2010), all of which are documented and described in detail. The island communities have in common that they were established as British colonies and that they received a founding stock of English settlers who were embedded in different language-ecological contact situations and share parallels, so close in fact that two of them (St Helena and Tristan da Cunha) have close historical connections via human traffic.

We begin with an outline of the social, historical and sociolinguistic development of the four communities, with special emphasis on potential founding groups and population demographics (the discussion of the Bermudian context is slightly more extensive as it is less researched than the South Atlantic islands; Sudbury 2000; Schreier 2003, 2008). An in-depth understanding of these conditions is necessary for reconstructing the sociolinguistic development of local varieties in the respective locations and also for discussing their relevance for models of English as a world language.

1.1 Bermudian English

Bermuda, a self-governing, geographically isolated British colony (Trudgill 2002), lies approximately 600 miles to the east of Cape Hatteras in North Carolina. It is an archipelago of approximately 120 islands, with seven main islands and a total land area of circa twenty square miles. The question of whether or not Bermuda belongs to the Caribbean sociolinguistically is a debated one, but it is often associated with that region, since the proximity of the Gulf Stream creates an almost sub-tropical climate, which has had an impact on the island's economic development.

In the early years of colonization, the mild climate and fertile soil led Bermudians to pursue agriculture, especially tobacco cultivation, even though the scarcity of land available for plantations meant that Bermuda was in no way comparable to competing colonies on the American mainland, which had the advantage that they were closer to major harbors, trading places and shipping routes (Bernhard 1985, 1999). After the Somers Islands Company lost its claim on Bermuda and the island became a royal colony in 1686 (Bernhard 1985), Bermudians – no longer subject to the Somers Islands Company's trade restrictions – turned to the sea, which became the prime factor of Bermudian economy (Jarvis 2002: 592). Trading, shipbuilding, wrecking, as well as occasional privateering partly replaced agriculture in this period, and from the late seventeenth to the late eighteenth centuries (with intermissions; Bernhard 1999: 167) Bermudians even established a salt trade route between Bermuda, the Turks Islands and North America. They "exported Turks Island salt to the British colonies in North American [sic] from Newfoundland to South Carolina and traded it for grain and salt-fish. This trading sequence became the backbone of Bermuda's economy during the eighteenth century" (Cutler 2003: 55).

In recent years, international business and tourism have become the most important sectors of the Bermudian economy (Slayton 2009), with both of these aspects considerably influencing the current social situation in Bermuda. Tourism, on the one hand, is a major factor that leads to Bermudians continuously interacting with foreigners (with over 80 percent of tourists coming from the United States). The numerous foreign companies with headquarters or dependencies in Bermuda, on the other hand, account for a considerable level of migration, since quite a large number of foreigners come to Bermuda on work permits. The (2010) Census of Population and Housing lists the island's population as 64,237, 50,565 of whom have Bermudian status. Some 82 percent

(41,575) of these with Bermudian status were born in Bermuda, as opposed to 6,230 foreign born people. Fifty-four percent of the population selected black as their racial group and 31 percent selected white. Bermuda is also home to considerable emigrant communities from the Azores and Philippines (among others).

The sociolinguistic evolution of BerE can be summarized as follows (see Eberle 2017 for a longer and more detailed discussion): while it is uncertain when Bermuda was discovered – (according to Zuill [1983: 3]: "Who discovered Bermuda and when they did is not clear. What is known is that in 1511 a map was published in an atlas called the Legatio Babylonica, which included Bermuda under the name La Bermuda") – it has been suggested that the island was discovered and first settled between 1503 and 1511 (Zuill 1983; Trudgill 2002). Prior to the shipwreck of the *Sea Venture* in 1609 and the start of a proper colonization process in 1612 with the arrival of the first larger group of permanent British settlers, little attempt was made to settle Bermuda and, consequently, the British encountered a *tabula rasa* situation in the sense that "the founders of the community did not come into contact with pre-existing language varieties" (Schreier 2005: 146). There were hardly any founder effects (in Mufwene's [2001] sense that those who establish colonies are likely to have a sociolinguistic impact on the development of emerging contact varieties): the survivors of the *Sea Venture*, shipwrecked near Bermuda on its way to Virginia, traveled onwards to the American colonies in May 1610; only three of them stayed in Bermuda (Hallett 2007: 15).

Consequently, Bermuda is the oldest continually inhabited colony (Tucker 1975; Bernhard 1999) and Bernhard (2010: 678) has claimed that it is "the smallest and most geographically isolated of England's New World colonies" (this would be even more valid for Tristan da Cunha and St Helena; see below). During this early period, the settlement processes led to a rapid development of Bermudian society and to a steady increase of the number of settlers, especially after the establishment of the Somers Islands Company in 1615, which "assume[d] administration of the colony and sent over another thousand settlers over the next seven years" (Jarvis 2002: 588). As early as 1625, the entire land mass was either inhabited or under cultivation and "the infrastructure of a settled colony was largely in place" (Jarvis 2002: 588). In fact, "Bermuda became [so] overcrowded by the late 1620s, [that it sparked] the emigration of Bermudian settlers to Virginia, Providence Island, and other English colonies throughout the 17th century" (Jarvis

2002: 591). Similarly, the high number of settlers (in a confined space) led to out-migration in the early years of the colony, and there were also – at least in one instance – religious disputes. "[I]n 1648, a group of British settlers seeking religious freedom left Bermuda and founded the first permanent colony on Eleuthera, in the northern Bahamas" (Reaser and Torbert 2012: 169). Subsequently, the island's population further increased so that "[i]n 1660 the colony had a total population of about 3,500 inhabitants" (Bernhard 1999: 103).

A second population group, the slave population, added to the community's feature pool (used here to refer to all possible variants that compete for adoption when new norms emerge), as Bermuda was one of the earliest colonies to start the process of slave importation (Jarvis 2002: 588). The first slaves were brought from the West Indies in 1617: "according to a contemporary account, she [the *Edwin*] 'brought with her ... one Indian and a Negroe (the first thes Ilands [sic] ever had)'" (Bernhard 1985: 63). From that point forward, Afro-Bermudian as well as Native American slave populations grew steadily; from very early on slaves formed a tight-knit community (Jarvis 2002: 590). Compared to other colonies at that time, the situation on Bermuda was different: the Afro-Bermudian population, for instance, was "mostly native-born [and consequently] more stable" and did not have a "continued influx of unacculturated newcomers from Africa" (Bernhard 1999: 200). This aspect – combined with the fact that restricted space and working opportunities prevented the importation of a higher number of slaves from outside Bermuda (Jarvis 2010) – increased societal stability on the island:

> The fact that Bermuda's acculturated population of blacks, Indians, mulattos, and mustees – nearly 3,000 by the 1670s – lived almost elbow to elbow with over 4,000 whites in an area of only 21 square miles would make the history of slavery and race relations in Bermuda quite different from that of England's other colonies. (Bernhard 1999: 96)

By comparison, Jarvis finds that "large sizes of both black and white families produced a racially integrated colonial society in which constant daily interracial interaction was the norm" (2002: 602). The native-born slave population further increased subsequently from 38 percent of the population by the end of the seventeenth century to 47 percent by the 1770s; "whites remained a narrow majority until the next century" and only in the early 1800s did blacks outnumber whites (Bernhard 1999: 98–99).

Only little is known about the precise origins of the Afro-Bermudian population. Since "[t]he vast majority of Bermudian slaves lived with their white owners" (Jarvis 2002: 610), it is virtually impossible to find historical traces and sources that provide detailed information about the black population's origins. It seems clear that most slaves came to Bermuda via the West Indies. While Bernhard states that "[s]ome of them could well have been Africans taken directly from West Africa by Spanish or Portuguese traders and later captured at sea by English or Dutch privateers [and o]thers . . . were West Indian blacks taken from Spanish settlements in the Caribbean" (1999: 23), Jarvis argues that "[f]ew of the . . . black arrivals before 1623 were apparently African-born; most were taken by English privateers from Spanish colonies in the Caribbean" (2002: 588). It is thus practically impossible to locate from where the slaves originated. In contrast, the putative origins of the Indian slave population are better reported. "Members of the Pequot, Mohican, Wampanoag, and Narragansett tribes from New England are the most likely to have been brought to Bermuda" (Bernhard 1999: 114), and some were brought from Jamaica as well (Bernhard 1999: 56). All things considered, the history and development of these populations in the early years of the colony remains fragmentary because written sources and records are scarce.

The final factor that considerably influenced the colony's development is the nature of socio-historical relationships between Bermuda and the United States. Bermuda established strong ties with North America on various levels. Trade was so crucial that it was "the centrepiece of US-Bermudian relations" (Slayton 2009: 19) over the centuries; economic ties were maintained in periods of tension between Great Britain and the United States. During the American Civil War, the Bermudian government recognized the Confederate states of America's government, while "Bermudian traders openly supported the Confederacy. Bermuda's proximity to the US South had helped to forge close commercial and social ties that would continue throughout the US Civil War" (Slayton 2009: 20). In the twentieth century, the tourism industry emerged as a major sector as the number of tourists from the United States increased from 13,000 in 1920 and over 82,000 in the 1930s to 651,000 in 2011 (Government of Bermuda, *Facts and Figures 2012*: 10).

The ties with the United States were strengthened during the twentieth century. Bermuda's position in the middle of the Atlantic Ocean proved to be of strategic and geopolitical relevance with regard to US defense efforts during the world wars and the Cold War (Slayton 2009: 20). Bermuda granted the US military forces a land lease where army bases were subsequently established (Zuill 1999). Consequently, a significant number of US military forces were stationed in Bermuda for an extended period of time during the twentieth century, which led to immediate and everyday contact between Bermudians and US military personnel and strengthened already thriving US-Bermudian relations.

1.2 Tristan da Cunha

Tristan da Cunha lies in the South Atlantic Ocean, some 2,800 kilometers west of Cape Town; the population as of 2010 was 264. Though insignificant in terms of speaker numbers, Tristan da Cunha English (TdCE) is important for the study of World Englishes in that it has a rather unique evolutionary development: the island was practically uninhabited when it was settled in the early nineteenth century, its founder stock can be located in extraordinary detail, and the social history has been researched and reported.

The sociolinguistic development was as follows (for more detailed accounts see Brander 1940; Munch 1945; Crawford 1982; Schreier 2003): the island was discovered by the Portuguese (in 1506) but the Dutch were the first to explore it (in 1643; Brander 1940). Towards the end of the eighteenth century, the American fishing industry expanded to the South Atlantic Ocean, and Tristan da Cunha became an occasional resort to the sealers and whalers. The island was settled in 1816, when the British Admiralty formally annexed Ascension Island and Tristan da Cunha and a South African military garrison was dispatched to the island. When it withdrew after only one year, some army personnel stayed behind and settled permanently: two stonemasons from Plymouth, a non-commissioned officer from Kelso, Scotland, named William Glass, his wife, "the daughter of a Boer Dutchman" (Evans 1994: 245), and their children. The population increased when shipwrecked sailors and castaways arrived and in 1824 the settlers included the Glass family, Richard "Old Dick" Riley (from Wapping, East London), Thomas Swain (born in Hastings, Sussex) and Alexander Cotton (from Hull/Yorkshire) (Earle [1832] 1966). The late 1820s and 1830s saw the arrival of a group of women from St Helena and three settlers from Denmark and the Netherlands and the population grew rapidly. By 1832, there were thirty-four people living on the island, twenty-two of whom were young children or adolescents. The 1830s and 1840s saw a renaissance in the whaling industry, and numerous ships docked in Tristan da Cunha to barter for fresh water and supplies; more American whalers arrived, some of whom also settled permanently.

The second half of the nineteenth century, in contrast, was a period of growing isolation, since the influx of settlers dwindled, and a weaver from Yorkshire and two Italian sailors were the only new arrivals in the second half of the century (Crawford 1945). This state of isolation lasted well into the twentieth century. When visiting the island in 1937, the Norwegian sociologist Peter Munch found that the islanders lived in pre-industrial conditions (Munch 1945) and Allan Crawford, the cartographer of the expedition, noted that only six out of a total of 190 Tristanians had ever left the island. This changed in April 1942, when the arrival of a British navy corps saw economic changes; a South African company obtained exclusive rights to establish a permanent fishing industry on the island, employing practically the entire local workforce. The traditional subsistence economy was replaced by a paid labor force economy, and the traditional way of life was modified as a result of the creation of permanent jobs with regular working hours. These social changes had sociolinguistic consequences, even more so during a period of economic prosperity in the 1970s and 1980s, which led to an increase in mobility (mostly for secondary education and further job training) and a quick opening-up of the community.

There are two main reasons why, though sociodemographically and politically insignificant, Tristan da Cunha is an important research site. First, the community's founders found themselves in *tabula rasa* conditions and present-day TdCE formed via direct contact of the inputs in the first half of the nineteenth century. Chambers (2004: 134) has called Tristan da Cunha the "sociolinguists' Galapagos." There was no contact with indigenous varieties since the island was uninhabited when the garrison arrived, which is rare. We can attempt to trace features and reconstruct how settlement history and population dynamics shaped the development of an indigenous variety (Lim and Ansaldo 2015). Second, the English input varieties to TdCE are well known, as is the development of the local population (there is an entire genealogical tree). The feature pool hosted dialects from the British Isles (the founders came from the Scottish Lowlands, East Yorkshire, East London and Hastings), the United States (the most influential American resident was a native of New London, Massachusetts) and St Helena. Moreover, though it was certainly an important factor (Schreier and Trudgill 2006), TdCE did not form via koinéization alone. There was some admixture from second-language (L2) forms spoken by settlers with Danish, Dutch and Italian as first languages (perhaps also early Afrikaans). Several kinds of linguistic contact operated during the genesis and formation periods of TdCE, which formed in a sociolinguistic environment that involved British and American English, L2 forms of English and St Helenian English (StHE), triggering intense language and dialect contact.

1.3 St Helena

The volcanic island of St Helena lies in the mid-central South Atlantic Ocean, 1,930 kilometers west of Angola and just south of the equator. St Helena covers 122 square kilometers, and its topography mostly consists of steep, relatively barren and rocky territory. The island's capital is Jamestown, although there are other smaller settlements such as Halftree Hollow, Blue Hills, Sandy Bay and Longwood (the latter being the residence of Napoleon Bonaparte, who lived in exile on the island from 1815 to his death in 1821).

At the end of 2017, the St Helenian population amounted to 4,846 people, with an estimated 4,761 residents and 4,267 persons with St Helenian status (St Helena Government post, January 29, 2018). The population stock is of mixed European, African and Asian origin, and English is the only language spoken on the island. The social history can be sketched as follows (see Gosse 1938 and Schreier 2008 for more detail): the island was discovered by the Portuguese in 1502, who used is as a refreshment station and sickbay. The island was not settled until it was claimed by the British East India Company (EIC) in 1658 (Gosse 1938). Then, a concerted settlement policy was implemented, and soldiers, servants and planters (employed and contracted by the EIC, who held direct control over the island until the 1830s) were recruited to St Helena, along with slaves (see below). Even though the origins of the British settlers are not known, there is socio-historical evidence from the origin of family names that they came from various English regions (Schreier forthcoming). Moreover, the St Helena Consultations suggest that the majority of the planters had working-class origins as the EIC recruited many of its soldiers (and settlers as well, for that matter) from among the unemployed in England (Gosse 1938: 72).

The origins of the non-white population are somewhat better documented. Slaves were first imported from the coast of Guinea, later on they were brought from the Indian sub-continent and Madagascar and to a lesser extent from the Cape and Larger Table Bay area, the West

Indies, Indonesia and the Maldives. In 1789, the importation of slaves officially ended, and Chinese indentured laborers arrived. However, very few, if any, stayed permanently, and slavery was finally abolished in 1832 (Melliss 1875). In 1815, the total population was 3,342: 694 whites, 1,517 slaves, 933 non-permanent army personnel, as well as some 300 indentured laborers from China. The situation changed when the administration was transferred to the British government and when St Helena officially became a Crown colony in 1834. Poverty led to out-migration, and the remainder of the nineteenth century was characterized by extreme hardship, an increase in mobility and ethnic mixing. Governor Charles Elliot remarked in 1868 that "there can be no position on the face of the earth where it would be more difficult to discriminate between the various strains of blood of which the body of the population is composed than here in St Helena" (quoted in Gosse 1938). The twentieth century saw economic hardship and out-migration (first to the Cape, subsequently to England) and the community relied heavily on government support as there was no local industry. More recently, this has changed due to the construction of an airport, but it remains to be seen what effects (economic, social, sociolinguistic) the tourist sector will bring to the island (Schreier 2008).

Sociolinguistically, there is no doubt that St Helena has a complex contact history, one that is at the same time multidialectal and multilingual. The development of StHE involved both dialect and language contact. To start with the dialect situation: even though we lack detailed information on settler origins, the British stock most likely came from various regions in England (perhaps with a strong input from southern [south-eastern] varieties, and the city of London and its surroundings [though this is disputed, Gosse 1938]). The language contact situation is clearer and it is documented that up to a dozen different varieties coexisted on the island at various stages: these came from Europe (English, Dutch, Portuguese, French; including Dutch-derived Afrikaans), Africa (unspecified, though from the Gold Coast, Nigeria and Southern Africa) and Asia (mostly Cantonese, various West Indian languages), and, if this can be included here, Malagasy. Not all of these varieties were of equal sociodemographic weight and importance. Some groups were numerically inferior (the slaves from the African mainland or the Maldives, the French Huguenots), others were not integrated into the community to the extent that they could have transmitted their language features to the newly developing variety (here we can include the indentured laborers from Canton, the liberated slaves from West Africa or later on the Boer prisoners; Schreier 2008). This means we can minimize or exclude the potential impact of a good number of varieties brought to the island, such as French, Afrikaans or Cantonese, on account of the fact that speakers of these languages were insignificant in number, that they arrived too late to have an impact or that they were simply not integrated in the community, leaving at the first opportunity.

The important varieties in the feature pool were English and Malagasy. These were the donors which fed into the feature pool most prominently (at least on sociodemographic grounds) and shaped the evolution of the local variety.

1.4 Falkland Islands

The final location included in this survey is the most southern one: the Falkland Islands (alternatively referred to as the Islas Malvinas). These islands also have an extensive colonial history. Although the British first charted them in 1690, settlement only dates back to the mid-1830s (Gough 1990: 270). According to Pascoe and Pepper (2008: 18–19), there were thirty-three residents at the time, along with an Argentinian garrison of twenty-six soldiers and their families. The garrison was forced to leave (which marked the beginning of a long and intense political dispute over ownership) and the residents were given the option of staying or leaving. Some twenty stayed behind (12 Argentinians, 4 Charrúa Indians from Uruguay, 2 British, 2 Germans, 1 French and 1 Jamaican; Pascoe and Pepper 2008: 20). However, the Admiralty instated no official presence on the islands; colonial status was expressed in that "storekeeper William Dickson was instructed to hoist a British flag on Sundays and when a ship approached" (Pascoe and Pepper 2008: 20; cf. which was also practice on Tristan da Cunha). However, when five settlers were murdered by resident gauchos a few years later, the Navy established a presence by establishing up a permanent garrison on the islands (Royle 1985: 205). The presence of the garrison did not straightforwardly lead to the development of a viable colony. Population numbers remained low and unstable. The 1838 census counted forty-three people (including fourteen sailors and seven temporary gauchos); only ten of the inhabitants listed in 1838 were still among the forty-nine (non-military) residents four years later (Royle 1985: 206). The island community consisted of independent settlers, travelling missionaries, temporary gauchos and sealers, a private group of horticulturalists and fish-curers and temporary government workers (Royle 1985: 206).

During the initial planning of a concerted settlement policy and efforts to have an organized settlement policy to attract permanent settlers, it was suggested that due to the climate and agricultural conditions, "there seemed to be general agreement that the best colonists would be Scottish islanders" (Royle 1985: 207). As a result, the population began to increase and censuses reported a population of 384 in 1851 (including 140 children under fifteen years, Pascoe and Pepper 2008: 24, which means that families must have arrived), 540 in 1860 and 662 in 1867 (Royle 1985: 211). There were more than 2,000 settlers by the end of the century, most of whom arrived from the British Isles, while there were few migrants from South America (Spruce 1996: one estimated that there were no more than circa 100, most of whom had left the Falkland Islands by 1900). However, the nineteenth-century population was in a state of flux: many of the workers were under contract and stayed a few years, others could not adapt to the harsh climatic conditions of the Falklands and returned to the United Kingdom (see Sudbury 2000, 2001).

Throughout the twentieth century, the total population remained at about 2,000 but the demographic instability continued; in 1952, over 12 percent of the population emigrated from the islands whereas 9 percent arrived to settle (Sudbury 2000: 26). There was a general decline in the population between World War II and 1982 – a fall of over 19 percent between the censuses of 1946 and 1980, caused by economic decline and the gradual fall of the price of wool on international markets, a key Falkland export at the time.

After the 1982 Falklands War, the investment into the local infrastructure improved the economic situation for the islanders. The establishment of a fisheries licensing zone in 1986 attracted workers and there was an upsurge in migration by more than 30 percent. The population urbanized quickly. Some 85 percent of the population live in Stanley, with the rest living in small rural settlements, and Sudbury (2000: 29–30) reported that the population was more stable. According to the 2006 census, the largest expatriate groups were from Great Britain (838 people, or 28.4 percent of the population), St Helena (394, 13.3 percent), Chile (161, 5.4 percent) and Australia (36, 1.2 percent). Fifty-five percent of the population was born outside the islands, coming from sixty-two different countries (Pascoe and Pepper 2008: 38). The islands may be small in terms of population but they are not demographically homogeneous or monocultural.

As for the sociolinguistic history of Falkland Islands English (FIE), it is once again difficult to establish the origins of the earlier settlers.

As Sudbury (2000: 119–121) outlines, many of the records have been lost or destroyed. Although dominated by the English, the origins of the very early residents of the Falklands in the mid-nineteenth century were diverse (Spain, Ireland and Scandinavia). By the late 1860s, the British settlement policy led to a steady increase in migration, especially from Somerset, Devon and other parts of the south west of England, from Hampshire in the South of England, and Scotland (Strange 1993; Trehearne 1978). As Trehearne notes, "a great proportion ... were of Scottish origin, often emigrants from the Western Highlands and Islands, especially Lewis ... Applicants from the Western Isles would have obtained favorable consideration for these free passages, coming as they did from a part of Britain not unlike the Falklands in climate and way of life" (1978: 124). Indeed, William Blain, a shepherd from Dumfries, noted on his arrival in the Falklands in 1878 that "Scotland has equally as good a claim to the Falklands as England. At the time I am speaking of, the majority of the inhabitants was Scotch or of Scotch descendants. Besides, the Scotch language was fairly well represented" (quoted in Cameron 1997). It is not known how long Gaelic was spoken in the Falklands, but Sudbury (2000) does not report any usage in the twentieth century. As for the dialects in contact, there is some dispute on the varieties that were most important in the formation phase of FIE, but it appears that the most important English donors can be traced to the south and south west of England and the north west of Scotland. This is rather special: in most overseas territories, there were sizeable non-English-speaking population groups and extensive language contact (see Schneider 2007). The local Falklands variety was predominantly formed by founders who arrived from two main regions of the British Isles, so that the local evolution patterns consisted mostly of dialect contact and koinéization (Trudgill 1986). Of course, the migrants from the Scottish Highlands and Islands may well have been Gaelic monolinguals or English/Gaelic bilinguals, but the impact of languages other than English (Spanish spoken by the South American gauchos) was small and restricted to the lexicon (Sudbury 2000, 2001).

2. DISCUSSION: BLURRED BOUNDARIES

We have now presented four distinct patterns of sociolinguistic evolution as found in lesser-known varieties of English in the South Atlantic: Bermuda, St Helena, Tristan da Cunha and the Falkland Islands. It has become clear that the four scenarios differ on a number of accounts and there is no coherent set of internal and external parameters that shaped their evolution and sociolinguistic development. The question of particular interest here is how these locally specific conditions lend themselves to theorizing and how they fit into current models of English as a world language, and this will be explored with reference to settlement history, identity formation and contact-linguistic innovation. Extra- and intra-territorial forces (as detailed in Buschfeld and Kautzsch 2017) involve a constant interaction of mutually influencing factors, both on PCEs and non-PCEs, that operate simultaneously on several levels: nationality, speech community (including transnationalism and diasporic settings), ethnicity, social cohort, and so on. The question with regard to lesser-known varieties in the Atlantic is what extra- and intra-territorial forces are at work in each of the four locations; we will first look at the characteristics of the varieties and then single out general and locally specific forces. The discussion needs to focus on the nature of various coexisting dialects (traditionally defined as ENL, ESL and EFL) in the early contact scenarios while taking into account that they straddle current dividing lines between social and ethnic communities in the locations, touching upon the interplay of colonial and postcolonial factors in the self-expression of identity and the contact scenarios that gave rise to local varieties. Buschfeld and Kautzsch (forthcoming) argue that we need to identify criteria that account for the interplay of extra- and intra-territorial forces in the formation of new Englishes (and perhaps English in general). I would argue that the most important extra-linguistic criteria in an LKVE (Lesser-Known Varieties of English) context are colonization and colonial history, including language and settlement policies, whereas formation and expression of attitudes towards colonization is a driving intra-linguistic factor. External and internal forces can be neatly divided in these cases; this is attested by the fact that there are accounts of the settlement histories of all four locations, whereas a microscopic (anthropological) approach to attitudes is perhaps only available for Tristan da Cunha (Peter Munch's sociological work). However, the picture becomes more complex as there is extensive overlap of extra- and intra-linguistic forces with regard to the sociodemographic background of communities and speakers. Obviously, external push and pull factors (see below) would be crucial in the first stage, but the unprecedented contact with other speaker groups (South Americans in the Falklands, St Helenians in Tristan da Cunha and Portuguese in Bermuda) would have led to local processes. In line with ecolinguistic criteria, particularly the well-known dictum "the ecology rolls the dice" (Mufwene 2000: 39), the focus must be on the population groups (and thus the speakers) who formed the new varieties (which essentially are nothing else than a by-product of colonization).

I argue that the settlement history is a key factor and that the South Atlantic varieties that have been discussed thus far provide good case studies. Two varieties are among the oldest colonial varieties we know (Bermudian and St Helenian English, established in the sixteenth and seventeenth centuries; Schreier 2008) and two are among the youngest ones that have undergone nativization (in the sense of Schneider 2007): Tristan da Cunha and Falkland Islands English emerged from the 1820s onwards and have only about nine to ten generations of speakers. Crucially, and this is of importance externally, all four varieties considered here involved a founding stock of British founders, who migrated from various regions from the British Isles to the four respective locations. The British founding populations varied in size, regional and social origins, and in their motivation for settlement. In the case of the South Atlantic, the British founding stock of the Falkland Islands comprised dialects from two regions principally (the English south west and the Scottish Highlands). In other words, there was little influence from other languages (only some Spanish loanwords are attested) and today's native-born population is mostly monolingual. As for the other South Atlantic islands, Tristan da Cunha had a Scottish input as well (the founder of the colony, William Glass, was a native of Kelso in the Scottish Lowlands) though the island dialect's feature pool is composed of dialects from various regions in England (south west, Yorkshire, London, Hastings, and so on) and the United States (eastern Massachusetts). The St Helenian and Bermudian colonies, however, were settled so early that we have practically no detailed information on the founders (other than some analysis of the regional provenience of their last names); though we know from official records that English settlers and colonists arrived, their exact origins are simply not known.

At the same time, it is clear that the status and influence of English was so strong that the koineization period saw a (complete) language shift in all four locations. Though the originally present varieties included languages other than English (we know that Malagasy and Portuguese were spoken on St Helena well into the seventeenth century, and that the Italian migrant on Tristan da Cunha still spoke Italian in the 1930s), these disappeared from the local sociolinguistic ecologies as subsequent generations of speakers adopted English as their native language. There are several ways of explaining why such a shift occurred: social stratification (in Bermuda), small numbers of slaves living in close proximity to the white population (St Helena), minority status as well as some pre-existing knowledge of English (Tristan da Cunha), extradition and removal of foreign settlers from the island (Falkland Islands), and so on.

Crucially for the EIF Model, the arrival of settlers was either the result of political decisions (notably by the East India Company, which regulated the transfer of planters and settlers and also decided on the total numbers and origins of slaves imported, for example on Bermuda and St Helena, which is a de facto extra-linguistic factor), or was haphazard and unplanned, as was the case on Tristan da Cunha, where most of the British founders (with the exception of Corporal Glass, who stayed behind when the military garrison left in 1816) consisted of shipwrecked sailors and seamen from various regions in England (see Schreier 2003). Still, it is remarkable from an intra-linguistic perspective that all four communities have strong colonial ties and perceive themselves as colonial outposts with a strong allegiance to the mother country, and did not suffer from an "Event X" (Schneider 2007). One can make a case in point that this is both extra- and intra-territorial. In the early phases extra-territorial forces were paramount since they were conscientiously enforced by the colonizing country (this also includes Tristan da Cunha, which was settled in 1815 as a military operation). However, in later stages it was the decision of the local population (thus intra-territorial, though external factors such as economic development, political representation and administration continue, thus blurring the boundaries).

This involves several of the major potential sub-categories identified by Buschfeld and Kautzsch (2017), for instance foreign policies and tourism. To give one example, for more than ten years there was a lively debate in St Helena whether or not to endorse the construction of a local airport (which meant that a substantial part of the island would need to be sacrificed for the runway). Discussions centered around economic prosperity, including tourism and increased contact with the outside world (including possibilities for St Helenians residing in England or the Falklands to revisit their families), or the negative impact (ecological consequences, changes of the local infrastructure), which was felt as a loss of local identity (in the words of an islander: "I suppose it could serve good purposes, got advantages and disadvantages. It bring more employment, the people can fly to the UK to visit their family, but more drugs coming in as well"). In other words, there is a constant struggle between those who endorse economic change in order to modernize and keep up with the world, and those who refuse it for fear of losing authenticity and identity. External and internal factors co-act strongly here.

It should thus be pointed out (and at the risk of some generalization) that the communities' colonial orientation (both intrinsic and extrinsic) is a crucial self-defining component that draws on both intra- and extra-territorial factors. We saw in the discussion above that a very strong sense of sociocultural belonging to the British Empire was reinforced via authorities such as the East India Company or local government representatives, who also served as local role models for a British way of life (and were in the most socially influential positions). On the other hand, the majority of the settlers had a deep conviction that they represented colonial outposts (Schneider 2007) and belonged to – and indeed were part of – Great Britain. It is no coincidence that symbols were proudly produced as icons of allegiance, the most notable here certainly being the Union Jack. On the Falkland Islands, a storekeeper was instructed to hoist a British flag when ships approached (Pascoe and Pepper 2008: 20) so as to mark the territory as a British possession, and in December 1859 the Captain of the visiting Ship HMS *Sidan* gave the chief islander on Tristan da Cunha, William Green, a flag, instructing him to fly it over his house when vessels approached at the island. On Tristan, it was reported that the community's founders had great pride in being British: "My three other companions have all been private seamen, who have remained here at different times in order to procure sea elephant oil and other oils, to barter with vessels touching here; and they all partake greatly of the honest roughness of British tars" (Earle 1832). The strong British character of the community was further noted in the early 1850s when Captain Denham visited the island in 1852: "The fine, healthy, and robust fellows, clad and speaking as Englishmen, gave the impression that they were from an island of Great Britain; even the Dutchman had become English" (quoted in Schreier and Lavarello Schreier 2011: 71; note that the "Dutchman" was Peter Green, who had anglicized his name from Pieter Willem Groen, who later served as Chief Islander for more than forty years). Munch (1964) addressed this loyalty from an anthropologist and sociologist stance; he distinguished between the British superculture and local subcultures "in the sense of a partially distinct cultural system within a larger system" (369). With regard to the outlook of the Tristan da Cunha islanders, he noted as follows:

To this isolated community, as I saw it in 1938, the whole "Outside World" had become a mysterious and remote superculture, which made sporadic and intermittent appearances in the form of passing ships, resident missionaries, and an occasional visit by the British Navy. Prominent in this superculture, as the Tristan Islanders conceived it, was the powerful authority that came from the prestigeful greater tradition of the British Commonwealth, of which the Tristan Islanders always regarded themselves as loyal members. (Munch 1964: 370)

The case was similar on St Helena. Captain Daniel Beeckman, who visited the island on June 9, 1715, wrote that all the white inhabitants were "English" and that they owned a large number of slaves. Moreover, it struck him that the local feeling was very much one of dependence on the mother country and one of a colonial outpost rather than of an independent colony: "They all have a great desire to see England, which they call home, though many of them never saw it, nor can have any true idea thereof" (quoted in Gosse 1938: 139). This feeling of cultural belonging, which we might also call colonial nostalgia, went hand in hand with a sense of local inferiority, which was particularly strong when representatives of the British government visited the islands. Still to the present day, elderly St Helenians address foreigners as "Sir," even if kindly asked not to do so, and the respect (almost admiration) for visitors of Great Britain is very high in present-day Bermuda as well (Eberle 2017). In other words, a feeling of colonial dependence and historical adherence to the British Empire was so strong that all four communities regard themselves as representing the Commonwealth (in fact, Bermuda and St Helena send athletes to the Commonwealth Games). When the British government reallocated British citizenship to inhabitants of former Dependent Territories in 2000, there were spontaneous parties, which further attests to the strong sense of sociocultural belonging.

This strong feeling of belonging to the United Kingdom politically was further strengthened due to the fact that there were other languages (and speakers of different, often heteroglossic, speech communities) present. Speakers of English – and the varieties they spoke – thus came to be in competition with other languages (Spanish in the Falklands, Dutch, Danish, Italian on Tristan da Cunha, Portuguese and Malagasy on St Helena, Portuguese and various Amerindian languages in Bermuda). Though this was certainly an important factor, the varieties did not form via koinéization alone and there was some admixture from second-language (L2) forms of English and various other languages. Several kinds of linguistic contact operated when the four varieties formed and indigenized, and the context of intense language and dialect contact further strengthened the language shift and the strong hegemonic views towards English (in fact, Tristan da Cunha may be one of the most monolingual communities in the English-speaking world). Historical approaches to the origins and development of BerE are representative in this context. Cutler et al., for instance, propose that "[t]he formation of Bermudian English must have taken place in an environment similar to that found later in the early colonial Bahamas" (2006: 2066). They base their assessment on the argument that close contact between blacks and whites as well as having similar occupations caused blacks to adopt the variety spoken by Bermudians of British descent, especially during the early years of the colony, when close contact was unavoidable and whites had not yet been outnumbered by blacks (2006: 2066).

English had the advantage that it was the language of the influential classes and the vehicle of communication with the mother country, and in all cases the Anglophone represented the majority. Notwithstanding, the presence of other languages arguably fostered the symbolic value of English as the language of ancestors, which had to be preserved in order to maintain the connections with the colonial epicenter, which was perceived as the home and authoritative figure. These values may have been transported via human traffic between the four communities (St Helenians were instrumental in the formation phase of TdCE and represent a major workforce on the Falkland Islands). Similarly, Ayres (1933) carried out the first substantial examination of Bermudian English phonology and aligns Bermudian English with American English (1933: 3), based on an impressionistic assessment and subsequent discussion of selected phonological features: "It [Bermudian English] has the level tone of American speech, the briskness of the coastal type, a characteristic crispness, and would create least remark, if indeed any at all, between, say, Norfolk, Virginia, and Charleston, South Carolina" (1933: 4). In their discussion of Ayres's article, Cutler et al. emphasize that "it is interesting that Ayres should draw parallels between Bermudian and Gullah, the creole spoken in the South Carolina and Georgia lowlands and offshore Sea Islands; these shared features underscore the view of a historical Bermuda-Bahamas-Carolina triangle" (2006: 2067; see Zullo et al. in press). Migration patterns would have had an impact on the transport of language attitudes as well, which seems to be an important factor. The feeling of colonial belonging and identity likewise would have been transported.

3. CONCLUSION: . . . AND WHAT ABOUT THE THEORY?

In this chapter, we have provided a close sociolinguistic analysis of four lesser-known varieties of English spoken throughout the Atlantic and have attempted to show their validity for the EIF Model. We saw that there is a very strong sense of colonial belonging in the speech communities that have no initiatives to become politically independent (mostly for economic reasons). The four communities have strong colonial ties and perceive themselves as colonial outposts with a strong allegiance to the mother country and did not suffer from an Event X (Schneider 2007). All four varieties have undergone full nativization and have high percentages of monolingual English speakers, yet they have extensive and intricate histories of contact with languages and dialects accompanied with a language shift towards English.

With regard to the model discussed, some sort of historic "push and pull" occurred between extra- and intra-territorial forces in all four varieties, and I have tried to demonstrate that there are domains where the two types cannot be subdivided (attitudes to tourism and immigration) and that external factors (such as settlement policy) have provided the petri dish for the enactment of internal forces at a later stage. As Buschfeld and Kautzsch (2017) suggest, tautological taxonomies of World Englishes should move beyond the nation state, as Englishes increasingly have transnational value and are not bound to political dividing lines, as previous models suggested (cf. Mair 2020). Intra-territorial forces, on the other hand, operate on local or in-group levels and shape the evolution of sociolinguistic and linguistic developments from within the country or speaker group, for instance via language attitudes and hegemonic values (cf. Buschfeld and Kautzsch 2020). Although it is crucial to have an early focus on colonization and colonial ties from an external point, intra-territorial correlates, namely enduring self-definition as a colonial outpost, are a subsequent internal process that depends on various factors (economic and social).

The comparative analysis suggests how important it is to reduce the long-standing conceptual gap between postcolonial and non-postcolonial Englishes. This would be another step towards questioning static categorizations made on the basis of speaker status and variety type and would allow us to concentrate on their development, evolving linguistic forms and features and usage contexts. In the end, all Englishes are shaped by their very own evolutionary processes, contact conditions and demographic factors (cf. Schreier and Hundt 2013).

REFERENCES

Aceto, Michael. 2010. Dominican Kokoy. In Daniel Schreier, Peter Trudgill, Edgar W. Schneider and Jeffrey P. Williams, eds. 2010, *The Lesser-Known Varieties of English: An Introduction*. Cambridge: Cambridge University Press, 171–194.

Ayres, Harry Morgan. 1933. Bermudian English. *American Speech* 8.1: 3–10.

Bernhard, Virginia. 1985. Bermuda and Virginia in the seventeenth century: A comparative view. *Journal of Social History* 19.1: 57–70.

Bernhard, Virginia. 1999. *Slaves and Slaveholders in Bermuda. 1616–1782*. Columbia and London: University of Missouri Press.

Bernhard, Virginia. 2010. Religion, politics, and witchcraft in Bermuda, 1651–55. *The William and Mary Quarterly* 67.4: 677–708.

Brander, Jan. 1940. *Tristan da Cunha 1506 – 1902*. London: Allen and Unwin.

Britain, David and Andrea Sudbury. 2010. Falkland Islands English. In Daniel Schreier, Peter Trudgill, Edgar W. Schneider and Jeffrey P. Williams, eds. 2010, *The Lesser-Known Varieties of English: An Introduction*. Cambridge: Cambridge University Press, 209–223.

Buschfeld, Sarah and Alexander Kautzsch. 2017. Towards an integrated approach to postcolonial and non-postcolonial Englishes. *World Englishes* 36.1: 104–126.

Buschfeld, Sarah and Alexander Kautzsch. 2020. Theoretical models of English as a world language. In Daniel Schreier, Marianne Hundt and Edgar W. Schneider, eds. 2020, *The Cambridge Handbook of World Englishes*. Cambridge: Cambridge University Press, 51–71.

Cameron, Jane 1997. Catalysts of Change: The Impact of War and Prosperity on a Small Island Community. Paper presented at the International Conference on the Cultural Heritage of Islands and Small States, Malta, May 1997.

Chambers, J. K. 2004. Dynamic typology and vernacular universals. In Bernd Kortmann, ed. 2004, *Dialectology Meets Typology*. Berlin and New York: Mouton de Gruyter, 127–145.

Crawford, Allan. 1945. *I Went to Tristan*. London: Allen & Unwin.
Crawford, Allan. 1982. *Tristan da Cunha and the Roaring Forties*. London: Allen and Unwin.
Cutler, Cecilia. 2003. English in the Turks and Caicos Islands: A look at Grand Turk. In Michael Aceto and Jeffrey P. Williams, eds. 2003, *Contact Englishes of the Eastern Caribbean*. Amsterdam: John Benjamins, 51–80.
Cutler, Cecilia, Stephanie Hackert and Chanti Seymour. 2006. Bermuda and the Bahamas. In Ulrich Ammon, Norbert Dittmar and Klaus J. Mattheier, eds. 2006, *Sociolinguistics: An International Handbook of the Science of Language and Society*. 2nd edn. Vol. 3. Berlin: Walter de Gruyter, 2066–2073.
Earle, Augustus. [1832] 1966. *Narrative of a Residence on the Island of Tristan D'Acunha in the South Atlantic Ocean*. 1st edn 1832. Oxford: Clarendon Press.
Eberle. Nicole. 2017. 'They're trying to hear English, which they are hearing, but it's Bermudian English'. Bermudian English – Origins and Variation. PhD thesis, University of Zurich.
Evans, Dorothy. 1994. *Schooling in the South Atlantic Islands 1661–1992*. Oswestry: Anthony Nelson.
Gosse, Philip. 1938. *St Helena 1502–1938*. London: Cassell and Co.
Gough, Barry. 1990. The British reoccupation and colonization of the Falkland Islands, or Malvinas, 1832–1843. *Albion: A Quarterly Journal Concerned with British Studies* 22: 261–287.
Government of Bermuda. 2012. The Cabinet Office. Department of Statistics. *Facts and Figures 2012*, http://www.gov.bm/portal/server.pt/gateway/PTARGS_0_2_980_227_1014_43/http%3B/ptpublisher.gov.bm%3B7087/publishedcontent/publish/cabinet_office/statistics/dept___statistics___additonal_files/2012_facts___figures_0.pdf (last accessed January 31, 2013).
Hackert, Stephanie and Magnus Huber. 2007. Gullah in the diaspora. Historical and linguistic evidence from the Bahamas. *Diachronica* 24.2: 279–325.
Hallett, Hollis. 2007. *Butler's History of the Bermudas. A Contemporary Account of Bermuda's Earliest Government*. Bermuda: Bermuda Maritime Museum Press.
Jarvis, Michael J. 2002. Maritime masters and seafaring slaves in Bermuda, 1680–1783. *The William and Mary Quarterly* 59.3: 585–622.
Jarvis, Michael J. 2010. *In the Eye of All Trade: Bermuda, Bermudians and the Maritime Atlantic World, 1680–1783*. Chapel Hill: Published

for the Omohundro Institute of Early American History and Culture, Williamsburg, Virginia, by the University of North Carolina Press.

Lim, Lisa and Umberto Ansaldo. 2015. *Languages in Contact*. Cambridge: Cambridge University Press.

Mair, Christian. 2020. World Englishes in cyberspace. In Daniel Schreier, Marianne Hundt and Edgar W. Schneider, eds. 2020, *The Cambridge Handbook of World Englishes*. Cambridge: Cambridge University Press, 360–383.

Melliss, John C. 1875. *St. Helena: A Physical, Historical, and Topographical Description of the Island, Including Its Geology, Fauna, Flora, and Meteorology*. London: Reeve and Co.

Mufwene, Salikoko S. 2000. Language contact, evolution, and death: How ecology rolls the dice. In Gloria Kindell and M. Paul Lewis, eds. 2000, *Assessing Ethnolinguistic Vitality: Theory and Practice, Selected Papers from the Third International Language Assessment Conference*. Dallas, TX: SIL International, 39–64.

Mufwene, Salikoko S. 2001. *The Ecology of Language Evolution*. Cambridge: Cambridge University Press.

Munch, Peter A. 1945. *Sociology of Tristan da Cunha*. Oslo: Det Norske Videnskaps–Akademi.

Munch, Peter A. 1964. Culture and superculture in a displaced community: Tristan da Cunha. *Ethnology* 3.4: 369–376.

Pascoe, Graham and Peter Pepper. 2008. Getting it Right: The Real History of the Falklands/Malvinas: A Reply to the Argentine Seminar of 3 December 2007. Unpublished manuscript.

Patrick, Peter. 1999. *Urban Jamaican Creole: Variation in the Mesolect*. Amsterdam: John Benjamins.

Reaser, Jeffrey and Benjamin Torbert. 2012. English in the Bahamas. In Bernd Kortmann and Kerstin Lunkenheimer, eds. 2012, *The Mouton World Atlas of Variation in English*. Berlin: Walter de Gruyter, 171–179.

Royle, Stephen. 1985. The Falkland Islands, 1833–1876: The establishment of a colony. *The Geographical Journal* 151.2: 204–214.

Schneider, Edgar W. 2007. *Postcolonial English: Varieties Around the World*. Cambridge: Cambridge University Press.

Schreier, Daniel. 2003. *Isolation and Language Change: Sociohistorical and Contemporary Evidence from Tristan da Cunha English*. Basingstoke and New York: Palgrave Macmillan.

Schreier, Daniel. 2005. *Consonant Change in English Worldwide: Synchrony Meets Diachrony*. Basingstoke and New York: Palgrave Macmillan.

Schreier, Daniel. 2008. *St Helenian English. Origins, Evolution and Variation*. Amsterdam: John Benjamins.
Schreier, Daniel. Forthcoming. Can Family Names be Used to Reconstruct Donor Varieties? Unpublished manuscript.
Schreier, Daniel and Marianne Hundt, eds. 2013. *English as a Contact Language*. Cambridge: Cambridge University Press.
Schreier, Daniel and Karen Lavarello Schreier. 2011. *Tristan da Cunha and the Tristanians*. London: Battlebridge.
Schreier, Daniel and Peter Trudgill. 2006. The segmental phonology of 19th-century Tristan da Cunha English: Convergence and local innovation. *English Language and Linguistics* 10.1: 119–141.
Slayton, Marina I., ed. 2009. *Four Centuries of Friendship. America-Bermuda Relations 1609–2009*. Bermuda: Bermuda Maritime Museum Press.
Spruce, Joan. 1996. Falkland Words. Unpublished manuscript.
Strange, Ian. 1993. *The Falkland Islands*. 3rd edn. Newton Abbott: David and Charles.
Sudbury, Andrea. 2000. Dialect Contact and Koineization in the Falkland Islands: Development of a Southern Hemisphere Variety? PhD thesis, University of Essex.
Sudbury, Andrea. 2001. Falkland Islands English: A southern hemisphere variety? *English World-Wide* 22.1: 55–80.
Trehearne, Mary. 1978. *Falkland Heritage: A Record of a Pioneer Settlement*. Ilfracombe: A. H. Stockwell.
Trudgill, Peter. 1986. *Dialects in Contact*. Oxford: Blackwell.
Trudgill, Peter. 2002. The history of the lesser-known varieties of English. In Richard Watts and Peter Trudgill, eds. 2002, *Alternative Histories of English*. London: Routledge, 29–44.
Tucker, Terry. 1975. *Bermuda. Today and Yesterday. 1503–1978*. London: Robert Hale Limited.
Zuill, William S. 1983. *The Story of Bermuda and Her People*. 2nd edn. London: Basingstoke.
Zuill, William S. 1999. *The Story of Bermuda and Her People*. 3rd edn. Oxford: Macmillan
Zullo, Davide, Simone E. Pfenninger and Daniel Schreier. In press. A pan-Atlantic 'multiple modal belt'? To appear in *American Speech*.

CHAPTER 15

English in Ireland: Intra-territorial Perspectives on Language Contact

Patricia Ronan

1. INTRODUCTION

Theoretically, contemporary Ireland is a bilingual country in which Irish is the first official language and English has secondary status. Practically, English is the dominant language, and Irish is a minority language that has first-language status for a small number of the population only and is acquired in school like a foreign language by the majority of children in Ireland. However, the historical spread of the English language in Ireland is comparable to the spread of English in a number of countries in which English now has the role of a second language, and which can be called 'Outer Circle' countries of English language use (Kachru 1992). In Ireland, English colonial history started in the late twelfth century; Irish English thus is the oldest overseas variety of English (Kallen 2013: 1). The linguistic situation in Ireland may therefore provide an early example of the spread of English as a postcolonial language in line with Schneider's (2003, 2007) Dynamic Model. However, the rise of the English language, as observed during the late medieval and Early Modern period, has neither been straightforward nor uncontested until the establishment of the language accelerates during the nineteenth century (cf. Hickey 2007; Kallen 2013: 1).

Considering the applicability of the Dynamic Model to the development of medieval language in Ireland, Ronan (2017) found that the development of English in Ireland in the medieval and Early Modern period are not yet fully explicable by the model. The current study elaborates on and extends the discussion beyond the early period. It aims to investigate in how far the spread of the English language in Ireland in this early period can be captured with by the modifications made to the Dynamic Model by the Extra- and Intra-Territorial Forces Model (Buschfeld and Kautzsch 2017). In order to do so, this study correlates socio-historical developments with linguistic features. Examples are taken from the Corpus of Irish English (Hickey 2002) for early materials and from the Ireland component of the International Corpus of English (Kallen and Kirk 2008) for contemporary data. These findings are then examined in the contexts of both Schneider's Dynamic Model and the Extra- and Intra-Territorial Forces Model (Buschfeld and Kautzsch 2017). The current study is organised as follows: after this introduction, key points of Schneider's (2003) Dynamic Model and the EIF Model (Buschfeld and Kautzsch 2017) are outlined briefly. Then, the data sources used in this study will be described. This is followed by a correlative discussion of the socio-historical situation of Ireland and the linguistic developments of the respective periods. These results are then discussed in the light of the Dynamic and the EIF Model and a conclusion is offered.

2. KEY ELEMENTS OF THE DYNAMIC AND THE EXTRA- AND INTRA-TERRITORIAL FORCES MODELS

According to Schneider's Dynamic Model of the developments of postcolonial varieties of English (Schneider 2003, 2007), different stages can be observed during the evolution of the variety of a language. Initially, the use of the language is introduced by the arrival of its speakers in an area during the foundation phase. Then the language stabilises on the basis of its source varieties, that is, exonormative stabilisation takes place. As more local speakers make use of the language, a process of nativisation happens, which introduces features of local languages. This eventually leads to the adoption of an internal linguistic norm, endonormative stabilisation. In a final stage, the variety of the language can develop differences, such as regional differentiation.

While endorsing the Dynamic Model overall, Buschfeld and Kautzsch (2017) suggest adaptations that allow us to take into account the development of non-colonial varieties and to improve explanatory power for postcolonial varieties of English. The Extra-and Intra-Territorial Forces Model postulates the (continued) impact of both extra-and intra-territorial forces on the emerging English language variety. In Buschfeld and Kautzsch's approach, the main systematic difference between postcolonial and non-postcolonial varieties is the presence and absence of colonisation and the resulting attitudes to the coloniser in the target country.

These forces – with the extra-territorial force given first and the intra-territorial force second in each case – are: colonisation versus attitudes to colonisation, language policies towards the target country by the coloniser or other external powers versus language policies and language attitudes in the target country, globalisation versus acceptance of globalisation, foreign policies towards the target country versus foreign policies of the target country, and the sociodemographic background both of the colonising or external power and in the target country (Buschfeld and Kautzsch 2017: 114).

Buschfeld and Kautzsch (2017: 116) point out that one of the biggest differences which the model assumes between postcolonial and non-postcolonial varieties is that the presence of English colonisers in the foundation phase of the Dynamic Model is replaced in non-postcolonial contexts by the presence of the English language by political decisions (such as introducing English teaching in school) or by trade relationships. However, as no direct language contact takes place between colonisers and local population groups, the local community has a less urgent need to learn English. We may further argue that even in the absence of colonisers, attitudes to the spread of English may exist on the basis of what is known or assumed about the countries from which the spread of the English originates – Britain and America – in the English as a Foreign Language context.

3. DATA AND METHOD

This study is largely theoretical in its approach. However, in order to corroborate the theoretical observations, corpus data are used to illustrate the outcomes of the socio-historical and sociolinguistic changes. For this, a corpus which provides a broad overview of linguistic developments will be used as well as a broadly sampled corpus of Standard Irish English. The earlier corpus materials are taken from *A Corpus of Irish English* (Hickey 2002). This consists of about ninety texts from the documented period of Irish English between the fourteenth and the twentieth centuries. The historical data is necessarily written data. However, spoken language is emulated by drama texts, which provide written-to-be-spoken language.

Examples of contemporary Irish English are taken from the *International Corpus of English – Ireland Component*, *ICE-Ireland* (Kallen and Kirk 2008). The ICE corpora consist of approximately one million words each. The written data consist of 200 files of about 2,000 words each that provide a cross-section of different textual categories. The spoken materials consist of 300 files of about 200 words each from different categories of spoken language. The ICE corpora, including *ICE-Ireland*, aim to represent standardised, not vernacular, basilectal forms of the investigated varieties of English.

These data are then used to illustrate the sociolinguistic developments taking place during the development history of Irish English.

4. THE ENGLISH LANGUAGE IN IRELAND

This section discusses how far the different phases outlined for the development of postcolonial varieties of English by Schneider (2003, 2007) can be identified in the linguistic history of Ireland. In the following, an overview of the historical, political and linguistic developments according to Schneider's model is given. Where possible, features of identity construction and sociolinguistics are taken into account. Extra- and intra-territorial forces as discussed by Buschfeld and Kautzsch (2017) are incorporated.

4.1 The Foundation Phase

In this phase, according to the Dynamic Model (Schneider 2003, 2007), English speakers colonise target countries, the local population loses land, and bilingual contacts exist at limited levels; language contact is restricted to topographic borrowings.

4.1.1 History and politics

Before the English language came to Ireland, Irish-speaking population groups are thought to have arrived in the country in the second half of the first millennium BC (cf. e.g. Ó Corráin 1989: 1). There is no evidence of social changes until the arrival of Christianity in Ireland, probably in the late fourth and fifth centuries (Ó Corráin 1989: 8), which brought with it Latin learning and the foundation of monasteries. Some Anglo-Saxon and Viking raids occurred until the eighth century. During the ninth century, Vikings set up camps and settlements in Ireland, which were to develop into towns (Ó Corráin 1989: 31–33).

Ó Corráin (1989: 25–26) notes that there might have been between eighty and 100 local petty kingdoms, which were frequently fighting each other, and the real power was wielded by the five or six provincial kings. It is against this background that the first grasp of power was made by England in Ireland (cf. Ronan 2017).

In the mid-twelfth century, the king of a Leinster kingdom, Dermot MacMurrough, was dethroned. He approached Henry II of England for support in 1166 (Simms 1989: 56–57). Richard fitz Gilbert de Clare, the Earl of Pembroke, also known as 'Strongbow', was offered the succession to Leinster and MacMurrough's daughter in marriage for his support, his followers were to receive Wexford.

The Anglo-Norman conquests in 1169 and 1170 succeeded. In 1171, King Henry II arrived himself with a fleet and with soldiers to take tributes and fealty from Strongbow, and from kings and chieftains from most parts of Ireland except for Connacht in the west and parts of the north. Kallen (2013: 11–12) notes that Henry II appears not to have been an English speaker as he used French-language translators to communicate with English speakers. The Connacht king Ruaidrí Ó Conchobair remained High King of Ireland outside Leinster, Meath and Waterford. When Ó Conchobair retired in 1183, English influence spread, but was not unchallenged. The new lords strengthened their grip and imported tenants. There was considerable feuding, including among the colonisers (Simms 1989: 59–60, 63).

4.1.2 Sociolinguistics of contact and identity construction

According to their surnames, free tenants, burgesses and artisans seem to have come from England, Wales and Flanders, while unfree tenants had Irish names. The original Irish landowners had to move to uncolonised areas (Simms 1989: 66). The new nobility spoke Norman French, the lower-class colonisers English. Kallen (2013: 13) points out that due to the small numbers of settlers, strong contacts with the Gaelic population groups had to take place, and intermarriages were frequent. In these cases, French, Latin and Irish were high prestige languages, English and Irish were used in low prestige contexts (Kallen 2013: 14).

4.1.3 Linguistic developments

In the foundation phase of linguistic settlement, we would expect mainly toponymic borrowing (Schneider 2003: 245). As the language of the colonising nobility was French, evidence of this can be found in an early Anglo-Norman composition, 'The Song of Dermot and the Earl', which describes Strongbow's arrival in Ireland (example 1).

> 1. . . . Mes en **Leschoin** i out un reis, **Ororic** out nun en yrreis, En **Tirbrun** mist la hiduse, Tere lede e boschaguse. Mes **Ororic**, li riche reis, Femme aveit bele a cele feis, La fille al rei **Malathlin**, '[But] in **Leath-Cuinn** there was a king, **O'Rourke** he was called in Irish, In **Tirbrun**, the barren, he dwelt, A waste and woody land. But **O'Rourke**, the rich king, Had a beautiful wife at this time, The daughter of King **Melaghlin**.' (Conlon 1992: 223–244)

This extract shows the use of Irish personal and place names. The phonology of the Gaelic language words is adapted to French phonology.

Even though the nobility spoke Anglo-Norman French, tenants of English origin used the English language. Kallen (2013:12) observes that the variety of English settler dialects that spread through Ireland at the time, from Devon, Cornwall, Exeter, Lancashire, along with speakers from northern France and the Netherlands, resulted in dialect mixing and provided the foundation for a new dialect of English in Ireland (cf. Kallen 2013: 12). Concerning cross-linguistic contacts, however, we do have a situation where only select elements of the two population groups interact. Language contact involving English is most likely to have taken place mainly between Irish tenants and English-speaking landholders. These developments are typical for the foundation phase of the Dynamic Model (Schneider 2003: 244).

4.1.4 Overall developments during the foundation phase

In the foundation phase, few English settlers arrived in Ireland. Many seem to have belonged to the francophone Anglo-Norman high social classes and mixed with local, Gaelic population groups. Use of the English language was restricted to the lower classes (Simms 1989). Concerning the correlation of these developments with the Dynamic Model, the picture is complicated by the fact that the highest social strata in the settler community did not speak English, but French. This is a, originally extra-territorial but ultimately also intra-territorial, sociodemographic fact which must be taken into account in order to understand the linguistic developments during the early phase of the development of Irish English.

4.2 'Exonormative Stablization' I – Irish Style

In the second phase, according to the Dynamic Model, a stable colonial status has been reached, settlers develop an English plus local identity. A largely standardised English language is used by the settlers, indigenous populations show elite bilingualism. Lexical borrowing takes place.

4.2.1 Historical background

From the thirteenth century, the remaining Gaelic kingdoms came under English control and were administered by Anglo-Norman barons. In order to retain their land, the Gaelic lords submitted to the English crown (Simms 1989: 79–80). A period of bad harvests and diseases in the mid-fourteenth century made the estates unprofitable and unattractive. The decreasing revenues from Ireland were blamed on incompetent administration and excess Gaelicisation of the Anglo-Irish nobility by the English crown (cf. Ronan 2017).

When Henry VIII took power in England in the early sixteenth century, the Gaelic tradition was strong. Concomitantly, efforts were made to tighten the English hold on Ireland. On the one hand, this was by a policy of re-granting lands to both Gaelic and Anglo-Irish nobility under new charters during the sixteenth century to strengthen these nobles' attachment to the English crown (Kallen 2013: 20). The strong connection between Gaelic and Anglo-Irish is also shown by the fact that both Anglo-English and Gaelic lords formed part of the Irish parliament meeting in 1541.

On the other hand, further settlements of English colonists followed. Elizabeth I confiscated lands in the southern province of Munster and gave it to English colonisers who were to clear the land of the native Irish population. By the early seventeenth century, an estimated 14,000 English settlers were then found in Munster. By 1641, there were 22,000 settlers, which brought the total number of English settlers in Ireland up to about 20 per cent (Kallen 2013: 22).

4.2.2 Sociolinguistics of contact and identity construction

Concerning identity construction, Kallen (2013: 13–14) points out that the small numbers of Anglo-Normal nobles, even though relations were unstable, had strong contacts and ties with Irish-speaking Gaelic nobles. He argues that the prestige languages of the time in Ireland were French, Latin and Irish. Irish was associated with social nationhood and traditions leading back to early medieval times whereas English was developing into the language of colonial power. At this early time, the status of the English language was fragile and various sources express fear that both the English language and even the English colony in Ireland might be lost. Kallen (2013: 15) quotes a Kilkenny representation to King Edward III from 1361, which argues that the colony is *en point d'estre perdu* ('on the point of being lost'). According to the *State Papers* only parts of the counties Louth, Meath, Dublin, Kildare and Wexford obeyed the King's laws, and otherwise, outside the walled towns, English people had taken on Irish customs and the Irish language (Kallen 2013: 19).

As a result, to keep the Anglo-Irish nobility apart from native Irish culture, laws such as the Statutes of Kilkenny were enacted in 1366. These statutes prohibit the use of Irish customs and language by the colonisers and were written in Norman French (Simms 1989: 83–88). Similarly, in 1492–1493, the Waterford Ordinance stipulates that Irish is not to be used in the city court, and all business is to be transacted through English, if necessary, with the help of a translator. If, however, one of the participants is from the country, then the use of the Irish language is allowed. These two pieces of legislation illustrate the socially and regionally constrained status of the English language in the thirteenth and fourteenth centuries (Bliss 1979: 13; Kallen 2013: 15–16).

Thus, concerning the sociolinguistic situation in early Ireland, as in England we had a small elite of French speakers ruling the country and the indigenous ruling classes, as well as the lower classes, speaking the indigenous language, here Irish. But in addition, there were free and tradespeople who were English speakers. Repeated interventions by English rulers were needed to stem a shift of the Anglo-Irish elite to Irish language and culture.

4.2.3 Linguistic developments

We can understand earliest evidence of Anglo-Irish writing against this background. Fourteenth-century administrative records like the Dublin Guild Merchant Roll are written in Latin (Kallen 2013: 14). It is from the fifteenth century onwards that the English language made significant inroads into formal official writing such as the statutes of the Irish parliament, which had previously been written in French.

The limited number of texts from the Middle and Early Modern Irish English Period show features of both southern and northern varieties of English, as well as innovations (cf. Hickey 2007: 54–66; Kallen 2013: 212–215). Notable features are a lack of contrast of the phonemes /v/ and /w/ and the use of stops instead of fricatives to express the voiced and voiceless /ð/ and /θ/ sounds, as well as a partial merger between /s/ and /ʃ/.

An example of prose writing is represented by the religious poetry known as *The Kildare Poems*. These are thought to have been compiled between 1330 and 1340 (Lucas 1995) and mainly consist of English, but also of some Latin, verse. The opening poem, *The Land of Cokaygne* (ed. Lucas 1995) blends strong native imagery with a probably satirical, partly bawdy, description of monastic life (example 2):

> 2. Fur in see bi west Spayngne / Is a lond ihote Cokaygne (l. 1–2)
> Though Paradis be miri and bright, / Cokaygn is of fairir sight (l. 5–6)
> The met is trie, the drink is clere, / To none, russin and sopper. I sigge for-soth, boute were, / Ther nis lond on erthe is pere, Vnder heuen nis lond iwisse, / Of so mochil joi and blisse. (l. 19–24)
> 'Far away in the sea, to the west of Spain, is a land called Cokaygne.
> Though Paradise may be merry and bright, Cokaygne is of a fairer sight.
> The food is excellent, the drink is clear, for lunch, for afternoon meal, for supper. I say truthfully, without doubt, that there is no land on earth which is equal. Under the Heaven there is not a land indeed of so much joy and bliss.'

The language of the poems is Middle English with few discernible influences of language contact apart from occasional loan words. The linguistic background of the author, or authors, is unknown, but he may be from close to Dublin. The poems show a number of dialect features, some of which have been argued to be distinctive of an emerging Irish English variety (cf. Hickey 2007).

Other examples of early Irish English show the strong allegiance with English politics and the considerable grip of English linguistic standards on the English administered parts of the country. This is particularly obvious in the east of the country, as the early fifteenth-century example (example 3) from James Yonge's *Secreta Secretorum* illustrates.

> 3. This wyrchipphul knight Syr Stewyn Scrope, in kynge Recharde-is tyme and Kynge Henry-is tyme the fourth Also, Hauyng*e* the gou*er*naunce of Irland*e*, many extorcionys did, Lyu*ere*ʒ takynge, lytill good Paynge, moche he traualit, lytille espolid in the Iryssh, enemys he had al the mene tyme. Atte the last the excellent lord, Thomas of lancastre, oure lege lorde is brodyr, that now is lieutena*n*t of Irland, makyd Stephyn his depute, Irland to governe. (Steele 1898: 133) 'The worshipful knight, Sir Stephen Scrope, in King Richard's time and King Henry IV's time, also having the governance of Ireland, did many extorsions, taking liveries, little good paying, much he labored, got little spoils in the Irish, he had enemies at the same time. At last the excellent lord, Thomas of Lancaster, our liege-lord's brother, who is now lieutenant of Ireland, made Stephen his deputy, Ireland to govern.'

In these two extracts we can see examples of two different traditions that were present in fourteenth- and fifteenth-century Ireland: on the one hand, English language use in the native Irish literary tradition, comprising Irish loan words and Irish imagery, as in example 2. On the other hand, we can see strong allegiance to the English crown, and identification with the rulers of England in the loyal part of the Anglo-Irish administration as represented by example 3.

4.2.4 Overall developments during the 'exonormative stabilization' phase

During early settlement phases, it was only a small group of settlers who came to Ireland. However, large elements of these groups acculturated in Ireland and the use of the English language was repeatedly under threat in Ireland from the native Irish language, and the political hold on the country was equally instable. In this respect, the stable colonial status assumed after the foundation phase in the Dynamic Model (Schneider 2003, 2007) does not hold for the early situation in Ireland (cf. Ronan 2017). The early development of English linguistic history of the country can thus only be explained by taking into consideration both extra- and intra-territorial forces.

Extra-territorially, the English crown maintains pressure on English settlers not to assimilate, and, in spite of repeated interventions, it is only moderately successful in doing so at first. As a further extra-territorial force, the prestige of the Anglo-Norman language also dwindled in England due to a fraught relationship with France, which is likely also to have had a negative effect on the use of Anglo-Norman in Ireland (cf. Hickey 2007). Intra-territorially, the social and sociolinguistic situation in Ireland is such that Anglo-Normans represented the new social elite while English speakers belonged to lower social classes. When the prestige of the Anglo-Norman language was dwindling, various members of the Anglo-Norman elite chose connections with the native Irish elite both culturally and linguistically over cultural adaptation to lower classes of English speakers in Ireland. It was due to continued intervention of English rulers that English was able to turn from a mainly lower- and middle-class language into a language that was suitable for high status uses such as official discourse.

4.3 Nativisation – Or Not

In the Dynamic Model, the nativisation stage takes place once the colonised countries' ties with England weaken. Both population groups identify as permanent residents of the (former) colony, bilingualism is widespread, heavy language contact phenomena arise.

4.3.1 Historical background

While the English language made restricted inroads into the use of Irish until the start of the seventeenth century, this changed with the plantations of Ulster in the north at the beginning of the seventeenth century, and the plantations of the south from about 1650. At the end of the sixteenth century, various rebellions arose especially in Munster and Ulster after private colonisation ventures and the imposition of a land tax. Irish resistance was crushed despite the support of a Spanish armada landing in Kinsale, Co. Cork, in 1601. The native lords had to flee, and the land was granted to English landlords. From 1603, King James I encouraged the redistribution of lands in Ulster to settlers from Scotland, especially the Lowlands, and from the north of England. These newly arriving settlers brought with them northern and Scots-influenced varieties of English, which formed the basis of the English of Ulster till the present day. Shortly after these settlements, further revolts broke out in Ulster, and these were equally crushed, and the largest part of the native Irish nobility fled to the Continent in 1607 (cf. Canny 1989: 127–134).

After a new rebellion in 1641, and the slaughter of Protestant settlers, new English forces were sent under the command of Oliver Cromwell. As a result, between 1649 and 1652 counties in the midlands and the south of Ireland were recolonised in a ruthless campaign, with the loss of many lives of the native Irish population. Previous landowners were resettled in the less fertile western province of Connacht (Canny 1989: 144–148). Cromwell's soldiers, who mainly yielded from the middle and the south of England, were predominantly paid in land grants.

This second, resettlement of English settlers changed the political but also the social and eventually the linguistic landscape in Ireland. The new settlers' variety of English built the foundation for the later English-based varieties of the southern counties of Ireland. Gaelic society received a heavy blow with the defeat of Catholic forces under King James II in the Battle of the Boyne and in the Battle of Aughrim in 1690 and 1691, after which Catholics were excluded from higher social and political positions.

4.3.2 Sociolinguistics of contact and identity construction

According to state papers from the sixteenth century, the use of English was mainly confined to walled cities and towns in the early years of that century, while the rural population retained the Irish language and Irish culture. Correspondingly, Henry VIII promoted legislation fighting increasing Gaelicisation throughout Ireland (Kallen 2013: 19). In 1537, the Irish parliament passed an act proscribing the use of English culture and language, which argued that the inhabitants of the country are kept in 'a certaine savage and wilde kind and maner of living' due to the 'diversitie that is betwixt them in tongue, language, order, and habite' (cited from Kallen 2013: 19).

Nevertheless, when Henry VIII assumed the title of King of Ireland in 1541, his proclamation in the Irish parliament was read out in Irish, which Kallen (1994: 153–154, 2013: 21) holds to have been a symbolic act to incorporate the Irish nobility within a new state organisation. Irish continued to be used in some official state matters (Kallen 1994: 154). Interestingly, according to the Irish chronicler Stanyhurst, both in the Fingal area of North County Dublin, and in the baronies of Forth and Bargy in County Wexford, the use of Middle English dialects had survived. Stanyhurst further denounced that the language of the English population showed strong Irish language contact phenomena (Kallen 1994: 154, 2013: 23). While towns and cities and areas around Dublin followed English traditions, in other towns, particularly Waterford and Cork, both Anglo-Irish and Gaelic citizens are reported largely to have used Irish among themselves by the opening years of the seventeenth century. However, Kallen reports that women in particular may have been conscious users of English, which seems increasingly to have developed into a higher prestige language. This situation is identified as a case of multilingualism in high registers by Kallen (2013: 24).

The linguistic landscape changed with the arrival of new settlers from England and the large-scale resettlement of native as well as 'Old English' landowners in the less fertile west in Connacht (cf. Bliss 1979: 19). Linguistically, the result of the land grants to English soldiers was that English was now also introduced into the low domains by these new settlers. Hickey (2007: 37–38) points out that large numbers of Gaelic population groups now shifted to English, partly due to the Penal Laws sanctioning the use of Irish, and partly due to the social advantages that could be gained from English.

The linguistic impact of these new settlers was not equally felt throughout the country. According to Census data from 1659, the largest groups of English speakers are found in the County of Ulster, accounting for between 25 per cent and 54 per cent of the population. Dublin had an English-speaking population of 45 per cent while the other counties had decreasing percentages of English speakers, the western county of Clare having only 3 per cent (Kallen 1994: 157–158). Larger percentages of English speakers were again only found in the towns, with fewer English speakers in the suburbs (Kallen 2013: 26–27). But as the largest part of local administration and trade was in the hand of English speakers, the importance of competence in English was growing for Irish speakers.

4.3.3 Linguistic developments

During this phase, we find linguistic evidence of both fully standardised, but also of vernacularised varieties. Exonormatively standardised English can be found in official communication, here with the King of England (example 4).

> 4. Great Monarch, If our Affection to Your Majesty could digest and abuse that proved so Fatal to Your Prerogative, We should rejoyce at the defection of England, that sent us the opportunity of kissing your hand in this your Loyal Kingdom of Ireland; Where, as the Honour of your Majesties presence was unexpected, so are our Eruptions of joy unspeakable. (*The Irish Recorder*, Kilkenny 1689)

By contrast, evidence of the outcome of language contacts is found in literary representations of Irish English from around the start of the seventeenth century. For example 5, printed in 1605, the composition date is assumed to be 1596 (Bliss 1979: 31).

> 5. *Oneale* Fate is the token? fate siegnc that *Brian Mack Phelem* said he would hang oot?
> [O] *Han*[lon] I feate I kno not ask the Shecretary. (Bliss 1979: 77)
> '*Oneale*: What is the token? What sign [is it] that Brian Mac Phelem said he would hang out? *O Hanlon*: I, faith, I know not, ask the secretary.'

This short passage illustrates various features commonly ascribed to early vernacular Irish English. Here these are the use of <f> for <wh>, /t/ for /θ/, as well as continued confusion of /s/ and /ʃ/. However, the intention behind such compositions is potentially derogatory and it is well possible that the linguistic peculiarities of the speakers have been exaggerated for comic effect.

Further, early English varieties, varieties of 'Chaucer's English' or 'broken Saxon' were retained as late as the late seventeenth century, or according to other accounts even till the late eighteenth century (Bliss 1979: 22). This refers to the baronies of Forth and Bargy in County Wexford, and to Fingal in County Dublin. A larger intermixture of Irish is reported for the Fingal dialect due to the long contact between the two languages (Bliss 1979; Hickey 2007: 83). Example 6 is an extract from a Fingallian text.

6. Dear Joy, St *P*atrick, vil dou hear / Dee own Cheeld *Nees* make his Pray-ere, / Dat never did, or I'm a Teef, / so much before in all mee Leef (. . .). (*The Irish Hudibras*, 1689; Bliss 1979: 126)
'Dear joy, St. Patrick, will you hear your own child Nees make his prayer, who never did, or I'm a thief, so much before in all my life.'

In example 6 we find typical Irish confusion between /w/ and /v/, /d/ and /t/ for /θ/ and /ð/, coupled with the Middle English vowel qualities /iː/ for /ei/ or /ai/ in the word *leef* 'life' (cf. Hickey 2007: 84).

In any event, it is in these examples of seventeenth-century Irish English that we find examples of exonormatively standardised English on the one hand, and on the other hand heavily contact-marked varieties (cf. Kallen 2013: 23), which could be seen as typical markers of ongoing nativisation of the English language in Ireland.

4.3.4 Overall developments in the period

Developments during this period show us that large amounts of the two main population groups are converging in terms of culture, but also linguistically. This development is conditioned by the sociodemographic background of the speakers: examples can be found of both Anglo-Irish nobility becoming more Gaelicised and Gaelic population groups becoming more Anglicised. While we can speak of ongoing exonormative stabilisation of the newly arrived British population groups, other population groups, possibly of Gaelic and also of 'Old English' origin, display features of a nativisation of English language and culture. This disparity can be explained by additional forces: both internal and external politics. Language policies promoted the English language in Ireland, while settlement policies pursued in Britain led to a resettlement of the country.

These developments illustrate that even after long-standing colonisation, foreign and language policies and sociodemographic background played important roles in the establishment of the English language in Ireland.

4.4 The Second Establishment of the Irish English and Resulting Endonormative Stabilisation

According to the Dynamic Model (Schneider 2003, 2007), the endonormative stabilisation phase is reached at a post-independence stage. Population groups identify as members of the new nation, a positive attitude to local language norms is developed and the variety becomes codified.

4.4.1 Historical background

After the considerable political upheaval mentioned in 4.3.1, penal laws were enacted in 1695 and 1704 which banned Catholic clergy, and restricted the rights of Catholics to own land or horses, bear arms or obtain education. These laws were relaxed only slightly with relief acts in the 1770s, which allowed land-lease and inheritance rights, followed by loosening of trade restrictions and some access to the professions by Catholics in the following decades due to social and political pressure in Ireland. Pressure on England increased with the foundation of the United Irishmen in 1791. After uprisings in 1794 and 1796, martial law was imposed in 1798 and was followed by an uprising in Wexford. After these events, an Act of Union was enacted in 1800, which created the United Kingdom of Great Britain and Ireland, and the Irish parliament in Dublin was abolished, with the legislative moved to London (Foster 1989).

The nineteenth century, too, was a period of considerable political and social unrest. In the 1840s, bad climatic conditions prevailed which led to the failure for a number of consecutive years of the most staple diet of the rural Irish population – the potato crop. In the resulting famine, an estimated one million people starved and population density roughly halved after the period due to starvation as well as to the emigration of large amounts of the population (cf. Foster 1989; Hickey 2007: 46–47). Concomitantly, Irish social and political resistance increased again with the formations of the Irish Republican Brotherhood (1858), the Home Rule League (1873) and the Irish Parliamentary Party

(1880) under Charles Stewart Parnell. In 1913, major strikes took place in Dublin, and paramilitary organisations were formed just before the outbreak of World War I. At Easter 1916, a major rising resulted in an Irish Republic being proclaimed. However, the rebels had to surrender and were executed, guerrilla warfare took place from then on. In 1921, a peace treaty was signed between Irish rebel forces and the British government, which lead to the creation of an Irish Free State, with the exception of six counties in Ulster. The complete independence of the former Irish Free State was finally achieved in 1948 but again did not include the six counties in Ulster (Fitzpatrick 1989).

4.4.2 Sociolinguistics of contact and identity construction

In a classic article, Wall (1969: 82–85) points out that in their fight for recognition, the Catholic middle classes protested their loyalty to the English crown and in this abandoned the Irish language, which resultingly became the language of the rural population and the less educated. During the eighteenth century, bilingualism also spread among the less educated, mainly through the medium of hedge schools, that is, local schools run by communities. Wall argues that the rise of English was driven by the new English-speaking middle classes, as well as by the growing political awareness of the population in the late eighteenth century (Wall 1969: 88). Famous Irish authors of the period writing in English included Jonathan Swift, Thomas Sheridan and Richard Brinsley Sheridan (cf. Hickey 2007). In order to promote the cause of an Irish Republic in England and overseas, the medium of English was made use of. A situation of diglossia started to emerge, in which English was increasingly used in all domains while Irish was relegated to daily life particularly in rural areas. Here, we can speak of a second nativisation process of the English language. English made further inroads when a National School system was introduced in 1831, and the death blow was dealt to the language by the depopulation of rural areas during the famine years in the 1840s (Wall 1969: 86–87).

The growing importance of English, especially in the economy and in politics, led to a steady decrease of Irish speakers in all areas of the country. Over time, the widespread Irish monolingualism turned into bilingualism and was replaced by English monolingualism. Arguably, it is this spread of English as the first language of the education system and the increasing loss of the Irish contact language which caused the endonormative stabilisation of the language.

The loss of the Irish language experienced some reversal after the foundation of the Irish Free State (table in Kallen 1994: 161). Mandatory Irish language teaching was introduced in state schools. While the number of first-language (L1) speakers could not be increased, the number of L1 English speakers with second-language (L2) competence in Irish has increased. According to the 2016 census, 73,803 speakers (4.2 per cent of the population) use Irish on a daily basis and 1.76 million speakers (39.8 per cent) state that they are able to speak Irish (Central Statistics Office 2017).

In addition to the obvious consequences for the Irish language, the massive decrease of L1 speakers of Irish is also likely to have influenced the development of Irish English over time. The change of the linguistic situation in Ireland provides an example of a language shift from the by-now less socio-economically powerful erstwhile majority language towards the former minority language of the now socio-politically dominant group.

4.4.3 Linguistic developments

Linguistic development in Ireland is a good example of language contact between majority and minority languages as described by Heine and Kuteva (2005: 237–239). During the seventeenth, eighteenth and early nineteenth centuries we have an example of large-scale L1 competence in Irish, during which largely untutored acquisition of English takes place. This scenario fits Heine and Kuteva's description of L1>L2 replication, in which the linguistic structures of the language spoken by the majority of the population (here Irish) lead to replication of these patterns in the target language, English (cf. Ronan 2013). This was very much the case in the formative years of Irish English, where the large-scale language shift to English led to the replication of Irish structures into well-known features of Irish English, such as distinct phonology (e.g. Hickey 2007), the tense and aspect system with the *after*-perfect (example 7), *do be* habituals (example 8) as well as pragmatic features such as extensive *it*-clefting (example 9). Various studies have highlighted their use in traditional or non-urban vernacular speech (Filppula 1999; Hickey 2007; Kallen 2013) or in literature (Taniguchi 1972; Bliss 1979).

7. But we seen a lot of people that were dead, laid out where they'*re after being shot*, in the rooms [. . .]. (Filppula 1999: 99)

8. And err, when I *do be listen'* to the Irish here, I *do be* sorry now, when you're in a local having a drink, nobody seems to understand it. (Filppula 1999: 130)

9. [Have many people left this area at all, or – or given up farming at all – or?]
Ah, very little's give up farming round this area. It's *looking for more land* a lot of them are. (Filppula 1999: 250)

These examples of traditional Irish dialects still show features that are due to nativisation processes as defined by the Dynamic Model (Schneider 2003, 2007). However, when we consider contemporary speech by not explicitly traditional speakers in urban Ireland, we find that specific vernacular features, particularly in grammar and lexicon, are overall not very frequent, as can be verified in the contemporary *ICE-Ireland* corpus (Kallen and Kirk 2008). Compare example 10.

10. The publishing, selling or distribution of literature advocating birth-control was also deemed an offence under the Act. Theatre in the Saorstát in the 1920s enjoyed freedom from censorship. However, when the Abbey Theatre performed Sean O'Casey's The Plough and the Stars, there were vocal protests against the bringing of the tricolour into a public house and to the presence there of a prostitute, Rosie Redmond. The play ran for two weeks but with the lights on in the theatre and with gardaí lining the passages at the sides of the pit. (*ICE-Ireland*, Popular Humanities South, W2B-010)

Phonological specifics are not indicated here, but the text does not contain specifically Irish grammatical features. However, we find the use of official terminology derived from the Irish language, *Saorstát* 'Free State', and *gardaí* 'police'. Such official terms arguably are the most visible examples of Irish language influence in contemporary acrolectal, urban Irish English. Overall, we can argue that endonormative stabilisation has taken place in contemporary Irish English.

4.4.4 Overall developments during the second stabilisation period

In the time after the extensive English settlements of the seventeenth century, the English language was strengthened in Ireland. The settlers again brought diverse varieties to Ireland, so that linguistically we can talk about accommodation and a second exonormative stabilisation during the seventeenth century. Large-scale language shift during the eighteenth and nineteenth centuries resulted in language shift varieties of English with new nativised features, a process that can be called a second nativisation stage. In contemporary Irish English, we find both traditional varieties, typically in non-urban regions, and non-traditional varieties.

This cyclical behaviour, in which we observe exornormative and nativisation phases twice during the course of the development of the language, is not unprecedented and shows some similarities to developments in American English (compare Schneider 2007: 251–306).[1] The development in Ireland can be explained by taking into account extra- and intra-territorial developments. In effect, we find two colonisation phases, with the second one starting in the seventeenth century, 600 years after initial settlements. Extra-territorial and intra-territorial language policies after this second settlement were considerably stricter, and the use of English, as well as the suppression of the Irish language, were enforced rigorously. Intra-territorially, the necessity to submit to the English language and culture was also stronger from the seventeenth century on than after the initial, twelfth-century settlements.

4.5 Is There a Differentiation Phase?

According to Schneider (2003, 2007), a young nation differentiates internally, and new group identities are created within the nation. Networks are created and new dialects are born.

Contemporary English in Ireland has clearly distinct varieties. Most evidently these are Northern Irish English (Corrigan 2010) and Southern Irish English. Further subdivisions, such as Dublin North Side versus Southern Dublin English, are clearly visible as well (Hickey 2007; Corrigan 2010; Kallen 2013). Due to the complex settlement and social history of interaction between Britain and Ireland outlined above, dialect variation developed early in the colonial history of Ireland and at early stages they were particularly influenced by early colonial settlement patterns and resulted from social and geographic distribution during exonormative and nativisation phases. Necessary conditions are strong variety differences in the input varieties of English in Ireland,

---

[1] I am grateful to Edgar Schneider for pointing this out to me.

such as settlers from Northern England and Scotland on the one hand, and from the south and the midlands on the other hand. Strong social differentiation may also play a role, as was the case in early Ireland, where very distinct high and low classes developed differently. We must further consider the external and internal political circumstances. In the case of the Irish developments, these are in particular the two consecutive waves of English settlement in Ireland: the early settlements from the eleventh century, and the much larger-scale settlements, accompanied by strong political pressure, in the seventeenth century.

4.6 The Application of the Dynamic and the Intra- and Extra-territorial Forces Models to the Development of the English Language in Ireland

Schneider's different stages can be observed in Irish English, as is also argued in Ronan (2013, 2017). Irish English has passed the stage in which it mirrored English English varieties, then local features have been increasingly introduced and a distinct variety emerged, particularly when large population groups shifted to English. However, in Ireland we observe two distinct settlement processes (cf. Ronan 2017: 126) and, due to circumstances of colonial settlement, language policies and changing sociodemographic backgrounds, these have different outcomes.

Dialect differentiation has not only taken place after Schneider's endonormative stabilisation, but already at an exonormative stage because settlement processes differed in the north and the south of the country. Further, distinct local varieties are increasingly being levelled. This is most probably due to increased contact with standard varieties of the language in education and modern media in contemporary Ireland.

Thus, the Dynamic Model describes some key stages of the postcolonial development of English also in Ireland appropriately, but there are developments due to both external and internal circumstances that cannot be captured. English nobles in Ireland adopted Irish customs and language first; political repressions, both as an extra- and an intra-territorial force, reversed these developments in later periods. Important extra- and intra-territorial factors which impact on the development of this variety are the changes in self-identification and thus in the sociodemographic background of the country: originally native speakers of English or Anglo-Norman did not continue to identify as English/Anglo-Norman but took up Irish customs and language. Only after pressure came to bear, did a shift back to English take place. Due to further increased military pressure and forced settlements and resettlements, the English language then finally gained a stronghold in seventeenth-century Ireland.

This is a clear example of the crucial importance of taking extra- and intra-territorial factors into consideration. In the case of Irish language history, these are language policies and extra-territorial foreign policies in particular, but also the intra-territorial force of identity construction of settlers and indigenous population groups, where, by bringing to bear extra-territorial force, settlers were first prevented from 'going native' and in a later process the use of indigenous languages and customs were increasingly repressed.

What neither of these two models provides for, however, is an increasing homogeneity of international varieties of English that arguably does not move towards differentiation but increasing internationalisation. A case in point might be transnational developments of varieties such as Mid-Atlantic English, comprising features of both British and American English (e.g. Modiano 1996), or epicentre approaches, which argue for centre-functions of varieties (Leitner 1992, but critically Hundt 2013), in geographic regions.

5. CONCLUSION

This study has shown in how far the Dynamic Model and the Extra- and Intra-Territorial Forces Model can model the rise of the English language in Ireland. It can be seen that while key stages of the development of English as a colonial language can be observed, other developments – particularly the large-scale loss of English by the first settler population, the slow adoption of English by the indigenous Irish population groups, and the early diversification of English into distinctive dialects – are not accounted for by the Dynamic Model. In order to account for these developments, further features must be considered. These further features can be captured to a large extent if extensions proposed in the Extra- and Intra-Territorial Forces Model are taken into account. This study has put particular emphasis on the influence of both external and internal language policies and the sociodemographic contexts of both settler and indigenous population groups.

This study gives a broad overview of developments. Due to space constraints, details could not always be discussed. In further research, a more fine-grained approach to different periods of the development of the English language in Ireland would be desirable. Also, while the issues of identity and identity construction have been discussed, language attitudes towards language and the colonising power have largely been left out of consideration. These issues would profit from further research.

REFERENCES

Bliss, Alan. 1979. *Spoken English in Ireland 1600–1740*. Dublin: Cadenus Press.

Buschfeld, Sarah and Alexander Kautzsch. 2017. Towards an integrated approach to postcolonial and non-postcolonial Englishes. *World Englishes* 36.1: 104–126.

Canny, Nicholas. 1989. Early Modern Ireland. In Roy F. Foster, ed. 1989, *The Oxford Illustrated History of Ireland*. Oxford: Oxford University Press, 104–160.

Central Statistics Office of Ireland. 2017. *2016 Census*, https://www.cso.ie/en/releasesandpublications/ep/p-cp10esil/p10esil/ (last accessed 1 August 2019).

Conlon, Denis J. 1992. *The Song of Dermot and Earl Richard Fitzgilbert: Le chansun de Dermot e li quens Ricard fiz Gilbert*. Frankfurt/Main: Peter Lang.

Corrigan, Karren. 2010. *Irish English Volume 1 – Northern Ireland*. Edinburgh: Edinburgh University Press.

Filppula, Markku. 1999. *The Grammar of Irish English. Language in Hibernian Style*. London: Routledge.

Fitzpatrick, David. 1989. Ireland since 1870. In Roy F. Foster, ed. 1989, *The Oxford Illustrated History of Ireland*. Oxford: Oxford University Press, 213–274.

Foster, Roy. F. 1989. Ascendancy and Union. In Roy F. Foster, ed. 1989, *The Oxford Illustrated History of Ireland*. Oxford: Oxford University Press, 161–212.

Heine, Bernd and Tania Kuteva. 2005. *Language Contact and Grammatical Change*. Cambridge: Cambridge University Press.

Hickey, Raymond. 2002. *A Source Book for Irish English*. Amsterdam: John Benjamins.

Hickey, Raymond. 2007. *Irish English. History and Present-Day Forms*. Cambridge: Cambridge University Press.

Hundt, Marianne. 2013. The diversification of English: Old, new and emerging epicentres. In Daniel Schreier and Marianne Hundt, eds. 2013, *English as a Contact Language*. Cambridge: Cambridge University Press, 182–203.

The Irish Recorder. 1689. The speech of the Irish Recorder Wing. *Early English Books Online*, https://eebo.chadwyck.com (last accessed 1 May 2013).

Kachru, Braj B. 1992. Models for non-native Englishes. In Braj B. Kachru, ed. 1992, *The Other Tongue: English Across Cultures (English in the Global Context)*. 2nd edn. Urbana: University of Illinois Press, 48–74.

Kallen, Jeffrey L. 1994. English in Ireland. In Robert Burchfield, ed. 1994, *The Cambridge History of the English Language*. Vol. 5. Cambridge: Cambridge University Press, 148–196.

Kallen, Jeffrey L. 2013. *Irish English Volume 2: The Republic of Ireland*. Berlin: Mouton de Gruyter.

Kallen, Jeffrey L. and John M. Kirk. 2008. *ICE-Ireland: A User's Guide*. Belfast: Cló Ollscoil na Banríona.

Leitner, Gerhard. 1992. English as a pluricentric language. In Michael Clyne, ed. 1992, *Pluricentric Languages: Differing Norms in Different Nations*. Berlin: Mouton de Gruyter, 179–237.

Lucas, Angela M., ed. 1995. *Anglo-Irish Poems of the Middle Ages*. Dublin: Columba Press.

Modiano, Marko. 1996. *A Mid-Atlantic Handbook: American and British English*. Lund: Studentlitteratur.

Ó Corráin, Donnchadh. 1989. Prehistoric and Early Christian Ireland. In Roy F. Foster, ed. 1989, *The Oxford Illustrated History of Ireland*. Oxford: Oxford University Press, 1–52.

Ronan, Patricia. 2013. L'évolution de la langue anglaise en Irlande. Ireland and its Contacts/L'Irlande et ses contacts. *Cahiers de l'ILSL* 38: 73–91.

Ronan, Patricia. 2017. Language relations in early Ireland. In Raymond Hickey, ed. 2017, *Sociolinguistics in Ireland*. London: Palgrave Macmillan, 113–129.

Schneider, Edgar. W. 2003. The dynamics of New Englishes. *Language* 79.2: 233–281.

Schneider, Edgar W. 2007. *Postcolonial English: Varieties Around the World*. Cambridge: Cambridge University Press.

Simms, Katharine. 1989. The Norman invasion and the Gaelic recovery. In Roy F. Foster, ed. 1989, *The Oxford Illustrated History of Ireland*. Oxford: Oxford University Press, 53–103.

Steele, Robert. 1898. *Three Prose Versions of the Secreta Secretorum. Early English Text Society*. Extra Series, 74. London: Kegan Paul, Trench, Trübner & Co.

Taniguchi, Jiro. 1972. *A Grammatical Analysis of Artistic Representation of Irish English, With a Brief Discussion of Some Phonological and Grammatical Features*. Tokyo: Shinozaki Shorin.

Wall, Maureen. 1969. The decline of the Irish language. In Brian Ó Cuív, ed. 1969, *A View of the Irish Language*. Dublin: Stationary Office, 81–90.

CHAPTER 16

English in Gibraltar: Applying the EIF Model to English in Non-Postcolonial Overseas Territories[1]

Cristina Suárez-Gómez

1. INTRODUCTION

Gibraltar is a British Overseas Territory located at the southern tip of the Iberian Peninsula. As a British territory, English is its official language, although due to the Spanish roots of part of the population, as well as the coexistence of other ethnic groups historically (Maltese, Genoese, Jewish, Moroccans, among the most notable), it has developed a local vernacular language, known as Yanito, which has coexisted with Spanish and English. However, a recent increase in the use of English at home among younger Gibraltarians has been reported (Kellerman 2001: 91–93; Levey 2008: 58, 95–98; Weston 2013) and English is becoming the first language of most Gibraltarians, to the extent that an emerging variety of English appears to be in the process of becoming nativized, labeled Gibraltar English (Kellerman 2001; Levey 2008; Weston 2011), which "carries an identity function for its users" (Weston 2011: 361; see

---

[1] I am indebted to Elena Seoane for her help with earlier versions of this chapter and to two anonymous reviewers for their thorough and valuable comments. I am also grateful to Dr. Jennifer Ballantine Perera, Director of the Garrison Library and the University of Gibraltar's Institute for Gibraltar and Mediterranean Studies, and to M. G. Sanchez, a Gibraltarian writer, for affording me a better understanding of the current linguistic situation in Gibraltar. Any errors remain my sole responsibility. For generous financial support, I am grateful to the Spanish Ministry of Economy and Competitiveness (Grant No. FFI2017-82162-P). Finally, my heartfelt gratitude to Sarah Buschfeld and Alexander Kautzsch for beginning this challenging project and for editing this volume, which is dedicated to Alex, whose company and wisdom I had the honor to share.

also Levey 2015: 51). The aim of this chapter is to consider how this new variety of English fits within the most influential models of analysis within World Englishes and then to apply the latest model, known as the Extra- and Intra-territorial Forces Model (EIF Model), developed by Buschfeld and Kautzsch (2017). The chapter is structured as follows: section 2 briefly describes the demographic, historical, and sociocultural situation of Gibraltar; section 3 analyzes the status of English in Gibraltar from a historical point of view, as well as the emergence of Gibraltar English, a new variety of English resulting from the language contact situation in Gibraltar; section 4 presents Gibraltar English according to the most influential analytical frameworks of World Englishes; section 5 analyzes the current status and linguistic forms of Gibraltar English from the EIF perspective; finally, section 6 presents some conclusions.

2. GIBRALTAR: DEMOGRAPHY, HISTORY, AND SOCIOCULTURAL BACKGROUND

Gibraltar is a territory located on the southern coast of the Iberian Peninsula, bordered to the north by Spain. It has an area of almost 7 km^2 and a population of 32,194 people (see Figure 16.1), according to the latest census report (Census of Gibraltar 2012), of which 25,111 (78 percent) are considered Gibraltarians, 4,249 (13.2 percent) British, and the remaining 2,501 (7.8 percent) form a heterogeneous group, of which the most numerous are Moroccans (522). Historically, however, the population of Gibraltar was less homogeneous and much more diverse than it is nowadays and was described as "a melting pot of peoples from different cultural backgrounds" (Moyer 1998: 216), reflecting its historical development. As recorded by the census compiled by the British administration in 1774, Genoese, Portuguese, and British names are interspersed with Spanish surnames like Sanchez, Jimenez, Gomez, Rodriguez, and Garcia. This is also highlighted by Alvarez, who describes Gibraltarians as "a rich mixed salad of immigrant genes" (Alvarez 2000: 11).

Gibraltar has been subject to British sovereignty since 1713, with the signing of the Treaty of Utrecht, and it still remains as such, being considered a British Overseas Territory for administrative purposes. However, between 1462, the time of the *Reconquista*, and 1713, Gibraltar was a Spanish territory, and before the fifteenth century, like the rest of the Iberian Peninsula, it was an Arab territory, from which the current

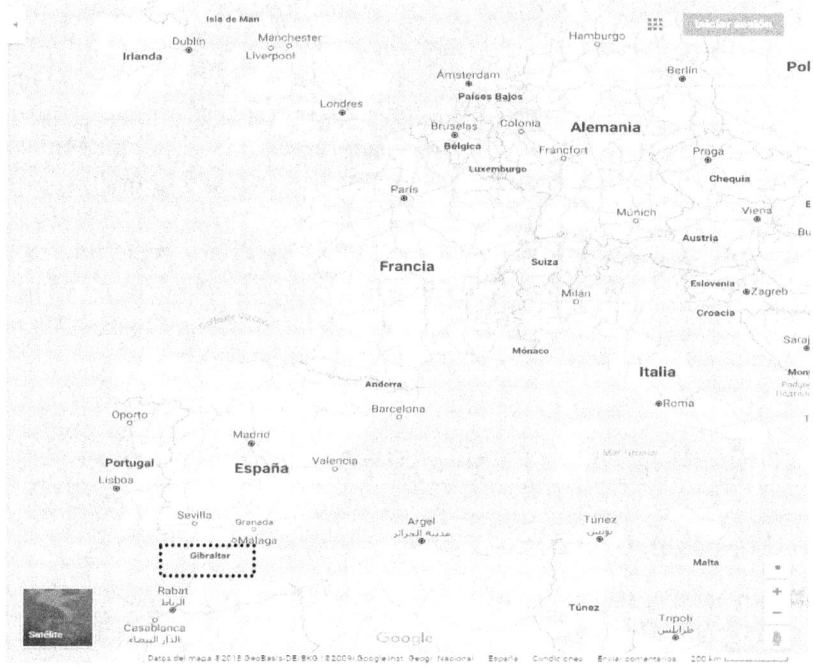

Figure 16.1 Gibraltar in Europe
Source: Google Maps.

toponym comes: the name Gibraltar derives from the Arabic name *Jabal Ṭāriq* (جبل طارق), meaning "Mountain of Tariq" (a well-known Muslim commander).

During the twentieth century there were several attempts by Spain to regain Gibraltar, especially in Francoist times (1939–1975). These began during the Spanish Civil War (1936–1939), when the victory of nationalist forces, led by Franco, compelled republicans to seek refuge in Gibraltar (c. 9,000 people). As a consequence, Gibraltar became an object of hatred for the Spanish regime and a focus for its nationalistic propaganda, in that it was seen as the "enemy" by Franco's dictatorship. One of the most important consequences of this political situation was the closure of the frontier in June 1969, which had an impact mainly on Spanish workers and on the Gibraltarian population with family ties to Spain. In 1982 the border was partially reopened, with only limited access for Gibraltarians and the Spanish. In 1985 a full reopening took place, this being a condition of Spain joining the ECC (European Economic Community). Between 1989 and 1996 passage across the frontier was fluid, with little (if any) traffic queues, and with a situation of conviviality in terms of social and cultural exchanges between both communities. However, a number of "border crises" have arisen over the years. These sometimes made crossing the frontier difficult, especially in 2013 during the government of Mariano Rajoy, when the Spanish Foreign Minister of the time, Mr. García-Margallo, frequently attacked Gibraltar in the media.

In this century, the British government held two referendums in Gibraltar (1967 and 2002). In both of them, the Gibraltarian population voted overwhelmingly to remain under British, rather than Spanish, rule (almost 96 percent in 1967 and 99 percent in 2002).

3. ENGLISH IN GIBRALTAR AND GIBRALTAR ENGLISH

3.1 English in Gibraltar

English became the official language of Gibraltar in 1713, when Gibraltar was subject to British sovereignty, and has remained the official language since then. The use of English was at first restricted to the military sphere and among the British themselves, who, having arrived in the area naturally came into contact with Spanish, which had been the official language of Gibraltar since the Middle Ages. English soon became the "high" language, used exclusively in formal and public contexts. English was the language of administration, government, education, religion, and military issues, and, hence, the language that had to be learned by anyone with professional aspirations. Nevertheless, due to language contact with Spanish, the roots of a large part of the population, and obvious geographic reasons, Spanish has continued to be one of the languages of Gibraltar, spoken with its own distinct Southern Spanish or Andalusian accent. Together with Spanish, which was until recently a language used in everyday life in Gibraltar as well as among family and friends, there also exists Yanito, a local vernacular language of Gibraltar, defined as "an Andalusian Spanish-dominant form of oral expression which integrates mainly English lexical and syntactic elements as well as some local vocabulary" (Levey 2008: 3; see also Moyer 1998: 216).

Interesting as this is, the complex linguistic situation in Gibraltar has been studied only in the last few decades (cf. especially West 1956; Ballantine 1983, 2000; Kramer 1986; Lipski 1986; Moyer 1993, 1998; Cal Varela 1996, 2001; Kellerman 2001), and only recently incorporated into studies of World Englishes (McArthur 1992: 440–441; Levey 2008, 2015; Weston 2011, 2013, 2015; Seoane et al. 2016; Loureiro-Porto and Suárez-Gómez 2017), and has also been overlooked by Spanish sociolinguistics. One of the earliest works to deal with the sociolinguistic situation of Gibraltar is West's (1956) brief overview of bilingualism in the territory. Following this, it was not until the final years of the twentieth century that the topic again attracted interest. Material published on the sociolinguistic situation of Gibraltar since then can be divided into two main groups: on the one hand, publications which focus on sociolinguistic issues such as language contact, bilingualism, and language choice (Ballantine 1983; Lipski 1986), code-switching (Moyer 1993, 1998; Weston 2013; Loureiro-Porto and Suárez-Gómez 2017), attitudes towards the languages (Kramer 1986; Fierro Cubiella 1997; Kellerman 2001; Fernández Martín 2003), and domains of use, in particular those of home and school (Ballantine 1983); on the other hand, several studies have concentrated on purely linguistic matters, covering mainly lexis and phonetics (Kramer 1986; García Martín 1996; Cal Varela 2001; Kellerman 2001; Levey 2008; Krug et al. 2019), and, more recently, grammar (Loureiro-Porto and Suárez-Gómez 2017).

Historically the linguistic situation of Gibraltar can be described as one of diglossia, typical of many countries and regions with language coexistence (Lipski 1986; see also Moyer 1993: 116; Cal Varela 1996: 41).[2] More recent studies by Kellerman (2001: 91–93) and Levey (2008: 58, 95–98) confirm this situation; nevertheless, they have also noticed an incipient increase of English at home among young Gibraltarians, and English has become a language used at home between children and parents (see also Weston 2013). This increase of English use has been located within the pre-adolescent generation (9–12 years old) and is explained in terms of the global prestige that English currently enjoys, making it a requirement for success in the professional sphere. In the case of Gibraltar, this is also because many young people know that they will end up in higher education in the United Kingdom. In fact, what has been currently observed is a distribution determined by age rather than a distribution of languages in terms of degrees of formality (Weston

---

[2] The role of education and social class in the choice of language in Gibraltar is noted by both Dr. Jennifer Ballantine Perera, Director of the Garrison Library and the University of Gibraltar's Institute for Gibraltar and Mediterranean Studies, and M. G. Sanchez, a Gibraltarian writer (Seoane 2017: 223 and 2016: 256, respectively).

2013; see also Kellerman 2001 and Levey 2008), according to which five different generations of speakers are distinguished:

- 60 and older. These are mostly grandparents of the pre-adolescent generation (9–12 years old). The language of everyday communication is Spanish and the Gibraltarian community has little or no knowledge of English; Spanish and Yanito are the languages of communication.
- 40–59 years old. The languages of communication are still Yanito and Spanish and English remains a "high language"; there is a greater exposure to English and, therefore, more inter-speaker variation. One of the reasons for the spread of English is the evacuation of the local civilian population of this generation during World War II (WWII), to places where their children (this 40–59 age group) received education in English-speaking countries. According to Dr. Jennifer Ballantine Perera, Director of the Garrison Library and the University of Gibraltar's Institute for Gibraltar and Mediterranean Studies, the evacuation explains the progressive decay of Spanish which would begin with this generation, since evacuees were forced to cut off any contact with the Spanish language (cf. Seoane 2017: 224).[3] Additionally, Spanish was spoken by the lower-class workforce, which also explains why Spanish starts to be looked down on.
- 26–39 years old. English shifts from being a "high" language to a language for intra-national communication among Gibraltarians and is used as an everyday language. The knowledge of English is much higher and communication between peers (brothers and sisters in particular) is expected to be in English. This is the generation of the closure of the border, which served as "a catalyst for language change" (Levey 2015: 66) and they are also the descendants of the evacuated population (post-WWII generation), who started to use English at home.
- 14–25 years old. Adolescents show a preference for English over Spanish and Yanito. This is particularly evident in the home domain where increasing numbers of children are communicating in English

---

[3] Dr. Jennifer Ballantine Perera disagrees with such a classification. According to her, the 40–59 age cohort does not switch between Yanito and English but uses essentially English. In her opinion, we are probably facing variation within the same age group according to position, job, and type of social relationships (Seoane 2017: 223–224), a kind of variation which clearly deserves future research in Gibraltar English.

with their parents. This situation seems to be accelerated not only by professional pressures but also by political and sociological ones, and seems to be reinforced by a more intense exposure to English. English, then, seems to be turning into the first language of most Gibraltarians, and an increase in the use of English at home among youngest Gibraltarians is observed (Kellerman 2001: 91–93; Levey 2008: 58, 95–98; Weston 2013). One of the reasons often mentioned for this change is the progressively more negative attitude towards Spanish as a consequence of the closure of the border under Franco's regime (1968), which fostered a strong "Hispanophobia" in the territory (also in 2013, see section 2).
- Pre-school children: English is the in-group language (Levey 2008; Weston 2013: 18; see also Seoane 2017: 224).

In sum, although English has been the official language of Gibraltar for the last 300 years, Spanish has traditionally been widely spoken there. Spanish and Yanito were used on a daily basis in almost every verbal interaction. Nevertheless, a recent linguistic shift towards English has been suggested by Levey (2008), who concludes that the variety of English used in this colony is losing Spanish-contact features and moving towards a British norm. Will Standard British English become the only language of Gibraltar, or will the emergent Gibraltar English become consolidated as a variety of prestige? There is need for systematic research here, including formal fieldwork and data collection. If this "new" variety is becoming nativized, will it also become institutionalized? It is too early to tell. As Kellerman has pointed out, "the New English of Gibraltar is still very new" (2001: 415).

3.2 Gibraltar English, a Nativized Variety?

As seen in the previous section, language coexistence has been the norm in Gibraltar, but the status of the coexisting languages has shifted in line with the different historical events that have affected the territory. Recently, the exposure to English has been increasing and English has already become the in-group language, especially for the younger generations (Weston 2013: 18). In fact, the latest research shows that English is turning into the native language of most Gibraltarians, to the extent that an emerging variety of English appears to be in the process of becoming nativized, labeled Gibraltar English (Kellerman 2001; Levey 2008, Weston 2011; Seoane et al. 2016; Loureiro-Porto and

Suárez-Gómez 2017), which "carries an identity function for its users" (Weston 2011: 361; see also Levey 2015: 51).

Gibraltar English is the nativized local variety which has emerged as the result of a language contact situation influenced by British English, the superstrate of the contact process, and Spanish and Yanito as the dominant local substrates (as well as other coexisting languages such as Hebrew). As a consequence, "complex patterns of contact linguistics, including lexical transfer, code switching and code mixing, and discoursal and syntactic change and accommodation" (Bolton 2006: 261) are very likely to occur (see also Thomason and Kaufmann 1988). Following Thomason (2001: 63) I assume that in situations of language contact, all language levels can be affected, and "anything" can be taken from the languages in contact, from vocabulary, to phonological or structural features. However, it is generally agreed that language contact is especially clear in the case of lexis and phonology, and less so in syntax and pragmatics, the latter requiring very intense contact, as shown on Thomason and Kaufmann's borrowing scale (1988: 74–76).

Although no comprehensive description of Gibraltar English exists to date, several studies list linguistic features of this variety of English, especially at the level of phonology and lexis (Kellerman 2001: 281–409; Levey 2008: 99–164, 2015; Suárez-Gómez 2012; Krug et al. 2019). At the phonological level, the most frequently observed phenomena are the mergers of long and short vowels (e.g. *kit/fleece, foot/goose, lot/thought, trap/strut/start*) and the merger of certain consonants (e.g. /b v/, /ʃ tʃ/, /dʒ ʒ j/); the opening realization of diphthongs, rather than centring; the non-existence of schwa /ə/ in weak syllables; epenthesis in the cluster /s/ + consonant (e.g. *start*); rhotic realizations (e.g. *shirt, nurse*); H-dropping in inter-vocalic contexts (e.g. *behind*) and initial <hu> sets (e.g. *human*); TH-stopping (e.g. *this, that*); and clear /l/ in all positions (e.g. Levey 2008: 158) (see Suárez-Gómez 2012 for further details of these features). Although all these phenomena have been mentioned in relation to the variety of English spoken in Gibraltar, scholars agree that they are less common among the youngest speakers, who rather show ongoing phonological phenomena reported for British English, such as TH-fronting and T-glottalling (e.g. Levey 2008: 164).[4] In terms of

---

[4] This variation in the pronunciation of Gibraltar English is clearly described by Levi Attias, a Gibraltarian lawyer, writer, and musician, belonging to the second generation of speakers, as follows (e-mail communication): "[T]here are a number of Gibraltarian accents. When we speak English, it is authentic 'English'.

prosody and rhythm, the distinctive characteristic of Gibraltar English is that "it has a syllable-timed rhythm rather than a stress-timed one and weak forms are rarely used" (Levey 2015: 61; see also Kellerman 2001: 307–308). Regarding lexis, it reflects interference between Spanish and English, and the semantic fields most affected are cultural terms related to food (e.g. *greivi* 'gravy', *saltipina* 'salted peanuts'), specialized vocabulary related to docks and constructions (e.g. *cren* 'crane', *doquia* 'dockyard'), vocabulary related to the classroom (English as the language of education) (e.g. *cho* 'chalk'), and the use of false friends (e.g. *aplicacion* 'job application') (see Suárez-Gómez 2012 for further details). A recent study by Krug et al. (2019) on "how British is Gibraltar English" in terms of vocabulary shows no clear tendency towards British English or American English. What they observed is that the lexical pairs under scrutiny have to be treated as individual categories and both a British and an American orientation exist depending on the lexical item selected.

Less information exists on the grammar of Gibraltar English, since corpus studies here are only now beginning to be conducted, although features at the interface between grammar and lexis have been noted, such as the use of mixed expressions in the periphrastic constructions *ir* ('go') + *-ing* form (e.g. *voy shopping*) or *hacer* ('do') + *-ing* (e.g. *hago shopping*). Recently, however, the compilation of the ICE-GBR (subcorpus of Gibraltar English within the International Corpus of English) allows the linguistic community to analyze current data of Gibraltar English.[5]

There may be local idioms. But there are a number of local accents: 1. English pronounced loosely 2. More conscientious pronunciation of English and anything in between!"

[5] In 2014 the research unit Variation in English Worldwide (with Elena Seoane, coordinator, Lucía Loureiro-Porto and Cristina Suárez-Gómez as main researchers) was commissioned to compile the Gibraltar component of the ICE project (2009). The ICE project was initiated in 1988 by Professor Greenbaum, then Director of the Survey of English Usage at UCL. Nowadays, it is coordinated by Professor Marianne Hundt (University of Zurich). The original aim of the project is that of creating parallel corpora of English worldwide for their linguistic study (Nelson 2006: 736–740). It contains parallel corpora of varieties of English as a Native Language (e.g. Canada, New Zealand, Ireland), English as an Institutionalized Second Language (i.e. official or widely used language for intranational communication, such as education, media, administration, e.g. India, Singapore English), English as a Second Dialect (ESD, e.g. Jamaican English), and varieties of English spoken in places where its exact status is debatable (e.g. Maltese English). The compilation of the Gibraltar English component of the International Corpus of English started with the written part, specifically with

In fact, a preliminary study of Gibraltar English based on a selection of texts from the still incomplete ICE-GBR shows the effect of language contact at the level of grammar (Loureiro-Porto and Suárez-Gómez 2017) by studying the use of passive voice and relativizers, as well as the presence of code-switching. The results from this research show a lower frequency in the use of passive periphrastic structures in Gibraltar English than in British English. This has been attributed to language contact, since in Spanish the periphrastic passives are scarcely used, as opposed to English, where passive periphrases are very common. Language contact is also a possible factor in explaining the more frequent use of the invariable relativizer *that* compared to British English, mirroring the situation of Spanish, in which invariable *que* "that" is the default relative marker irrespective of antecedent, function, or type of relative clause.[6] Finally, the results from the analysis of code-switching in ICE-GBR (see also Weston 2013 for a study of code-switching), the most obvious consequence of language contact, constitute important evidence for the influence of Spanish on Gibraltar English, in that results from the corpus study reflect the fact that Gibraltarian speakers seem to have a tendency to insert Spanish words and expressions occasionally, even in written registers such as press news reports.

4. REVIEW OF MODELS OF ANALYSIS

Gibraltar English has been considered a new "New English" (Kellerman 2001) and has recently been described as such. One of the first models of classification of Englishes around the world was Kachru's Three Circles Model (Kachru 1985), which classifies varieties of English in three concentric circles according to whether English is a native language (Inner Circle), a second language (Outer Circle), or a foreign language (Expanding Circle). Most of the "New Englishes," nowadays, are located in the Outer Circle. However, this is debatable in the case of Gibraltar, since it is true that from the classification provided in section 3, many of

---

the following text types: academic writing, popular writing, reportage, persuasive writing, and creative writing. Next, our aim is to compile other written registers to which access is proving extremely difficult (e.g. student writing and letters).

[6] Here we cannot exclude the possibility of UsE either, a variety which chooses *that* to introduce relative clauses more frequently than the pronominal *wh*-words (Leech et al. 2009: 229).

the speakers are very likely ESL speakers, represented by the two oldest cohorts of age, whereas the youngest ones are ENL speakers: they are the post-WWII speakers and the descendants of the evacuees who were educated in England, most of whom had the chance to attend university in the United Kingdom. In terms of analyzing how things are evolving in Gibraltar, the best way to describe the linguistic situation following this model of analysis is to look at the transition from the Outer to the Inner Circle. In the 1960s, Gibraltar English could have been located within the Outer Circle (ESL variety); nowadays, it is closer to –if not within– the Inner Circle (ENL variety).

Another very popular model of analysis is the Dynamic Model of postcolonial Englishes devised by Schneider (2003, 2007). This model has not been conceived to apply to varieties that have not been decolonized, as is the case of Gibraltar English, since Gibraltar still remains a British territory (see section 2), and, hence, key socio-political and sociolinguistic factors of the model cannot be applied. Nevertheless, an attempt has been made by Weston (2011, 2015). Schneider's model adopts an evolutionary perspective to postcolonial varieties of English from the moment the intervening languages enter into contact (colonization) with the current status of the language. He distinguishes five phases in the evolution of the varieties, starting from the moment the territory is colonized by a colonial power. In order to classify the variety of English into the different phases, Schneider uses the following parameters: socio-political background, identity constructions, sociolinguistic conditions, and linguistic consequences. After a careful analysis of census data, available documents, and colonial reports of Gibraltar, Weston concludes that the local variety with which the Gibraltarians identify themselves has already reached the phase of "endonormative stabilization" (fourth phase). The application of the model by Weston (2011, 2015) can be summarized as follows.

- Phase 1, Foundation (Weston 2011: 341–345): the first phase is characterized by the first contact between English-speaking settlers and indigenous people and their languages in non-English-speaking territories. In Gibraltar this happened in 1704, when the British Empire conquered the territory during the War of Spanish Succession. English was brought by the settler strand (STL), formed not only by the British, but also by Genoese, Jews, and Portuguese. By this time, the indigenous strand (IDG) that remained in Gibraltar (most of the IDG population left Spain when the territory was colonized in 1704) and the STL shared an unfriendly relationship and the only contact was for utilitarian purposes. In order to communicate, this multilingual territory developed a new pidgin language or lingua franca to communicate between the various nations, mainly Genoese, Jews, British, Portuguese, and Spanish, which coexisted at that time in Gibraltar (Weston 2011: 342, 343).

- Phase 2, Exonormative Stabilization (Weston 2011: 346–353): the second phase is identified linguistically by the use of a British variety of English imposed by the British officials who resided in Gibraltar. This goes back to the nineteenth century. By this time, English was the language of administration and legislation, associated with prestige and power, and was disseminated through education. It is at this point that intermarriages are documented, with "Spanish wives" marrying members of the local population and thus a local-plus-English identity develops.[7] Unavoidably, these mixed marriages fostered the expansion of Spanish, while English was still considered a prestige language.
- Phase 3, Nativization (Weston 2011: 353–357): this is the phase in which both STL and IDG populations start to build a common identity. According to Weston, this phase started at the beginning of the twentieth century. In the Dynamic Model, this is one of the most important phases, as this is when the colonized territory becomes (politically and sociolinguistically) independent. Although this was not the case in Gibraltar at that time, and indeed Gibraltar has remained ever since a British Overseas Territory, a common identity as well as an association of the local population with the territory started to develop and is confirmed by the end of the century.[8] This was also reinforced by the rejection of Spain during Franco's regime, which began to foster a sentiment of Hispanophobia together with one of Anglophilia (Weston 2011: 356). Linguistically, this phase corresponds with the first and second groups' speakers described in section 3, whose language of communication is mainly Yanito, with English remaining a high language.

---

[7] In fact, the majority of Spanish names tend to be on the female side of the family (M. G. Sanchez, pc).

[8] This is clearly reflected in Sir Peter Richard Caruana's words, the Chief Minister of Gibraltar between 1996 and 2011: "Our identity is distinct, separate and unique. As a community, the only way in which we can be accurately described is therefore as Gibraltarians. We are distinct from mainland Britons and distinct from our Spanish neighbours. We regard ourselves as British Gibraltarians" (*Panorama* 1519, July 29, 1996, quoted from Kellerman 2001: 42).

- Phase 4, Endonormative Stabilization (Weston 2011: 357–361): this phase is characterized by the development and consolidation of a local variety of English, accepted and positively seen by the local community. In Gibraltar this was also fostered by the closure of the border in 1969. In fact, "Spain's decision to close the border with Gibraltar in 1969 [...] is precisely the type of catastrophic event that would count as 'Event X'" (Weston 2015: 680). Although in the case of Gibraltar, this Event X has not led to independence, it did carry a reinforcement of self-identity.[9] It also contributed to the development of a local variety of English which has an identity function for its users, with traces of nativization at different linguistic levels, especially at the level of pronunciation (Cal Varela 2001; Kellerman 2001; Levey 2008), as already noted in section 3.
- Phase 5, Differentiation: it is not clear how Gibraltar and the local variety which identifies Gibraltarians are going to evolve, especially with the political events of the twenty-first century. The Gibraltar Referendum of 2002 on shared sovereignty of Gibraltar between Britain and Spain ended with a 99 percent rejection, the local population thus refusing any kind of governmental link with Spain. This is also reinforced by the progressive shift towards English as the only language, as shown in section 2, represented by the 4th and 5th cohorts of speakers, and closure of the Instituto Cervantes in 2015, as will be seen in section 5. It is difficult to assess what the consequences of Brexit will be for Gibraltar, however, the issue of Gibraltar is currently an issue covered in the news at the time of writing this chapter.[10]

---

[9] For a thorough description of what being Gibraltarian means, see M. G. Sanchez's novels, in particular *The Escape Artist* (e.g. "'I am Gibraltarian,' he said in a tone which made it clear that he was no longer kidding" [Sanchez 2013: 5] or "No, I'm not Spanish. I'm from Gibraltar, mate" [Sanchez 2013: 14]) or the recently released paper "Representing Gibraltarianess" (Sanchez 2018), where he describes Gibraltarianess as "in-betweeness" (2018: 5), "our hybrid Gibraltarian identity" (2018: 6) or "the signs of hybridity are everywhere around you" (2018: 7).

[10] It is not clear yet how Brexit will affect Gibraltar, but the border could close again and leave Gibraltar isolated and cut off, as it was from 1969 to 1982, with subsequent linguistic consequences. In a recently published paper, Modiano speculates that a European variety of English may develop "in much the same manner as other second-language varieties" (2017: 319), contra Schneider (2017) or Jenkins (2017), who dismiss the idea of Euro-English as an independent variety. The case of Gibraltar is different at this respect because it already has English as an L1.

Mair's (2013: 260) 'world system of Englishes' model attempts to overcome the limitations of the Dynamic Model by capturing the ecological complexity of multicultural contexts which World Englishes theory currently has to deal with. His model is intended to apply not only to postcolonial varieties but also to varieties of English that have emerged as a result of global mobility. In this model, adapted from de Swaan's (2013) approach to global multilingualism, he establishes a fourfold classification which divides varieties into "hypercentral," "super-central," "central," and "peripheral," according to parameters of number of speakers, institutional support, and geographic diffusion. According to this model, Gibraltar English would be classified as a "peripheral" variety, mainly because of the low demographic weight and reduced diffusion due to its geographic isolation.

To face the challenges derived from the current expansion of English beyond postcolonial territories, either as an international universal language or as a lingua franca (the territories located in the Expanding Circle by Kachru), Schneider himself also acknowledges certain limitations of applying the Dynamic Model to non-postcolonial scenarios and proposes an adapted version of the model by introducing the concept of "Transnational Attraction." By updating some of the parameters (Schneider 2014), the notion of globalization as a relevant factor irrespective of the variety is also incorporated, already advanced to some degree by Edwards (2016), in her "foundation-through-globalisation" notion used to describe English in the Netherlands, a general notion which reflects influences of the United States externally via the internet and other cultural phenomena, such as the cinema or music industries.

5. A NEW INTEGRATIVE MODEL: THE EIF MODEL

The Extra- and Intra-territorial Forces (EIF) Model has been proposed by Buschfeld and Kautzsch as a consequence of the necessity to face the challenges derived from the expansion of English to territories traditionally classified within the Expanding Circle. It has been devised as a complementary model to previous models, especially Schneider's Dynamic Model, to cover emergent varieties of English without a colonization process in the countries in which they emerged. The limitations of the Dynamic Model have already been discussed by Schneider himself in relation to non-postcolonial varieties. This would be the case with territories such as Namibia (Buschfeld 2014) or the Netherlands (Edwards

2016) which have ESL as a consequence of globalization but have never been colonized by an English-speaking country. Limitations have also been shown by Weston (2015) for Gibraltar English and for Hong Kong (as well as for the Falklands and Northern Ireland). These territories have suffered political pressures from their neighboring countries, and this has led them to maintain a British allegiance longer.

All these attempts to complement Schneider's Dynamic Model paved the way for the development of the EIF Model. In it, Buschfeld and Kautzsch (2017) sought an "integrative framework which captures exactly these developments, help describe the diverse forms of English world-wide and relates them to each other, not only in terms of their development but also with respect to their current status and linguistic forms" (2017: 105). It is compatible with the Dynamic Model in that it complements the route traced therein by adapting it to varieties from territories that lack a colonial trajectory, and that therefore do not comply with some of the socio-political and sociolinguistic parameters established by Schneider's Model. In effect, the EIF Model is an integrative model of postcolonial and non-postcolonial Englishes in a unified framework (Buschfeld and Kautzsch 2017: 113). To that end, Buschfeld and Kautzsch incorporate the notion of "extra- and intra-territorial forces." The most significant innovation of the model is the incorporation of a set of extra-territorial forces, which includes "any factor entering the country from the outside" (Buschfeld and Kautzsch 2017: 112). These forces cooperate with the group of intra-territorial forces such that they "mainly operate on a local, that is, national or regional, level and therefore influence the cultural and linguistic development from within" (Buschfeld and Kautzsch 2017: 113). This model goes beyond Schneider (2014) and Edwards (2016) in that "it meets not only the problem of lacking a foundation phase but also the missing settler strand as well as the external colonizing power" (Buschfeld and Kautzsch 2017: 115).

In the previous section of this chapter, the role of English in Gibraltar has been traced from different viewpoints. The current section attempts to capture the development of English here by applying the EIF Model. So, in what respects does the EIF Model complement the Dynamic Model in the case of Gibraltar?

English was introduced to the territory of Gibraltar in 1704 by extra-territorial forces when the British colonial power defeated Spain in the War of Succession. From that moment, and as predicted by the foundation phase of the Dynamic Model (see section 4), English became the language of prestige, used at the level of administration and education, and coexisted with Spanish, as the indigenous language, and Yanito, a code-switching variety developed in the nineteenth century for purposes of inter-group communication. The situation of bilingualism (with a diglossic distribution) has been the norm in Gibraltar since the introduction of English. It was observed during the twentieth century and is still the case for the oldest generations today: Spanish or Yanito as the home language and English as the high language. This illustrates the shift from exonormativity towards endonormativity, already seen in the brief summary of Weston's application of the Dynamic Model. However, the sociolinguistic reality now sees a shift towards the phase of differentiation, reflected in a monolingual situation of only English, especially in the younger generations. This has also been motivated by extra-territorial forces: on the one hand, the evacuation of the civil population to the United Kingdom as a consequence of WWII, whose children were educated in English; on the other hand, the difficult political relationship with Spain during Franco's regime also contributed to this development towards the phase of endonormativity. The political turmoil of the time led to decisions on treaties and diplomatic relations which have had cultural and linguistic impact and consequently affected the popularity of a certain culture and/or language in the country. One of these consequences was the closing of the Instituto Cervantes in 2015, the official Spanish Language and Cultural center whose aim is to promote the teaching of Spanish throughout the world and to foster the knowledge of the cultures of Spanish-speaking countries. At the same time, a formalized state education system in Gibraltar was imposed and the current language policies developed; both are associated with the phase of endonormative stabilization. English thus becomes the only medium of instruction, and Spanish is considered a secondary language, no longer useful for professional success. The presence of English also dominates the media. Gibraltar Broadcasting Corporation (GBC) is the main TV station, with 100 percent of its programs in English.[11] GBC coexists with Radio Gibraltar as the most influential radio station. In terms of newspapers, the *Gibraltar Chronicle* (published in Gibraltar since 1801) and *Panorama*, in print since 1975, together with the weekly newspapers *7 Days*, *The New People*, and *GibSport*, are the most sig-

---

[11] In the past, this station used to broadcast programs in Yanito, as in the case of Talk about Town, where local issues where discussed, and Pepe's Pot, a cookery program.

nificant and are all written exclusively in English.[12] This situation is also reinforced by the results from two referendums carried out (1967 and 2002) in which the majority of the population expressed a wish to remain British, reaching almost 100 percent in the latter case.[13] In terms of education, Gibraltar follows the English system (established when the children of WWII evacuees returned). The primary education curriculum is based on the national curriculum for England, as set out by the United Kingdom's Department of Education, although "there are specific differences in respect of Spanish and other subjects (including Religious Education) reflecting local realities" (quoted from the Department of Education). The same applies to secondary schools; according to the Department of Education, they follow the "national curriculum legislation." For higher education, people moved to the United Kingdom until 2015, when the University of Gibraltar started offering some degrees, especially those related to Business, Sports, Health, Tourism and Hospitality Environment, and Life Sciences, Gibraltar and Mediterranean Studies. In terms of language policy, the Clifford Report of 1944 gave a central role to English. According to the Gibraltarian Department of Education, "[s]chools are all co-educational and English is the language of instruction. Spanish is introduced formally as a subject in middle school (year 4) but may be employed earlier as a teaching aid in special circumstances." Therefore, the attitudes towards English have been positive since the evacuation of the civil population to the United Kingdom during WWII. Such positive attitudes were further reinforced as a consequence of the closure of the border and the fact that at the time of the evacuation, Spanish was mainly spoken by blue-collar workers.[14] More recently, with the expansion of English as a global language, English is a language of prestige and professional success.

---

[12] Since Gibraltar is so close to Spain, Spanish newspapers are also easily available, but while nowadays the only local newspaper written in Spanish is the weekly *El Faro de Gibraltar*, before World War II there were three daily newspapers: *El Calpense*, *El Anunciador*, and *El Espectador*.

[13] While the results of the referendums show loyalty to Britain, nationalist traditions have been developing in Gibraltar and Union flags are no longer seen as frequently as they used to be since the victory of the Gibraltar Socialist Labour Party (GSLP) in the 1988 elections (Alvarez 2000: 15).

[14] According to Alvarez, Spanish "was widely regarded as being culturally inferior to English" and schoolchildren "were often reprimanded for speaking Spanish in front of [their] teachers" (Alvarez 2000: 9). Weston (2013: 8), however, points out that many still see speaking two languages as an advantage.

In terms of linguistic effects, a local variety of English exists, as already described in section 3, which gives "Gibraltarians a linguistic and cultural space for themselves" (Manzanas-Calvo 2017: 29, quoting Adami 2013) and is accepted by the local population. This parameter would place the variety in the phase of nativization. In the case of Gibraltar, it goes beyond this phase because it is codified and used by local writers (e.g. M. G. Sanchez, Vanessa Webster, Mary Chiappe, Sam Benady, Rebecca Faller, Trino Cruz, Giordano Durante, as well as a few others) (see Stotesbury 2014 for a description of Gibraltarian fiction in English). The shift towards an English monolingual situation is not incompatible with the emergence of a national local identity fostered by the historical coexistence of ethnically different peoples, not only Spanish and British but also Maltese, Genoese, Jews, and Moroccans. The identity which this has created, which itself is associated with endonormative stabilization, is nowadays considered as a central element in Gibraltarian identity (see Alvarez 2000: 5; see also footnote 11 this chapter). This is independent of both Spanish and British identities, as is also seen in the sociodemographic profile of the territory in the 2012 census (78 percent Gibraltarians).

Another important factor for the entrenchment of English at the expense of Spanish is the force exerted by globalization, especially through the internet. The influence of American English in global media and language contact brought about by the spread of the internet, as well as in modern communications generally, has been reported as a major influence on Englishes worldwide (Mair 2013), motivated by the United States as a major cultural and economic power. In the case of Gibraltar, this external force may also help to justify a shift towards English as the only vehicle of communication among the young, who have adopted English as a symbol of modern identity and cosmopolitanism, and the evolution of Gibraltar English towards the phase of differentiation, already advanced in section 4.

Table 16.1 summarizes the position of Gibraltar English within the Extra- and Intra-Territorial Forces Model:

6. CONCLUSION

This chapter applies the recently developed model of 'Extra- and Intraterritorial forces' proposed by Buschfeld and Kautzsch (2017) to account for varieties of English around the world. The model complements

Table 16.1 Gibraltar English in the EIF Model

	Extra-territorial forces	Intra-territorial forces
Foundation	1704: War of Succession and introduction of English in Gibraltar	Diglossia: English, language of the settlers, and language of prestige
Exonormative Stabilization	Establishment of British workers (mostly civil servants)	Spanish and Yanito, indigenous languages, and home languages
Nativization	WWII: evacuation of a large group of the civilian population to the UK	Shift towards English as the in-group language Development of a nativized variety
Endonormative Stabilization	1967 Referendum 1969: closure of the border Political turmoil during Franco's dictatorship (1936–1975)	1944, Clifford Report: English becomes the only medium of instruction and Spanish is only a formal subject Development of the current language policies and expression of local language attitudes Emergence of a Gibraltarian identity Literary production by local writers
Differentiation	2002 Referendum 2011–2016: political difficulties with Spain (Foreign Minister García-Margallo) Expansion of English as a global language (globalization) and English as the language of the media	Closure of Instituto Cervantes (2015) Opening of the University of Gibraltar (2015) Primary and secondary education curricula based on the national curriculum of England Media (100% English): Gibraltar Broadcasting Company and Radio Gibraltar Local newspapers in English: *Gibraltar Chronicle*, *Panorama*, *7 Days*, *The New People*, and *GibSport*

previous ones in that it can also be applied to ESL varieties that had been overlooked before, because they became ESLs as a consequence of globalization (e.g. English in the Netherlands or Namibia), or even because the territories where they emerged remain under the colonial power (e.g. Gibraltar, a British Overseas Territory).

Historically, Gibraltar has been a multilingual territory, with the coexistence of English, Spanish, and Yanito; however, it is steadily shifting towards a monolingual English territory. English in Gibraltar is nowadays considered a native language and the first language of most speakers (ENL territory). Although non-decolonized, an adaptation of the Dynamic Model to Gibraltar English (Weston 2011) convincingly shows that it has reached the phase of endonormative stabilization and it is already showing traces of advancing towards the phase of differentiation. Nevertheless, it is the EIF Model which makes it possible to fully capture the situation of Gibraltar English, since it incorporates the influence of both external forces and internal forces to the configuration of the local reality. Regarding external forces, the current situation and evolution of English in Gibraltar, after its introduction in 1704, can only be explained and understood historically as a consequence of the evacuation to the United Kingdom of civilians after WWII and the political pressures of Spain, as well as the result of globalization more recently. Consequently, to a great extent, it was these external phenomena that motivated the construction of a national local identity, one which was neither British nor Spanish, also aided by the development of a local linguistic variety, Gibraltar English. This is also fostered by the fact that English is the only medium of instruction in primary, secondary, and higher education as well as the language used in the media: radio stations, newspapers, and magazines have become almost exclusively available in English.

REFERENCES

Adami, Esterino. 2013. Interview with M. G. Sanchez. *IRIS Uni Torino, AperTO*. Torino: Università degli Studi di Torino, http://aperto. unito.it/retrieve/handle/2318/150037/26278/E%20interview%20 G%20M%20Sanchez.pdf (last accessed January 31, 2018).

Alvarez, David. 2000. Colonial relic: Gibraltar in the age of decolonization. *Grand Valley Review* 21.1: 4–26.

Ballantine, Sergius J. 1983. A Study of the Effects of English-medium

Education on Initially Monoglot Spanish–speaking Gibraltarian Children. MA dissertation, University of Valencia.
Ballantine, Sergius J. 2000. English and Spanish in Gibraltar: Development and characteristics of two languages in Gibraltar. *Gibraltar Heritage Journal* 7: 115–124.
Bolton, Kingsley. 2006. World Englishes today. In Braj B. Kachru, Yamuna Kachru and Cecil L. Nelson, eds. 2006, *The Handbook of World Englishes*. Oxford: Blackwell, 240–269.
Buschfeld, Sarah. 2014. English in Cyprus and Namibia: A critical approach to taxonomies and models of World Englishes and Second Language Acquisition research. In Sarah Buschfeld, Thomas Hoffmann, Magnus Huber and Alexander Kautzsch, eds. 2014, *The Evolution of Englishes: The Dynamic Model and Beyond*. Amsterdam: John Benjamins, 181–202.
Buschfeld, Sarah and Alexander Kautzsch. 2017. Towards an integrated approach to postcolonial and non-postcolonial Englishes. *World Englishes* 36.1: 104–126.
Cal Varela, Mario. 1996. Hacia una concepción prototípica de *comunidad de habla*: Gibraltar. *Atlantis* XVIII (1–2): 37–52.
Cal Varela, Mario. 2001. *Algunos aspectos sociolingüísticos del inglés gibraltareño: Análisis cuantitativo de tres variables a nivel fónico*. Santiago de Compostela: Servizo de Publicacións, Universidade de Santiago de Compostela.
Census of Gibraltar. 2012. https://www.gibraltar.gov.gi/new/census (last accessed January 31, 2018).
Departament of Education. www.gibraltar.gov.gi/new/department-education (last accessed January 31, 2018).
de Swaan, Abram. 2013. Language systems. In Nikolas Coupland, ed. 2013, *The Handbook of Language and Globalization*. Malder: Blackwell, 56–76.
Edwards, Alison. 2016. *English in the Netherlands: Functions, Forms and Attitudes*. Amsterdam: John Benjamins.
Fernández Martín, Carmen. 2003. *An Approach to Language Attitudes in Gibraltar*. Madrid: Umi-ProQuest information on Learning.
Fierro Cubiella, Eduardo. 1997. *Gibraltar: aproximación a un estudio sociolingüístico y cultural de la Roca*. Cádiz: Servicio de Publicaciones de la Universidad de Cádiz.
García Martín, José M. 1996. *Materiales para el estudio del español de Gibraltar. Aproximación sociolingüística al léxico español de los*

estudiantes de enseñanza secundaria. Cádiz: Servicio de Publicaciones de la Universidad de Cádiz.
Instituto Cervantes. www.cervantes.es/sobre_instituto_cervantes/informacion.htm (last accessed January 31, 2018).
Jenkins, Jennifer. 2017. An ELF perspective on English in the post-Brexit EU. *World Englishes* 36.3: 343–346.
Kachru, Braj. 1985. Standards, codification and sociolinguistic realism: The English language in the Outer Circle. In Randolph Quirk and Henry G. Widowson, eds. 1985, *English in the World: Teaching and Learning the Language and Literatures*. Cambridge: Cambridge University Press, 11–30.
Kellerman, Anja. 2001. *A New New English. Language, Politics and Identity in Gibraltar*. Heidelberg: Heidelberg Schriften zur Sprache und Kultur.
Kramer, Johannes. 1986. *English and Spanish in Gibraltar*. Hamburg: Helmut Buske Verlag.
Krug, Manfred, Ole Schützler and Valentin Werner. 2019. How British is Gibraltar English? In Paloma Núñez-Pertejo, María José López-Couso, Belén Méndez-Naya and Javier Pérez-Guerra, eds. 2019, *Crossing Linguistic Boundaries: Systemic, Synchronic and Diachronic Variation in English*. London: Bloomsbury.
Leech, Geoffrey, Marianne Hundt, Christian Mair and Nicholas Smith. 2009. *Change in Contemporary English. A Grammatical Study*. Cambridge: Cambridge University Press.
Levey, David. 2008. *Language Change and Variation in Gibraltar*. Amsterdam and Philadelphia: John Benjamins.
Levey, David. 2015. Gibraltar English. In Daniel Schreier, Peter Trudgill, Edgar W. Schneider and Jeffrey P. Williams, eds. 2015, *The Lesser-Known Varieties of English*. Vol 2. Cambridge: Cambridge University Press, 51–69.
Lipski, John. 1986. Sobre el bilingüismo anglo-hispánico en Gibraltar. *Neuphilologische Mitteilungen* LXXXVIII: 414–427.
Loureiro-Porto, Lucia and Cristina Suárez-Gómez 2017. Language contact in Gibraltar English: A pilot study with ICE-GBR. *Alicante Journal of English Studies* 30: 93–119.
McArthur, Tom. 1992. *The Oxford Companion to the English Language*. New York: Oxford University Press.
Mair, Christian. 2013. The world system of Englishes: Accounting for the transnational importance of mobile and mediated vernaculars. *English World-Wide* 34.3: 253–278.

Manzanas-Calvo, Ana Mª. 2017. The line and the limit of Britishness: The construction of Gibraltarian identity in M. G. Sanchez's writings. *ES Review: Spanish Journal of English Studies* 38: 27–45.

Modiano, Marko. 2017. English in a post-Brexit European Union. *World Englishes* 36.3: 313–327.

Moyer, Melissa G. 1993. Analysis of Code-Switching in Gibraltar. PhD dissertation, Universitat Autònoma de Barcelona.

Moyer, Melissa G. 1998. Bilingual conversation strategies in Gibraltar. In Peter Auer, ed. 1998, *Code–Switching in Conversation: Language, Interaction and Identity*. New York: Routledge, 215–234.

Nelson, Gerald. 2006. World Englishes and corpora studies. In Braj Kachru, Yamuna Kachru and Cecil L. Nelson, eds. 2006, *The Handbook of World Englishes*. Oxford: Blackwell, 733–750.

Sanchez, M. G. 2013. *The Escape Artist. A Gibraltarian Novel*. Huntingdon: Rock Scorpion Books.

Sanchez, M. G. 2018. Representing Gibraltarianess. *Gibraltar Chronicle*, http://chronicle.gi/2017/12/representing-gibraltarianness/ (last accessed January 31, 2018).

Schneider, Edgar W. 2003. The dynamics of New Englishes: From identity construction to dialect birth. *Language in Society* 79.2: 233–281.

Schneider, Edgar W. 2007. *Postcolonial English. Varieties Around the World*. Cambridge: Cambridge University Press.

Schneider, Edgar W. 2014. New reflections on the evolutionary dynamics of world Englishes. *World Englishes* 33.1: 9–32.

Schneider, Edgar W. 2017. The linguistic consequences of Brexit? No reason to get excited. *World Englishes* 36.3: 353–355.

Seoane, Elena. 2016. Telling the true Gibraltarian story: An interview with Gibraltarian Writer M. G. Sanchez. *Alicante Journal of English Studies* 29: 251–258.

Seoane, Elena. 2017. A Gibraltar in the making: Interview with Dr. Jennifer Ballantine Perera. *Canarian Journal of English Studies* 74: 217–225.

Seoane, Elena, Cristina Suárez-Gómez and Lucía Loureiro-Porto. 2016. The ICE Project Looks at Iberia: The International Corpus of Gibraltar English. Paper presented at the 40th AEDEAN Conference, Universidad de Zaragoza, November 8–10, 2016.

Stotesbury, John A. 2014. The Rock and the Barbary Macaque in 21st-century Gibraltarian fiction in English. *The European English Messenger* 23.2: 34–39.

Suárez-Gómez, Cristina. 2012. English in contact with other European languages (Italian, Spanish, Slavic). In Alexander Bergs and Laurel J. Brinton, eds. 2012, *Historical Linguistics in English: An International Handbook*. Vol 2. Berlin: De Gruyter, 1738–1753.
The ICE Project. 2009. The design of ICE corpora, http://ice-corpora.net/ice (last accessed November 30, 2017).
The University of Gibraltar, www.unigib.edu.gi/ (last accessed January 31, 2017).
Thomason, Sarah G. 2001. *Language Contact: An Introduction*. Edinburgh: Edinburgh University Press.
Thomason, Sarah G. and Terrence Kaufmann. 1988. *Language Contact, Creolization, and Genetic Linguistics*. Berkeley and Los Angeles: University of California Press.
West, Michael. 1956. Bilingualism in Gibraltar. *Oversea Education* 27: 148–153.
Weston, Daniel. 2011. Gibraltar's position in the Dynamic Model of postcolonial Englishes. *English World-Wide* 32.3: 338–367.
Weston, Daniel. 2013. Code-switching variation in Gibraltar. *International Journal of Bilingualism* 17: 3–22.
Weston, Daniel. 2015. The lesser of two evils: Atypical trajectories in English dialect evolution. *Journal of Sociolinguistics* 19.5: 671–687.

CHAPTER 17

English in Ghana: Extra- and Intra-territorial Forces in a Developmental Perspective

Thorsten Brato

1. INTRODUCTION

Huber (2014: 87–91) discusses the development of English in Ghana against the background of the Dynamic Model of the Evolution of Postcolonial Englishes (Schneider 2007) and claims that the variety can be located between the nativisation and endonormative stabilisation phases. However, at the same time he makes an important point about the divergence of Ghanaian English from the prototypical path laid out by Schneider, who suggests (2007: 31–32) that one of the most important driving forces in the development of a new variety of English is the interplay between colonisers (settler or STL strand) and colonised (indigenous or IDG strand). Ghana was an exploitation colony (cf. Mufwene 2001: 8 footnote 3), not a settler colony. Therefore, the number of British in the country over the whole colonisation period and after independence was very small in comparison to the local population. In addition, those Brits who stayed in the colony would often not stay long enough to lose their ties with the mother country. This leads Huber (2014: 88) to conclude that 'convergence and identity construction [. . .] did and does take place not so much *between* the STL and IDG groups but rather *within* the IDG strand' (emphasis in the original).

With the absence of a sizable IDG strand, one main explanatory factor underlying the Dynamic Model is not met. In the Extra- and Intraterritorial Forces (EIF) Model proposed by Buschfeld and Kautzsch (2017), colonial interactions are just one of a set of factors contributing to the developmental history of a variety. It may therefore prove more useful in accounting for the evolution of Ghanaian English and its current sociolinguistic manifestations. I will argue in this chapter that on the intra-territorial side, educational and language policies as well as sociodemographic realities play a major role. Together with the country's colonial history as the major extra-territorial force, they have shaped Ghanaian English in the foundation (beginning in 1632) and exonormative stabilisation phases (1844–1957). They also account for some linguistic patterns found today.

Since independence in 1957, which marks the formal onset of the nativisation phase of Ghanaian English, the number of speakers of English has expanded greatly (in both absolute and relative numbers) and while many Ghanaians still struggle to accept a local standard model of English, many distinct Ghanaian features exist on every linguistic level, some of which even show sociolinguistic stratification (such as /t/-affrication, Huber 2014; Brato 2015). As elsewhere, globalisation has taken its toll, surfacing linguistically in an Americanised pronunciation referred to as a 'locally acquired foreign accent' (Shoba et al. 2013). Furthermore, many children in the urban areas now grow up either as English monolinguals or acquire it as a (dominant) language alongside a local one, which will further influence the linguistic development of English in Ghana. The role of foreign policies as a force is only minor.

In the following, I will first give a general overview of Ghana as it stands today. I will then outline previous outlines of the development of English in Ghana before turning to the discussion of extra- and intra-territorial forces in the evolution of the variety. The final section will show some difficulties in applying the model and make some suggestions for future research.

2. GHANA

Ghana is a country with about 28 million inhabitants (2018 estimate; CIA The World Factbook 2019) which borders the Gulf of Guinea. It is bordered by Côte d'Ivoire to the west, Burkina Faso to the north and Togo to the east. As of 2018 the country is divided into ten regions (see Figure 17.1).[1] The population is concentrated in the southern half of the country and the coastal regions are overall more populous than the inland. More than half of the population is under the age of twenty-five.

---

[1] Following a referendum held in December 2018 the regional division will be reorganised and six new regions will be introduced.

Figure 17.1 Map of Ghana with current regions

As most African countries, Ghana is multi-ethnic and multilingual. Akans (inhabiting mainly the Western, Central, Eastern, Ashanti and Brong-Ahafo Regions) account for about 48 per cent of the population, followed by the Mole-Dagbon in the Northern Region, and the Ewe in the Volta Region. The Gas are the fourth major ethnic group and traditionally come from the Greater Accra region. More than eighty languages are spoken in Ghana (Lewis et al. 2013). Belonging mainly to the Niger-Congo family, they can be divided into the Gur branch in the North and the Kwa branch in the South. Varieties of Akan (Fante, Twi, Brong and others) are the most widely spoken and the first two serve as lingua francas across the south of the country. In the north, Dagomba is used most frequently. Hausa enjoys some currency as a lingua franca in the north but may also be heard in parts of the larger cities. English is the de facto official language, used in all public domains. According to the 2010 Census (Ghana Statistical Service 2012: 41), 46.8 per cent of the population aged eleven and above claim to speak English and a Ghanaian language, 20.1 per cent say they speak only English and 7.0 per cent speak only a Ghanaian language.

3. PREVIOUS WORK ON THE EVOLUTION OF GHANAIAN ENGLISH

The current chapter is not the first to discuss the socio-historical developments of English in Ghana. Sackey (1997: 126) proposes three phases:

1. The first arrival of the British on the Gold Coast (1550s–1820s).
2. Colonial administration and missionaries (1820s–1957).[2]
3. Post-independence (1957 and after).

He argues that the first phase is characterised mainly by trade relations between Africans and various European powers. Following the marginalisation of the other European powers, the British were left as the only colonisers. He concludes that this phase brought languages into contact and that there was some borrowing of English terms into Ghanaian languages (interestingly, he does not mention that this happened the other way around, as would be expected in the foundation stage; Schneider 2007: 36) but that social changes, because of contact with the English language, were very limited. During the second period, the British government started taking control of the administration, which hitherto was mainly in the hands of the merchants, and mission-established schools, the majority of which were located near the coast. Bilingualism spread rapidly among a small educated elite as English was seen as a motor of social advancement. Following independence and the large-scale education expansion, more people obtained access to English. It is still a key to getting into secondary and tertiary education as well as better-paid jobs.

Huber provides a succinct overview of the historical background of Ghanaian English (2004: 842–845) and also places it into Schneider's (2007) Dynamic Model (Huber 2014: 87–90). He proposes the following divisions:

1. Foundation phase (1632–1844).
2. Exonormative stabilisation phase (1844–1957).

[2] Sackey does not state these years explicitly.

3. Nativisation (1957 onwards).
4. Endonormative stabilisation (incipient).

Although the English had traded with the Gold Coast since 1553, it was not until 1632 that they set up the first permanent post and started trading on a more regular basis. The onset of the exonormative stabilisation phase, he argues, is not the official proclamation of the Gold Coast Colony in 1874, but rather the Bond of 1844, in which eight coastal peoples accepted British legal jurisdiction and the area became a protectorate. Independence is the most important socio-political factor for the onset of the nativisation phase, which Ghana reached in 1957. Huber (2014: 90) suggests that the vibrant English-language literary scene and the first attempts at codifying Ghanaian English should be seen as indicators of progression into phase 4. As mentioned in the introduction, Huber (2014: 88) notes that Ghana may not serve as a very good example of the Dynamic Model because of the absence of a sizable STL strand.

The near absence of the STL strand is the major sociodemographic factor. Together with the colonial history and educational policies, it has had a considerable influence in the evolution of English in Ghana. I will also show that the temporal division that Huber suggests largely reflects colonial and political developments but does not always match developments in other areas such as language or education policies.

4. THE EIF MODEL AND GHANAIAN ENGLISH

The following should be seen as an initial attempt at modelling the development of Ghanaian English against the background of the EIF Model as I can only address some of the many issues that have played a role. The individual forces are often strongly interwoven and interact with one another. It is therefore more convenient to discuss them in a chronological perspective rather than addressing them in turn.

I will show that colonial developments, sociodemographics, including the contact of Africans and Europeans at different times, and the educational and language policies play vital roles for understanding the history of English in Ghana, whereas language attitudes and globalisation are rather important for the more recent developments. Foreign policies do not seem to play a major role.

4.1 First Afro-European Contacts (1470s–1632)

When the first Europeans set foot on the Guinea Coast in what today is the Central Region of Ghana in the late fifteenth century, they encountered African civilisations that had already been established in the region for over several hundred years. The most powerful and historically most important people in the context of Afro-European contact were the Asante. Following a series of attacks against neighbouring states in the early and mid-seventeenth century, they established themselves as the leading power in the region and by the 1820s controlled the modern Ashanti and Brong-Ahafo regions. Their expansion also brought them in regular contact with the peoples from the coast, Fantes in today's Western and Central regions, Ga-Adangbes around Accra and Ewes in the Eastern and Volta regions (McLaughlin and Owusu-Ansah 1994; Owusu-Ansah 2005: 29–33).

Several European powers established trade relations with the local tribes from the 1470s onwards. The British started trading in 1553, and in 1555 they took four captured Africans to Britain to train them as interpreters for future voyages. In terms of attitudes between locals and Europeans, we must assume that at this early stage these were primarily friendly, or at least indifferent as all parties were involved in trading and no territorial claims were made by Europeans (Huber 2004: 842). However, this was soon about to change. The British merchants lost interest in the Gold Coast and the Portuguese and Dutch started claiming land and erecting forts.

4.2 Foundation (1632–1844)

The first permanent English settlement was erected in Kormantin in 1632 and this year marks the onset of the foundation phase of Ghanaian English. Several European states fought for power and the Dutch captured Kormantin Castle from the English in 1665. The competition was purely commercial and there was no intention to colonise or settle the area (Bourret 1952: 14). Until the abolition of slavery by the British government in 1807, the slave trade became a large-scale business in the coastal regions. Systematic trade began in the middle of the seventeenth century and was an early manifestation of globalisation as part of the Atlantic triangular slave trade. African slaves were taken to the Americas where they worked on plantations, the raw materials were shipped back to Europe, and the goods manufactured from these were brought back to Africa. This was only possible because European and African powers cooperated. The Asante, who ruled much of the coastal hinterlands, provided the British with slaves, who were mainly prisoners of war. This period also saw the establishment of castle schools and the first emergence of western education and language policies. The earliest castle schools were run by the Portuguese (from 1529) and the Dutch (from 1637) and it was not until 1694 that the British Royal African Company set up a short-lived school in Cape Coast Castle as they required 'literate interpreters' (Graham 1971: 2). A new school, mainly aimed at teaching children of mixed origin, was opened in 1712, and by 1740 more than three-quarters of the forty-five pupils were Africans, including five girls. The medium of instruction at these castle schools was that of the European power running the school and no regard was given to the African way of teaching or using a local language (Boampong 2013: 141).

In 1754, three African boys were sent to England to receive their education there. As the castle schools were mainly attended by the sons of chiefs, the English hoped that the indigenous 'would value the friendship and in a good measure adopt the views of the British Government' (Graham 1971: 6). Scholars disagree as to whether the castle schools were successful in achieving these goals. Whereas Foster (1965: 45) points out that apart from children of mixed descent, only some children of wealthy local traders and even fewer children of chiefs attended these schools; Graham (1971: 10) stresses that other parts of the population also demanded for their children to be educated. However, both agree that it was mainly those who were peripheral to traditional society who would be educated.

Returning to the colonial aspects, we can move forward to 1817, when the only remaining European powers – the British, Dutch and Danish – were forced to accept that the Asante had increased their territory to include large areas of the coast and the peoples living there (cf. McLaughlin and Owusu-Ansah 1994: 11–13). The Fante, who had also collaborated with the British in the slave trade, as well as the Gas relied on British protection against their powerful neighbour. The relationship between Asante and British remained strained until a peace treaty was drawn up in 1831.

The educational system was expanded in the first half of the nineteenth century. A mulatto schoolmaster was appointed in Cape Coast in 1815 to teach African children, and when the British government took over the forts from the merchants in 1821, 'English became firmly established as the medium of instruction' (Boampong 2013: 141). The

'Colonial School' in Cape Coast at this time had about 200 pupils, some of whom later filled key roles in the colonial administration and government. Among these scholars was George Blankson of Anomabu, who became the first pure African member of the Legislative Council in 1861 and a leader of the Fanti Confederation (a movement for self-government) in 1867.

From 1828 onwards, missionary schools were established. The Wesleyan schools were mainly located in the coastal urban centres where there was a demand for education and a desire to learn English; therefore, English was used as a medium of instruction. The Basel Mission, on the other hand, largely went to the hinterland and deemed a local language more useful. In terms of language policies this marks a first change, as a European language was no longer the only language used in education, but practices varied greatly.

Reports on language attitudes in the foundation phase are scarce. Boampong (2013: 149) – citing Saah and Baku (2009) – reports that:

> during the early stages of European intrusion into Africa, there was an 'unbridled adoption' of European lifestyle [by some Africans] manifested in their language, dressing and other social aspects. This was the time when the policy of assimilation was at its peak and European culture was idealized to the detriment of Gold Coast culture; as colonial Ghanaians 'uncritically mimicked' European lifestyle.

At the other end of the social scale of African speakers of English were the so-called 'Cape Coast Scholars' (Foster 1965: 69), poorly educated boys who were frowned upon by both the Europeans and the well-educated Africans.

4.3 Exonormative Stabilisation (1844–1957)

From a colonial-political perspective, the onset of the exonormative stabilisation phase is marked by the Bond of 1844, in which the Fante chiefs acknowledged British jurisdiction and agreed to have serious crimes such as murder tried before a British court. The British neither officially declared it as a protectorate, nor did they make any territorial claims. Nevertheless, this changed the relationship between British and locals substantially and it is therefore considered the foundation stone of later formal colonisation (Huber 2004: 842). It has been often commented on

Table 17.1 Summary of population figures for the exonormative stabilisation phase

Year	Africans	British/Non-African[a]		Area
1846	~275,000	37	British	Protectorate (6,000 square miles)
1851	~400,000	?		Protectorate (8,000 square miles)
1873	651,000	?		
1891	969,508	48	Non-African	Colony (24,335 square miles)
1901	1,696,965	716	Non-African	Colony, Ashanti (24,750 square miles), Northern Territories (31,100 square miles)
1911	1,835,000	1,625	Non-African	
1921	2,298,000	1,629	British	As above + British Togoland
1931	3,163,568	1,843	British	
1948	4,118,450	4,211	British	

[a] Only some statistics differentiate between different groups of non-Africans

Source: summarised from Engmann (1986: 50–105).

that this meant that Africans gave up their sovereignty. One advantage for the coastal tribes was that the agreement also protected them from the attacks of the Asante Empire that they had been exposed to so far.

With regard to other forces at play at the time, we can only reliably identify language policies and sociodemographic factors. As mentioned above, the advent of the missionary schools brought the first change in language policies and exposed more locals to a western type of education. However, at this stage their number was still so irrelevant that the colonial force was clearly the most important and we should, therefore, adopt 1844 as the onset of the exonormative stabilisation phase. In terms of sociodemographics, this date is also convenient. Despite the Gold Coast not yet being a colony, the British started collecting and publishing statistics as part of their colonial 'Blue Books'. The first edition for the Gold Coast came out in 1846, and over the years these became considerably more complex and today are an invaluable source of data on many aspects of the colonial history, including population. Initially, estimates were very rough, but in later years they became more solid. (see Table 17.1). In 1846, the population stood at about 275,000 Africans over a territory of about 6,000 square miles along the coast and about sixty miles inland. The number of British was as low as thirty-seven. When the Danes ceded their previous possessions and forts in 1851 to the British, the number of Africans increased to approximately 400,000 over roughly 8,000 square miles (Engmann 1986: 48–49).

In terms of colonial developments, the first constitution was drawn up in 1850. The administration now lay in the hands of a governor, who was assisted by an Executive Council, exclusively made up of Europeans, and a Legislative Council. The latter included the members of the Executive Council and so-called unofficial members, appointed by the governor. These included Africans (Owusu-Ansah 2005: 80).

With regard to the expansion of western education, two developments occurred at the same time. The government implemented an official education policy in 1852 (Graham 1971: 107), but the bulk of schoolchildren were taught by missionaries, initially located mainly in the coastal towns (Jedwab et al. 2018: 37). By 1881, a total 139 schools, which catered to about 3,000 pupils, had been established.

The relationship between the British and Asante remained strained during this period. The Asante invaded the Protectorate in 1863, 1869 and 1872. Following the transfer of power at Elmina from the Dutch to the British, they were the only remaining European power in the region.

In July 1874, following the defeat of the Asante in another war, the British officially declared the Gold Coast, mostly the area that was already a protectorate at the time, a colony. Unlike in the Bond of 1844, the local peoples were not consulted, but were largely indifferent because the British made no further land claims.

Meanwhile, the loss of an overarching government in Asante led to several civil wars among the various groups. Despite being begged by the former Asantehene (paramount chief) to restore order, the British refused to help. This took a further heavy toll on the relationship between the two groups (Bourret 1952: 22). In 1896, following agreements between the local tribes, the French in the Ivory Coast and the Germans in Togoland, the British felt the need to establish their power in the hinterlands. They forced the Asantehene to accept Asante as a British protectorate, and in 1902 the former kingdom and the Northern Territories became part of the Gold Coast Colony. The area under British control had increased more than threefold, but the two areas were only sparsely populated. While there were about 900,000 Africans in the colony – the name refers to the territory claimed in 1874 – only 345,000 resided in Ashanti and just over 300,000 in the Northern Territories. The British established a resident commissioner in both regions, but they stuck to the system of indirect rule, that is, they left much of the administration in the hands of local rulers. This system had some advantages for the British. They set the rules and instructed the chiefs, but at the same time they completely disrupted the societal structures, which, so they hoped, would help in keeping peace among the African population (McLaughlin and Owusu-Ansah 1994: 20).

Despite early advocates promoting the use of local languages in the second half of the nineteenth century (Saah and Baku 2011: 79–92), '[b]ilingualism became a hall mark of the educated African' (Sackey 1997: 133), basically separating this group from the vast majority who did not speak English. Yet, English was the force uniting the (educated) Gold Coasters as it was not a tribal language. The multitude of local languages would basically have made it impossible to disseminate ideas as most of them did not have a written form. However, through the use of the common language of English it was possible to reach the whole (educated) society (cf. Sackey 1997: 134). Therefore, English in a way also paved the way for the first nationalist movement in the Gold Coast. The elite became increasingly dissatisfied with the British administration as they were deprived of the higher-paid and in-demand jobs. Many of the African civil servants started leaving the administration and turned to law or medicine instead (Foster 1965: 93–94), and became early nationalists opposing the colonial system. The Gold Coast Aborigines' Rights Protection Society (ARPS) was founded by traditional leaders and the educated elite in 1897. Originally formed to oppose a bill threatening traditional land tenure, which they successfully managed, the ARPS raised awareness across West African intellectuals, who formed similar groups, such as in Nigeria in 1912. Whereas Webster and Boahen (1980: 246–247) claim that the ARPS was not very successful in the following years, Bourret (1952: 41) holds that it opposed government policies the group considered contrary to African rights until 1925. Yakohene (2009: 3) argues that they should even be considered as laying the foundation of opposition that ultimately led to independence.

The situation regarding education changed in 1882, when the British decided to take stronger control of the education sector. In addition to the handful of government-run schools, there was a growing number of so-called 'assisted' schools, which were maintained and run by missions or private sponsors but were eligible for public funding, for which the minimal requirements included, among other things, the teaching of reading, writing, the English language and – optionally – English grammar (Foster 1965: 82). Education in Ashanti had only begun after 1874 (George 1976: 24) and the first school in the Northern Region was opened no earlier than 1909 (Bening 1990: 5), and so the number of schools and pupils – and therefore western-educated Africans – was strongly lagging behind the colony.

The post-World War I administration under Governor Guggisberg laid the foundation for modernising the Gold Coast on all levels, including improvements in transportation, sanitation and public buildings like hospitals and schools. The Constitution of 1925 brought the introduction of Provincial Councils of Chiefs, who could elect members to the Legislative Council and increased the active participation of Africans in administration. However, the educated elite perceived this as a move to avoid having elections or too much of an influence of the native Gold Coasters (McLaughlin and Owusu-Ansah 1994: 20–21) in the colonial administration.

The new constitution also brought a major change in language and educational policies. A local language was going be used as the sole medium of instruction in primary school; a European one should be learned as early as possible, ideally beginning in kindergarten (Guggisberg and Fraser 1929: 86). By the time pupils reached Standard VII (that is ten years of education; Foster 1965: 118), they should be fully bilingual in English and their mother tongue. At the same time, Guggisberg and Fraser (1929: 87) maintain that the Europeans involved in education should also be fully bilingual, which in reality rarely happened. An indigenous language was used – as much as possible – in the first three years of primary school and English thereafter.

Between 1881 and 1920, the number of primary schools had increased from 139 to 216 and catered to about 28,500 pupils, up from about 5,000. However, once we put this number into perspective and break it down to the regional level, it becomes clear that only a tiny proportion of Gold Coasters were receiving a basic western education. George (1976: 29) reports that about 2.2 per cent of the population of the Colony attended school – 0.6 per cent in the Ashanti Region and a mere 0.04 per cent in the Northern Region. Since then, there has been a massive increase in schools and pupils (see Figure 17.2) so that by 1949 almost 300,000 children attended a primary school and some even went on to the newly established secondary schools; however, strong regional differences in school attendance remained.

Since the late 1930s, the elite called for self-government. But it was only after World War II that the struggle for independence fully took off. The 1946 Constitution led to an African majority in the Legislative Council but the Executive Council was still dominated by the British (Webster and Boahen 1980: 280). This resulted in the formation of two political groups, the United Gold Coast Convention (UGCC) in 1947 and the Convention People's Party (CPP) in 1949. The UGCC

Figure 17.2 Number of pupils attending primary school (left) and secondary school (right) for selected years between 1881 and 1949
Source: based on George (1976: 26).

leadership criticised the Legislative Council as being composed mainly of chiefs and not the well educated, and stated that it would, therefore, reinforce the colonial status rather than represent the interests of the Africans. The CPP under Kwame Nkrumah was more radical in nature, which brought them greater support from workers, petty traders and youth.

In 1951, following a new constitution which further increased the political power of the native Gold Coasters and a landslide victory in the following elections to a general assembly, Nkrumah became the Leader of Government Business, a de facto Prime Minister (cf. McLaughlin and Owusu-Ansah 1994: 28). After the 1956 elections, parliament passed a motion that the colony become independent. As the first sub-Saharan country, Ghana gained independence on 6 March 1957. As '[p]olitical independence is a precursor of linguistic in-dependence' (Greenbaum 1996: 11; cited in Schneider 2007: 41), this date can formally mark the onset of the nativisation phase, although I argue that the foundation for linguistic nativisation was the 1951 Accelerated Development Plan, whose consequences I will discuss in the following section.

Summing up, with regard to the colonial force, the exonormative stabilisation phase was characterised by the British extending their power from small pockets on the coast to the hinterland and then in 1902 towards the Ashanti and Northern Regions. There was always only a very small number of British/Non-Africans in the colony at any given time as shown in Table 17.1 (also cf. Huber 2014: 88). In the early years of the exonormative stabilisation phase and after the formal establishment of the colony in 1874, the number of British was diminishingly low, and even at a later stage the ratio of Africans to British or Non-Africans stood between 2,370 and 978 to 1. In other words, there was hardly any contact between Gold Coasters and their colonisers in everyday life.

The decision to integrate the Northern Territory into the colony was largely due to foreign political reasons as the British feared that the French or Germans could take possession. Attitudes towards the colonisers varied. While the coastal tribes began to accept the presence of the British, the Asante remained hostile. Also, towards the end of the nineteenth century, the local elite became increasingly dissatisfied with the situation and the first nationalist movements were organised.

With regard to language policies, there were two important developments. With the advent of the missionary efforts, local languages became a medium of instruction at least in some of the mission schools. In 1925, using a local language as medium of instruction became part of the constitution. Language attitudes varied, but in this respect we should note that the number of Africans who had some command of English was still very small. In my discussion of sociodemographic developments I focused largely on the spread of a western education system, which is the key to understanding later developments leading towards independence.

The situation at the end of the colonial period and before the onset of the nativisation phase is best captured by the following quote:

> The nature of expansion from the coast had resulted in a markedly uneven pattern of social and economic change. At one extreme were the coastal peoples who had been exposed to over three centuries of European contact, with the concomitant growth of urban centres and an exchange economy; at the other were the northern peoples whose traditional social structures and subsistence economies were barely affected by the imperial power. (Foster 1965: 112)

4.4 Nativisation (since 1951/1957)

The formal onset of the nativisation phase falls together with political independence in 1957. However, the foundations for the spread of English and its linguistic nativisation were laid before that, namely in the 1951 Accelerated Development Plan. Over the next twenty to twenty-five years, several developments, mainly concerning intra-territorial forces, came together in the political, economic, education and infrastructure sectors. All these had a massive impact on the sociodemographic realities and linguistic expansion of English in the country.

Figure 17.2 showed that, by 1950, great efforts had already been taken to provide education to the local population. The implementation of the Accelerated Development Plan aimed to rapidly expand the entire pre-tertiary educational system over a five-year period from 1952 to 1957 so that every child of school-going age could receive at least six years of primary education (George 1976: 37). By 1960, more than 40 per cent of all children attended school, but these figures varied greatly, from a mere 11.7 per cent in the Northern Region to almost 60 per ent in Accra (Foster 1965: 189). However, this led to a sudden and serious lack of qualified teachers. While in 1951 there were about 7,200 teachers, of whom 52.4 per cent were trained, in the following year, the number of teachers had more than doubled, but only 28.3 per cent were trained. So-called 'pupil teachers', graduates who had gone through ten years of schooling, were employed to fill the gap. This situation was only going to get better slowly, and by 1972 there were 48,000 teachers of whom more than two-thirds had received teacher training.

This was paired with a change in language policy, namely the return to English as a medium of instruction after the first year of primary school, which had negative concomitant effects. The reasons behind this decision were manifold. Most importantly, the government hoped that English could develop into the uniting national language to avoid conflicts arising between ethnic groups and their languages (Foster 1965: 186). The direct consequence was a sudden and massive fall in standards of English (Huber 2004: 844). English was made the official language when Ghana became independent, thus cementing its status as the language of power. The movements made in the 1960s to make Akan the national language were rejected. Critics claimed that it was not developed enough, for example with regard to technical vocabulary, and that English was a binding force because of its tribal neutrality (Sackey 1997: 136).

There was some continuity regarding leadership as the Gold Coast became independent. Nkrumah was named prime minister of Ghana and the Queen remained head of state, represented by a governor-general until 1960, when Ghana became a republic and Nkrumah its first president. Ghana's foreign policy at the time was based on three principles: pan-Africanism, neutralism, and world peace (Webster and Boahen 1980: 328). Nkrumah was well known for his aim to completely liberate Africa from its colonial domination and he believed in a political union of African States, which he tried to pursue actively. He tried to establish good relations with both the United States and the Soviet

Union. In his later years, Nkrumah continued his pan-African aspirations, but increasingly he propagated his socialist views and oriented rather towards the Eastern bloc. He was ousted in a military coup d'état in February 1966.

Economically, the ties with the former coloniser remained strong, particularly in the initial years after independence, as the economy was almost completely in the hands of foreigners. Webster and Boahen (1980: 327–328) report that over 90 per cent of the imports and all seven goldmines belonged to expatriate companies, as did most of the manufacturing and construction firms. Ninety per cent of the banking business was run by two British companies and the traders saw competition from North African, Indian and British companies. Between 1961 and 1965, all major industries as well as the banking and insurance sector (cf. e.g. Evans 2009 on the evolution of Hong Kong English) were nationalised but could not be run profitably, and by 1964 the country was basically bankrupt. The economic hardships resulted in a first wave of out-migration and several more followed until the 1980s, mainly to other places within Africa (such as Côte d'Ivoire and Nigeria; Peil 1995: 347), but there are now large communities in Toronto and, most notably, London, where about two-thirds of the Ghanaians in the United Kingdom reside as of 2011 (Office for National Statistics 2012).

At the same time, this period was characterised by a massive population growth. By 1960 the total population stood at over 6.7 million, and ten years later it had already reached 8.6 million. That means that in the twenty-two years since the last pre-independence census the population had more than doubled. In comparison to the locals, the relative number of British and Irish in the country in 1960 remained stable at about 0.1 per cent, but by 1970 it had dropped to a mere 0.04 per cent (Huber 2014: 88). Primary school attendance had grown more than fivefold and that of secondary schools almost tenfold. Furthermore, since the opening of the first university in 1948, several thousand students had graduated.

Following Nkrumah's fall, Ghana became politically unstable and remained so until the declaration of the Fourth Republic and the return to civilian and democratic rule in 1992. Nevertheless, foreign policy largely remained stable. Ghana advocates pan-Africanism and considers itself to be a non-aligned country which aims to maintain friendly relations with other countries (cf. Ministry of Foreign Affairs and Regional Integration 2019).

The years following independence were also characterised by their changing language policies. Up to 1966, no Ghanaian language was used as a medium of instruction. From 1967 to 1969 a local language was to be used once more, but only in the first year of instruction. Until 1973, local languages were used up to the sixth year of primary school. Between 1974 and 2002 one of eleven – so-called government-sponsored – Ghanaian languages was used in the first three years (Owu-Ewie 2006: 77), but practice varied. Markin-Yankah (1999; cited in Anyidoho 2018: 232) reports the results of a study carried out in the Western Region, where the dominant language is Fante. She found that about a third of the teachers in a local primary school used Fante as a medium of instruction and that the vast majority held the view that the policy should be changed to English-only as it was the language used in exams and aided upward social mobility.

The period between 1951 and the early 1970s was one of constant change and had severe effects on the identity constructions of Ghanaians as well as on Ghanaian English. Therefore, we must take into account the sociolinguistic situation at the time. The social elite in the years leading up to independence usually attended the most prestigious schools in the colony before taking up their studies in the United Kingdom or the United States. Their English was strongly exonormatively oriented and often showed traces strongly resembling conservative RP, such as the near-triphthongal realisation of the NEAR vowel (also cf. Huber 2017) or /r/- liaison (cf. e.g. Travelfilmarchive 2010; also cf. Huber 2017). These speakers have been characterised by Sey (1973: 6) as a group that 'would not endanger their social prestige in bold attempts at linguistic innovation or in the sort of easy and unguarded linguistic habits that might result in "impure" or "foreign" English'. At the other end, there was a large group of mainly younger speakers of English who had already benefited from the educational expansion and had a basic working knowledge of English. Many of these became pupil teachers and, therefore, 'primary transmitters' (Schreier 2014) in the absence of parents speaking to their children in English. Therefore, it is likely that this led to a stronger vernacularisation of English as the older control mechanisms no longer worked.

A case in point is the rapid spread of /t/-affrication, that is the pronunciation of /t/ as [ts] as in <time> [tsaɪm] and <kit> [kɪts], which today is 'a pan-ethnic, endonormative [...] feature of educated [Ghanaian English]' (Brato 2015). The affricate is an allophone of /t/ in Fante, which occurs before /i/, /ɪ/ and /ɛ/ (Adjaye 1989: 30). /t/-affrication is not documented in recordings or commented on until at least the 1970s (neither Brown and Scragg 1950 nor Sey 1973 mention it). Huber (2014: 96) argues that it emerged as an intra-territorial feature in the 1970s. As such, it makes sense that it was first attested as a regular feature in the speech of some Ghanaians in the early 1980s (Adjaye 2005). While the variant was in the feature pool, possibly as a basilectal variant in the English of the early Fante speakers, it did not spread into the group of higher-educated speakers at first. Once pupil teachers took over in the 1950s – for sociodemographic reasons many of which would have been Fantes – they spread the feature initially from below (Brato 2015: 69) until it became established as an accepted and even desirable feature later on.

4.5 The Current Situation – Towards Endonormative Stabilisation

I summarised the basic demographic facts of Ghana today in section 2 and Huber (2014: 90) provides several indications for the assumption that Ghanaian English is moving into the endonormative stabilisation phase; here I will confine myself to describing the current extra- and intra-territorial forces and recent developments not covered in his paper. Since 2004, the current educational and language policy has been in place. Education is free of charge and is compulsory between the ages of four and fifteen. Following kindergarten, at the age of six, children move on to primary school and at twelve they attend junior secondary school. The medium of instruction is English, which should be complemented by one of the government-sponsored languages between kindergarten and primary three. However, private schools may ignore this policy and teach a Ghanaian language as only a subject rather than using it as a medium of instruction (Quarcoo 2014). Furthermore, the position that English holds in the world has led to a marginalisation of the Ghanaian languages in the school context (Anyidoho and Kropp Dakubu 2008: 151). This situation is only made worse by the fact that textbooks and other materials are usually only available in English, despite the founding of the Bureau of Ghanaian Languages in 1951 which states its mission as the provision of

> [. . .] effective and excellent services for the development, promotion, orthographic control and learning of Ghanaian languages and other cultural aspects through pragmatic strategies and influencing government policies. (National Commission on Culture 2006)

Access to senior secondary school is competitive, as fewer than half of the pupils taking the Basic Education Certificate Exam can move on. English is one of four core subjects; a Ghanaian language may be selected as part of the arts programme. After three years, pupils take the West African Senior Secondary Certificate Examination (WASSCE), which allows them to proceed to tertiary education (cf. US Embassy in Ghana 2019).

Dako and Quarcoo (2017) provide detailed insights into the current language attitudes Ghanaians have, and I shall only summarise their key findings. English is the most prestigious language and the authors confirm the findings from several previous studies that competence in English is highly regarded. Despite RP still representing the official target, speakers sounding too British are frowned upon, whereas the local speech form – Ghanaian English – is becoming conceptualised and accepted, in contrast to what Sey (1973) and Anderson (2009) report. Lexical peculiarities are deeply entrenched in not only the spoken but also the written language (Dako 2003) – and many have been attested as far back as the 1960s and 1970s (Brato 2019). This could be interpreted as a sign that the variety is beginning to move forward into the endo-normative stabilisation phase. American English enjoys some currency, particularly among younger speakers, who may use an approximated form referred to as LAFA (locally acquired foreign accent; Shoba et al. 2013).

The importance of English in the education system has also led to an attitudinal change in many – mainly urban – parents. English is gradually assuming L1 status as parents speak English to their children to prepare them for being educated at an English medium-only school. Many parents assume that their children will grow up speaking one or more local languages anyway just because they are in a multilingual environment.

Attitudes to the local languages are not negative per se, but they do not enjoy the same status as English. Dako and Quarcoo (2017: 22) report that university students do not consider it an asset to be bilingual in English and a Ghanaian as 'the knowledge of the local language hardly ever has any economic value' and that they may not even list these languages in a curriculum vitae. Despite this, students still consider Ghanaian languages to be an integral part of their identity. This is also mirrored in the results collected from a survey taken in Tema, a major port city close to Accra. Office workers strongly disagreed (89 per cent) when asked whether English should replace the Ghanaian languages, but only 40 per cent agreed when asked whether a Ghanaian language should become the official language of the country.

Recent studies also suggest that there is some robust sociolinguistic variation. Not only did /t/-affrication spread vigorously over the last decades, it is also a gender-related variation in the fact that females use it more frequently than males (Huber 2014: 97). Brato (2015: 69) also suggests in an experimental study that the variant may also be spreading in apparent time as younger (middle-class) speakers use the variant more frequently than older ones. In terms of the use of English, Ofori and Albakry (2012) show that there are robust social class differences in Accra. Upper-class speakers were much more likely to learn English at home and use it more frequently than middle- and lower-middle-class speakers with their family, friends, in church, and even when praying in private.

5. DISCUSSION AND OUTLOOK

The EIF Model is a greatly welcomed extension of the Dynamic Model as it suggests and calls for a more fine-grained analysis of the factors contributing to the evolution of a variety of English. Forces are often at play at the same time and may interact. In the Ghanaian context, this is the case in the expansion of the colony to include the Northern Territories with regard to the colonial, foreign political, globalisation and sociodemographic forces. At the same time, this greater level of granularity may also complicate matters, particularly when comparing the evolutions of varieties.

I think that our understanding of postcolonial Englishes can be greatly enhanced by applying the EIF Model. It has provided a new perspective on the development of Ghanaian English and can also help explain some of the linguistic patterns that we find today. The extended EIF Model proposed in Buschfeld et al. (2018: 25) now also takes care of the difference between a rather abstract level of variation and variability (as is suggested in the Dynamic Model and criticised by Huber 2014: 104) and internal linguistic variability as an expression of sociolinguistic variation beyond acrolect and basilect at every evolutionary stage. In the Ghanaian context, this is certainly the case for /t/-affrication, which has spread from a sub-ethnic marker to the prestige form and shows gendered variation within a socially homogenous group of speakers.

Table 17.2 Language policies from the pre-colonial era to today

Periods	1st year	2nd year	3rd year	4th year
1529–1925				
a. Castle school era	–	–	–	–
b. Mission era	+	+	+	+
1925–1951	+	+	+	–
1951–1955	+	–	–	–
1957–1966	–	–	–	–
1967–1969	+	–	–	–
1970–1973	+	+	+	+
1974–2002	+	+	+	–
2002–2006	–	–	–	–
2008–	+	+	+	–

Source: from Quarcoo's (2014) adaptation of Owu-Ewie (2006: 77).

In my discussion of the evolution of Ghanaian English, I have largely adopted the categorisation that Huber (2014) proposes on the basis of political events. However, it can be difficult at times to pinpoint a particular year or period signifying the move towards the next phase, as each force may proceed at a different pace and at different times. So, in a way the EIF Model can also complicate our modelling of the evolution of World Englishes as more factors need to be taken into account. If we look at language policies, for example, it would make more sense to use a different classification, such as the one proposed by Owu-Ewie (2006: 77) shown in Table 17.2 (whereby + indicates that a Ghanaian was used as [additional] medium of instruction and - indicates that no Ghanaian language was used). Even if we do not want to break this down to such a small level of granularity and only take into account the period since the British appeared on the scene, we could still argue for at least four periods, of which only the last one coincides with the division I drew above:

1. Castle schools period (1694–1830s).
2. The advent of the mission schools (1830s–1880s).
3. Colonial language and education policies (1880s–1950s).
4. Educational expansion and reforms (1950s onwards).

In this chapter I could only sketch some of the most important factors in each of the forces that contributed to the evolution of English in

Ghana, but my research has clearly shown that linguists should pay more attention to sociodemographics, which is also why I would suggest that the *sociodemographic background force* should be relabelled as *sociodemographic factors* (cf. e.g. Evans 2009 on the evolution of Hong Kong English). In a globalised world, migration plays an ever more important role. But even within a colony or country like the Gold Coast, there has always been migration, such as from north to south and back, from rural places to the cities, and within West Africa (Engmann 1986). I could also only outline a tiny fraction of the developments in the education sector, for which there is a large and detailed body of existing research that we should integrate into our work, as I tried to by showing one possible path for the emergence of /t/-affrication. One other area that should be taken into account in subsequent research is the evolution of the media. Finally, I would argue that the EIF Model calls for more diachronic studies (such as Huber 2017 on the vowel system in the 1950s or Brato forthcoming on noun phrase complexity in Ghanaian English) and apparent-time studies (for example Fuchs and Gut 2015 on the progressive in Nigerian English).

REFERENCES

Adjaye, Sophia A. 1989. Fante: The orthography versus speech. *Journal of the International Phonetic Association* 15.2: 23–33.

Adjaye, Sophia A. 2005. *Ghanaian English Pronunciation*. Lewiston: Mellen.

Anderson, Jemima A. 2009. Codifying Ghanaian English: Problems and prospects. In Thomas Hoffmann and Lucia Siebers, eds. 2009, *World Englishes – Problems, Properties and Prospects: Selected Papers from the 13th IAWE Conference*. Amsterdam: John Benjamins, 19–36.

Anyidoho, Akosua. 2018. Shifting sands: Language policies in education in Ghana and implementation challenges. *Ghana Journal of Linguistics* 7.2: 225–243.

Anyidoho, Akosua and Mary E. Kropp Dakubu. 2008. Ghana: Indigenous languages, English, and an emerging national identity. In Andrew Simpson, ed. 2008, *Language and National Identity in Africa*. Oxford: Oxford University Press, 141–157.

Bening, R. Bagulo. 1990. *A History of Education in Northern Ghana: 1907–1976*. Accra: Ghana Universities Press.

Boampong, Cyrelene A. 2013. Rethinking British colonial policy in the Gold Coast: The language factor. *Transactions of the Historical Society of Ghana* 13: 137–157.

Bourret, Florence Mabel. 1952. *The Gold Coast: A Survey of the Gold Coast and British Togoland 1919–1951*. Oxford: Oxford University Press.

Brato, Thorsten. 2015. A pilot study of acoustic features of word-final affricated /t/ and /ts/ in educated Ghanaian English. In Rita Calabrese, J. K. Chambers and Gerhard Leitner, eds. 2015, *Variation and Change in Postcolonial Contexts*. Newcastle: Cambridge Scholars Publishing, 61–78.

Brato, Thorsten. 2019. Lexical expansion in Ghanaian English from a diachronic perspective: A structural and semantic analysis. In Alexandra Esimaje, Ulrike Gut and Bassey E. Antia, eds. 2019, *Corpus Linguistics and African Englishes*. Amsterdam: John Benjamins, 259–291.

Brato, Thorsten. Forthcoming. Noun phrase complexity in Ghana-ian English. *World-Englishes*.

Brown, Philip Penton and John Scragg. 1950. *Common Errors in Gold Coast English: Their Cause and Correction*. London: Macmillan.

Buschfeld, Sarah and Alexander Kautzsch. 2017. Towards an integrated approach to postcolonial and non-postcolonial Englishes. *World Englishes* 36.1: 104–126.

Buschfeld, Sarah, Alexander Kautzsch and Edgar W. Schneider. 2018. From colonial dynamism to current transnationalism: A unified view on postcolonial and non-postcolonial Englishes. In Sandra Deshors, ed. 2018, *Modeling World Englishes: Assessing the Inter-play of Emancipation and Globalization of ESL*. Amsterdam: John Benjamins, 15–44.

CIA The World Factbook. Ghana. 2019, https://www.cia.gov/library/publications/the-world-factbook/geos/gh.html (last accessed 5 March 2019).

Dako, Kari. 2003. *Ghanaianisms: A Glossary*. Accra: Ghana Universities Press.

Dako, Kari and Millicent A. Quarcoo. 2017. Attitudes towards English in Ghana. *Legon Journal of the Humanities* 28.1: 20–30.

Engmann, E. V. 1986. *Population of Ghana: 1850–1960*. Accra: Ghana Universities Press.

Evans, Stephen. 2009. The evolution of the English-language speech community in Hong Kong. *English World-Wide* 30.3: 278–301.

Foster, Philip. 1965. *Education and Social Change in Ghana*. Chicago: University of Chicago Press.

Fuchs, Robert and Ulrike Gut. 2015. An apparent time study of the progressive in Nigerian English. In Peter C. Collins, ed. 2015, *Grammatical Change in English World-Wide*. Amsterdam: John Benjamins, 373–387.

George, Betty S. 1976. *Education in Ghana*. Washington, DC: US Department of Health, Education and Welfare.

Ghana Statistical Service. 2012. 2010 Population & Housing Census: Summary Report of Final results, Accra, http://www.statsghana.gov.gh/docfiles/2010phc/Census2010_Summary_report_of_final_results.pdf (last accessed 13 July 2016).

Graham, C. K. 1971. *The History of Education in Ghana from the Earliest Times to the Declaration of Independence*. London: Cass.

Greenbaum, Sidney. 1996. Introducing ICE. In Sidney Greenbaum, ed. 1996, *Comparing English Worldwide: The International Corpus of English*. Oxford: Clarendon Press, 3–12.

Guggisberg, Frederick G. and Alexander Gordon Fraser. 1929. *The Future of the Negro: Some Chapters in the Development of a Race*. London: Student Christian Movement.

Huber, Magnus. 2004. Ghanaian English: Phonology. In Edgar W. Schneider, Kate Burridge, Bernd Kortmann, Rajend Mesthrie and Clive Upton, eds. 2004, *A Handbook of Varieties of English: A Multimedia Reference Tool. Vol. 1: Phonology*. Berlin: Mouton de Gruyter. 842–865.

Huber, Magnus. 2014. Stylistic and sociolinguistic variation in Schneider's Nativization Phase: The case of Ghanaian English. In Sarah Buschfeld, Magnus Huber, Thomas Hoffmann and Alexander Kautzsch, eds. 2014, *The Evolution of Englishes: The Dynamic Model and Beyond*. Amsterdam: John Benjamins, 86–106.

Huber, Magnus. 2017. Early recordings from Ghana: A variationist approach to the phonological history of an Outer Circle variety. In Raymond Hickey, ed. 2017, *Listening to the Past: Audio Records of Accents of English*. Cambridge: Cambridge University Press.

Jedwab, Remi, Felix Meier zu Selhausen and Alexander Moradi. 2018. The Economics of Missionary Expansion: Evidence from Africa and Implications for Development. *CSAE Working Paper Series* 07: 1–26, https://www.csae.ox.ac.uk/materials/papers/csae-wps-2018-07.pdf (last accessed 21 March 2019).

Lewis, M. Paul, Gary F. Simons and Charles D. Fennig. 2013. *Ethnologue*

- *Languages of the World: Ghana*, http://www.ethnologue.com/country/GH (last accessed 26 April 2013).
McLaughlin, James L. and David Owusu-Ansah. 1994. Historical setting. In LaVerle B. Berry, ed. 1994, *Ghana: A Country Study*. Washington, DC: Federal Research Division, 1–58.
Ministry of Foreign Affairs and Regional Integration. 2019. Foreign policy, https://mfa.gov.gh/index.php/foreign-policy/ (last accessed 12 March 2019).
Mufwene, Salikoko S. 2001. *The Ecology of Language Evolution*. Cambridge: Cambridge University Press.
National Commission on Culture. 2006. *The Bureau Of Ghana Languages-BGL*, http://www.ghanaculture.gov.gh/index1.php?linkid=331&page=2&sectionid=602 (last accessed 1 July 2014).
Office for National Statistics. 2012. *2011 Census: Key Statistics for Local Authorities in England and Wales, London*, http://www.ons.gov.uk/ons/rel/census/2011-census/key-statistics-for-local-authorities-in-england-and-wales/rft-table-qs203ew.xls (last accessed 21 March 2019).
Ofori, Dominic M. and Mohammed Albakry. 2012. I own this language that everybody speaks: Ghanaians' attitude toward the English language. *English World-Wide* 33.2: 165–184.
Owu-Ewie, Charles. 2006. The language policy of education in Ghana: A critical look at the English-only language policy of education. In John M. Mugane, John P. Hutchison and Dee A. Worman, eds. 2006, *Selected Proceedings of the 35th Annual Conference on African Linguistics: African Languages and Linguistics in Broad Perspectives*. Somerville, MA: Cascadilla Proceedings Project, 76–85.
Owusu-Ansah, David. 2005. *Historical Dictionary of Ghana*. Lanham, MD: Scarecrow Press.
Peil, Margaret. 1995. Ghanaians abroad. *African Affairs* 94.376: 345–368.
Quarcoo, Millicent A. 2014. Language policy and language of education in Ghana: A reality or an illusion? *Wisconsin Journal* 4: 49–59.
Saah, Kofi K. and Kofi Baku. 2009. "Do not rob us of ourselves": Language and Nationalism in Colonial Ghana. Paper presented at the Great Hall, University of Ghana, Accra.
Saah, Kofi K. and Kofi Baku. 2011. "Do not rob us of ourselves": Language and nationalism in colonial Ghana. In Helen Lauer, Nana A. Amfo and Jemima A. Anderson, eds. 2011, *Identity Meets Nationality: Voices from the Humanities*. Accra: Sub-Saharan Publishers, 74–99.

Sackey, John A. 1997. The English language in Ghana: A historical perspective. In Mary E. Kropp Dakubu, ed. 1997, *English in Ghana: Proceedings of the Inaugural Meeting of the Ghana English Studies Association, held at the University College of Education, Winneba, June 13–15, 1996*. Accra: Ghana English Studies Association, 126–140.

Schneider, Edgar W. 2007. *Postcolonial English: Varieties Around the World*. Cambridge: Cambridge University Press.

Schreier, Daniel. 2014. On cafeterias and new dialects: The role of primary transmitters. In Sarah Buschfeld, Magnus Huber, Thomas Hoffmann and Alexander Kautzsch, eds. 2014, *The Evolution of Englishes: The Dynamic Model and Beyond*. Amsterdam: John Benjamins, 231–248.

Sey, Kofi A. 1973. *Ghanaian English: An Exploratory Survey*. London: Macmillan.

Shoba, Jo A., Kari Dako and Elizabeth Orfson-Offei. 2013. 'Locally acquired foreign accent' (LAFA) in contemporary Ghana. *World Englishes* 32.2: 230–242.

Travelfilmarchive. 2010. Ghana New Nation, 1957, https://www.youtube.com/watch?v=XY2SrD1zAwM (last accessed 12 March 2019).

US Embassy in Ghana. 2019. Educational system of Ghana, https://gh.usembassy.gov/education-culture/educationusa-center/educational-system-ghana (last accessed 12 March 2019).

Webster, James Bertin and Alfred Adu Boahen. 1980. *The Revolutionary Years: West Africa Since 1800*. London: Longman.

Yakohene, Afua B. 2009. Overview of Ghana and regional integration: Past, present and future. In *Ghana in Search of Regional Integration Agenda*. Accra: LECIA; Friedrich-Ebert-Stiftung, 1–22.

CHAPTER 18

Synopsis: Fine-tuning the EIF Model

Sarah Buschfeld

1. ASSESSING THE EIF MODEL: PERSPECTIVES FROM AROUND THE WORLD

The sixteen contributions to the present volume all make a significant contribution to World Englishes theorizing and shed important light on the strengths and weaknesses of the EIF Model. The contributions are very different in nature and set-up, coming from different directions and with slightly different objectives and foci. Some are mainly critical in nature, many others "simply" apply their case studies to the EIF Model and thus show that indeed it works; some glean rather anecdotal evidence, others present empirical data; some focus on a broader set of forces, others concentrate on a single particular force. I welcome this heterogeneous composition of the volume since it highlights the flexible character of the model and its valuable contribution to World Englishes theorizing, as well as some of its weaknesses.

Most of the articles seem to agree on (1) how "important it is to reduce the long-standing conceptual gap between postcolonial and non-postcolonial Englishes" (Schreier: 317); (2) that "[t]he EIF Model indeed allows for more internal differentiation by positing a range of extra- and intra-territorial factors [. . .] and by explicitly incorporating variety-internal heterogeneity as a third dimension [. . .]" (Labade et al.: 90); (3) that "[t]he EIF Model is a greatly welcomed extension of the Dynamic Model as it suggests and calls for a more fine-grained analysis of the factors contributing to the evolution of a variety of English" (Brato: 390); and (4) that "[t]he EIF Model [. . .] can make an important contribution by providing new ways of looking at varieties, while at the same time accounting for the complex use of English in the ever-shifting speech communities of the twenty-first century" (D'Angelo and Ike: 179). Cristina Suárez-Gómez explicitly states that "it is the EIF Model which makes it possible to fully capture the situation of Gibraltar English, since it incorporates the influence of both external forces as well as internal forces to the configuration of the local reality" (366) and Schröder and Zähres point out that

> Namibia (and NamE for that matter) may not be "a very prototypical case" (Buschfeld and Kautzsch 2017: 119) for a non-PCE, but may be an excellent test case for the EIF-Model, which does this country and its socio-historical linguistic situation far more justice than any other model of [World Englishes] to our knowledge. (58)

I would like to take the opportunity to thank all contributors for their valuable feedback, comments, and suggestions on the model, their largely positive assessments as well as their critical feedback and suggestions for modification and extension. In the following, I will present a variety of the suggested modifications and additions to the repertoire of forces and discuss the negative criticism raised in some of the chapters.

Not all contributions make suggestions for modifications or further forces to an equal extent, which is why I do not elaborate on all chapters to an equal extent. This, however, by no means suggests anything regarding the usefulness and impact of the individual chapters on the fine-tuning of the EIF Model. Some of the chapters simply point out how the model can be successfully applied to their contexts and, therefore, will be mentioned less in the synopsis. Still, they are of high value for the EIF Model since they reinforce its strengths and underline its usefulness.

2. AN EXPANSION OF THE REPERTOIRE OF FORCES

In eight reflections on cornerstones and phases of the development of the English language in its mother country, England, Clive Upton has impressively worked out the peculiarities of the development of the parent variety of all World Englishes. He puts particularly strong influence on the heterogeneity found in English in England from the initial phases onwards and how this can and has also been assumed for the global context. He points out how factors that are already part of the original conception of the Dynamic Model can be "reconceptualized" (or at least "relabeled") as intra- and extra-territorial forces in the sense of the EIF Model, for example the process of linguistic accommodation and "the need for language to act as a symbol of unity" (27). He finally transfers the heterogeneity found in English English to contexts beyond the mother country and argues that

> the regional and class backgrounds of the colonial settlers and administrators, who will have been linguistically influential in any particular territory overseas, have properly to be taken into account in the deeper analysis of the forms of English in use there. (30)

Conclusively and convincingly, he suggests that "psycho-social forces operating within a specific culture might usefully be examined as regards attitudes to deference to authority, formality, correctness and consequent language change" (33) and therefore to add "attitude to variation" to the list of forces operating within and upon a country. These are, of course, in themselves variable, their exact manifestations in the intra-territorial realm being influenced by a variety of factors, depending on how prescriptive the language policies pursued by the respective governments are (cf. the intra-territorial force of language policies suggested by Buschfeld and Kautzsch 2017: 11) or whether they occur in PCE or non-PCE contexts.

At the total opposite end – and at first sight contradictory to what Upton suggests – Anne Schröder and Frederic Zähres propose to take epicenter status (in their context SAfE) into account as an extra-territorial force. Assuming the existence of epicenters would presuppose the existence of linguistic homogeneity, which, as Upton convincingly argues, does not exist. On the other hand, epicenter orientation is not solely a linguistic phenomenon but also an attitudinal one as it primarily deals with people's perceptions and norm orientations. This is indeed a factor also pointed towards by Schröder and Zähres, who assume that language attitudes towards not only the English(es) spoken in the country, but also towards the English(es) and other languages spoken in neighboring countries, in short, the sociolinguistic influence of neighboring countries, play an important role, in particular in situations such as Namibia and South Africa. They "believe that when applying the EIF Model to the Namibian case, the influence of South Africa, SAfEs, and South African (language) policies, in the past and present, should be acknowledged as decisive extra-territorial forces" (54). They propose that multilingualism should be given more prominence in the EIF Model as a major intra-territorial force, and the model should "discriminate between strongly multiethnic entities [that is, nation-states] and strongly monolingual ones" (Bruthiaux 2003:164, as quoted in Schröder & Zähres)

Investigating English in the United Arab Emirates, Saeb Sadek comes up with yet another interesting observation, namely "that the STL strand is not exclusive to native speakers of English in the case of the Emirates" (75). His assumption is based on the observation and argument that "[s]ince using English has become a necessity in almost all domains in the UAE, any expatriate living in the UAE could be considered a settler in the sense of the Dynamic Model" (75). This is a highly interesting interpretation and reconceptualization (or rather broadening) of the notion of the settler strand (as defined by Schneider 2003, 2007) and the question of who would be part of it. It has both an extra-territorial and an intra-territorial side to it and the influence this deviation from the typical STL strand might have on the spread and development of the English language (in Sadek's case the heterogeneity or even fragmentation of the STL strand into so many different groups) can clearly be captured in terms of extra- and intra-territorial forces. In fact, his argument appears similar to what Upton suggests about the heterogeneity of the "traditional" English settler strands.

Two further interesting additions to the original set of forces are provided by Sofia Rüdiger. Drawing on the Korean case, she shows how the presence of English in the linguistic landscape and the L1 of a respective country/people as well as cultural phenomena such as the so-called Korean wave (*Hallyu*) can be conceptualized as intra-territorial but also to some extent extra-territorial forces. Lionel Wee makes a similar suggestion regarding the Singaporean context. He argues that the commodification of Singlish is a widely neglected but very important aspect to consider in the spread and development of Singapore English. However, he argues that both the Dynamic Model and the EIF Model cannot account for such developments (see the follow-up discussion of that in section 3.2). Rüdiger, however, aptly shows that this is not necessarily true and how such current developments can indeed be conceptualized as forces in the sense of the EIF Model.

In their account of English in Australia, Kate Burridge and Pam Peters illustrate how AmE influence can be and actually has to be singled out from the larger force of "globalization" (see Schneider's contribution to the present volume for a similar suggestion on the Canadian context) and that it has both an extra-territorial and intra-territorial side. They show how AmE successfully entered the Australian linguistic landscape (as it has entered so many countries and varieties of English around the globe) and how its acceptance but also strong resistance against it have shaped the development of Australian English. They acknowledge that such influences are not equally at work at all times in all varieties (see Buschfeld and Kautzsch's [2017: 14] assumption about the nature of the forces in general), but that it is, of course, not unique to the Australian context.

Philipp Meer and Dagmar Deuber further suggest "outward mobility" as an important force with both extra- as well as intra-territorial facets, for example to be found in "[t]he relatively high degree of outward mobility of tertiary students [. . .] and general outward migration [. . .] to the United States, Canada, and the United Kingdom" (286). This is clearly something to be found not only in the Caribbean but also in other postcolonial and non-postcolonial contexts and therefore adds a valuable force to the overall repertoire of extra- and intra-territorial forces. They further suggest that

> the attitudinal dispositions of the informants show that persistent outside influences need to be taken into account to describe the outcomes of norm reorientation processes in postcolonial speech communities [. . .] especially in those, perhaps, that are relatively small in terms of sociodemographic size, geographically close to a powerful English-speaking country, and in which different linguistic norms interact due to a high degree of migration, tourism, presence of different linguistic norms in (new) media, or outward mobility of (parts of) the population. (283)

This observation once again brings up the idea of epicenter influence as an important extra-territorial factor (see the suggestion made by Schröder and Zähres). At the same time, it has led the authors to suggest an important and welcome reconceptualization and relabeling of the phase of endonormative orientation as further discussed in section 3.2.

Edgar Schneider, in his chapter on English in North America, argues that psychological factors such as identities and attitudes deserve a prominent place among the intra-territorial forces. Saya Ike and James D'Angelo make a similar point in their case of the Japanese context. Both factors are indeed of crucial importance and are present in the original conception of the EIF Model, but I would like to take this as an opportunity to reinforce their importance. If these are not featured prominently enough in earlier versions of the EIF Model, we should definitely do so in the revised version.

Schneider further postulates that "extra-territorial forces such as migration and demographic proportions are decisive in early phases of variety emergence while intra-territorial forces, notably socio-psychological ones such as attitudes and identities, become increasingly important and influential towards the later developmental phases" (244). This is a very interesting observation and it might well be that it accounts for other contexts as well, but its universal validity would, of course, be subject to further empirical testing. He further suggests that

> a new force [but maybe not all that new, see his comment on page 245] has arisen in the western world over the last few years which may have the potential of threatening and possibly stopping globalization and, with it, the further spread of English, namely nationalism and isolationism. Strong indicators include the Brexit vote in the UK, the election of Trump to the presidency of the US, and growing internal and nationalist orientations in several countries (such as Poland, Hungary, Turkey, and others). (245)

These can be conceptualized as parts of the forces of domestic and foreign policies but they may indeed require special attention in that they constitute a destabilizing force in today's global economy, which certainly also has important repercussions on global linguistic developments.

Patricia Ronan makes another valuable addition to one of the overarching core forces at work in the development of Englishes. She suggests that

> even in the absence of colonisers, attitudes to the spread of English may exist on the basis of what is known or assumed about the countries from which the spread of the English originates – Britain and America – in the English as a Foreign Language context. (324)

This is an interesting and important observation in that it shows that attitudes are not only speaker or people bound, but that also varieties and their global prestige are met with attitudinal stances. AmE is certainly a case in point here (see also the contribution by Burridge and Peters, this volume). Further, she observes for the case of Ireland – and this is certainly also true for other contexts – that "distinct local varieties are increasingly being levelled. This is most probably due to increased contact with standard varieties of the language in education and modern media in contemporary Ireland" (342). This being both an extra- as well as intra-territorial force can aptly help explain the often-observed phenomenon of glocalization. Related to this latter aspect, Ronan points out that what "neither of these two models [the EIF and Dynamic Models] provides for [. . .] is an increasing homogeneity of international varieties of English that arguably does not move towards differentiation but increasing internationalisation" (343). This is certainly a good and important point to consider in the interplay and complex repertoires of extra- and intra-territorial forces.

Last but not least, Thorsten Brato, again, shows that "linguists should pay more attention to sociodemographics, which is also why I would suggest that the *sociodemographic background* force should be relabelled as *sociodemographic factors*" (392, emphasis in original). Even though this is already part of the set of forces, this, too, is an important observation, which elevates the position of sociodemographic factors among the set of forces.

To sum up, the individual chapters have yielded additional forces, both quite unique to the specific contexts under investigation but also, even more prominently, forces that at least some of the countries share. I will refrain from presenting a summary of these forces due to spatial limitations but will certainly account for them in more detail in future publications.

3. MEETING THE CRITICS

Beyond the discussion and addition of further forces, some contributions point out general weaknesses of the EIF Model which I seek to address and clarify (if possible) in the following.

3.1 Fuzzy Forces, Fuzzy Boundaries

A number of chapters mention the vagueness inherent in the forces approach – most of them, at the same time, acknowledging its flexibility and appropriateness. Following his very positive general evaluation of the EIF Model, Brato, for example, remarks that "this greater level of granularity may also complicate matters, particularly when comparing the evolutions of varieties" (390). Schröder and Zähres are even more specific and ask "[i]n which of the categories or developmental phases do factors such as multilingualism, norm orientation (including epicentric influences), mass media, and tourism play what role?" (58). These are, indeed, important questions to consider, but the answer can also be vague at best. In principle, these factors can play any role in any category or phase, as this depends on the individual case. Determining these aspects and exact manifestations remains the task of the researcher. The EIF Model can only assist in this process and, at the same time, serve the purpose of a general, and, certainly in many aspects, oversimplified framework. This, of course, makes it vague but flexible at the same time.

Also commenting on the "fuzziness" of the forces, Labade et al. remark that

> [f]rom the currently available descriptions of the model, it is not quite clear how the extra- and intra-linguistic forces are to be conceptualized – rather cumulative, descriptive, and open-ended, or as analytical categories with specific manifestations at specific stages of the model. (108)

In a similar way, Ike and D'Angelo remark that "the distinction between extra-territorial and intra-territorial forces needs additional clarification. We find that often the same forces in EIF simultaneously act externally and internally" (194) and that "the interconnected and dynamic nature of each of the intra- and extra-territorial forces needs to be carefully analyzed" (194).

That extra- and intra-territorial forces cannot always be kept apart is also shown by Schreier, who reports "some sort of historic 'push and pull' [. . .] between extra- and intra-territorial forces in all four varieties" (317) that he investigated. He demonstrates that "there are domains where the two types cannot be subdivided (attitudes to tourism and immigration) and that external factors (such as settlement policy) have provided the petri dish for the enactment of internal forces at a later stage" (317).

The idea of translocality, suggested by Meer and Deuber as a "useful alternative perspective for conceptualizing the forces" (291), accounting for "complex socio-spatial interactions" (Greiner and Sakdapolrak 2013: 376) is a welcome refinement to the EIF Model but, in my opinion, does not warrant a new model. It is implicitly entailed in the observation that extra- and intra-territorial forces interact and can have both an external as well as an internal side. Taking into account the fruitful comments and discussion provided by Meer and Deuber – and in particular entertaining the idea that local varieties, corresponding attitudes, and norm orientations may emerge but can always retain a certain degree of heterogeneity and can be influenced by outside forces and norms provided by other neighboring or superpower varieties – I will suggest a relabeling of that phase in section 3.2. This multinormative and translocal approach also allows one to take into account epicenter influences as discussed by Schröder and Zähres for the Namibian context and the influence of AmE as illustrated by Burridge and Peters for the Australian context, and as also mentioned as an important extra-territorial force in the development of Gibraltar English by Suárez-Gómez. I am grateful to Philipp Meer and Dagmar Deuber for bringing up these two important issues.

All of these observations and suggestions are fruitful and appropriate remarks and additions to the EIF Model. However, as mentioned above, the fuzzy character of the forces and the model in general can also be interpreted as flexibility. As we have seen in many of the case studies presented in the volume, forces can indeed act in a cumulative fashion; they can be external and internal at the same time; they may be descriptive and, at the same time, open-ended as there is no principled restriction as to what constitutes a force and what does not, and at what time or in whatever combination with other forces they operate on the development of a particular type of speech form. Full flexibility or exact preciseness naturally come at the expense of the other; I would like to argue that, though certainly far from perfect, the EIF Model constitutes a successful compromise between the two extremes.

3.2 After Phase 3: Reconceptualizing the Later Stages of the Model

A number of contributions comment on the particular fuzziness and the probable untenability of the boundaries and conceptions of phases 4 and 5 of the model. Schröder and Zähres, for example, suggest conflating the two. This may indeed make sense, in particular since they are not the first to criticize the set-up and interaction of these two phases (for example, Deuber 2013: 253; Edwards 2016:184; Mesthrie and Bhatt 2008: 35 on the Dynamic Model). They further suggest highlighting the fluid character of the phases in general by changing the monodirectional arrows on the developmental axis by bi-directional arrows. I will take both into consideration in the revised illustration of the model (see Figure 18.1, section 4 below).

Meer and Deuber's findings on the use and attitudes of Standard English in Trinidad show that, in the educational domain, a multidimensional norm orientation, incorporating exo- and endonormative tendencies, exists. This does not constitute the addition of a concrete force to the original repertoire of forces but rather a conceptual and terminological modification. Instead of assuming a phase of endonormative stabilization, they propose to relabel this phase and suggest "multinormative stabilization" as an alternative. This is indeed a very promising and convincing terminological refinement. Even if Meer and Deuber's suggestion is more an alternative for the phase of endonormative orientation in the Dynamic Model, it fruitfully shows that a restriction to endonormative stabilization alone is indeed too short-sighted for PCEs and non-PCEs and this should be reflected within the EIF Model. On the other hand, endonormative stabilization does not, per se, imply that only one homogenous, endonormative standard can emerge. Regarding phase 4, Schneider (2007) points out that endonormativity in phase 4 "is not to say that PCEs are really free of variation" (51); he refers to it as "putative homogeneity [. . .] not in an absolute sense" (54). In the first place, the notion of endonormative stabilization was meant to indicate that speech communities may ultimately develop an intranational standard and let go of their rigid and sole orientations towards the traditional native varieties – this is indeed something that happened in a variety of contexts (see, for example, the case studies in his 2007 monograph). That this is not an absolute and necessary development in all contexts and that at least some degree of heterogeneity exists in all speech communities is explicitly taken care of by the EIF Model (cf. Figure 1.2 in the Introduction). As mentioned several times already (for example in the original conception of the model, in the Introduction to this volume, and earlier in the present chapter), differences between the different contexts exist. In some contexts we do find endonormative stabilization while others remain oriented towards exonormative standards (be that BrE or AmE or both; see, for example, Ike and D'Angelo's contribution to this volume); yet other contexts are characterized by multinormativity. Indeed, models of World Englishes should be able to account for this heterogeneity. Considering both the "insecure status" and heterogeneous character of what was originally labeled the phase of endonormative stabilization and the fuzzy boundaries between phases 4 and 5, I suggest merging the two and relabeling it the "multinormative post-nativization stage." This stage then leaves room for different normative developments (as suggested in Meer and Deuber's modified version of the model in Figure 13.1) and different degrees of heterogeneity and thus "differentiation" (see Figure 18.1, section 4 below). I would also like to point out here that the phases, even if admittedly a prominent part of the visualization of the model, were never at the heart of our initial conception. The focus should definitely be on the forces and not on the phases, which is why dissolving the rigid boundaries between the latter comes not as a loss for the EIF Model, even if, of course, it may further increase its fuzzy character.

Another important question related to the later phases of the model is raised by Lionel Wee in his contribution on English in Singapore: What happens to PCEs, and non-PCEs respectively, beyond phase 5? He argues that globalization and changes in the nature of social space go beyond the initial developmental phases suggested in the Dynamic Model. "Singlish [for example] is not simply limited to being used *within* Singapore and by *only* Singaporeans," he states (117, emphasis in original). "Many Singaporeans working and living overseas use Singlish to express their national identity and to create a sense of community" (117). This is related to the force of "outward mobility" as put forth by Meer and Deuber (see section 2) and can be found in many other contexts around the globe (as, for example, in the Greek-Cypriot community living in the London Borough of Haringey). Wee further points to the commodification of Singlish "as a cultural product that is exportable" (117). As pointed out earlier, this is not an isolated case; Rüdiger observes a similar trend for the Korean case. To account for these recent developments, I will add an additional potential developmental layer to the multinormative post-nativization stage, called "global dispersion."

Wee further remarks that

> [b]ecause the EIFM argues that non-PCEs go through similar phases as PCEs [...] it therefore can be described as adopting a strategy of parallel development by trying to integrate PCEs and non-PCEs. But unless there is some deeper explanation as to why both PCEs and non-PCEs develop along parallel lines, the EIFM, too, runs the risk of treating the similarities in the development of both kinds of Englishes as simply a remarkable concurrence of events. (113)

He acknowledges the importance of keeping apart the early developmental phases and the reasons for the spread of English in PCE and non-PCE contexts but ultimately suggests not conceptualizing the similarities between the two scenarios as an instance of parallel development but rather in terms of convergence.

> Under convergence, both PCEs and non-PCEs can be acknowledged to have different development phases rather than the similar ones that the EIFM is committed to emphasising. Both PCEs and non-PCEs, however, converge in the era of late modernity given the effects of extra- and intra-territorial forces. (113)

This is an interesting and valid observation, which, however, is not necessarily excluded in the original version of the EIF Model. What I must admit, however, is that, of course, the depiction in the graphic representation of the model is highly misleading in that respect and indeed suggests parallel but clearly separate developments. This will be accounted for in the updated version (see Figure 18.1; section 4 below; and, of course, the same will then apply to Figure 1.2 as presented in the Introduction).

3.3 On the Nature of Model Making

A third type of general criticism is raised in the chapter by Hackert et al. (and also partly by Schneider). The authors address general questions and problems of model making and World Englishes theorizing in that they question

> that varieties are discrete entities which may be "transported" or "translocated" somewhere or even "travel" and "spread" themselves; that such varieties are describable in terms of a set of more or less consistent but clearly identifiable features; that a variety's most natural basis is the nation; and that all varieties of English undergo evolution, that is not just change but teleological development, whose designated end point is the coming-into-being of autonomous standard varieties. (253)

These are all valid and important questions to ask, some of which have been discussed in the more recent literature (see, for example, the "post-varieties" approach by Seargeant and Tagg 2011). I would argue that some of these issues are at least implicitly accounted for in the EIF Model. The current version of the EIF Model as presented in Buschfeld et al. (2018), for example, explicitly envisages intra-varietal variation and heterogeneity. In principle, the model is also open for application to contexts beyond the nation state as suggested by Buschfeld et al. (2018) but of course "this would require a reformulation into external and internal forces to get rid of the nation state-oriented perspective encoded in the term 'territorial' (or a metaphorical understanding of the notion of 'territory')" (2018: 38). Let us stick to the notion of extra- and intra-territorial forces for the time being and the purpose of the present volume, but, of course, this could be taken as a starting point for any contribution seeking to apply the model to non-territorial contexts. When it comes to Hackert et al.'s criticism questioning the nation state as the most natural basis of a variety in general, I would like to make a general remark: First of all, I agree with the observation that a solely nation-based account does not reflect recent linguistic realities in principle. Yet, that does not render the nation-based approach invalid since nation-based varieties still do exist. It is, once again, a matter of what we are interested in and from what perspective and level of granularity we approach the English Language Complex: They are just two different but, I would say, equally valid approaches.

Bolivar, for example, does not concentrate on a strictly nation-based variety as she investigates one piece of the complex picture of the English language as used in the Philippines. She approaches the hybrid variety of Bislish. In this respect, she points out that "[i]t is important to note [. . .] that hybrid forms, being products of translingual processes rather than actual varieties, may not fit the mold of PCE and non-PCEs" but that "[t]he EIF Model accommodates the unique nature of hybrids" (151). Bislish, of course, is not a transnational variety in Seargeant and Tagg's (2011) sense, but still Bolivar's account offers some first hints that the EIF Model may well be transferred to contexts that are not nation-bound in the strict sense. As Bolivar points out, "Bislish has a regional, almost anti-national, dimension [and] it may be difficult to conceive of it as a nativized version of the English transplanted by the settler population during the American colonial period" (151). She further recommends "that other cases of hybridity be studied under the EIF lens as a way of unearthing forces that may have significant social and political implications" (152).

4. CONCLUDING REMARKS ON THE NECESSITY OF MODEL MAKING

As we have seen, attitudes towards the very same model can be very different, not only depending on the particular case study one is working on but also on one's very own attitudes when it comes to more general questions of linguistic conceptualization and model making. The criticisms raised against the EIF Model and against model making in general are certainly valid and offer perspectives and insights that should be taken into consideration when theorizing linguistic variation. It always depends on the perspective we take and the level of granularity, the latter of which reinforces the validity of the Dynamic Model, as it was not Schneider's aim to account for all varieties of English but for the postcolonial ones. I believe that the EIF Model offers some alternative perspectives and useful additions to the Dynamic Model, but it was never meant as a competing framework.

As presented in Figure 18.1, I finally suggest some revisions to the visualization of the model as presented in the Introduction. Based on the aspects raised in the individual chapters and what has been discussed in section 3 above, I have revised three major aspects of the model, as briefly commented on in the following:

First of all, I changed the set-up and labeling of the later, post-nativization stages of the model: I resolved the clear-cut and consecutive character of the phases of endonormative stabilization and differentiation and suggest a phase of "multinormative post-nativization," allowing for exo-, endo-, or even multinormative stabilization (reacting to the suggestions made by Meer and Deuber), differentiation, and also global dispersion. This last aspect is meant to account for the "post-phase 5" phenomena addressed by Wee (and also described, even if not criticized as a shortcoming of the model, in Rüdiger's contribution). The dashed lines indicate that the three aspects are by no means obligatory. Countries may or may not go through these sub-phases or not necessarily through all of them or in the exact same order. Phases may be skipped or taken at the same time, again depending on the exact manifestations of forces and the overall developments of the contexts under investigation.

Second, I introduced fuzzy boundaries between the phases and concepts. This is illustrated by the dashed lines between the phases and the EFL, ESL, and ENL categories as presented in Figure 18.1. In a similar way, the bi-directional arrows indicate that the development that varieties take is not necessarily a monodirectional one but that reverse

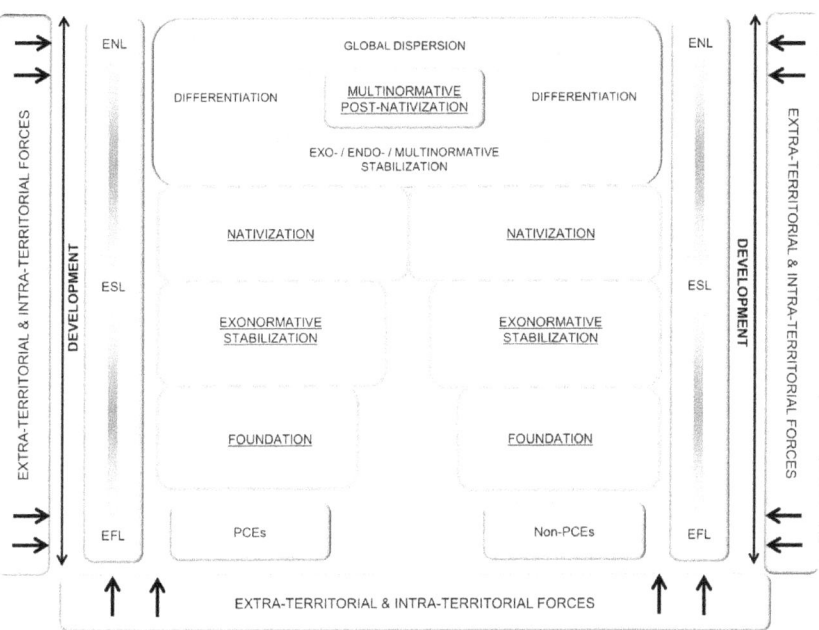

Figure 18.1 The revised Extra- and Intra-territorial Forces Model

development (as suggested by Schröder and Zähres) and thus full permeability between variety types and developmental phases is envisaged.

Last but not least, I take up the idea that PCEs and non-PCEs may undergo convergence in the later stages of development (as suggested by Wee). This is indicated by the fact that the phases PCEs and non-PCEs go through move closer and closer together and that, in the later phases of their development, they may undergo convergence, in particular in more recent times due to general forces of globalization, gradually leveling the initial differences between the types. Wee's suggestion that at some point the initial differences are overruled by converging forces of globalization is scientifically appealing in view of current sociolinguistic developments. However, I would like to emphasize here that we never assumed that PCEs and non-PCEs develop in an exactly parallel but distinct fashion. Most importantly, the development of non-PCEs started much later than the development of most PCEs, the general evolutionary paths still being comparable. And of course, convergence not necessarily sets in with the nativization phase. The model is and will always be abstract, pointing out general developmental trends and not making any predictions about exact manifestations in particular phases.

Of course, convergence could set in prior to or after the nativization phase, once again depending on the exact developmental paths of the individual cases. For reasons of illustrative clarity, Figure 18.1 no longer contains the four parameters of the Dynamic Model (Schneider 2007) as seen in the original version of the model as "history and politics," "identity rewritings," "sociolinguistic conditions," "linguistic developments" (Buschfeld and Kautzsch 2017: 107, 117; see also Figure 1.1 in the Introduction). However, their importance to the model remains the same; in fact, many of them can actually be conceptualized as parts of the complex network of forces.

Furthermore, we can certainly argue that a nation-based perspective is too narrow for recent times and that we should expand our focus to varieties of English, speech communities, and communities of practice that go beyond the classical borders of the nation state. Again, this depends on our perspectives and aims, and it does not render the nation-based approach invalid in principle. Political borders still play an important role in popular perceptions and political recognition of languages and speech forms, and do contribute a good deal to the identity conceptions of people and whole nations (see, for example, the hotly contested notions of "pluricentricity" and "pluriareality" in particular among linguists aiming to conceptualize the spread, norms, and standards of the German language, e.g. Scheuringer 1996, Muhr 2013, Dollinger 2019, Elspas et al. 2017). Furthermore, it remains to be seen whether the EIF Model cannot in fact account for these transnational communities of practice primarily found in computer-mediated communication but also other forms of cross-border or non-territorial communication such as lingua franca or grassroots contexts (for the latter notion, see, for example, Han 2013; Schneider 2016; Buschfeld forthcoming). Research investigating and conceptualizing such "emergent contexts" (for the notion, see Schneider 2014) is still in its early stages and is definitely needed to come to a full understanding of the English Language Complex. I would like to take this chance to invite scientific contributions on the topic to test the EIF Model against the background of such emergent contexts and to make suggestions for further modifications. I do not believe that model making is bad in itself; understanding and conceptualizing things we encounter around us is an essential part of human nature and that of scientists in particular. However, we should be open to perpetually verifying and, if necessary, modifying and revising our approaches. Powerful and innovative World Englishes theorizing should factor in ongoing developmental processes and aim at explanations for the blurring between major variety types such as ESL (English as a Second Language) and EFL (English as a Foreign language), or ESL and ENL (English as a Native Language). To capture current linguistic realities, I still believe that it is necessary to jointly approach postcolonial and non-postcolonial settings in which varieties of English have been emerging. Schreier, too, confirms this by pointing out that

> [t]he comparative analysis suggests how important it is to reduce the long-standing conceptual gap between postcolonial and non-postcolonial Englishes. This would be another step towards questioning static categorizations made on the basis of speaker status and variety type and would allow us to concentrate on their development, evolving linguistic forms and features and usage contexts. In the end, all Englishes are shaped by their very own evolutionary processes, contact conditions and demographic factors (cf. Schreier and Hundt 2013) (317).

When it comes to model making in general, I would like to conclude with Karl Popper's words: "Science may be described as the art of systematic oversimplification" – but without it we would give up on a central element of human existence.

REFERENCES

Bruthiaux, Paul. 2003. Squaring the circles: Issues in modeling English worldwide. *International Journal of Applied Linguistics* 13.2: 159–178.

Buschfeld, Sarah. Forthcoming. Grassroots English, learner English, second-language English, English as a lingua franca ..: What's in a name? In Christiane Meierkord and Edgar W. Schneider, eds. forthcoming, *The Growth of English at the Grassroots*. Edinburgh: Edinburgh University Press.

Buschfeld, Sarah and Alexander Kautzsch. 2017. Towards an integrated approach to postcolonial and non-postcolonial Englishes. *World Englishes* 36.1: 104–126.

Buschfeld, Sarah, Alexander Kautzsch and Edgar W. Schneider. 2018. From colonial dynamism to current transnationalism: A unified view on postcolonial and non-postcolonial Englishes. In Sandra C. Deshors, ed. 2018, *Modelling World Englishes in the 21st Century:*

Assessing the Interplay of Emancipation and Globalization of ESL Varieties. Amsterdam: John Benjamins, 15–44.

Deuber, Dagmar. 2014. *English in the Caribbean. Varation, Style and Standards in Jamaica and Trinidad*. Cambridge: Cambridge University Press.

Dollinger, Stefan. 2019. *The Pluricentricity Debate: On Austrian German and other Germanic Standard Varieties*. Abingdon: Routledge FOCUS.

Edwards, Alison. 2016. *English in the Netherlands. Functions, Forms and Attitudes*. Amsterdam: John Benjamins.

Elspaß, Stephan, Christa Dürscheid and Arne Ziegler. 2017. Zur grammatischen Pluriarealität der deutschen Gebrauchsstandards – oder: Über die Grenzen des Plurizentrizitätsbegriffs. *Zeitschrift für deutsche Philologie* 136: 69–91.

Greiner, Clemens and Patrick Sakdapolrak. 2013. Translocality: Concepts, applications and emerging research perspectives. *Geography Compass* 7.5: 373–384.

Han, Huamei. 2013. Individual grassroots multilingualism in Africa Town in Guangzhou: The role of states in globalization. *International Multilingual Research Journal* 7.1: 83–97.

Mesthrie, Rajend and Rakesh M. Bhatt. 2008. *World Englishes: The Study of New Varieties*. Cambridge: Cambridge University Press.

Muhr, Rudolf. 2013. The pluricentricity of German today – Struggling with asymmetry. In Rudolf Muhr, Carla Amorós Negre and Carmen Fernández Juncal, eds. 2013, *Exploring Linguistic Standards in Non-Dominant Varieties of Pluricentric Languages – Explorando estándares lingüísticos en variedades no dominantes de lenguas pluricéntricas*. Frankfurt am Main: Peter Lang, 55–66.

Scheuringer, Hermann. 1996. Das Deutsche als pluriareale Sprache: Ein Beitrag gegen staatlich begrenzte Horizonte in der Diskussion um die deutsche Sprache in Österreich. *Die Unterrichtspraxis* 29.2: 147–153.

Schneider, Edgar W. 2003. The dynamics of New Englishes: From identity construction to dialect birth. *Language* 79.2: 233–281.

Schneider, Edgar W. 2007. *Postcolonial English. Varieties Around the World*. Cambridge: Cambridge University Press.

Schneider, Edgar W. 2014. New reflections on the evolutionary dynamics of world Englishes. *World Englishes* 33.1: 9–32.

Schneider, Edgar W. 2016. Grassroots Englishes in tourism interactions. *English Today* 32.3: 2–10.

Schreier, Daniel and Marianne Hundt, eds. 2013. *English as a Contact Language*. Cambridge: Cambridge University Press.

Seargeant, Philip and Caroline Tagg. 2011. English on the internet and a 'post-varieties' approach to language. *World Englishes* 30.4: 496–514.

Index

adstrate, 75, 122, 234, 279
African American English, 239
African Englishes, 245; *see also* Ghanaian English; Namibian English; South African English(es)
Afrikaans, 39, 41, 42–55, 306–8
after-perfect, 339
American English (AmE), 11, 34, 49, 54, 55–6, 88, 119, 158, 161, 202–24, 228–33, 236–41, 244–5, 259–60, 262, 280, 306, 316, 341, 343, 355, 389
  as hyper-central variety, 245
  see also Standard English; World Englishes
American expression, 213
American influence, 202–24, 259–61, 287, 364
  attitudes to, 205–13, 222–3, 280
  evidence of, 203–5, 210–12, 214–22
American pronunciation, 206–7, 209–12, 238, 280–2
American spelling, 207–9, 218, 220, 236
Americanisms, 208, 210, 214–18, 220, 223, 233, 236, 260; *see also* American expression
Americanization, 245, 260–1, 267
American-style dates, 211, 220–1
analytic language, 22–3
Anglo-Irish, 328–32, 334, 336

Anglo-Norman, 22, 326–9, 332, 342
  conquests, 326
  see also Norman Conquest
Anglo-Saxon, 18–24, 26, 28, 237, 325
  Anglo-Saxons, 19–20, 21
Arabic language, 67–71, 77–80
AusE *see* Australian English
Australian English (AusE), 202–6, 208–10, 212–14, 216, 218–23

Bahamian Creole, 255, 261; *see also* creole; pidgin
Bamboo English, 158; *see also* The Bahamas
Baster(s), 47, 48
  as an ethnic group, 42, 46, 51
  culture, 45
  identity, 52,
  phonology, 51–2
  speech, 51–2
  see also Namibian English
Bermudian English (BerE), 299–310, 316
bilingualism, 40, 72, 78, 92, 190, 328, 332, 338, 351, 362, 374; *see also* cline of bilingualism
Bislish, 133–45, 149–52
borrowing, 53, 134, 185, 204, 209–10, 235, 325, 327, 328, 354, 374; *see also* lexical borrowing; loan word(s)
British Overseas Territory, 347, 348, 358, 366; *see also* overseas territory

INDEX   417

Cajun English, 239
Canadian English (CanE), 239–41
CanE *see* Canadian English
Caribbean, 228, 256, 257, 258–60, 264–5, 274–5, 278–81, 283, 284, 285–6, 289, 290, 291–2, 299, 300, 303
Cebu, 136, 140–1, 143–4, 146–8
  Cebuano, 133, 135–6, 139, 140–50, 152
Cebuano-Bisaya, 134, 136, 139, 140–1, 146, 149
  Bisaya, 133–4, 141, 142, 144, 148, 149, 150
CEFR *see* education
Celtic, 17, 20–1
Chicano English, 239
cline of bilingualism, 90–91, 99, 107; *see also* bilingualism
code-mixing, 21, 134, 139, 184, 354; *see also* code-switching
code-switching, 106, 134, 351, 354, 356, 362; *see also* code-mixing
colonial background, 2, 4, 276
  of Namibia, 40–1, 47–9, 51
  of the United Arab Emirates, 64–7, 75–6, 79
  of India, 89, 107
  of the Philippines, 134, 136, 145–7, 150, 151
  of Korea, 157–9, 171
  of Japan, 182–5
  of America, 231–4, 235–6
  of Canada, 240
  of The Bahamas, 253–7, 259–60, 261, 267
  of Trinidad, 278–9, 284, 287
  of Bermuda, 300–3, 313–14, 316, 317
  of Tristan da Cuhna, 304, 313–14, 315, 317
  of St Helena, 306–7, 313–14, 315, 317
  of the Falkland Islands, 308–10, 312–14, 317
  of Ireland, 322, 326–9, 332–5, 341
  of Gibraltar, 348–50, 353–4, 357–8, 361–3, 365
  of Ghana, 371, 372, 375, 376–84, 386
  see also colonial history; colonial heritage; colonial period; colonization; decolonization; Overseas Territory; subjection colony
colonial heritage, 74; *see also* colonial background; colonial history; colonial period; colonization; decolonization; Overseas Territory; subjection colony
colonial history, 51, 85, 112, 119, 121, 150, 255, 256, 261, 308, 311, 322, 341, 372, 375, 379
  (post)colonial, 85, 255, 256, 261
  see also colonial background; colonial heritage; colonial period; colonization; decolonization; Overseas Territory; subjection colony
colonial period, 48, 147, 151, 252, 284, 384, 409; *see also* colonial background; colonial history; colonial heritage; colonization; decolonization; Overseas Territory; subjection colony
colonisation *see* colonization
colonization, 2–4, 48, 88, 89, 113, 118, 119, 130, 133, 136–7, 155, 157–9, 182, 231–2, 240, 242–3, 252–3, 266, 282, 285, 301, 311, 317, 333, 337, 341, 371, 378–9
  attitudes towards, 4, 121–2, 230, 232, 242, 311
  attitudes towards (the) colonizing power, 4, 107, 155, 157–9, 172, 182, 232, 384
  British, 34–5, 39, 40, 228
  lack of, 114, 181, 324, 360
  period, 371
  see also colonial background; colonial period; decolonization; Overseas Territory; subjection colony
Commodore Perry, 181, 183
competition
  between languages, 88, 315
  English proficiency level, 126
  see also norm competition
complaint tradition, 203, 222–3
counter-forces, 186, 191, 193, 185
creole, 234, 253–9, 264–5, 278–9, 280, 289, 299, 316
  continuum, 265, 275
  formation, 256, 267, 265
  see also Bahamian Creole; pidgin; Trinidadian English Creole

creolization, 256
Cromwell, 231, 333

Declaration of Independence, 236
decolonization, 146, 257, 262, 282, 285
　lack of, 89, 357, 366
　see also colonization; Declaration of Independence
democratization, 162, 237
demography, 243, 348–50; see also sociodemographic background
Deterministic Model, 276
developmental model, 261–6
diachronic, 55, 265, 278, 392
　Americanism, 260
　aspect of the Deterministic Model, 276
　aspect of the Dynamic Model, 136, 264
　aspect of the EIF Model, 6, 55, 264, 278
　dimension, 19
　investigation, 54
　linguistic evidence, 265
　studies, 189, 392
dictionary, 91, 184, 208n, 216–18, 236, 241, 256
　Macquarie Dictionary, 205, 210
　Oxford, 188–9, 210, 214, 216, 219
　Webster, 219, 237
　see also Webster, Noah
differentiation (phase 5), 23, 34, 39, 55–6, 74, 112–13, 115–16, 129, 181–2, 278, 284, 292, 323, 341–3, 397, 403, 407, 410
　in England, 18–20, 33–4
　in Namibia, 46, 53–4, 57
　in Singapore, 118
　in North America, 229, 237–9, 243–4
　in Trinidad, 284
　in Ireland, 341–3
　in Gibraltar, 359, 362, 364–6
　see also Dynamic Model; English as a Native Language; heterogeneity
diglossia, 338, 351, 365
　diglossic distribution, 362
　see also bilingualism
DM see Dynamic Model
Dynamic Model (of the Evolution of postcolonial Englishes), 3–4, 6, 33, 38–9, 55, 85, 93, 112–20, 129, 137, 156, 180–2, 229–30, 251–2, 278, 287–93, 323–4, 325, 328, 332, 337, 360–1, 390, 398–9, 403, 407, 410
　Namibia, 38–9,
　United Arab Emirates, 63, 73–5, 400
　India, 86–93, 107
　Singapore, 123, 407
　Philippines, 135, 136–7, 150, 151
　Japan, 180–2, 194
　North America, 229–30, 241–2, 244–5
　The Bahamas, 253–67
　Trinidad, 276–7, 282–4
　Ireland, 322–3, 327–8, 340, 342–3
　Gibraltar, 357–60, 361–2, 366
　Ghana, 371, 374–5, 390
　see also differentiation; endonormative stabilization; exonormative stabilization; foundation; nativization; Schneider, Edgar W.

Early Modern English, 322, 330
East India Company (EIC), 64, 228, 306, 313, 314
education, 32
　Common European Framework of Reference for Languages (CEFR), 127–8, 188
　colonial, 31, 48, 150, 233, 375, 377–8, 381, 391
　English, 87, 92, 158 160, 172, 181–6, 186, 188, 190, 207
　English as a foreign language, 156
　English as a language of, 92, 94, 140, 184, 258
　English as the language of, 63, 88, 92, 279, 293, 350, 355, 358, 362–3, 366, 389
　English-medium instruction, 92, 122, 145, 160, 165, 186–7, 362, 365, 366, 377, 378, 385, 388, 389
　entrance exam, 165, 171, 388
　higher, 49, 69, 79, 92, 96, 165, 185, 192, 290, 305, 351, 352, 363, 374, 389
　in America, 233
　in Australia, 207, 209
　in Ghana, 372, 374–5, 377–8, 379–85, 387–9, 391
　in Gibraltar, 350, 351, 355, 357, 358, 362–3, 365, 366

in India, 94–6, 99, 101–6
in Ireland, 342, 337, 338
in Japan, 128, 181, 182, 183–8, 190, 191, 192
in South Korea, 156, 158, 160, 164, 165, 172
in The Bahamas, 254, 258, 259
in the Philippines, 134, 135, 138, 140–1, 143, 145–6, 150
in the United Arab Emirates, 66, 68–9, 71, 75, 79
in Trinidad, 274, 279–81, 287, 290, 292, 293–4
of language models (EIF/DM/WE), 34, 192
of survey participants, 43n, 97, 99, 101, 138, 140–1, 143, 145, 238, 259, 279–81
policies, 33, 158, 172, 181, 185–6, 187–8, 209, 254, 286, 337, 362–3, 365, 366, 372, 374, 375, 377, 379, 380, 381–91
private English, 69, 96, 160, 172, 183
spread of English, 73, 75, 338, 342
state (public), 28, 34–5, 68–9, 287, 362
see also English proficiency test; force(s)
Edwards, Alison, 4, 41, 73–4, 85, 96, 159, 181, 224, 360, 361
see also foundation-through-globalisation
EFL *see* English as a foreign language
EFL–ESL, 2, 71–3, 85, 413
continuum, 73, 80
distinction(s), 72, 91, 412–13
divide, 72
EFL–ESL–ENL, 72, 73, 165, 181, 410
continuum, 72, 412–13
distinction, 73, 91, 276, 410
EsuppL spectrum, 202–3
see also Dynamic Model; Three Circles Model
EIL *see* English as an International Language
ELF *see* English as a Lingua Franca
emigrant(s), 301, 310; *see also* emigration; migration; immigrant(s); immigration
emigration, 210, 292, 301, 309, 337; *see also* emigrant(s); migration; immigrant(s); immigration

endonormative stabilization (phase 4), 9, 74, 107, 112–13, 115, 264, 276–7, 288, 289, 292, 323, 406, 410
in England, 18, 23, 33
in Namibia, 39, 41, 51, 53, 55–7
in India, 87
in Philippines, 135,
in North America, 236–7, 243
in The Bahamas, 265–6
in Ireland, 337–42
in Gibraltar, 357, 359, 362, 364, 365, 366
in Ghana, 371, 375, 388–90
see also Dynamic Model; Event X; homogeneity
English as a Foreign Language (EFL), 1–2, 6, 71–3, 85–6, 90, 91, 99, 154, 156, 181, 202–3, 224, 243–4, 275, 276, 278, 324, 402, 410, 413; *see also* EFL–ESL; Expanding Circle; foundation
English as a Lingua Franca (ELF), 188, 190, 192; *see also* lingua franca(s)
English as a Native Language (ENL), 1, 6, 91, 99, 117, 154, 181, 203, 222, 224, 228, 243, 275, 298, 311, 355n, 357, 366, 410, 413; *see also* differentiation; EFL–ESL; EFL–ESL–ENL; Inner Circle
English as a Second Language (ESL), 1–2, 6, 67, 71–3, 80, 85, 86, 91, 117, 154, 156, 181, 202, 203, 228, 243–4, 275, 276, 278, 298, 311, 357, 361, 366, 410, 413; *see also* EFL–ESL; EFL–ESL–ENL; nativization; Outer Circle
English as an International Language (EIL), 192
English as an official language, 184, 187
English Fever, 160, 170, 172
English in the Philippines, 133, 135; *see also* Philippine English
English in the UAE, 63–81
functions, 68–71
status, 71–3, 78–80
English proficiency test, 125–6
Test of English as a Foreign Language (TOEFL), 34, 122, 165, 171, 188, 190
Test of English for International Communication (TOEIC), 165, 171, 188, 190
see also Education

ENL *see* English as a Native Language
epicenter, 40, 49, 54, 56, 58, 316, 343, 399, 401, 404, 405
ESL *see* English as a Second Language
EsuppL *see* Supplementary English
European Migration Period, 17
Event X, 88, 180, 313, 317, 359; *see also* Dynamic Model; Endonormative stabilization; Schneider, Edgar W.
evolution
  human, 68, 266
  in the Atlantic Ocean, 298, 301, 304, 308, 310–11
  of English in Gibraltar, 364, 366
  of English in Trinidad, 283, 284, 285, 287–90
  of English(es), 4, 17, 18, 22, 24, 28, 85, 116, 159, 192, 253, 266, 289, 292, 298, 317–18, 390, 397, 403, 408, 411, 413
  of Ghanaian English, 371, 372, 374–5, 390–2
  of Indian English, 86, 91, 411
  of non-PCEs, 277
  of (North) American English(es), 230, 231–41, 243, 244
  of PCEs, 33, 85, 156, 229, 251, 277–8, 282, 288, 289, 294, 323, 357
  of Singlish, 117
  see also Dynamic Model; force(s)
exonormative stabilisation *see* exonormative stabilization
exonormative stabilization (phase 2), 4, 115, 120, 181, 256, 323
  in England, 18, 33
  in Singapore, 120
  in South Korea, 155, 171
  in North America, 233–5, 243
  in Ireland, 328–32, 336, 341
  in Gibraltar, 358, 365
  in Ghana, 372, 374–5, 378–84
  see also Dynamic Model
Expanding Circle, 2, 6, 85, 93, 113, 156, 179, 180–1, 182, 191, 193–4, 276, 356, 360; *see also* English as a Foreign Language; Inner Circle; Kachru, Braj; Outer Circle; Three Circles Model
expatriate(s), 63, 67–9, 70–1, 72, 73, 75, 76, 77–81

extra-territorial force(s), 23, 34, 54, 80, 90, 121, 123, 145, 150, 170 183, 185, 186, 188, 189–90, 194, 224, 231, 240, 243–4, 252, 313, 324, 332, 343, 361–2, 365, 372, 399–400, 402, 405; *see also* American influence; colonial background; colonial heritage; colonial history; colonial period; colonization; education; epicenter; expatriate(s); force(s); globalization; immigration; intra-territorial force(s); language; migration; mobility; pop culture; settler strand; tourism
extra-territorial influence, 202–5, 213–22; *see also* American influence; extra-territorial force(s)

Falkland Islands English (FIE), 299, 309–10, 312
famine, 232, 337, 338
FIE *see* Falkland Islands English
Fiji, 245, 281, 289
Filipino, 135–6, 140, 141, 142, 143–9; *see also* Tagalog
Fingal, 334, 336
force(s)
  conservative, 88, 287–8
  progressive, 88, 287–8
  see also American influence; colonial background; colonial heritage; colonial history; colonial period; colonization; education; emigration; epicenter; expatriate(s); extra-territorial force(s); extra-territorial influence; foreign policy; globalization; identity; immigration; intra-territorial force(s); language; migration; mobility; pop culture; psycho-social forces; religion as a force; settler strand; sociodemographic background; psychological factor; tourism; translocal
foreign policy, 4, 35, 121, 122, 136, 182, 230, 266, 277, 324, 402
  in South Korea, 155, 163–4, 167, 172
  in Japan, 183
  in Australia, 205, 218
  in Trinidad, 285

in St Helena, 313–14
in Ireland, 343
in Ghana, 372, 375, 384, 385, 386, 390
see also force(s); globalization; language
Forth and Bargy, 334, 336
foundation (phase 1), 4, 6, 40, 56, 74,
113–15, 118–20, 137, 151, 181, 193,
195, 278, 323, 324, 327, 361
in England, 17–18, 19, 33
in Singapore, 120–1
in the Philippines, 137, 151
in South Korea, 159
in Japan, 181, 183, 193
in North America, 231–3, 243
in The Bahamas, 255–6
in Ireland, 325–8, 332
in Gibraltar, 357–8, 361, 365
in Ghana, 372, 374, 376–8
see also colonial background;
colonization; Dynamic Model;
English as a Foreign Language;
foundation-through-globalisation
foundation-through-globalisation, 159, 360;
see also Edwards, Alison; foundation;
globalization
founder effect, 255–6, 301
French, 24–6, 28, 35, 70, 95, 164, 209, 235,
238–9, 278, 307–8, 326–8, 329, 330,
380, 384
Norman French, 24–5, 28, 326, 327,
329
Old French, 25

Gaelic, 310, 326–7, 328–9, 333–4, 336
Germanic, 17, 18, 19–20, 21, 22, 44
West Germanic, 18, 20, 44
Ghana, 371–6, 383, 385–6, 388–9, 392
Ghanaian English, 371–2, 374–5, 376,
387–9, 390–2
globalisation *see* globalization
globalization, 85, 90, 105, 121–2, 124,
133–4, 136–7, 150, 155, 167, 171–2,
181–2, 186, 193, 230, 243, 245,
251–60, 360–1, 365, 375, 376, 392,
402, 407
acceptance of, 4, 90, 105, 108, 121,
136–7, 150, 155, 162–3, 182, 224, 243,
324

effects of, 4, 54, 162–3, 189, 252, 259,
266–7, 285, 364, 366, 372, 390
force(s) of, 3, 33, 78–9, 80, 124, 130, 134,
150, 151, 190, 224, 252, 267, 277, 285,
400, 411
spread of English, 73–4, 161, 245, 277,
364
see also extra-territorial force(s); force(s);
foundation-through-globalisation;
internet; intra-territorial force(s); pop
culture
globalization drive, 162
Gold Coast, 307, 371–92

habitual aspect
do be habituals, 339
heritage language, 234, 241
heterogeneity, 6–7, 19, 41, 50–4, 56, 57, 90,
93, 230, 278, 284, 290, 292, 294, 299,
397, 398–400, 405, 406–7, 409
Hindi, 67, 69, 86, 87, 88, 92, 94–5, 97–8,
100–7, 119
HMS Phaeton, 183
homogeneity, 152, 234, 257–8, 283, 284,
343, 399, 403, 406
hybrid, 2, 120, 133–9, 141, 149–52, 257,
281, 359n, 409
hybridity, 134–7, 138, 139, 151–2, 359n,
409

identity, 1, 27, 34, 53, 86, 118, 142, 180,
238, 240–1, 244, 256–7, 287, 311, 314,
317, 358–9, 364–5, 389
Baster, 52
carrier(s), 86, 89, 107, 239, 347, 354
conceptions, 6, 412
construction(s), 4, 39–46, 50, 57, 74, 86,
88, 91, 93, 107–8, 114, 180, 194, 252,
256, 260, 267, 325, 326, 329, 333–5,
338–9, 343–4, 357, 364–6, 371, 387
cultural, 46, 163
ethnic, 51, 134, 140, 147–50, 238
formation(s), 88, 157, 241, 257, 276, 311
language, 78, 96, 97–104, 107–8, 145, 389
linguistic, 17, 43, 46, 78
manifestations, 237
national, 117, 134, 140, 212, 216, 222,
224, 232, 407

identity (cont.)
  pan-Indian, 87–8
  pan-Namibian, 51
  regional (local), 27, 51, 72, 133–4, 136, 180, 238–9, 279, 286, 313, 328
  (re)constructions, 276
  religious, 77–8
  (re)writing(s), 3, 47, 89, 107, 108, 157–8, 194, 235, 258, 412
  social, 27, 29, 192
  sociolinguistic, 257
  see also language
IDG *see* indigenous strand
idiolect, 7, 50, 184, 195, 230, 239, 263
  idiolectal plane, 7, 230, 239
immigrant(s), 75, 94, 117, 120, 123, 232, 234, 237, 241, 243, 254, 348; *see also* emigrant(s); emigration; immigration; migration
immigration, 20, 64, 120, 189, 206, 234, 240, 242, 254, 255, 257, 259, 278; *see also* emigrant(s); emigration; immigrant(s); migration
IndE *see* Indian English
Indian Communicative Space, 86, 90, 91–3
Indian English (IndE), 86, 228
  in the Dynamic Model, 86–91, 107–8
  in the EIF Model, 90–1, 94, 99, 108
indigenization, 266; *see also* indigenized; nativization
indigenized, 89, 96, 316; *see also* indigenization; nativized
indigenous strand (IDG), 74–5, 78, 80, 89, 122, 232, 234, 255, 256, 276, 357–8, 371; *see also* foundation; settler strand
Inner Circle, 6, 192, 276, 356; *see also* English as a Native Language; Expanding Circle; Kachru, Braj; Outer Circle; Three Circles Model
interlanguage, 23
internet, 4, 73, 77, 78, 119, 120, 122, 124, 136, 137, 151, 156, 159, 171–2, 181, 187, 190, 224, 244, 259, 360, 364; *see also* media
intra-territorial force(s), 34, 35, 39, 40, 54, 56, 58, 74–80, 90, 108, 113, 115, 119, 121–3, 133–4, 137–8, 150–2,
155–7, 169, 171–2, 182, 184–6, 188, 189, 190, 193, 194, 224, 231–41, 243, 252, 266, 277, 284–93, 298, 311, 317, 323–4, 325, 332, 343, 361, 365, 384, 388, 399–404, 408, 409; *see also* education; extra-territorial force(s); force(s); foreign policy; globalization; identity; language; mobility; pop culture; psycho-social forces; sociodemographic background; socio-psychological factors
Ireland, 17, 28–9, 203, 310, 322–3, 325–9, 332–4, 337, 341–4, 361, 402–3
Irish English, 322, 323, 324–5, 238, 330–1, 335–6, 337–43
it-clefts, 339

Japanese English, 184, 188, 190–2; *see also* Japanized English
Japanized English, 184, 188; *see also* Japanese English

Kachru, Braj, 1, 2 6, 73 90; *see also* Three Circles Model
Kilkenny, 329
  Statutes of Kilkenny, 329
koine, 23
koinéization, 233, 305, 310, 311, 316

Language
  attitudes, 1, 4, 53, 79, 86, 93, 94–108, 138, 155, 159–62, 171–2, 180, 188, 191–3, 259, 75, 276, 279, 280, 290, 294, 316, 317, 324, 344, 365, 375, 378, 384, 389, 399
  choice, 142–3, 166–7, 351
  contact, 4, 22, 39, 41, 114, 119, 159, 164, 167, 180, 213, 256, 265, 307, 310, 324, 325, 327, 330, 332, 334, 335, 339, 348, 350–1, 354, 356, 364
  identity, 96, 97–8, 106, 107–8
  norms, 46, 282, 283, 286, 294, 323, 337, 401
  policy, 1, 4, 34, 40, 54, 90, 108, 115, 119, 121–2, 136, 145, 150, 155, 159–62, 168, 171–2, 181, 182, 186, 187–8, 193, 230, 235–6, 266, 277, 286, 324, 336–7, 341, 342–3, 343, 362, 363, 365, 372,

INDEX 423

375, 377, 378, 379, 384, 385, 387, 388, 391, 399
prestige, 28, 92, 97–8, 99, 100–8, 136, 213, 233, 260, 279–80, 287, 315, 326, 329, 332, 334, 351, 353, 358, 362–3, 365, 387, 390, 402
use, 7, 17, 39, 70, 94–107, 135, 139, 156, 180, 190, 252, 259, 267, 275, 279, 285, 294, 322, 331, 350–1, 366, 373, 378, 387
see also competition; identity; lingua franca(s)
lesser-known varieties of English, 38, 310–11, 317
lexical
  activity, 24
  borrowing, 204, 328
  choice, 203
  elements, 57, 169, 180, 210, 289, 350
  evidence, 205
  expressions, 116
  incursions, 222
  influence, 210
  investigation, 57
  knowledge, 207
  level, 57
  pairs, 355
  peculiarities, 211, 263, 389
  regularity, 31
  semantics, 203
  set(s), 50, 214–18
  transfer, 354
  usage, 237
  see also phonological; phonology; vowel(s)
lingua franca(s), 39, 41, 94, 358, 373
  English as a, 53, 67–8, 75, 92, 232, 360, 412
  see also English as a Lingua Franca
linguistic hybridity, 134, 139, 151
linguistic landscape, 76, 137, 145, 155, 168, 184, 189, 333, 334, 400, 401
  English in the, 155, 162, 167–8, 172
linguistic migration see migration
loan word(s), 162, 168, 171, 183, 184, 186, 188, 222, 312, 330, 331; see also borrowing; Spanish
local variety see variety
loyalists, 240, 254, 255, 259

Maharashtra, 86, 87n, 92, 94–8, 104, 106, 107
Malagasy, 307, 308, 312, 315
Malayalam, 67, 69, 95, 120
Marathi, 92, 94–107
ME see Middle English
media, 54, 63, 66, 69–70, 71, 73, 79, 94, 114, 115, 119–20, 124, 134, 137, 145, 146, 151, 160, 161, 165, 208, 211, 223, 254, 258, 287, 294, 350, 355n, 362, 365, 366, 392
  electronic, 190
  global, 119, 364
  mass, 28, 58, 119, 147, 404
  modern, 122, 171–2, 224, 259, 342, 403
  (new), 283, 285, 401
  social, 77, 136, 139, 141, 169
  see also internet; social networking services; see also YouTube
Meiji, 183–5
Middle English (ME), 22–3, 24, 330, 334, 336
migration, 64, 118, 146, 228, 231, 239, 242–3, 244, 254, 283, 286, 290–1, 300, 309–10, 316, 392, 401–2
  linguistic, 231
  out-migration, 302, 307, 386
  remigration, 290, 292
  see also emigrant(s); emigration; European Migration Period; immigrant(s); immigration
mobility, 10, 12, 150, 165–7, 263, 277, 283, 286, 291–2, 299, 305, 307, 401, 407
  economic, 133, 134, 145, 146, 150
  global, 112, 166–9, 360
  policy, 127
  political, 150
  social, 28, 86, 108, 133, 134, 145, 146, 150, 387
Mori, Arinori, 184, 185
Mufwene, Salikoko, 256, 301
multilingualism, 41–6, 50, 56, 58, 89–90, 93, 334, 360, 400, 404
multinormative
  approach, 405–6
  orientation, 259, 262, 288, 290
  stabilization, 288–90, 292–3, 406, 410
  see also mulitnormative post-nativization stage; multinormativity

multinormative post-nativization stage, 406–7, 410
multinormativity, 289–90, 406; *see also* multinormative
Mumbai, 86, 94–6, 106–7
Munch, Peter, 305, 311, 314–15

NamE *see* Namibian English
Namibia, 38–42, 44, 47–9, 51–4, 56, 58, 113–14, 263, 360, 366, 398, 399; *see also* colonial background; Dynamic Model; endonormative stabilization; Namibian English; nativization
Namibian English (NamE), 39, 41, 46, 49, 50–4, 56–8, 398
nation state(s) *see also* territory, 56, 116, 123, 244, 291, 317, 400, 409, 412
national language
  Akan, 385
  Bisaya, 134
  Bishlish, 151
  EE, 35
  English, 126, 134, 385
  Filipino, 136, 140, 143, 146–8
  French as the, 26
  Korean, 160
  policy, 145, 286
  Tagalog, 134, 140–1, 144, 146–8, 150
  see also English as an International Language
national variety *see* variety
nationalism, 26, 245, 402
  in England, 26, 27, 35, 245
  Hindu, 94
  in Japan, 185
  in America, 237
  in Canada, 241
  see also transnationalism
native speaker(s), 6, 52, 75, 117, 119, 128–9, 140, 160, 162, 172, 187, 191, 342, 400; *see also* non-native speaker
nativisation *see* nativization
nativised *see* nativized
nativized, 41, 51, 57, 89, 115, 116, 151, 188, 264, 299, 341, 347, 353–6, 365, 409; *see also* indigenized; nativization (the process of)

nativization (phase 3), 33, 41, 55, 56–7, 74, 115, 156, 181, 256, 265, 278, 284, 289, 332, 405–8, 411–12
  in England, 18, 33
  in Namibia, 40, 41, 51, 57
  in the United Arab Emirates, 63, 75, 78, 79, 80
  in India, 87–8
  in the Philippines, 135
  in South Korea, 155, 171
  in Japan, 191, 193
  in North America, 235–6, 243
  in The Bahamas, 256, 265
  in Trinidad, 284, 288
  in Ireland, 332–7, 338, 341
  in Gibraltar, 358–9, 364, 365
  in Ghana, 371, 372, 375, 383, 384–8
  see also Dynamic Model; English as a Second Language; indigenization; multinormative post-nativization stage
nativization (the process of), 18, 33, 50, 57, 72, 87–8, 112, 114, 118, 184, 188, 235–6, 265, 275, 279, 299, 312, 317, 323, 336, 338, 340, 359, 383; *see also* indigenization; nativization (phase 3); nativized
Nigeria, 307, 381, 386
Nkrumah, Kwame, 383, 385–6
non-native speakers, 119, 191, 264; *see also* native speaker(s)
non-PCE(s) *see* non-Postcolonial English(es)
non-Postcolonial English(es) (non-PCE), 2–8, 16, 30–5, 38–41, 55–6, 58, 64, 67, 73–4, 78–80, 93, 112–16, 118–19, 121, 123, 128–30, 136–7, 151–2, 156, 180–2, 193–5, 229–30, 243, 251, 261, 264, 266, 277, 311, 317, 324, 360, 361, 397–9, 406–9, 411; *see also* postcolonial English(es)
norm competition, 49, 54; *see also* competition
norm complexities, 287, 289, 293
Norman Conquest, 18, 24; *see also* Anglo-Norman
Normans *see* Anglo-Norman
Northern Cities Shift, 238; *see also* vowel(s)

INDEX   425

Northern Territories, 379, 380, 384, 390;
    see also colonial background; Ghana

OE see Old English
Official English Debate, 160
Old English (OE), 18, 19, 22, 23, 334, 336
Old Norse (ON), 22
ON see Old Norse
Outer Circle, 2, 6, 85, 232, 276, 322, 356–7;
    see also English as a Second Language;
    Expanding Circle; Inner Circle;
    Kachru, Braj; Three Circles Model
out-migration see migration
overseas territory, 30, 34–5, 310; see
    also British Overseas Territory;
    colonization

PCE see postcolonial English(es)
phase 1 see foundation (phase 1)
    see also Dynamic Model
phase 2 see exonormative stabilization
    (phase 2)
    see also Dynamic Model
phase 3 see nativization (phase 3)
    see also Dynamic Model
phase 4 see endonormative stabilization
    (phase 4)
    see also Dynamic Model
phase 5 see differentiation (phase 5)
    see also Dynamic Model
Philippine English, 133, 135, 137, 151, 245
phonological
    change, 210
    characteristics, 180
    development(s), 54, 180, 210
    feature(s), 53, 289, 316
    knowledge, 207, 354
    peculiarities, 263
    phenomenon, 52, 354
    regularity, 31
    specifics, 340
    standard, 53
    transfer, 210
    see also lexical; phonology
phonology
    AusE, 210
    Bermudian English, 316
    English, 17, 21, 28

    extra-territorial influence, 203
    French, 327
    Gaelic, 327
    Gibraltar English, 354
    in Namibia, 50–8
    Irish English, 339
    Rehoboth Basters, 51–2
    transfer, 50
    variation, 50–2, 276
    see also lexical; phonological
pidgin, 23, 184, 186, 234, 239, 265, 358
    "Indian Pidgin", 232
    Korean English pidgin, 158
    pidgin-creole life cycle, 265
    see also creole
plantations, 234, 279, 300, 376
plantations of Ulster, 333
policy mobility see mobility
pop culture, 139, 149
    American/US, 122, 156, 224, 259
    Hallyu, 167, 168–70, 171, 400
    in the EIFM, 119, 170
    K-pop, 119, 169–70
popular culture see pop culture
population
    analysis, 25–7, 42–6, 50, 63, 67–8, 75–6,
        78, 94–6, 104–5, 117, 164–5, 234, 240,
        255, 257, 285–7 298–310, 312–13,
        332–9, 342–3, 348–50, 357–9, 372–4,
        379–82, 386
    Gaelic, 326, 327, 328, 334, 336
    growth, 87, 164–5, 254, 302, 304, 309,
        386
    indigenous, 22, 39, 89, 120, 255, 276,
        328, 357–8
    local, 115, 120, 305, 324, 325, 352, 357–9,
        364, 371, 385
    mixing, 29, 136, 151, 157, 224, 232,
        256–7, 283, 298–9, 302, 306, 309, 312,
        327, 352, 362–4, 374
    native, 67, 76
    native-born, 312
    pre-colonial, 63
    rural, 86, 333, 338
    urban, 164–5
    see also identity; indigenous
        strand; settler strand; slavery;
        sociodemographic background

postcolonial English(es) (PCE), 1–6, 8, 16, 29–35, 38–9, 41, 55–8, 64–7, 73–4, 78, 80, 88–9, 91, 93, 112–16, 118–24, 128–9, 137, 151–2, 156, 180–2, 193–5, 229, 241, 253, 257, 261, 264–7, 276–8, 282–4, 287–9, 292–4, 311, 390, 398–9, 406–9, 411; see also Dynamic Model; non-postcolonial English(es)
prestige see language
psycho-social forces, 25, 33, 399, 401–2
  psycholinguistic, 25
  psychological and social levels, 25, 26, 27
  psychological independence, 258
  psychological resistance, 148
  socio-psychological accommodation, 257
  see also identity; intra-territorial force(s); language; force(s); socio-psychological factors

rankings of English language competence, 124–6
reflexive awareness, 126
regional language, 92, 94, 147
Rehoboth Basters see Baster(s)
religion as force, 67, 77–80, 81, 139, 257; see also force(s)
remigration see migration
rhotic, 233, 260, 281, 351

SAfE see South African English
StHE see St Helenian English
St Helenian English (StHE), 298, 299, 306–8, 312
Schneider, Edgar W., 3, 6, 29, 34, 49, 57, 74, 85, 86–9, 93, 107, 112, 115–17, 133–5, 151, 156, 164, 179–81, 194, 229, 235, 238, 251, 252, 255–7, 264, 265, 276–7, 341, 357, 360, 371, 374, 401–2, 406, 408, 410; see also Dynamic Model; Transnational Attraction
Schneider's Model see Dynamic Model
Schreier, Daniel, 404, 413
Scotland, 17, 28–9, 304, 310, 333, 342
Scots, 29, 333
Seargeant, Philip, 190, 252, 263, 409; see also Tagg, Caroline
settlement
  England, 20–1, 31

United Arab Emirates, 66–7, 75–6, 79
India, 89
Philippines, 146
Australia, 204, 205
North America, 231, 240
The Bahamas, 253–6
Bermuda, 301, 303, 311–12
Tristan da Cunha, 305, 311–12
St Helena, 306, 311–12
Falkland Island, 308–10, 311–12
Ireland, 326, 328, 332, 333–4, 336, 340–3
Ghana, 373
settler strand (STL), 4, 74–6, 78–80, 180, 244, 255, 357, 400
  lack of, 4, 39, 74–5, 78–79, 114, 115, 137, 180, 361, 400
  see also foundation; indigenous strand
Singapore, 6, 116–18, 120–1, 123, 126, 159, 164, 193, 400, 407
Singapore English, 355n, 400; see also Singlish; Standard Singapore English
Singlish, 116–18, 123, 151, 355n, 400, 407; see also Singapore English; Standard Singapore English
slavery, 47, 232, 234, 253–5, 257, 298, 302–3, 306–7, 313, 315, 376–7
SNS see social networking services
social networking services (SNS), 181, 190
sociodemographic background, 4, 121, 136, 155, 164–7, 172, 182, 230, 242, 266, 277, 285, 311, 324, 336–7, 342, 372, 375, 379, 384, 388, 390, 392, 403; see also demography
sociolinguistic monitor, 207
socio-psychological factors, 237, 242–3, 244; see also psycho-social forces
South Africa, 40, 54, 228, 289, 399
  influence of, 40–1, 46–50, 54, 56–8, 304, 305, 399
  see also colonial background; colonization; South African English
South African English(es) (SAfE), 7, 32, 40, 49–50, 52, 54, 399
  Afrikaans-influenced, 52
  Black, 46
  Cape Flats English, 52
  White, 38
  see also South Africa

South Carolina, 234, 254, 300, 316
Spanish
    armada, 333
    colonizers, 146, 228
    influence, 239, 315, 347, 348–50, 356
    language, 95, 239, 310, 315, 347, 350, 352–3, 354, 355–6, 358, 362–4, 365, 366
    loan words, 312
    settlements, 303
    Spanish Civil War, 349
    Spanish-American War, 236
    territory, 278, 348, 349
    traders, 303
stabilization, 181, 184, 186, 188, 191; *see also* exonormative stabilization
Standard
    American date-formatting, 211, 221
    American English, 49
    American speech, 280
    Bahamian English, 262
    British English, 49, 353
    British practice, 220
    dialects, 17, 22, 25, 26–7, 28–30, 33, 34
    dialects (non-standard), 17, 21, 27, 29, 32, 33
    English, 27, 31, 169, 203, 238, 253, 258, 274, 279, 283, 286–7, 290, 293–4, 406
    Japanese, 185
    language(s), 27, 262
    Singapore English, 123
    see also Singapore English; Singlish
steady states, 287–8
STL *see* settler strand
subjection colony, 66–7, 75–6
supplementary English (ESuppL), 202–3, 204
synchronic dimension, 19–20, 54, 55, 73; *see also* diachronic dimension
synthetic language, 23

Tagalog, 67, 69, 134, 136, 137, 140–1, 143–8, 150; *see also* Taglish
Tagg, Caroline, 190, 263, 409; *see also* Seargeant, Philip
Taglish, 134, 136, 141, 151; *see also* Tagalog
TdCE *see* Tristan da Cunha English
TEC *see* Trinidadian English Creole

territory, 48, 64, 285, 306, 314, 348, 353, 357–8, 364, 366, 377, 379–80
    Anglo-Saxon, 21
    as a nation state, 29, 123–4, 244–5, 409
    English in a, 6, 29, 30, 40, 41, 53, 74, 150, 158, 253, 255, 288, 353, 357–8, 361, 366
    expansion, 18, 47
    foreign, 243
    language(s) in a, 20, 22, 47, 351, 357–8
    postcolonial, 287
    see also British Overseas Territory; Northern Territories; overseas territory
The Bahamas, 251–62, 266–7
Three Circles Model, 1, 73, 202, 229, 275, 356; *see also* Expanding Circle; Inner Circle; Kachru, Braj; Outer Circle
tourism, 4, 58, 114, 194, 202n, 283, 313–14, 401, 404
    in the United Arab Emirates, 63, 66, 70, 76, 78
    in Singapore, 129
    in South Korea, 166–7, 172
    in Japan, 181, 189, 194,
    in The Bahamas, 254, 259–60
    in Bermuda, 300, 303
    in Gibraltar 363
    see also extra-territorial force(s); force(s)
translocal, 292, 294; *see also* Translocality
Translocality, 274, 291–4, 404; *see also* translocal
Transnational Attraction, 3, 4, 6, 55, 74, 85, 181, 202–3, 213, 264, 277–8, 291, 360; *see also* Dynamic Model; Schneider, Edgar W.
transnationalism, 85, 311; *see also* nationalism
Trinidadian English (TrinE), 274, 282, 285
Trinidadian English Creole (TEC), 274, 278–9, 282, 286–7, 294; *see also* Creole
Tristan da Cunha English (TdCE), 299, 304–6

Ulster, 333, 334, 338; *see also* plantations
uniformity of speech, 5, 229, 237
    lack of, 17, 53, 258

university entrance exam, 165, 172; see education
see also English proficiency test
urbanization, 87, 146, 164–5, 239, 309
  international, 343, 403
  local, 288, 290, 299, 308, 311, 342, 354, 357, 359, 364, 402, 405
  national, 7, 133, 135, 136–7, 150, 151, 195, 224, 261–3, 267
  of English, 54, 75, 114, 116, 141, 156, 203, 253, 274, 289, 322, 327, 333, 347–8, 353–4, 357–9, 364, 371, 390, 397
  transnational, 263, 409

variation, 18, 20, 24, 28, 31, 50–4, 91–2, 162, 212, 213, 261, 279, 288–9, 294, 390, 406
  accent, 279–80
  across registers, 52
  as a norm, 34
  attitude to, 34, 218, 399
  dialectal, 24–5, 55, 341
  ethnic, 50–1, 57, 241
  gender-related, 390
  internal, 25, 91
  inter-speaker, 352
  intra-varietal, 409
  linguistic, 29, 410
  linguists, 154
  morpho-syntactic, 259
  pronunciation, 259, 345n
  qualitative, 299
  sociolinguistic, 275, 390
  spelling, 207–9, 212
  spoken, 25
  unit, 355n
  written, 25
  see also variety
Vikings, 22–3, 325–6

vowel(s), 39, 50, 52, 238, 336, 354, 387, 392
  merger, 50–2, 354
  split, 50–3
  see also lexical; Northern Cities Shift

Wales, 17, 28–9
War of Spanish Succession, 358
Webster, Noah, 236, 262
West Saxon, 18, 24
World English(es) (WE), 8, 35, 38, 58, 154–6, 192
  American English, 202, 228, 245
  English English, 19, 29, 33, 34, 398
  evolution of, 391
  frameworks, 5, 348
  model(s), 5, 16, 154–6, 192, 202, 260–7, 274–8, 348, 406, 408
  modelling, 8, 33, 63, 154–6, 245, 260–7, 274–8, 283, 288–9
  paradigm, 179, 202
  perspective, 129, 192
  research, 2, 38, 64, 73, 75, 229, 276, 304, 351
  researchers, 2, 72, 90, 154, 245, 289
  taxonomies of, 317
  The World Englishes Enterprise, 192
  theorizing, 1, 8, 252, 263–4, 274, 274, 277, 360, 397, 408, 412
  see also Dynamic Model; Three Circles Model
World War I, 31, 48, 65, 205, 241, 304, 338
  post-World War I, 382
World War II, 48, 159, 171, 172, 185–6, 204–5, 238, 241, 304, 309, 352, 362, 363, 365, 366, 382
  post-war, 186
  post-WWII, 352, 357

Yanito, 347, 350, 352–4, 358, 362, 365, 366
Yokohama, 184, 186
YouTube, 117

EU representative:
Easy Access System Europe
Mustamäe tee 50, 10621 Tallinn, Estonia
Gpsr.requests@easproject.com

www.ingramcontent.com/pod-product-compliance
Lightning Source LLC
Chambersburg PA
CBHW051802230426
43672CB00012B/2605